SIMULATION, GAMING, AND LANGUAGE LEARNING

Edited by

David Crookall

and

Rebecca L. Oxford

The University of Alabama

NEWBURY HOUSE PUBLISHERS, New York

A division of Harper & Row, Publishers, Inc.
Grand Rapids, Philadelphia, St. Louis, San Francisco
London, Singapore, Sydney, Tokyo

Dedicated to three good friends

Richard C. Brecht

Leopoldo Schapira

Jonathan Wilkenfeld

Director: Laurie E. Likoff
Production Coordinator: Cynthia Funkhouser
Cover Design: Robin Hoffman
Compositor: Crane Typesetting Service, Inc.
Printer and Binder: McNaughton & Gunn

NEWBURY HOUSE PUBLISHERS
A division of Harper & Row, Publishers, Inc.

Language Science
Language Teaching
Language Learning

Simulation, Gaming, and Language Learning

Library of Congress Cataloging in Publication Data

Simulation, gaming, and language learning / edited by David Crookall
   and Rebecca L. Oxford.
       p.   cm.
    Includes bibliographical references.
    ISBN 0-06-632617-6
  1. Language and languages—Study and teaching—Simulation methods.
  I. Crookall, David.   II. Oxford, Rebecca L.
  P53.78.S56   1990
  418'.007—dc20   89-78536
                                                          CIP

63-26177   93 92 91 90 9 8 7 6 5 4 3 2 1

Contributors

Michael Brammer   Manufacture Michelin, 6 rue Camille Saint-Saens, 63800 Cournon d'Auvergne, France.

Nick Bullard   CAVILAM, Vichy, France.

Elizabeth M. Christopher   School of Business and Public Administration, Charles Sturt University—Mitchell, Bathurst, NSW 2795, Australia.

D. Wells Coleman   Department of English Language and Literature, The University of Toledo, Toledo, OH 43606-3390, USA.

David Crookall   MA TESL Program, Department of English, Morgan Hall, The University of Alabama, Tuscaloosa, AL 35487-0244, USA.

Martha Graves Cummings   Rochester Institute of Technology, Learning Development Center, 1 Lomb Memorial Drive, PO Box 9887, Rochester, NY 14623, USA.

Gail Ellis   British Council, High Scrubbs, Wyatts Road, Chorleywood, Herts, England.

James J. Fernandes   Gallaudet University Center on Deafness, University of Hawaii, Kapiolani Community College, 4303 Diamond Head Road, Honolulu, HI 96816, USA.

Robert C. Gardner   Department of Psychology, Faculty of Social Science, The University of Western Ontario, London N6A 5C2, Canada.

Marion Geddes   Freelance Teacher Trainer, Flat 4, 45 Cromwell Avenue, London N6 5HP, England.

Rhona B. Genzel   Rochester Institute of Technology, Learning Development Center, One Lomb Memorial Drive, PO Box 9887, Rochester, NY 14623, USA.

John J. Higgins   School of Education, University of Bristol, Bristol, England.

David Horner   British Institute, 11 rue de Constantine, 75007 Paris, France; or 27 rue Julien Périn, 92160 Antony, France.

Tom Hutchinson   Institute for English Language Education, The University of Lancaster, Bowland College, Lancaster LA1 4YT, England.

Richard Lalonde   Department of Psychology, York University, 4700 Keel Street, North York, Ontario M3J 1P3, Canada.

Linda C. Lederman   Director, SCILS, 4 Huntington Street, Department of Communication, Rutgers University, New Brunswick, NJ 08903, USA.

Andrew Littlejohn   Institute for English Language Education, The University of Lancaster, Bowland College, Lancaster LA1 4YT, England.

Kevin McGinley   The TEFL Training Institute of Ireland, 159 Lower Rathmines Road, Dublin 6, Ireland.

Douglas Morgenstern   Foreign Languages and Literatures, Massachusetts Institute of Technology, Cambridge, MA 02139, USA.

Rebecca L. Oxford   Area of Curriculum and Instruction, College of Education, Graves Hall, The University of Alabama, Tuscaloosa, 35487-0231, USA.

Hana Raz   Oranim, School of Education of the Kibbutz Movement, University of Haifa, Haifa, Israel.

Brent Ruben   Department of Communication, Rutgers University, New Brunswick, NJ 08903, USA.

Christopher Sawyer-Lauçanno   Foreign Languages and Literatures, Massachusetts Institute of Technology, Cambridge, MA 02139, USA.

Robin Scarcella   University of California, Irvine, 22 Mendel Court, Irvine, CA 92717, USA.

W. W. Sharrock   Department of Sociology, University of Manchester, Manchester M13 9PL, England.

Barbara Sinclair   British Council, 19 Albert Avenue, Chingford, London E4, England.

Larry E. Smith   Institute of Culture and Communication, East-West Center, 1777 East-West Road, Honolulu, HI 96848, USA.

Susan L. Stern   University of California, Irvine, 3902 Cedron Street, Irvine, CA 92714, USA.

Gill Sturtridge   Centre for Applied Language Studies, University of Reading, Whitegates, Reading RG6 2AP, England.

Robert V. Vernon   The University of Michigan, 814 Third Street, Ann Arbor, MI 48103, USA.

Edward B. Versluis   Department of English, Southern Oregon State College, Ashland, OR 97520, USA.

D. R. Watson   Department of Sociology, University of Manchester, Manchester M13 9PL, England.

Contents

v

List of tables

List of figures

Preface

Ever greater numbers of articles and books on a vast range of language learning topics and issues are being published. Some deal with theoretical issues in second language development, some look at bilingualism or cross-cultural communication, and others concern instructional materials and classroom procedures. This book focuses chiefly on the practical pursuits of learners and teachers in the classroom, and it does so from the unique vantage point of a particularly powerful and increasingly popular methodology known as simulation/gaming.

Versatility and need

Many language teachers' volumes and student textbooks include discussion on, or make use of, role-play or simulation/gaming. The language teaching profession is moving ineluctably toward a greater use of simulation/gaming, whether this be in general second or foreign languages, in languages for specific purposes, in computer-assisted language learning, or even within certain "schools" or "methods" of language instruction. Indeed, the word "simulation" is now used almost unawares, in contrast to a few years ago when it tended to raise eyebrows among language instructors.

And yet this is only the second major volume which has attempted to explore the issues, to outline some of the background, and to offer down-to-earth advice on practical concerns in language simulation/gaming. The first book to do this was published in 1982 by my friend Ken Jones. His book, written essentially from a simulation/gaming viewpoint, has had a quiet but steady influence on language teaching, and I would like to pay homage here, not only to his foresight in that book but also to his other books and to his simulation/games (which have been used by countless language teachers and others around the world).

So, despite the growing interest in, and widespread use made of, simulation/gaming in language learning, this edited volume is really the first comprehensive book to tackle the area from a language learning perspective. The authors show that the use of simulation/gaming for learning another language is just as worthy of attention and study as, say, curriculum design, testing, CALL, or learning strategies. Simulation/gaming has much to contribute to almost all areas in the language instruction arena, as the diversity of chapters in this volume amply testifies.

Experience and reflection

It has been said that taking part in a simulation/game is a little like scuba diving—you can only really know what it is like if you *do* it. This lies behind the adages that "you learn by doing" and "you learn what you do." So, in my workshops, only after participants have gained this common experience of participating in a few simulation/games do we talk about the methodology and attempt to link it to a more theoretical framework. In this way, participants can more vividly see the relationships between practice and theory; they can more clearly link new information to background knowledge—in keeping with the basic tenet of schema theory.

Even those chapters in this book which concern themselves with more theoretical issues are grounded in the ongoing and unfolding activity of simulation. There is no substitute for concrete experience followed by reflection and critical appraisal, and this applies as much to simulation/gaming as it does to many everyday pursuits of the language teacher, such as organizing the classroom, providing feedback to students, and designing learning materials. Doing it oneself and thinking are two different but complementary aspects of striving to help our learners learn.

Courses on simulation

Growing numbers of universities and teacher training units around the world are setting up courses, indeed whole programs, on simulation/gaming. The day is not far away when the first training program for language teachers (e.g., an M.A. in TESOL) will decide to devote a full-fledged, semester-long course to simulation/gaming in language learning. When this happens, it will no doubt be seen as a pioneer in the field, and the area of language learning through simulation/gaming will have come of age. That this should not have already happened is, at first sight, a little mystifying. After all, simulation/gaming is the object of increasing attention in language publications aimed at both learners and teachers.

If the present volume merely strengthens simulation/gaming components within existing courses, then it will prove to be a very useful reader and guidebook for teachers. If, though, this volume goes further and actually inspires the setting up of entire courses on the use of simulation/gaming in language learning, then not only will the trainees benefit enormously but the contributors to this volume will be extremely gratified.

What's in it for me?

The topics covered and the perspectives offered in this book are wide-ranging and include the *practice* of simulation/gaming (e.g., conducting and designing games), *specific applications* (e.g., reading and writing, business, science, teacher training, learner training, learning strategies, testing), *computers* and *theoretical background* (e.g., language acquisition, culture). In addition, one section contains two *ready-to-use exercises*, and there is a lengthy chapter of further *resources*.

The questions at the end of each section in the book are intended not so much as study questions, which have to be "worked through" in lieu of participation, but rather as catalysts for reflection and discussion on real experiences. Trainees might also be encouraged to generate their own questions for discussion and inquiry. Teachers using this book on their own can also gain much from reflecting on the questions, but they are also strongly encouraged to find a group of colleagues with whom to work and play, and to exchange ideas and share experiences.

Development of this book

Several years ago, I gradually became aware of how much simulation/gaming activity existed in the foreign and second language fields, and I thought that a book on the area would be valuable. I also felt that an area as vast as simulation/gaming, touching almost every conceivable aspect of language learning, needed the expertise of a range of authors rather than being confined to the experience of just one writer—hence, an edited volume.

When I first approached a number of authors about the possibility of editing a volume on the topic, I was overwhelmed by the response and enthusiasm. So much so, in fact, that I received enough proposals to fill two books. Some articles appeared in a special issue of *System*, 13:3 (which I guest-edited). Those that seemed to be better suited as book chapters were retained for the present volume, which, over the last few years, gradually took shape.

Acknowledgments

Many authors from many lands have contributed their expertise to this volume; without them this book would not have been written, and without any one contributor the book would be incomplete. My coeditor and I thank them heartily. We should also like to express our gratitude to our Newbury House editors, Leslie Berriman and Laurie Likoff (director of Newbury House), and to Cindy Funkhouser (production coordinator), for their encouragement and guidance throughout the last stages of this book. Thanks also to Jay Robbins (University of Alabama, USA) for helping to proofread.

My parents, Hilde and Robert, and my sister, Jean, have been of unswerving support ever since I can remember, and especially while this book was being put together. A great many colleagues and friends have inspired or helped me in numerous ways, and I cannot name them all here, but I particularly wish to acknowledge the following. Cathy Stein Greenblat (Rutgers University, USA, and past editor of *Simulation & Games*) has greatly influenced simulation/gaming around the world. I wish to record here my own gratitude to her for her friendship and encouragement. My friend Rod Watson (Manchester University, UK) has taken a close interest not just in this volume but in simulation more generally, and has been influential in my thinking. Alan Coote and Danny Saunders (both of Polytechnic of Wales, UK, and coeditors of *Simulation/Games for Learning*) deserve warm thanks for all that I have learned from them and for the fun we have had designing and playing games together. Alan Maley (formerly British Council, now Bell Educational Trust, UK) has inspired many a language teacher, including myself, and he provided much support during the initial stages of this book. A "thank you" goes to Norman Davies (editor of *System*) for his help with the special issue I had the privilege of guest-editing.

A great many other people should be mentioned for their encouragement or friendship during the time this book was being written. Among them, I particularly wish to mention Doug Coleman (University of Toledo, USA), Frank Frankel (British Council), Howie Giles (formerly University of Bristol, UK, now University of California, Santa Barbara, USA), Mike Grover (Multilingual Matters, UK), Henri Holec (CRAPEL, Université de Nancy II, France), Ken Jones (free-lance author, UK), Yves Luchaire (Université de Lille, France), June Robinson (Solent Simulations, UK), Robin Scarcella (University of California, Irvine, USA), Don Thatcher (Solent Simulations, UK), and Cath Walter (free-lance author, UK). I should also like to express my gratitude to my colleagues at the Université de Toulon et du Var (France), as well as to those at the University of Alabama (USA).

Many of my students have shown enthusiasm for simulation/gaming and provided invaluable critical feedback—especially my students over the years at the Université de Toulon et du Var (France). I am also indebted to those numerous interested teachers who have attended my workshops (both in Europe and in the United States). The challenges and ideas of all these have helped me better understand the intricacies, advantages, and problems related to the use of simulation/gaming for language learning.

This book is dedicated to Dick Brecht (professor of Russian and past dean of the College of Arts and Humanities at the University of Maryland, USA), Leo Schapira (professor of urban planning at the Universidad Nacional de Cordoba, Argentina), and Jon Wilkenfeld (professor of international politics at the University of Maryland, USA). We have worked together on what is probably the most exciting foreign language simulation yet to have been devised, a simulation which brings together peoples from around the world and which encourages the development of values and attitudes which real educators share: tolerance, open-mindedness, awareness and understanding of others, and the hope that the world will indeed one day become a peaceful global village. An account of this simulation, called ICONS, is provided in Chapter 13. With Leo, Jon, and Dick I have shared many disappointments, arguments, triumphs, and happy moments; all three have done much to enrich my life.

Finally, it was in part through ICONS that Rebecca Oxford and I came together. There were times when the Atlantic separated us, and our horrendous phone bills would have been astronomical had we not also been able to communicate using the computer networks that are at the heart of ICONS. And so it was that Rebecca accepted to help out, as coeditor, in the latter stages of this volume. The book as it now appears is largely due to her ideas and hard work; I sometimes wonder whether this book would have ever seen the light of day without her help. She has been instrumental in editing this volume, and my affectionate thanks go to her.

David Crookall

Le Pradet, France and Tuscaloosa, USA

Overview

Chapter 1

Linking language learning and simulation/gaming

David Crookall and Rebecca Oxford
University of Alabama

> I hear and I forget
> I see and I remember
> I do and I understand
> OLD CHINESE PROVERB

Imagine for a minute a small group of people intensely engaged in negotiations on how their countries should regulate the exploitation of fishing, oil, or deep-sea manganese nodules. Or think of detailed, indeed petty, wrangling between officials on what color their local buses should be painted. Or picture a large conference table around which are seated delegates from the European countries deeply involved in a heated and formal debate about quotas on wine or sugar production levels. These three snippets could be glimpses of the informal sessions of the actual United Nations Conference on the Law of the Sea, a local government agency meeting, or a Council of Agriculture Ministers meeting of the European Economic Community. But, in fact, they are examples of simulation sessions in language classes. Such sessions present situations, interactions, and practice opportunities which are very different from those found in many traditional language classrooms. A glance at the photographs (Figures 1.1–1.6) will provide a good idea of the dynamics of such sessions, as well as of the genuine concentration and involvement fostered by simulation/gaming for language learning. Indeed, one might not think they were photos of a language classroom at all, but they are; the students are actively engaged in the issues at stake and are communicating about them in a language which is not their mother tongue.

3

Figure 1.1   Photograph of a language simulation/gaming session.

Figure 1.2   Photograph of a language simulation/gaming session.

Figure 1.3   Photograph of a language simulation/gaming session.

Figure 1.4   Photograph of a language simulation/gaming session.

Figure 1.5   Photograph of a language simulation/gaming session.

Figure 1.6   Photograph of a language simulation/gaming session.

This book is about the use of the methodology of simulation/gaming in foreign and second language learning. Our authors explore the reasons why and the ways in which simulation/gaming may contribute to the achievement of certain language learning goals. Various aspects of simulation/gaming as a means of learning a new language are analyzed on a number of levels and from a variety of standpoints. The authors explore how simulation/gaming may be used to help learners acquire aspects of a foreign or second language and culture. Although the terms "foreign" and "second" are by no means synonymous, the use of simulation/gaming is just as effective for second as it is for foreign language learners, and the discussions contained between these covers are of relevance to both branches of language learning. Sometimes authors will refer to one or the other, but such reference is not intended as exclusive and should be taken as including both strands of interest. When reference is made simply to "language" (as in language learning or language learner) the term covers both foreign and second languages. Sometimes other words are also used—for example, a "new" or "another" language.

Most people have heard of simulation. The classic example is the airline pilot's training simulator: a mock cockpit which gives the trainee the impression of flying in a real aircraft. Another example, closer to the interests of language teachers, might be a situation in which one student is given a menu while another student takes the role of a waiter. Or again, it might be a meeting in which several students, representing diverse interests in a community, have to come to a decision on what route a new motorway should take or what new facilities should be built in the local school. The snippets given at the start of this chapter are also typical. Simulation can thus take an extremely wide range of forms.

Simulation/gaming techniques are proving to be an extremely powerful means of helping people to acquire certain foreign or second language skills. More and more language teachers are using an ever greater range of simulation/gaming methods in their classrooms and are doing so more and more regularly; indeed, some language courses are even based entirely around simulations and games. Basically, this increase in the use of simulation/gaming is due to the fact that communication plays such a vital role in many simulations, as it does in many social situations, and because simulation is an ideal way of developing communication skills.

It is also noteworthy that one of the areas of simulation/gaming application which has developed the most rapidly in recent years is precisely that of language learning. Just as simulation/gaming as a discipline has contributed much to language learning, and there can hardly be a language teacher who has not used some form of game or simulation at some time or other, so foreign/second language learning methodology has much to offer the simulation/gaming world (e.g., in its concern with language). It is in this perspective that this book also has much to offer to a wider readership than the second or foreign language teacher (e.g., first language teachers).

There are common points between simulation/gaming and the use of language (foreign, second, or native). Both language and simulation depend on rules, symbols, and codes. Both involve models, representations, realities, and negotiated meanings. (Later on, these and other complementary features will be discussed in a little more detail.) Our aim, in this chapter, is largely of an orientational kind; so, rather than outline each chapter individually, we shall confine ourselves to a more general commentary. Other chapters in this volume will provide more specific comments. Here we first summarize how the volume is organized. We then discuss the importance of communication in foreign/second language learning. Following this we outline some basic concepts in simulation/gaming. Finally, in tying together these various threads, we outline some of the ways in which simulation may help people to learn another language.

Organization of contents

Two of the implicit aims of this volume are to highlight the many links between the two fields of simulation/gaming and language instruction, and to show how they may be seen as mutually supportive, with an emphasis on how simulation/gaming contributes to language learning. The book is aimed mainly at teachers using, wishing to use, or studying simulation/gaming techniques as a means of encouraging the learning of a foreign or second language.

Seven sections have been selected for organizing the discussions in the book. At this point we must recognize the inherent problem associated with any work that covers a wide range of topics and crosses disciplines: organization of material. In short, there is more than one way of looking at a subject or writing about it. There are doubtless other alternative plans that would have been suited to the volume's broad aim, but the plan chosen has the advantage of being relatively simple; conceptually, the middle sections (B to E) move from the practical to the more theoretical. The seven sections are as follows:

Section A—Overview
Section B—Practical aspects
Section C—Specific applications
Section D—Using computers
Section E—Background
Section F—Sample simulation/games
Section G—Sources and resources

Section A contains just one chapter (this one)—a general overview of the links between language learning and simulation/gaming. Section B contains chapters of an essentially practical nature, which will be valuable to those who use or wish to use simulation/games now, but who do not need discussions on specific aspects or background rationale.

Section C is also concerned with practical matters, but it discusses specific areas of application—for example, language for specific purposes, testing, teacher training, learner training, and learning strategies. Section D discusses a number of practical and theoretical aspects of using computers in simulation for foreign/second language learning.

Section E provides some background discussion. Topics here include the relations among culture, communication, and language; social psychological aspects; language acquisition; the realities of participation; and ethical problems.

Section F brings us back to more practical concerns and offers a few simulation/games that can be used in the classroom. Section G contains an annotated a list of suggested further readings, as well as information on simulation/game associations and journals. In addition, the reference list (at the end of the book) contains a number of articles or books not cited in any of the chapters, but of potential interest to readers.

Communication in foreign/second language learning

The importance of being able to communicate in another language arises, not because of something intrinsic to that other language, but simply because communication, in any form and in any language, is a vital part of society and our social relations. The more forward-looking language instructional methodologies emphasize the communicative aspects of language learning. This emphasis does not exist simply because foreign/second language scholars or researchers have decreed it; it has come about because we now recognize more clearly that a new language, like one's own native tongue, is usually used as a means of communicating with others. Communication is not an adjunct to a language; rather, the target language is just one means of communication. Communication is the key thing, and it often takes place in many different languages. Rather than considering communication as a (subordinate) part of a new language, we emphasize the foreign/second language dimension of communication—communication remains the fundamental objective of learning another language.[1]

[1] For further discussion on some of the points made throughout this chapter, see Crookall et al. (1987, 1989), from which some of the ideas and phrasing in parts of this chapter have been taken.

Scope and nature of communication

Communication has, in recent years, become a popular theme for eclectic discussions that cannot easily be contained within any one conventionally defined discipline, and has attracted scholars from many areas. Communication is now widely recognized as a vital resource on many fronts. This is reflected, for example, by the heated debates going on in various international forums on the right to communicate, by the UN proclamation of 1983 as World Communications Year, by the rapidly expanding field of communications studies, and, above all, by the heightened awareness of the central importance of communication in many disciplines, such as language learning, sociology, social psychology, management studies, politics, international relations, media studies, and education. Here we present a definition of communication, outline its scope, summarize factors leading to a general increase in communication, touch on the concept of communication as a basic human right, and mention some barriers to communication.

Natural languages are not only humanity's most important sign system (Berger & Luckmann, 1966) but are ipso facto the major means of communication across the world. Just as our world would not exist without communication, much communication would hardly be possible without language. As Fisher (1982) succinctly puts it, "Life depends on communication . . ."; communication is thus crucial to the continuation of the human race. More specifically,

> Communication maintains and animates life. It is also the motor and expression of social activity and civilization; . . . it creates a common pool of ideas, strengthens the feeling of togetherness through exchange of messages and translates thought into action, reflecting every emotion and need from the humblest tasks of human survival to supreme manifestations of creativity—or destruction. Communication integrates knowledge, organization and power and runs as a thread linking the earliest memory of man to his noblest aspirations. . . . (MacBride et al., 1980)

Cheery (1957) reminds us that "communication is essentially a social affair." The socially constructed nature of communication implicitly places the priority on conversation and language. These involve human participants rather than inanimate senders and receivers pumping information along channels; or to put it another way, communication is more than two robots on the telephone. Communication is a complex, dynamic, and qualitative process involving the creation, interpretation, negotiation, and exchange of meanings by individuals and social groups (see, e.g., Fiske, 1982; O'Sullivan et al., 1983).

This perspective on communication puts language at the center of communication, and this has had a direct impact on the more recent language learning methods. Language instruction has begun to focus on aspects of negotiation and interpretation between parties who are actively involved with the social situation, its definitions and realities, and who construct a variety of meanings rooted in cultures and society. Thus, language instruction is beginning to see communication as embedding and embodying language and foreign/second language, rather than trying, as it were, to graft a communication component on to some formal and pre-social language system. Language exists because social relations require communication; communication remains the ultimate goal of language. It so happens that there is more than one language in this world, and this may often make communication problematic; cultural differences complicate things further.

Multilingual communication

The need to understand and deal with other cultures in today's global village is more urgent than at any time in the history of humanity. This has contributed to the increase in multilingual communication around the world. The sense of our planet as a global village and the phenomenon of multilingual communication have grown hand in hand. Today, about 60 percent of the world's population is multilingual, and the mastering of other languages as a means of cross-cultural communication has become crucial to the survival of the world. It is useful to look at some examples, for they highlight the necessity of being able to communicate in more than one language, and they help focus attention on the methods we use to learn other languages.

The exponential increase in multilingual communication at all levels of human activity can be seen in many areas. Whether the following examples are causes, effects, or symptoms is beyond our present discussion: population movements of various kinds and for a variety of motives; the growing self-awareness of ethnic groups, and often their desire for independence from nation states; the ever-increasing complexity of politics both within and between nations; the increase in travel, and the explosion in media (telephones, television, and satellites); the proliferation of publications of all kinds; the international concern with the never-ending depletion of natural resources (such as the Amazon forest); and last but not least, the wars waged in many corners of the world.

Paradoxically, some of the factors which have led to an increase in multilingual communication have also put up barriers to such communication. These include complexity (e.g., in international relations), speed (e.g., in satellite transmission), social and technological change, the assertion of ethnic identities, poor intergroup relations, and problems associated with multilingualism itself.

One way of overcoming such barriers is to increase the number of people who learn additional languages. But learning a new language as a body of unapplied rules does not help; people need to be able to *communicate* in that language. This requires more than rote language manipulation exercises. It needs a learning environment in which learners can use the language creatively for communicative ends.

When we speak of communication between cultures we necessarily speak of using a variety of languages, some of which may be new to at least one of the parties to the communicative act. The mastery of foreign and second languages has thus come to the forefront of educational activity and international concerns, and there is no reason to suppose that the importance of multilingual (and multicultural) communication will decrease. However, it is another question as to whether language teaching/learning techniques are as effective as they should be in achieving their objective of making such communication easier. The urgency for effective multilingual communication thus raises a key question: How well does present-day language teaching methodology meet the need?

Communication in language instruction

Communicative competence has become a major concern in most of the recent foreign and second language instructional approaches, methods, and techniques, but they do vary in the relative explicitness with which they aim to achieve communicative competence. Most of these practices recognize that an individual's motivational level and emotional state strongly affect language learning. Communication itself is an important element of motivation. A student who can see no (communicative) value in what is learned will probably not be particularly interested in learning with that method, especially if he or she actually needs to be able to communicate with others.

The communicative dimension of language teaching methods has waxed and waned over the centuries and seems now to be at a high-water mark. A spate of books and articles has recently been published about communicative language teaching and its close relative, proficiency-oriented instruction. However, this popularity begs the question of what is actually going on in the language classroom. In many institutions, some of the older methods linger on, and observations of real classroom behavior (e.g., Seliger & Long, 1983) show that communicative language teaching is sometimes more an ideal than a reality, even for teachers who are aware of communication as a major goal. And, even when teachers have accepted the general idea of communicative language instruction, they do not always know what it is or how to implement it.

Encouraging communication among students in the classroom requires a rather radical shift in roles and classroom organization. "It is now inconceivable to regard the teacher as sole arbiter and controller of what goes on in language classrooms" (Maley, 1984). Communicative language instruction changes the essential role of the teacher from that of a classroom conductor to that of a partner in the learning process (often also termed a resource person or facilitator of learning). Many teachers find this change to be a threat, especially when it necessitates letting go of cherished ideas and familiar habits inherited from their own teachers or encouraged by their employers. But, despite these problems, there are many language classrooms around the world in which communication is not only encouraged but also effectively taught.

The basic strategy behind a communicative language classroom is to put students in social situations and give them interesting activities and tasks, which, by allowing them to interact, create in them a desire to communicate. But thinking of such situations and activities is not such an easy thing, so the more enlightened language teachers are beginning to look elsewhere than to foreign/second language instructional theory and applied linguistics for ways of creating a communicative climate in the classroom. Such sources of ideas and materials include the social sciences, business training, and cross-cultural orientation. These areas already use some rather creative and interesting exercises, which capture the students' interest and imagination, and which therefore encourage them to interact. Examples of such activities used in language instruction include problem-solving activities, debates, tasks, trips, and the celebration of festivals and special cultural events typical of the country where the new language is spoken.

One of the most promising and increasingly popular techniques for encouraging communication in the language classroom has proved to be simulation/gaming. The more recent and more communicatively oriented language teaching methodologies have advocated, if only implicitly, greater use of simulation as an important language learning technique. This parallels the increase in simulation use in a wide range of other disciplines, particularly in those which recognize communication as essential to their full understanding and practice. But to understand fully these developments, we need to look at the nature of simulation, particularly as related to language learning, and it is to this which we now turn.

Simulation/gaming

We have discussed various aspects of communication and language instruction as a backdrop to our discussion on simulation. Here we will look at the nature of simulation/gaming, touch on the concept of simulation/

gaming as a "language" for education, training, and research, and analyze aspects of simulation as both representation and reality.

Simulation has witnessed a spectacular development in recent years and has come to be widely recognized as a valuable means of learning about a whole range of phenomena and fields, particularly those in which communication is important—for example, conflict, decision making, language behavior, intergroup relations, cultural values, and language learning, to name but a few. There has been widespread recognition, in a great many fields, of the powerful features of simulation as a tool of research, as an experiential study aid, and as a professional training instrument.

Simulation as a language for learning

Of particular relevance to language learning is the conception of simulation itself as being a language or a form of communication (Duke, 1974, 1989). Both simulation and language have their own vocabularies, syntax, meaning systems, and analytic tools. We learn about the world in learning a language, and likewise the activity called "simulating" is also learning about the world. Three ways of learning correspond to three main areas of simulation application: education, training, and research. In *education* and *training*, four interrelated reasons are often cited for using simulation. First, it motivates and is fun; second, it is more congruent with the learning process than chalk-and-talk teaching practices; third, it is more like the "real" world than the traditional classroom. Finally (and perhaps most significantly), simulation results in positive outcomes, such as more active participation, improved performance, greater retention, and better understanding of complexity. In *research*, simulations may be used to generate data (e.g., for statistical studies), as objects of study in themselves (to learn about what happens in them), as measuring instruments (to test students), and as predictors (to see how people will perform in a given situation, or to gain insight into possible futures).

Representation and reality

There are two main ways of viewing simulations, and both are relevant to language learning. One perspective sees them as merely *representations* of some other real-worldly system, and has been called the "representational" viewpoint. This is the view commonly adopted by language instruction methodology. In this view, simulation is seen as somehow representing some real-worldly system; simulation is a symbol with a referent and thereby draws its essential meaning from that referent. For example, an appointments board meeting can be simulated by having participants represent the various parties involved (essentially board members and candidates); an international relations simulation may have participants taking the roles of various ministers of, say, half a dozen countries.

Simulation is "brought to life" by participants. In being activated, however, it gains autonomy and takes on a reality of its own, thereby leaving the domain of pure representativity. During a simulation the notion or feeling of representativity fades.

Thus, another, less common, view sees simulations as *operating realities* in their own right—that is, as not necessarily having direct or explicit representational power or value. Participants do not necessarily see their activity as simulating. For them simulation is a very real experience; it establishes its own reality, which *might* also have relevance to some other world or system. In this lies the essential nature of the "reality" perspective. Simulation is often defined as real by participants, and it may thus be conceived as a real world in its own right. A simulation session on job appointments may seem very real to the participants, and they will argue at length about this or that candidate, even though there is in fact no actual job which the chosen candidate will take up afterwards. In an international relations simulation, the issues involved between countries may be based, say, on a past real-world international crisis, but the types of interactions and the outcomes of negotiations in the simulation may take paths very different from the real ones, and yet participants during the session will behave as though the issues and actions counted for real.

A real situation, whether simulation or any other, is one in which participants are personally involved. Indeed, during a performance, participants may not be explicitly aware of simulating; they do not continually ask themselves, "What does this represent?" in terms of the real (non-simulation) world. This is precisely because they get involved, and the performance becomes very real in its own terms. If simulation is regarded and treated as a reality taken for granted in its own right, then the experiences of participants become real, and the use of language becomes meaningful communication. Simulations thus encourage language participants to use their new language in the ways most people do in other (similar, but real) situations.

The two perspectives (representation and reality) are not necessarily incompatible. Neither is sufficient to explain the phenomenon of simulation; both are necessary for a full understanding of what constitutes simulation. *Debriefing*, the discussion period which follows a simulation session, can be seen as an essential link between the two perspectives, allowing parallels to be drawn between the reality of the simulation performance and that of the real world. These two perspectives have implications for two other important characteristics of simulation: their relative safety and their relatively inexpensive nature.

A relatively safe and inexpensive learning environment

Related to the above two perspectives on simulation (representation and reality) are two important and interrelated characteristics which account, at least in part, for its power as a learning methodology.

One of the purposes of a simulation is to broaden and deepen participants' perceptions and interpretations of the real world, while another is to refine their skills; both cases constitute learning. The drawback of performing for real, of learning in the real world, is that the learner is prone to making mistakes which may be costly for the system (including the learner him/herself). So we replace the system with a replica, in which the costs of making an error are greatly reduced and contained within the framework of the simulation.

Simulation thus protects people from the otherwise potentially severe consequences of making mistakes, and yet in so doing allows these mistakes to be examined. It provides learners with a relatively safe (or non-threatening) learning environment. The mistakes are made in the simulation, not in the outside world. For example, if a pilot makes a mistake in an aircraft simulator, she or he may come away feeling a bit jittery, but no real damage will have been caused—the plane will not have been damaged and no one will have been killed.

The relatively *low cost* of an error, compared with that of a similar error in the real system, means that participants are less constrained. They know they perform under conditions of relative safety, which in turn means that they can experiment with certain behaviors which would be too risky in the real world. However, learners do not lose all fear of making a mistake just because they are in a simulation, for a simulation can become a totally real situation for participants (as we saw above). Because participants define the simulation activity as real, the consequences of any errors are experienced as real, but errors have very low negative consequences *outside* the simulation. Language learners are thus freer to make mistakes and be creative with the language without the crippling fear of longer-term consequences, and yet when mistakes are made, they remain meaningful within the simulation itself.

The relatively inexpensive nature of simulation is not only related to the cost of errors but is also due to the fact that a simulation is cheaper to run than certain real events. For example, it is far cheaper for a dozen students to spend a day or two taking part in a large-scale foreign language simulation than it is to fly them across the Atlantic. This is not to say, of course, that simulation can replace real-world experience abroad. Simulation is useful because it is able to put participants in situations which resemble real ones, and thereby prepare them for real ones. Simulation can be seen as a bridge between the often ascetic traditional classroom and the flux of the outside world.

In addition, a particular situation may just not be practical or available in the real world. For example, it is hardly possible to let most students loose in a real UN Conference on the Law of the Sea, or let them represent a real company negotiating a major contract abroad, and yet it can be extremely instructive for learners to gain experience of using their language skills in these types of situations.

Keywords

There is little consensus on the terminology used in the simulation/gaming literature, and this is reflected in this volume, each author using the terms in his or her own way. A variety of terms abounds, which can, on first encounter, appear rather bewildering. We find such terms as "simulation," "game," "role-play," "simulation/game," "simulation-game," "game/simulation," "game-simulation," "gamed simulation," "role-play simulation," "role-playing game." Although the distinctions are not always crucial, it may be useful to discuss some of them, especially so that readers following up on the references do not worry unduly about the use of different terms. We accept the inherent ambiguity that arises from these terms; indeed, they also tend to be used interchangeably throughout this volume, as they are in much of the literature on this topic. Rather than detracting from a fruitful discussion on simulation/gaming, such fluidity may even contribute to the debate by keeping doors open, and allowing readers to come to their own conclusions. However, for newcomers to the area, it is worth outlining some main distinctions and making some tentative suggestions. Our own preference is to use "simulation" as a general category or short-form term, which may contain elements of games and/or role-play, and the term "simulation/gaming" to refer to the field as a whole.

We have discussed simulation, especially in terms of representation, reality, relative safety, and low cost. The word "game," however, is one of the most difficult to delineate and has probably engendered even more debate than simulation. Game is at once a narrower and a broader concept than simulation; much depends on how games are seen in relation to simulation. Here we shall delineate a strict or technical sense (where they are different but complementary concepts), and a broader or more general one (where "game" is equated with "simulation").

The fundamental difference between some game forms (in the strict sense) and a simulation lies in the two major features discussed above—i.e., representativity and negligible error consequence. In terms of representativity and error cost, games show almost the contrary effects to simulations. In contrast to a simulation, a game (in our technical sense) does not usually represent any real-world system (although it may have been inspired by one, e.g., CHESS), and costs of game errors can be high for the real world (e.g., losing money at POKER). Both effects are related; consequences may be costly precisely because a game is not a representation. A classic example is the nationalist fervor generated by the Olympic Games, which is expressed not only by the players but, well beyond the games themselves, by fans and sponsors. A game in the strictest sense, therefore, does not purport to represent any part of another system; it has no real-life referent, and it is a real-world system in its own right.

Despite this technical distinction, some activities often referred to as "games" actually simulate processes like decision making, and their substantive area is relatively unimportant. Thus, some games aim to mirror or represent various social, economic, or political processes, and this brings us to the more general sense of the term. General usage allows such terms as "political gaming" and "business game," but these should properly be regarded as simulation. Most instances of use require no distinction to be made, and writers follow their own individual preferences, often using the term "game" interchangeably with "simulation." Not inconsequentially, "game" is easier and more pleasant than "simulation," the former often thus being used in place of the latter. This may also be the reason why "gamer" is by far the most common term used in referring to those who carry out, design, or otherwise work with simulation/games. Other titles exists, such as "gamester," "simulationist," or even "simulator," the first also often being an alternative to "player," while the latter two appear unsatisfactory for fairly obvious reasons. Despite the fluidity in the use of such terms, debates about the formal differences between simulation and game continue, with many book and journal titles reflecting a healthy willingness to compromise.

In language instruction, the term "game" usually refers to small-scale activities (e.g., CHARADES or 20 QUESTIONS), which aim principally at allowing players to practice a language component or a narrow range of them (e.g., structures, asking questions). These types of language learning games do not claim much more than a rather tenuous representational value, although it can, of course, be argued that merely by using language in a relatively free and naturalistic speech situation, some representation is achieved. However, except in the use of language, such games do not generally purport to resemble real-world situations in any substantive or substantial way. Thus, the term "game" would seem to be the more apt one in such instances, and in these cases "game" is not a substitute for "simulation" (as noted above).

Let us now consider the term "role-play." It is useful to consider this as simply one aspect of simulation, as a component embedded within simulation, rather than as a totally separate type of activity. A role-play is always a simulation, but a simulation need not necessarily involve any significant role-playing. Role-play is usually defined as a social or human activity in which participants take on and act out specified roles, often within a predefined social framework or situational blueprint (a scenario). This view, however, does not explicitly express the simulation aspect of role-play and sees role-play as the general category, rather than as a particular aspect of a more general activity—that of simulation. The concept of role-play sometimes conjures images of theater or fantasy, where acting or performing rather than participating predominates. However, mainstream role-play is usually inspired by some kind of other external reality. It is because of this underlying representational property that role-play should really be seen as a component of simulation.

In our view, then, a role-play is always a simulation. The participant in a role-play activity is representing and experiencing some character type known in everyday life, and the interaction between participants is a simulation of a social situation. The distinction between between role-play simulation and non-role-play simulation is a question of degree, not of kind. In language learning, the term "role-play" tends to be used more than "simulation" or "simulation/gaming," perhaps because it sounds less technical and therefore less threatening to teachers. However, teachers need to recognize that role-play is essentially a form of simulation.[2]

Enhancing language learning through simulation

In Chapter 18, Gardner and Lalonde make the intriguing suggestion that all types of foreign/second language classroom activity can be thought of as simulations of actual language behavior. Extremely artificial language learning situations, such as those that require memorizing word lists or drilling dialogues, "can be viewed as instances of low-level simulation of language activity." Role-playing, games, and dramatic techniques, however, "exemplify simulation strategies that foster language development" of a more natural, authentic kind. This book is primarily about this latter type.

Simulation is much more than a Friday afternoon respite from more tedious exercises and is being used more and more as a standard feature in language learning situations. It is somewhat unfortunate that early applications of simulation (mainly in the form of unprepared and often stilted skits, led by inexperienced or unprepared teachers) resulted in the inappropriate criticism of simulations as time-killers that required little thought and skill.

Simulation, if effectively used, can be a means of overcoming certain limitations of the classroom as a language learning environment, or as

[2]For further discussions on terminology, see Duke (1974), Greenblat and Duke (1981), Crookall et al. (1987), Greenblat (1988), and K. Jones (1987, 1988).

Sharrock and Watson (1985) express it, for "declassrooming the classroom." Simulation thus "extends the range of experiences" (Greenblat, 1988) normally made available to learners. One of these experiences is using the new language communicatively (i.e., both accurately and fluently)—in a self-initiated and purposeful way. Simulation allows language learners to create their own communication realities, rather than being entirely dependent upon the teacher for providing a model; it allows participants to learn by doing—by doing it for themselves.

> Gaming-simulations have been successfully designed and utilized to meet a number of teaching and training objectives including the following: (1) Increasing motivation and interest . . . (2) Teaching: conveying information or reinforcing information already given in another format . . . (3) Skill development . . . (4) Attitude change . . . (5) Self-evaluation or evaluation by others. . . .
>
> In a gaming-simulation . . . the class members are *active learners*. They must make decisions, pay the consequences, articulate positions, and make the system work. . . . Students experience the topic as a whole. . . . Previously silent members of a class sometimes become the most vocal and active participants. . . . Gaming-simulations are particularly for conveying *system* characteristics. . . . A simulation . . . can be an even more potent teaching tool than a graphic model. . . . Gaming-simulations rely considerably on game-specific symbols, not simply on words. Thus students develop orientations to particular concepts. . . . While gaming-simulations will not solve all educational problems, it is clear that they offer exciting opportunities for teaching and learning about a great many social systems and social problems. (Greenblat, 1988; emphasis in the original)

As the above quote shows, simulation/gaming provides a richness in learning which appears to be unobtainable by other methods. Let us look at just a few of the more specific ways in which the above broad advantages of simulation/gaming can be seen to work when using simulation/gaming for learning an additional language. The language advantages both draw on and go beyond the advantages already noted.

The kind of language used in simulations is more authentic and richer than that usually found in a typical teacher-directed classroom, which means the problems of real communication can be explored. In a simulation, communication may proceed uninterrupted by teacher intervention, just as it does in most other situations, allowing participants to grasp and convey meaning in a more natural, free-flowing way. But, as Chapter 19 points out, active involvement in communication is essential. Simulation encourages such involvement by providing learners with an appealing and relevant context in which, collectively, they make decisions, solve problems, negotiate agreements, and the like. Moreover, apart from the tasks and problems in the simulation at hand, freer interaction is itself motivating and allows students to practice a wider variety of both communication and learning strategies (see Chapter 8).

As mentioned earlier, one important characteristic of simulation is its low error consequence for the real world; in other words, the real system and people being represented will not be greatly affected if errors are made in the simulation. When this principle is applied to a language simulation, it means that language communication gaffes made during the simulation, while real and meaningful in the simulation itself, will not have any serious effects on the outside world. This allows the language learner to make mistakes in the simulation that would be less acceptable elsewhere. As a result, the anxiety level is often lower in a simulation than it is elsewhere (including in teacher-directed classrooms). Simulation reduces anxiety in several other ways, as well. Participants are under less pressure to produce complex language than they may be in other situations, and K. Jones (1982) notes that anxiety is reduced in simulations because the teacher's role is reduced. In addition, since the focus of comparison is on peers, simulation "reduce[s] anxiety associated with communicating in a new language, . . . create[s] a sense of self-confidence . . . [and] permits the development of the non-verbal component" (Gardner & Lalonde, Chapter 18).[3] Harper (1985) emphasizes the advantage of simulation in helping language students to build a positive self-image. Reduced anxiety encourages the simulation participant to communicate more, and more spontaneously, although some tension can help in language learning (Brown, 1987). We should, however, be cautious about asserting the existence of a universal and inevitable reduction of anxiety and inhibition in simulations, especially if students already work in a competitive atmosphere or hostile environment. This is even more true if hostility and competition are created within a simulation (e.g., in STARPOWER) and not discussed and defused sufficiently during the debriefing session.

Another aspect of simulation that is especially pertinent to language learning is its ability to reflect the culture of the target language (Dubin, 1985; Sawyer-Lauçanno, 1987). Human communication is culture-bound; that is, membership in a particular culture determines the ways in which we communicate. At the same time, culture is defined and learned through communication, so there is a reciprocal relationship between culture and communication (see Chapter 17). Although some simulations are culture-generic, language simulations often embody elements of the specific culture surrounding the target language. Simulation, because of its participatory quality and because it not only simulates reality but also constitutes a reality in itself, allows the learner to communicate as a member of the temporary

---

[3]For a number of simulation/games designed specifically to deal with over-anxiety in language learners and teacher trainees, see Crookall (1990) and Crookall and Oxford (1990).

simulation culture. "Simulation and game designs familiarize participants with the cultural and social significance of a second language . . ." (Saunders & Crookall, 1985).

Additional advantages of simulation for language learning relate indirectly to communication. Simulation/games can be used to good effect for the learning of a few travel phrases, for "survival language" needs (Hare & McAleese, 1985; Raz, 1985), or for moving toward higher levels of proficiency. Because simulations can be designed to deal with a particular subject or skill area, they are uniquely suited to languages for specific purposes (LSP); for example, they are of great benefit to those who need to use the language for highly specialized, job-related purposes, such as in business, science, technology, and international relations (see Chapters 11, 12, and 13).

Because simulation/gaming is an extremely versatile tool, useful in a wide range of both skills and substantive areas, it is particularly useful for some specific aspects of the language learning process. Some of these are discussed in this book—for example, learner training (Chapter 7), learning strategies (Chapter 8), integrating language skills (Chapter 9), and testing (Chapter 10). In connection with the last, it is noteworthy that one of the major tests, the Oral Proficiency Interview (ACTFL/ETS/ILR), makes use of mini role-play/simulations. Teacher training is an extremely important part of the overall language learning scene, and we are lucky to have a lengthy chapter (6) on this which shows how simulation can be used for various aspects of teacher training/development.

Underlying the above advantages of using simulation in foreign and second language classrooms is the general principle of providing students with a relatively safe learning environment in which they may practice and develop a range of communication skills. Because simulation is essentially experiential (learning by doing), such skills can be transferred relatively easily to the outside world; simulation helps the language learner to move from the classroom to the real world (see, e.g., Chapter 18; Cunningsworth & Horner, 1985.)

It might be suggested that certain features of simulations (e.g., low anxiety and minimal error consequence) make simulations unrealistic because we must live with our errors and cope with consequent anxiety in the real world. The counterargument is that simulation is a stepping-stone, a gentle (but active) introduction to many of the demanding aspects of multilingual communication and cultural plurality. If, in the classroom, there is little significant learning of multilingual communication skills because of anxiety and punishment of errors, then there is little chance that the longer-term effects of such anxiety or punishment will miraculously disappear outside; and even if they do, the learner will anyway be left with few of the necessary target language communication skills. Simulation helps students learn more efficiently by making the language learning experience real, by taking the learning experience out of its more usual, purely academic setting, and by engaging the student in actively using the new language. Only by communicating with each other can simulation participants hope to tackle problems, make decisions, negotiate meanings, define realities, and the like. In simulation, as in the real world, communication forms the bedrock of human activity; simulation provides a useful training environment for the development of communication skills in the target language.

Simulation is uniquely suited to developing communication skills that play an important role in cross-cultural and multilingual interaction. This has resulted in two further developments. First, gamers are becoming more aware of the need to examine the communication patterns that evolve during simulation. Second, the introduction of simulation into language courses/programs inevitably increases the types, complexity, and importance of communication patterns used. This leads us to rethink the structure of language classrooms and teacher-learner relations.

Conclusion

The foregoing discussion has shown the usefulness of simulation/gaming in exploring multilingual communication processes and in developing communication skills in another language. Both communication and simulation involve the use of sign and symbol systems, such as language. Language, and to a lesser extent other sign systems, form the bricks and mortar of both simulation and communication; both depend upon language for their operation. Communication between people (and between people and technology) consists largely, though not exclusively, of language behavior. It may be said that simulation is both a form of language and a medium for learning another language.

The need to understand and to accept other cultures and languages is more urgent than at any time in the history of humankind. If handled with care, simulation/gaming can be a particularly fruitful methodology in helping people from different cultures to understand each other, particularly by helping them to develop effective foreign and second language communication skills.

To end the beginning of this volume, we should like to quote at length from one of our most creative and talented gamers. Although the occasion of the simulation session described in the quote was not explicitly for the purposes of learning another language or culture, it depicts vividly and illustrates impressively the power of simulation to foster communication across language and cultural boundaries.

One of the most frustrating (but ultimately one of the most rewarding) developmental tests I have ever done with a simulation was in Cameroon, West Africa, in early 1985. My fellow designers of CAPJEFOS (a simulation of village development) and I had arranged a field test at an agricultural school in Kumba, about two hours from where we were working. A few days before the run was to take place, we drove to Kumba and carefully checked out the facilities, the arrangements for lunch, the number of students to be brought together for the exercise, and so on. It did not occur to us to ask about whether all the participants spoke English, the language in which the simulation materials were written! Hence we were dismayed when we began the day-long session and were immediately informed that half the participants were French-speaking; most knew some English but they were not comfortable with it, and contended that they could understand neither us nor their simulation materials (such as role profiles).

Fortunately, two of us spoke some French. We were able to regain enough composure after the shock wore off to offer our introductory remarks and explanations in both languages, and to provide oral translations of the written materials. This slowed things down considerably, but at least we could proceed. The next problem was that participants needed to talk to one another to make the simulation operate. Several "farmers," for example, were English-speaking but found that they had French-speaking "spouses" with whom they needed to interact to make decisions. The "traditional doctor" was French-speaking, and his services were needed by all. And many of the villagers found that the "development agents," who offered the possibility of improvements in health and agricultural practices, sometimes did not speak their language, both literally and figuratively. They struggled to understand one another, however, and in most cases succeeded.

By the time we stopped for lunch, we were exhausted and were concerned that the session was proceeding much more slowly than planned. Our spirits were revived, however, when we heard the exuberance of the regular faculty of the school. They exclaimed that this was the first time they had ever seen the two groups of students (the English-speaking and the French-speaking) interact with one another in anything but a superficial (and sometimes hostile) manner. Challenged by the simulation and by their desire to participate successfully in it, however, students had made the first attempt to overcome the barrier of language difference—an effort we were told continued beyond the day's enterprise.

Too often, members of different cultures have no opportunities to interact, or have encounters which are analysed only with those of "one's own kind." Bringing members of different groups together in the context of a simulation, however, presents a rich opportunity for first generating the typical misunderstandings and then for collective consideration of these differences—i.e. for understanding the misunderstanding. (Greenblat, 1989:279–280)

Questions and activities

The questions at the end of each section are designed to help teachers come to grips with some of the main ideas and issues discussed in the chapters contained in that section. Some of the questions are reasonably straightforward and remain fairly factual, although teachers may come up with answers that differ from, or that supplement, those proposed in the chapters, and this should be seen as a healthy sign. However, many of the questions are more immediately open to a wide range of possible answers, and actually require some form of critical appraisal and original thought.

If possible, teachers should probably be asked, not to answer questions on their own, but rather to consider them in small groups. The questions should be seen, not so much as hurdles to be overcome or as some kind of test, but rather as triggers to cooperative discussion and as prompts for thoughtful dialog in which there are no right answers—merely a sharpening of perceptions and understandings. This applies to the questions below, as well as to those at the end of the other sections.

1. List five ways in which language learning and simulation/gaming are linked, and give examples where possible.
2. What are the role and the significance of communication in second or foreign language learning?
3. How would you define communicative competence? What elements constitute communicative competence, in your opinion? To what extent is communicative competence a goal in language classrooms today? In your language classroom?
4. Why is multilingualism on the rise? Give at least five reasons, either from this chapter or from your own personal observation.
5. Simulation has been called a "language." Why is this so?
6. Explain the difference between the *representation perspective* and the *reality perspective* in simulation/gaming. How do these two perspectives interact? How do these two perspectives relate to second or foreign language learning?
7. In what ways does simulation/gaming provide a safe, inexpensive environment for learning a new language? With other people, brainstorm as many ways as possible and list them on a large sheet.

Now, in light of this list, discuss the benefits simulation/gaming might bring to your own classes.

8. Say what *you* mean by the following key terms:

simulation	simulation/gaming	scenario
game	role-playing	player
simulation/game	gamer	

How and why do your ideas differ from those offered in the chapter?

9. In what ways can simulation/gaming "declassroom the classroom"? List at least three ways.

Practical aspects

Introduction

Practical aspects of using simulation/ gaming in language learning

This section contains four chapters, each considering a particular aspect of the practical side of simulation/gaming. The practical aspects of simulation/gaming are, of course, not always plain sailing. Classes are taught in institutional settings and within a certain educational ethos or (at least) an attitude on the part of fellow teachers and the educational establishment as to what constitutes "good teaching" (as, say, opposed to helping or facilitating learning). It is not always easy to resist pressure to do things in certain ways, especially if such things are seen as departing radically from orthodox practices. If you are at least aware of certain constraints, you will no doubt find it easier to run simulation/games and to encourage colleagues to try them out.

Chapter 2, on conducting simulation/games, takes us straight into the nitty-gritty of the activity itself. David Horner and Kevin McGinley provide a series of guidelines on how to run a simulation, and look at the many smaller problems and practical moves involved at each step in conducting a simulation/game session. Whether you are a newcomer to simulation/ gaming or an old hand, this chapter will be a valuable guide, but it cannot, of course, be any substitute for actually running a session yourself. Many teachers, especially those who have tended to keep tight control of the class, may understandably feel apprehensive when running a simulation/ game for the first time. As the authors emphasize, one of the tenets of simulation/gaming is that there is nothing like practice and practical experience for learning, and this goes too for learning to conduct simulation/ games. There is certainly nothing wrong in being cautious about running a simulation/game for the first time; indeed, we (and no doubt many of the writers in this volume, too) were nervous before we conducted our first game, and sometimes still are a little when we run a new game for the first time. However, once you have run a couple of games, you will gain considerable confidence and eventually wonder what all the fuss was about.

If you are a newcomer, there are a number of ways of getting initial reassurance in running simulation/games—in addition to the guidelines offered in Chapter 2. One way is to ask a colleague to run a game with you. The colleague may be a newcomer or an experienced gamer; both types have their advantages. A newcomer will be in the same boat as you, and this is reassuring; an experienced gamer will be able to provide you with may useful tips. Another way is to get experience as a participant, so you can see what your students will be doing later. This can be achieved by gathering a number of colleagues together to try out a few simulation/games or by attending a simulation/gaming workshop or conference. Workshops are probably the ideal form of learning about simulation/games since they are usually very practical and provide ample opportunities to experience and conduct a wide range of simulation/games over an extended period of time. Conferences held by various professional associations also provide a good opportunity to take part in these activities as well as to talk to experienced gamers. (Information on associations will be found in Chapter 24.)

Chapter 3, by Liz Christopher and Larry Smith, looks at a particular, and often neglected, part of conducting simulation/games. This is how form and content interact during a simulation/game session. The authors help us to see how form structures content—that is, how the organization and running of a simulation/game may modify the underlying message of the activity. Although newcomers to simulation/gaming should consider this chapter carefully, it will be especially useful to people who have gained a little more experience in conducting simulation/games.

Chapter 4, by Nick Bullard, examines two essential stages in any simulation/game. These are briefing and debriefing (sometimes also known as preparation and postgame discussion or critical appraisal) and are crucial to simulation/game sessions. The author provides a very thorough overview of these two phases and shows how the components of language and behavior may be briefed and debriefed. The author also emphasizes that several sessions, comprising briefing, the game itself, and debriefing, can be integrated in a cyclical fashion. Briefing and debriefing, as with running simulation/games, can be a delicate matter, and so careful preparation is essential. Experience in these aspects can be obtained by means similar to those outlined above for running games.

Before you can run a simulation/game, you must, of course, get hold of it. This means either selecting one that has been published, and possibly modifying it, or creating one for yourself. Martha Cummings and Rhona Genzel, in Chapter 5, provide us with a basic overview of the simulation/game design process. As the authors point out, this process is a lengthy one. If you have never taken part in a simulation/game, it is probably unwise to attempt to design one, especially if it is at all complex. However, even if you have not yet designed a simulation/game but have had experience in participating in a variety of exercises, it can be very rewarding to design your own simple simulation/games. Designing large-scale exercises should probably be left until you have gained experience in building a few smaller ones. However complex your simulation/games, testing is a critical stage; even though the basic idea may be good, it is nearly always necessary to modify the simulation/game once you have tried it out.

Chapters 2 to 5 in this section (B) cover the essential points concerning the practical aspects of simulation/gaming. More specific and detailed discussions will also be found in some of the works listed in Chapter 24. The next section (C) is also practical in nature but considers a number of more specific applications, such as using simulation for language testing or teacher training.

Chapter 2

Running simulation/games

A step-by-step guide

David Horner
British Institute

Kevin McGinley
TEFL Training Institute of Ireland

One of the main objectives of smaller-scale simulations in foreign or second language (L2) learning is to bridge the gap between controlled language learning and the uncertainties of the real world. To do this successfully, simulations need to be set up carefully, with thorough integration between the teaching of individual items and the final outcome (the simulation). Learners need to control the language necessary for the simulation, of course, but they need, even more, the freedom of the simulation to communicate realistically. The teacher also needs to monitor the simulation closely and prepare appropriate follow-up work. In this chapter, we seek to establish some guidelines which will help in the smooth running of a simulation. A number of important areas are deliberately excluded from discussion or are treated superficially, since they are discussed in full in other parts of the volume—for example, debriefing (Chapter 4), design (Chapter 5), and testing (Chapter 10). Table 2.1 displays the topics discussed in this chapter.

Integration

Integration is an important issue in using simulations for language learning, as indicated in Table 2.2. Simulations should be performed with a given purpose in mind and particular goals to achieve. And there are strong arguments in favor of building a course around simulations—especially in periodic intensive courses—rather than doing the odd simulation here and there. Simulations should therefore be viewed not as things

Table 2.1   An overview

Problems	Solutions, techniques, and considerations
Integration	Simulation integrated, use of "3P" approach, choice/design of simulation
Overcoming reticence	Learners, colleagues
Setup	Brainstorming, setting the scene, getting into character
Task	Setting a specific task, creating the need to share information
Instructions	Need for clarity
Management of the simulation	Setting up groups, managing groups, appointing roles, reaching decisions Teacher's role: observer, organizer, adviser, stimulator
Session appraisal	Debriefing, evaluation

apart but rather, like video or computers, as an essential part of any language course and be integrated accordingly. However, in most L2 courses around the world, the problem is one of introducing simulation into the curriculum in the first place, and this poses the problem of integrating simulations into course work.

There seem to be two common ways of doing this. First, the traditional "3P" procedure, moving progressively from the presentation of new language items, to controlled practice, then to free production. This places the simulation firmly within the course framework and allows the identification, preteaching, and practice of language items which may be necessary during the simulation.

Second, many teachers now use a "4P" procedure, which begins with a free production stage, from which one identifies the elements which are causing difficulty, presents them, and practices them, before going on to a second simulation which reuses them in a realistic way. This has the advantage of making learners aware of language items they are lacking or where they are using first language (L1) forms to express L2 functions.[1] Subsequent practice is then made much more real and immediate.

Both ways of proceeding are perfectly valid and appropriate to different groups and circumstances. Beginners, for example, will benefit more from a 3P approach, whereas a 4P approach will be more useful with intermediate groups with disparate learning backgrounds, or for diagnostic purposes.

---

[1]This is a common problem even among advanced students and leads to what is coming to be called "cross-cultural pragmatic failure," where learners fail to perceive the underlying significance of an utterance or are unaware themselves how to formulate it. For example, a Frenchman might suggest going for a drink by saying, "If we went for a drink?" which would leave native English speakers waiting for the end of a conditional, because they would formulate the suggestion differently ("What about a drink?").

Table 2.2   Integration

Problem	Solutions, techniques, and considerations
Need to integrate simulation	1. Use of traditional "3P" approach 2. Appropriate choice/design of simulation

Choosing a simulation is another essential aspect of integration. Many teachers feel, and published materials suggest, that student interest can be sustained only by choosing controversial topics. This is only partially true, because the intrinsic interest of the subject matter becomes less important if the task set for the learners is itself sufficiently challenging. A good simulation usually has challenging tasks, and the subject matter of the simulations should reflect students' interests. It is perfectly possible to design your own simulations, and, indeed, many teachers prefer this. One big advantage of doing so is that relevance can more easily be assured.

Overcoming reticence

Reticence of both learners and colleagues may pose problems (see Table 2.3). These problems can be reduced or eliminated in several different ways.

Learners

To a large extent overcoming the reticence of learners is a matter of learner training (see Chapter 6). Learners may feel inhibited about communicating in an unfamiliar language and losing face, or there may be a mismatch between learner expectations of how learning should take place, and what is expected during simulations. Learners from traditional school backgrounds, or older learners, for example, often have some difficulty accepting simulations as useful learning activities. Explaining to such people the reasoning behind simulations and pointing out their widespread use in all kinds of training programs, including business and the military, can be very helpful. It is also useful to indicate occasions when learning could not have taken place in a traditional learning situation.

Table 2.3   Reticence

Problem	Solutions, techniques, and considerations
Overcoming reticence	1. Learners: explain use, play recording of favorable discussion 2. Colleagues: discuss merits and learning theories, keep noise level down

Another useful way to create positive learner attitudes is to replay a video recording in which the question of the value of the simulation has been "floated," with the teacher taking a backseat and encouraging the students to answer one another's objections. This was discovered by accident,[2] and the result was a very interesting and frank discussion. We found the students to be very eloquent in making a number of points we could not have made so well or so convincingly.

Also, group work is generally less threatening than full-class activities; this encourages learners to express themselves more freely while at the same time placing them in a situation in which they are in charge of their own learning—thus encouraging increased responsibility, self-direction, and satisfaction.

A technique which sometimes works as a means of convincing students of the utility of simulation is to provide periodic intensive sessions of one or two days when learners are expected to demonstrate what they have "learned." If these sessions take place outside normal school time (e.g., weekends) or, even better, off the school premises, students feel more relaxed and hence more willing to "play the game." This can be even more effective if you can mix in one or two native or near-native speakers or even advanced learners. But this technique does far more than *convince* students of the usefulness of simulations—it is also a highly valuable language learning experience.

Colleagues

Colleagues may also be reticent or even hostile about your using simulation. Once again, this may arise from their own training and learning experience, leading them to expect a more directed learning environment. Often this kind of attitude can be overcome by discussing the merits of simulation and the learning theories behind it, and inviting colleagues to drop into your classroom as observers or "strangers." Or invite them to a student discussion on simulation (or show them a video recording).

Many teachers also worry about noise level, a legitimate concern. This arises from the acoustics of the physical setting as well as from group activity. Noise may irritate colleagues. But it may be threatening psychologically (not just acoustically) since it says, "That class is active and the students are interested and involved." In practice, the noise level is seldom a major problem that cannot be solved. Too much noise is disturbing to the groups themselves: Not only does it become difficult to make out what fellow participants are saying, but it also becomes tempting to listen to the

[2]Thanks to Andrew Morrison, University of Zimbabwe.

deliberations of other groups. When too much noise occurs, it is useful to separate groups physically. This is easy if one has access to several class-rooms or sound-absorbing movable partitions. Without these facilities, groups can still assemble in the four corners of the room.

Setup

Once you are ready to begin the simulation proper, the first, and in many ways most important, step is setting the mood. Time spent in al-lowing learners to build up their own reality around and within a simulation (see Chapter 20) helps generate interest and ideas that might otherwise be absent, by allowing students to abstract themselves away from the "pres-ence" of the classroom. The scenario and the role-cards play a considerable part here. Some possible techniques (shown in Table 2.4) include brain-storming, setting the scene, and getting into character.

Brainstorming

This is particularly useful in simulations where a lot of creativity is involved. It involves people sharing ideas freely, without criticism or cen-soring.

Setting the scene

Ask students to imagine the setting of the simulation, such as a board-room or a wrecked airplane. Photos can be a help here. Or, when simu-lations are supposed to take place in a particular kind of room or building, students can be asked to move furniture around and bring in realia. This all helps to increase learner involvement in the "reality" and success of the simulation and reduce feelings of awkwardness, perhaps caused by "performing" in a classroom.

Table 2.4   Setup

Problem	Solutions, techniques, and considerations
Setting the mood	1. Brainstorming 2. Setting the scene 3. Getting into character: use of role cards

Getting into character

Some role-plays provide extremely detailed background information about participants. However, a good guideline here is to provide any information that will give *sufficient* understanding of the character within the setting of the scenario and the constraints of time. Our own preference is to present this information in two parts. The first is more general and may include some or all of the following: job, brief occupational history, character. The second is the character's attitude during play. This information may be supported by quotations which contain the language items to be learned.

Other simulations depend less on such information for their outcome and consequently allow more learner creativity. Role-cards can then be restricted to facts, with learners encouraged to fill in the gaps: Are they married, where do they live, how old are they, what would they most like to do? A short session where all the participants sit around a pack of cards containing personal questions that must be answered in character can be an excellent mood-setter.[3]

In both cases, however, what is essential is that the students know exactly what is expected of them, so time spent answering queries and checking comprehension is vital.

Task

Several ways exist to enhance play and communication during the task itself, as shown in Table 2.5: setting a specific task and creating the need to share information.

Setting a specific task

Simulations are used because they allow the closest possible approximation inside a classroom to genuine language use. In real life, we rarely talk to no purpose: Communication is a means of achieving something. One feature which differentiates simulations from most other free production activities is their sense of purpose. Setting a task gives learners a real reason to communicate, in that the use of the target language becomes a means to a definite end and overcomes the tendency of undirected conversation to degenerate into sporadic talking or embarrassed silence.

---

[3]This technique was first suggested by Mavis Schiffer.

Table 2.5 Task

Problem	Solutions, techniques, and considerations
Ways to enhance play and communication via the task	1. Setting a specific task 2. Creating the need to relay/elicit information

Creating the need to share information

Participants both need information and need to communicate their information in order to act out the simulation. To stimulate interests and promote play, an uneven distribution of information is necessary—especially if one of the aims is to promote communication skills. Of course, action may be enhanced by other means—for example, by deliberately building conflict situations into some of the roles. This creates an "information gap." (There's nothing new about information gaps—you get them every time you put two people together. Simulation, because it simulates, merely recreates these information-gap situations.) In the event of the action flagging, additional information may be provided by the teacher in the form of media reports, rumor, etc.—which must, nonetheless, be credible in both form and source within the conventions of the game.

Instructions

If the task furnishes the ultimate goal of the simulation, the instructions provide the specific directions for reaching it. The aim[4] of the activity must be clear to the participants—for example, to lobby opinion, to discuss the merits of an action and come to a conclusion. This will obviously give the activity direction and the participants a sense of purpose. Instructions should therefore be kept simple and concise to minimize confusion (so as not to overstrain students' attention), although elaborate simulations might incorporate a number of ongoing instructions as subgoals are achieved on the way to completing the main task. For this reason, it is perfectly acceptable to outline the rules in the learners' L1 (see Table 2.6).

---

[4]The aim must, of course, be distinguished from the objectives of running the simulation. In addition to giving the participants experience of the situation, you will probably have linguistic objectives that you may/may not make explicit before running the simulation (e.g., providing practice in the use of certain functions).

Table 2.6 Instructions

Problem	Solutions, techniques, and considerations
Instructions	Need to provide clarity and specificity in instructions

Management of the simulation

As indicated in Table 2.7, the simulation proper raises the issues of setting up groups and determining the teacher's role. Many considerations are involved, and several solutions are available to resolve each of these.

Setting up groups

When the task and instructions have been made clear, learners can be organized into groups (but this depends a lot on the mechanics and structure of the game and its development). This can be a delicate matter, and it brings with it a whole range of problems.

One consideration is the use of *homogeneous versus heterogeneous groups*. Both have advantages: In the former, the teacher does not have to worry about grading input according to level, and all group members can participate equally (barring personality factors). The latter potentially allows weaker students to "acquire" target language via "comprehensible input" from their peers during communicative interaction, assuming that such input occurs.

A second consideration is *constant or changing membership*. Group members can be chosen by the teacher or by the learners themselves. The former allows the teacher to compose groups according to how s/he feels the best interaction will take place. The latter often assures optimum interaction by giving the learners the opportunity to work with people they know best. Alternatively, the teacher can ask for volunteers for certain parts (here

Table 2.7 Management of the simulation

Problem	Solutions, techniques, and considerations
Setting up groups	1. Homogenous or heterogeneous groups 2. Constant or changing membership 3. Appointed or natural roles 4. Group size 5. Majority or unanimous decision
Determining the teacher's role	1. Observer 2. Organizer with special reference to managing time and early/late finishing 3. Adviser 4. Stimulator

"natural" leaders may emerge) and assign roles to individuals according to estimation of suitability.

Many teachers favor changing group membership from one simulation to another. This improves class cohesion (everyone gets to know everyone else) and prevents the development of cliques, which can be a disturbing element where students get to know each other too well and sometimes revert to L1 as the language of intimacy.

Constant membership, on the other hand, can encourage the smooth running of simulations since group members get to know each other sufficiently well to be able to allot tasks, although this obviously depends on the students, type of courses, and similar factors. Pair work and other activities can then be used to create class cohesion. This does not mean, of course, that changes in group membership should never be made. One must take into account such factors as personality conflicts or the inability of some learners to express themselves in a particular group.

A third consideration related to setting up groups is *appointed versus natural roles*. Some published simulations require the selection of a spokesperson for the group. This is a matter of personal preference. Well-chosen leading roles can maintain interest and involvement in a simulation, and shy individuals can gain confidence by being placed in a position of trust and authority. On the other hand, natural leaders almost always arise, and shy learners can be overwhelmed by the responsibility.

Group size is a fourth consideration. This will obviously depend, to some extent, on the simulation itself: A role-play with seven roles usually requires seven members in a group. Unfortunately, class sizes are not always adapted to these demands. For this reason it is always necessary to keep some supplementary roles for extra people—a detective sergeant to help the inspector, an unexpected VIP dropping in. Or you can double up: Two people share the same role. Or you can leave out two roles.

The final consideration in setting up groups is *majority versus unanimous decisions*. Most simulations allow for majority decisions, and in most cases this is fine. However, if one of our aims is to refine learners' skills in presentation, explanation, persuasion, and argument, requiring a unanimous or consensus decision can be a particularly useful device.

Determining the teacher's role

Teachers have a natural tendency to control what is happening in a classroom. During a simulation, therefore, they often feel frustrated at apparently having nothing to do while their students are working together quite independently. It can therefore be helpful to leave the room. This not only reduces the nervous strain on the "unoccupied" teacher but also removes restraints imposed by the presence of an authority figure and can lead to quite dramatic improvements in learner interaction (captured, of course, by recording).

This may give rise to problems with less motivated groups who revert to the L1. However, showing confidence in the learners, giving them the initiative, and setting a task are usually sufficient to overcome this problem. Should problems still arise, recording the simulation usually helps, since guilty conduct is made apparent and can, if necessary, be negatively sanctioned (within or outside the rules of the game).

One role the teacher can take is that of *observer*. After the simulation, there will be a feedback or debriefing session, described in Chapter 4. During the simulation the teacher observes the students and collects data to share during the debriefing. The simplest observation method is note taking, whereby the teacher wanders around either jotting down mistakes or filling in error sheets (see Figure 2.1). These sheets may or may not be individual, but it helps if they are easy to complete and easy to correct by the students.

The teacher's observational role might also include tape-recording. This has the advantage of capturing speech in action, so that the context is there to help the learners reconstruct what they wanted to say. It does, however, pose a problem if several groups are working separately: Few institutions have sufficient tape recorders available. Moving recorders from one group to another is not recommended unless absolutely necessary because it may affect spontaneity. Increasingly, video (with audio) is being used to record simulations. This has the advantages of the tape recorder and is often even more motivating.

Recording equipment, however, suffers from the drawbacks of being

Error sheet	Name _____		
function	structure	vocabulary	pronunciation

Figure 2.1   Error sheet.

obviously present and potentially causing inhibition. However, most students quickly get used to recording equipment. Recordings also need sufficient time for full analysis. One useful analysis method is to replay the recording, asking the students to indicate when they want the tape stopped in order to comment on selected aspects, including language use. This is useful only so long as students pay adequate attention and try not to forget. Thus, the use of recordings is greater for aftergame discussion than for control.

In addition to observing, teachers might take on the role of *organizer*. For the most part, they should remain observers and merely "facilitate" play—i.e., ensure its continuance. They should only exceptionally interfere, since their nonpeer image might diminish spontaneity. In fact, any "organizing" that should prove necessary during the play should be assumed by the students who have the lead roles, and this should be made clear to them. In case of doubt, they can consult the teacher.

The organizational role frequently concerns time management. Time is often an important constraint on the running of a simulation. Clearly, the simulation should be designed around the blocks of time available. It is disappointing for participants and the teacher to have to finish before things get moving. On the other hand, some teachers like to halt play before a simulation reaches its natural conclusion and, therefore, like to dictate time. Ending a simulation, in fact, can be a tricky business. Where several groups are involved, they will almost inevitably finish at different times. The teacher's role is then to keep the early finishers busy—and hence not bored—while preventing the others from going on too long. In fact, both early and late finishers pose problems.

Ending early may result from a number of things: a group's finding the correct "solution" rapidly, or a group's having found little to discuss because of lack of interest in the simulation (an unchallenging task?) or because they do not value the activity. In any event, the teacher should always provide follow-up work, which can be linked theoretically or linguistically to the simulation, to keep early finishers busy. This can be fairly traditional (e.g., grammar exercises based on structures that could be expected to crop up, or comprehension texts concerning some aspect or other) or more creative (e.g., continued discussions in pairs or small groups).

The problem of stopping simulations from going on too long, either because some groups have already finished or because a class period is coming to an end, can also create some awkward moments. It is therefore probably a good idea for teachers to set deadlines and to make sure that learners are aware of them and that they stick to them. This does not mean, incidentally, that simulations must be completed within a single class period. In most cases, this is far too short a time, but one should try to avoid the frustration caused by having to interrupt a simulation that is almost finished simply because one has run out of time. Nonetheless, timing remains essentially a question of "feel": Experience will tell you when a simulation is coming to an end, even when the deadline has not been reached, and similarly, where interest is still intense it would be pointless to bring a simulation to a close because an arbitrarily imposed deadline has been reached.

Yet another potential role for the teacher is that of *adviser*. If any language problems or doubts about the development of the simulation crop up, the teacher should be readily available to advise. A final teacher role is *stimulator*. If the simulation seems to be getting bogged down, the teacher can contribute new information or, as a last resort, an idea to stimulate further debate. It is important that s/he does not directly intervene as "the teacher," especially if any decision is to be made. Any intervention must occur within the conventions of play—for example, sending information via a note from a concerned party. If the participants try to ask the teacher, "Is this a good decision?" or "Can we choose this?" the teacher should reply, "That's something I can't answer. You have to decide yourself according to the situation you are in." If they ask, "Can we do this?" the reply should be "Well, what would you be able to do in this type of situation?" or "What do *you* think?"

Session appraisal

As Table 2.8 shows, there are two considerations in session appraisal: debriefing and evaluation (see Chapter 4 for more details). Debriefing provides the students with the opportunity to comment on all aspects of the simulation, although teachers should try, of course, to structure the discussion. This can be combined with replaying the recording in segments in which the students are also interested in the language used. You should make it clear that everything is up for discussion (scenario, roles, the task, the operation) and suggested modifications are welcome. Teachers are also, of course, vitally interested in the teaching effectiveness of the simulation. Some evidence of this will come out during debriefing, but, additionally, a formal evaluation questionnaire can be used. Since there should be no requirement to write names, you can elicit opinion from every student on a range of issues: usefulness of the approach, value to the student, as well as questions on specific areas that may have been suggested during debriefing.

Table 2.8 Session appraisal

Problem	Solutions, techniques, and considerations
Appraisal	1. Debriefing
	2. Evaluation

Conclusion

Clearly, there are many considerations in running simulations. We have touched on many of the key considerations in the foregoing description. These have arisen not only out of the variety of situations in which simulation is used but also because of the nature of simulation, which attempts to represent some form of reality—and reality, of course, is infinitely variable. The running of simulations, however, follows a number of fairly well-established steps, which offer an element of control in a situation with often unpredictable, free-flowing language use. Free language use is a noticeable feature of the "outside" world and one in which simulation is very helpful in giving students valuable practice.[5]

[5]Thanks to Gillian Porter Ladousse, Mavis Schiffer, and David Crookall for comments on earlier drafts of this chapter.

Chapter 3

Shaping the content of simulation/games

Elizabeth M. Christopher
Charles Sturt University—Mitchell

Larry E. Smith
University of Hawaii

Simulation/games are models of social organization in the "real" world. Therefore, teachers' fundamental beliefs about the nature of social organization—their "worldview"—will affect the structure and organization of any simulation/game they design and/or present. The content of any dynamic structure is in continual interaction with the form in which it is arranged and presented. Therefore, the content of all simulation games—*irrespective of their ostensible subject matter*—will inevitably reflect the worldview of their creators, whether they are consciously aware of it or not.

This chapter argues there are basically two models of game structure, each representing a different and opposing value system. The chapter identifies the salient characteristics of each model, suggests how these will affect the responses of the game participants, and offers guidelines for game presenters to enhance or subvert either model at will, depending on their teaching needs.

Simulation/games as world models

Social scientists argue over two basic and general perspectives on the nature of social organization—respectively called here a "convergent" and a "divergent" worldview. According to the *convergent* view, societies solve their problems by referring them to social and cultural norms that appear "natural" and "instinctive." Thus, specific solutions emerge that are assumed—by consensus—to be "good," and any opposition is assumed to be "wrong" and/or "bad." A *divergent* view of the world sees nothing "natural" about social values, which appear to be no more than moral pressures exerted by powerful and elitist minorities to maintain and expand their economic, social, and political power. Thus—according to this divergent argument—the assumptions underlying social organization need continually to be identified, questioned, and reviewed.

The structures of all simulation/games assume predominantly either a convergent or a divergent view of the way societies work. Choice of structure, however (including the social assumptions that accompany such a choice), is not necessarily or even frequently the result of conscious decision by the game designer. Furthermore, teachers who organize and present simulation/games have the power—whether they know it or not—to support or subvert the original structure of any simulation/game. Experienced users of simulation/games, though adept at restructuring them to serve specific teaching needs, may not always locate their expertise within a theoretical framework of social organization. Therefore, a systematic analysis of the relationship between structure and content in simulation/games may benefit experts and newcomers alike. It may provide new insights to the nature of the forces that are created within the game which move participants into *apparently* spontaneous actions and interactions—and by extension may suggest some new guidelines for designing and directing simulation/games as learning techniques.

Convergent models

The classic and historic model of a simulated world, in themes that can be traced through countless variations in traditional drama, poetry, and prose, depicts a stable situation that becomes disturbed in some way. After various fortunes and misfortunes, the disturbance is cathartically resolved—the final situation being even more satisfactory than in the beginning because "good" has been rewarded and "evil" punished. This model is the archetypal structure of narrative, that begins "Once upon a time . . ." and ends ". . . happily ever after" (Beckerman 1970; Propp 1968). It promotes consensus and reconciliation, celebrates shared social norms, values, and beliefs. It is essentially a consensus or convergent model, not because it contains no conflict—on the contrary, conflict is essential to demonstrate the value of consensus—but because it works toward *closure*. Differing views converge toward a socially acceptable standard, even if this final agreement is that people have the right to differ.

This is the model that experienced game designers choose and directors implement—even if unaware—when they need a simulation/game that makes value judgments between good and bad, right and wrong. For example, convergent model simulations will convey linguistic, mathematical, and scientific principles—i.e., *right answers*. They also promote ideologically "sound" social, political, religious, and economic views, such as a particular interpretation of history, or a generally accepted version of literary texts, language usages, or effective negotiation skills in management training.

Convergent, consensus-seeking simulation/games are built on assumptions which make the end appear an *inevitable* outcome of the situation set up in the beginning. They demonstrate a linear, logical progression of events, converging toward and culminating in a resolution of conflict that simultaneously celebrates and explains why some behavior is "good" and why other kinds of behavior are "bad" and/or "foolish." The effects of this consensus structure can be seen clearly in many commercial board games, such as MONOPOLY. Here the players impersonate real-estate property speculators, owners, and tenants. In order to win, they must follow the rules appropriate to this represented setting—which also means they must be willing to bankrupt their friends and/or drive them to suicide (voluntary withdrawal from the game). This behavior is seen as inevitable and necessary, even fun!

Children respond to games more directly than adults; that is, very young players tend to treat games as reality. With increasing emotional maturity, participants become more inclined to view games as simulations or representations of reality and to remain relatively emotionally detached from the experiences of winning or losing. However, sometimes these experiences can cut too close to the bone. Therefore, organizers of learning games need to sensitize themselves to the degree of emotional resilience their players possess—in general, and in relation to the theme or topic of the game. For example, a simulation about growing old and dying could be an unbearable experience for players who in real life were facing these situations. Likewise, MONOPOLY might be a threatening experience for somebody, say, who has recently been dispossessed of his or her home through inability to pay the rent.

Generally speaking, however, MONOPOLY creates an entertaining ambience within which to validate a free market economy, including the unsentimental assumption of market societies that "business and friendship don't mix." It discourages players from thinking about—and perhaps questioning—whether the effect of this assumption is entirely beneficial. The game represents a movement of convergence toward the social consensus under which capitalism operates. It can be played usefully as part of a course in real estate, town planning, or any kind of competitive trading.

Divergent models

An alternative to this convergent model is one that illustrates a process of erratic leaps and bounds, an opposition of one viewpoint against another without suggesting that one is better than the other. This divergent scenario inclines participants to question social assumptions that some things, people, events, and actions are intrinsically more important than others. In game versions of this model, the players are led to ask what "winning" and "losing" really mean in terms of human endeavor. In the divergent model, conflict is evoked for a different purpose than in the convergent. In convergent models, conflict is deliberately built into the scenario in order to demonstrate its basically dysfunctional nature, like an illness in the body social. In divergent models, the conflict arises out of the game's dynamic and the synergy of the players—it appears constructive rather than destructive, healthy as opposed to sick. Divergent models are appropriate for the *invoking of insights*—for brainstorming a topic, for revealing multiple perspectives without implying any necessity for value judgments, action, choices, or conclusions. The emphasis is on *reflective observation*. This takes place in a climate of inquiry that encourages the growth and development of what in convergent models are seen as minority and subversive views.

In foreign or second language learning, divergent simulation/games perform three valuable functions: They encourage players to communicate a variety of views, they increase the confidence of the participants by creating a nonjudgmental climate of interaction, and they stimulate creative enthusiasm for learning. On the other hand, if teachers want their students to learn via a simulation/game the generally accepted meanings, syntax, and structure of a language and its vocabulary, they should use a convergent game model.

The director's leadership style and its effects on game structure

Though experienced game directors do not hesitate to reshape the content of a simulation/game to serve their teaching needs, less experienced game leaders may hesitate to do this. As a result, if they have not understood the power of *form* to structure *content*, they may be disconcerted by unexpected responses from the participants.

A short simulation concerning management-worker relations, called PINS AND STRAWS, offers a good example of interaction between form and content. The players, in small groups, have to build competitive sculptures from drinking-straws and pins. The finished models are judged in competition on the criteria of beauty, size, and stability. Each group leader is privately instructed to behave in a certain way: One is told to act in a very authoritarian way, another to behave democratically, and a third to be *laissez-faire*. Differences in the finished sculptures are then related back to the behavior of the respective groups and their leaders.

Perhaps a game director might want PINS AND STRAWS to demonstrate—say, to management trainees—that democratic leadership is the most effective way for a small company to manufacture a quality product in a competitive market. Thus, the director wants a convergent game structure (which essentially is the basis of PINS AND STRAWS anyway) because the teaching objectives are judgmental; they aim to demonstrate the "intrinsic value" of democratic ways.

On the other hand, game organizers might want PINS AND STRAWS to demonstrate to a group of industrial psychology students some of the behavior that characterizes a breakdown in management-worker relationships. In this case organizers need to impose a divergent model on the game, because they are interested in setting up a situation rather than creating a problem that needs solving by a particular kind of action. The aim is for students to view a number of phenomena from relatively objective but critical stands.

Tables 3.1–3.4 present comparisons between the respective leadership styles of a director of a convergent and a divergent version of PINS AND STRAWS.

Options

In practice, no simulation/game is ever structured to a totally convergent model, or to one that is completely divergent. The two extremes described above are the two ends of a continuum of techniques in game design and direction. For example, the closed, consensus structure of MONOPOLY can be opened by a teacher who wants to use it to demonstrate an alternative economic model to that of private ownership of land. If the game's rules, which work on a cause-and-effect basis, are modified to permit the formation of cooperatives and communally owned property, this will result in the subversion of its linearity to a much more open structure. Within this structure many options are open to the players that are not available to them in the original version.

For example, they may choose to develop the board sites as a group, abolish the jail, pool all the money that accrues as the players progress

Table 3.1   The represented setting

Convergent model	Divergent model
"This is the problem; how shall we solve it?"	"This is the situation; what will we do?"
The action has a "past." The director sets a story that begins long before the game starts, including the criteria for a "winning" sculpture. Thus, players begin the game at a *moment of crisis*.	All the action takes place "on stage." The director gives virtually no background. The story begins when the game begins. Players embark on a journey and decide their criteria.

Table 3.2   The players' impersonation

Convergent model	Divergent model
The director typecasts leaders' roles and puts the more assertive players under an authoritarian leader to ensure conflict, in order to demonstrate later its negative quality (for this group's sculpture may be relatively smaller and less stable).	The director casts leaders' roles and forms groups at random. S/he wants to create a *situation*, not necessarily a conflict. If conflict arises, it will manifestly be the choice of the players, not the result of circumstances beyond their control.
The few roles are personalized; players assume responsibility for interpreting (not creating) the "givens" of their roles.	The director adds extra roles, casts players as "trade union representatives," "industrial spies," "dissatisfied employees," etc. The players create their *own* personal and detailed versions.
Roles are given in detail; players are constrained to behave in particular ways.	Roles have no constraints; players virtually play themselves AS IF they were in the represented situation.

around the board, and become a powerful land conglomerate. All that is needed to encourage this kind of divergence among the players is for the organizer to add a rule that all other rules, structures, and givens can be changed. Or the players may choose to form small power cliques, as partners or small subgroups, and become, in effect, a number of independent states, each with its own frontier and economy. Alternatively, following the principle of *Lebensraum*, they may end by invading each other's territory; the possibilities are endless.

Table 3.3   The dramatic action

Convergent model	Divergent model
The organizer processes the action in carefully timed sequences, each building on the one before. S/he promotes tension.	The organizer makes no formal steps or sequences. The action depends on the arbitrary decisions of the players. Players indicate the pace and rhythm of the action.
Players' choices become increasingly limited. They are bound by the criteria by which the sculptures will be judged. They have increasingly little control.	Building the sculptures becomes less important than group negotiation, communication processes, and interpretation of meanings.
The action is linear and logical, and proceeds with gathering speed toward a definite conclusion, guided with authority by the game director.	The action is nonlinear; minor actions spin off from major ones in an apparently irrelevant way. The director does not intervene or seek to influence.

Table 3.4   Observation (pulling the learning experience together)

Convergent model	Divergent model
Attention becomes more and more focused on "what will happen?"; it is future-looking, goal-oriented.	Attention becomes more and more focused on what the players do; it is located in the present; goals become relatively unimportant. Some of the sculptures may never be completed.
The end is seen in terms of the beginning. There is a single view. The behavior of the groups and their leaders is judged to be good or bad in terms of their sculptures, i.e., on criteria that have been set before the game began, so that they—and therefore the results—seem inevitable, "natural."	The end appears to bear very little relation to the beginning. There are multiple perspectives on the action and value judgments are difficult. The preset criteria do not seem inevitable and may have been rejected by the players.
The director debriefs the game by telling players "what happened" (e.g., even if the winning sculpture was by the *laissez-faire*, not the democratic group, the director may ask questions designed to reveal that its leader interpreted the *laissez-faire* role in a democratic way).	The director debriefs the game by asking players to describe their versions of what happened, thus keeping analysis open.

Implications

Thus, simulation/game organizers have an alternative, and theirs is the final decision as to whether their game will have a convergent or a divergent structure. This decision will in turn determine to a large extent the nature of the learning their players acquire. Participants will be more or less inclined to negotiate meaning, depending on how closely the game conforms to its appropriate model. Game directors are the final arbiters of structure; it is their responsibility to decide whether to push their players toward convergence, closure, and consensus or whether to leave issues open to their divergent ideas.

If directors want their players to "know" that two and two make four, that there are scientific laws, that murder is wrong, that race prejudice is to be deplored, then they must create convergent models even from games that were designed to be divergent. They must channel players' actions to be *convergent* and their observations *deductive*. If they want the participants to live with uncertainty, to accept insecurity, to remain open-minded, they will promote open models whose dramatic action is *divergent*, and which evoke observations that are *inductive*.

In discussion after the game, directors of convergent models will focus attention on how the players solved the problem presented in the game. They will emphasize that some solutions were more effective than others—without mentioning that "effectiveness" has been defined in terms of the game's "givens"—for example, the assumptions in PINS AND STRAWS that size and stability are desirable qualities for a sculpture. In fact, many directors of PINS AND STRAWS are probably not fully aware of the game's assumptions about what makes a "good" sculpture, because they are concealed in the heart of a convergent structure that synthesizes a variety of player responses into what appears to be self-evidently a single "right answer." Directors who create divergent game sessions do so because, whether fully aware of it or not, they are more interested in revealing the assumptions of both the game and the players and in keeping discussion open, rather than working toward a group decision that will close the investigation and come to a definite conclusion.

Players of divergent games will come instead to realize there is more to the game situation than meets their eyes; that consensus, though satisfying, is the end of argument; and that learning also consists of learning that there is more to learn. These realizations may make them thoughtful, uncertain, even angry because they feel confused, whereas the players of a convergent simulation are more likely to feel relieved and satisfied that some truth, previously hidden or unclear, has now been revealed and they now know more than they did before.

Conclusion

It can be said that all teaching, including foreign and second language instruction, is essentially a manipulative or persuasive act by which teachers attempt to influence their students to share their worldview. They are more likely to succeed if they understand that structuring the form of simulation/games will also structure their content. A metaphor serves to summarize the difference in content between the two basic concepts of social behavior on which all simulation/game forms are based. It can be said that a convergent model teaches its players that beauty is truth and truth beauty; a divergent model suggests that there is no Grail, only a Quest.

Chapter 4

Briefing and debriefing

Nick Bullard
CAVILAM

The process of running a simulation usually involves stages which precede and which follow the running of the simulation itself. Preceding the simulation we usually have a period of *briefing*, during which participants are prepared, or prepare themselves, for the roles they are to use during the simulation. Following the actual simulation we would expect a *debriefing* phase, where some form of feedback and analysis of the simulation can take place. In this chapter I shall examine some of the more important aspects of these two phases, from the point of view of the language teacher in particular.

Many simulation managers in language teaching are inclined to overlook the importance of these two phases, yet the effectiveness of a simulation is likely to hinge on successful briefing. And full linguistic benefit is usually largely dependent on a successful debriefing phase. In courses built around simulations, indeed, the briefing and debriefing make up the ordinary classroom lessons, sandwiching the simulations and providing the opportunities for language input. They are times when students meet and reflect upon new lexes or structures. The simulation itself, on the other hand, is mainly an output activity, providing language practice.

The processes of briefing and debriefing have a double application when used in language teaching. They apply both to the performance of the simulation as an activity and to the performance of the target language used in the simulation. K. Jones (1982) uses the terms "behavior debriefing" and "language debriefing" to distinguish between the two, and I shall be using these terms with reference to both briefing and debriefing.

Language and behavior

Language briefing and *language debriefing* refer to all aspects of the use of the target language, its structure, lexis, and so on, as well as any problems related to its use. *Behavior briefing* and *behavior debriefing*, on the other hand, concern all aspects which are not specifically concerned with target language use—such matters as might equally well arise in native speaker simulations. There is, of course, a substantial gray area between the two, occupied notably by the sort of cultural problem which, although not related to language, would not occur with native speakers.

The relative weight attached to behavior or language in briefing and debriefing in language teaching simulations is something which can be worrying to some teachers. It may be argued that language teachers should concern themselves only with language teaching, and therefore that they should ignore any problem arising in a simulation that is not linguistic. Because the line between language and behavior is not a clear one, however, this gray area is often one into which teachers will be obliged to venture. Even leaving aside cultural considerations, we find that many of the problems which arise in language teaching simulations relate to the use of language at the discourse level. Let us suppose, for example, that in a simulation of a meeting the chairperson repeatedly interrupts other participants, thus rendering the effective exposition of a problem impossible. This apparently behavioral problem may in fact conceal language difficulties. It may be that the other participants are too polite or too reserved to combat the interrupter, but it may also be that they do not command the language necessary for holding the floor in such a discussion. Their inability to resist interruption or to fight back may be a behavioral trait, or it may reveal a language inadequacy. Similarly, the chairperson may be a domineering personality or may have inadequate language skills for encouraging full participation from others. In both cases, of course, it is very likely to be a combination of the two. Additionally, the problem may be cultural. It may be that the participants come from a culture where interruption is more or less acceptable than it is in English-speaking countries. In such cases the teacher is obliged to move beyond strictly linguistic considerations.

The willingness of the teacher to move over into more explicitly behavioral or cultural aspects will very much depend on the kind of learner involved. With younger learners the teacher will almost certainly feel that behavior-oriented briefing may be more appropriate than with older learners, who might feel that a discussion of their performance which went beyond the language, or at most the cultural aspects, was interfering with their personalities. This area will be discussed more thoroughly in the section on debriefing.

Whether we concentrate on behavioral or cultural aspects of briefing and debriefing or on both, it is important to bear in mind that briefing and debriefing are integral parts of the simulation process, not mere subsidiary possibilities. The rest of this chapter will be devoted primarily to examining the processes and their integration. Much of this integration, as we shall see, can be of a cyclical nature; the debriefing of one simulation can become the briefing of a subsequent one, the problems revealed in one simulation being dealt with in the debriefing, which also serves as briefing for the next.

Briefing

What do our learners need to know in order to participate effectively in the simulation? Answering this question helps us establish what information or capabilities the participants will need to acquire during the briefing session. Such sessions usually tend to be either teacher-centered or centered around an input text or texts which carry the background information. There are, however, a number of ways in which learners can be led to participate actively in briefing, and it will be valuable to encourage such participation. In language learning terms it is more likely that the information in the briefing will be assimilated if there is active participation. In addition, the more closely the learners are involved in the briefing, the more likely they are to become involved in the simulation itself. Such involvement will motivate the participants more rapidly than merely handing out a series of texts, allocating roles, and leaving the participants to get on with it. Even simulations with a high intrinsic interest will get going more rapidly if there has been student involvement from the outset.

Behavior and situation briefing

Simulations not specifically designed for language teaching frequently have a heavy content input. Participants are required to assimilate a considerable quantity of general and role-specific background information before embarking on the simulation. Frequently this means reading through several pages of text, and this is best done the night before the simulation so that participants can come in prepared the next day. Such an approach can work well with certain categories of learners, especially the so-called captive students in higher education, provided that attention is paid to the language level of the input. In other language teaching situations, however, it may be unrealistic to expect such "homework" to be done effectively by all the participants. This will clearly make it difficult to get the simulation off to a good start, and class time will be wasted before it does.

When all the participants have the same native language, one possible way around this problem is to use the native language in the input material. An additional advantage here is that such an approach may well be very close to what happens outside the classroom. A German businessman

preparing for a meeting usually would approach that meeting with doc-
umentation and ideas put together in his own language, whether or not
the actual meeting is to take place in that language or in a foreign one.
One very real problem he faces is that he has to adapt the ideas in his first
language to the second. Thus, using the first language for simulation input
can effectively reproduce this situation in the classroom, enabling learners
to develop strategies for dealing with it. In addition, of course, the use of
the first language for input makes the whole process of assimilating the
background information less tedious. And for students who are pressed
for time or who are relatively weak in the language, this can be a big
advantage.

The first language is unlikely to be used on a regular basis in many
classes, and in situations where learners come from different language
backgrounds the possibility does not arise. Another approach is for the
teacher to take a more active role, and for the information to be conveyed
orally in the classroom rather than through the printed word. In this case,
the teacher can simply explain the background of the simulation to the
class, using visual or other support material where necessary, letting the
context of the simulation gradually unfold. One advantage of such an
approach is that certain elements of the language briefing—especially
vocabulary—can be handled alongside the nonlanguage input. A further
advantage is that the teacher using this approach can involve the participants in the development of the background of the simulation, even to the
extent of modifying the situation in response to student suggestions. Experienced teachers will feel able to accommodate quite far-reaching modifications to their own original plans, provided they are able to make a
careful (but immediate!) assessment of the implications. Less experienced
teachers, working with a situation they know less well, will obviously limit
themselves to such minor modifications as they feel able to handle. Of
course, the integration varies considerably according to the type of simulation in use. Computer-based simulations, for example, may or may not
be designed for teacher modification, and the possible modifications may
depend on the teacher's programming know-how.

One advantage of the gradual expository approach is that the roles
will emerge and fill out little by little, and it will probably be easier for
participants to take them on when required. Another real advantage is that
a simulation which is not text-based is easier to adapt to classes of different
sizes or different language levels.

An extension of the teacher exposition approach is to make the development of the simulation even more participant-centered, the teacher
laying down only the basic guidelines while the details and the character-
ization emerge by negotiation at class level. Such an approach usually
implies that both teacher and participants already have some experience
of using the more traditionally structured simulations; otherwise the sim-

ulation which emerges from negotiation may well prove less successful than hoped.

Many published simulations handle the problem of information input creatively. One approach is to contextualize a series of simulations within an ongoing story which develops over a number of video or audio episodes. The situation shown in the story can then be the starting point of a simulation, and the participants do not need to spend a long time assimilating the background information.

Another approach is to move toward the simulation through a number of inputs of different kinds—written, visual, audio, and so on—all of which can in themselves be exploited for language learning purposes. The vocabulary and to some extent the structures to be used in the simulation are gradually introduced by these inputs, and the context of the final simulation emerges from their realization.

Language briefing

In the language learning classroom we would usually expect a simulation to be used in the context of a language learning program. In this case, a particular simulation will have been chosen because the teacher feels it appropriate to the development of a particular language skill, a skill which may well have been seen already in some other classroom context.

It is probably preferable in an initial briefing stage to keep the quantity of new language introduced fairly small. Some of the language will already have been seen in some other context not specifically related to the simulation. Attention is, however, focused more sharply on the language in the particular simulation which has been chosen. It is usually better to make use of the simulation as a way of capitalizing on this previously seen language, for the participants cannot be expected to assimilate very much new material in a briefing session. Nevertheless, some specialist vocabulary and expressions may form part of the context of the simulation in any case. Generally, learners will find it possible to use new lexis during the running of the simulation, while they will find new structures more difficult to handle effectively. Some published simulations give participants lists of useful expressions for their particular roles. But few students will be able to use these effectively and appropriately in the context of the simulation, and effective assimilation is unlikely to take place.

Language structures central to the simulation should thus already be at least a little familiar to the participants before briefing, although the teacher may wish to go over them again, or at least point out that they will be of use. Some new lexis may well be introduced in the briefing stage, but in general it is advisable not to overload participants with language during briefing.

Debriefing

The teacher will almost certainly have been a nonparticipant in the actual simulation, but will have been far from passive. The teacher's observations of the way the simulation has developed, and of the problems encountered, coupled with the participants' own observations, are the raw materials of the debriefing phase: a phase, incidentally, which may take up more time than did the simulation itself. If only for this reason, we have to consider the debriefing as being at least as important as the simulation itself.

Behavior debriefing

The controversial nature of behavior debriefing in the context of language learning has already been touched upon in the introduction to this chapter. Many of the less acceptable features of behavior debriefing can, however, be avoided, if some basic conditions are observed. One could, of course, eliminate behavior debriefing in some contexts, but it seems a pity to eliminate a phase unconditionally when it has the potential of being linguistically rich.

Ideally, the principal contributors to a behavior debriefing should be the participants rather than the teacher/observer, although where cultural issues are at stake this may not be possible. Furthermore, behavior debriefing should be seen as yet another opportunity to use the target language communicatively, rather than as a period of self-criticism. One useful consideration here is that the kinds of language function required by the students while actually debriefing are usually rather different from those elicited by the simulation.

By asking the participants to be the prime movers in the debriefing process, we can do both of these things at once. In addition, because of the participation the debriefing will probably be both more valuable and more memorable. Moreover, if a particular group of people is not given to public introspection (a right to be respected), they will not be forced into an analysis which is against their nature.

The role of the teacher in a behavior debriefing session is essentially that of the chair, though with some groups even this role might be filled by a participant. In this way the teacher can control the discussion, ensuring that anyone who wishes to contribute can do so, and thus not be seen as a critic of behavior—for some learners may react against the teacher's going beyond the role of *language* teacher.

Probably the most effective way of beginning a debriefing session is quite simply to go over the simulation more or less chronologically, letting the participants comment on the way things evolved. Frequently this mere reliving of the simulation will lead to a discussion of, for example, alternative routes the simulation might have taken. The teacher will usually have to be careful, however, of not stepping over the boundary between what happened, or might have happened, and what, in his or her opinion, *should* have happened.

If there was a problem-solving element within the simulation, or if its context required some sort of decision to be reached, the debriefing should also examine whether the problem was in fact solved or whether a decision was reached. Because of the linguistic handicaps under which participants were operating during the simulation, crucial issues like these may well have been overlooked and will need to be brought to light in the debriefing. It may even be possible and desirable to revive the simulation momentarily in order to deal with such an oversight.

Teachers' overt participation in behavior debriefing may be limited to points like this or to cultural issues where an outsider's view is essential. With younger participants, however, who might reasonably be expected to have organizational problems in role-playing in their own language, more teacher participation will probably prove necessary, and a teacher may gradually develop participants' awareness of behavior issues over a cycle of simulations.

A more formal approach to debriefing is the use of debriefing checklists handed out to the participants, which enable them to evaluate their performance through a series of guiding questions. Such a checklist can be a useful support to any debriefing and can be particularly effective in clarifying whether or not certain tasks were carried out.

Language debriefing

It is in the area of language debriefing that the teacher is obliged to occupy a more central role in the classroom. Yet even here, participants can and must take on an active role, for the teacher can in general only be concerned with what has been said. What has *not* been said may be of equal importance, and one of the teacher's first questions here may be something along the lines of "Was there anything you wanted to say during the simulation which you didn't say because you didn't know how to?" Such a question will bring out some of the real needs of the learners in the context of the simulation and is likely to elicit language of real value, precisely because it reflects a real need. Clearly, then, we should ask participants to note such problems as the simulation is going along—if necessary using the mother tongue to do so.

The investigation of what could not be said is probably one of the best ways to begin a language debriefing. The teacher's own language analysis, on the other hand, is probably best left till later, if only because the teacher's analysis requires him or her to adopt a central role, and it may subsequently be difficult to relinquish this.

Even leaving aside audio and video recording techniques, there are a number of different techniques used by teachers when noting language problems during a simulation. Assuming the teacher does actually take notes, one of the first considerations is whether all errors can be noted together or whether individual student headings should be used. As a general rule, it is preferable not to point the finger at individual participants, at least in front of their peers, so unless separate notes need to be kept for marking purposes, it is probably simpler to keep collective notes for the class.

Most of the errors noted by teachers during simulations fall into one of three categories: structural, lexical, and pronunciation. During the simulation there will also have been errors at the discourse level, which are more difficult to handle because they require the manipulation of large quantities of text for students to understand where the problems lie. In addition, many teachers find it extremely difficult to provide hard and fast discourse rules which can help students realize where things have gone wrong. Some discourse problems will need to be dealt with prior to a rerun, but in many cases discourse problems may have to be kept for those times when recording techniques are used, because it is here, especially when video is used, that students can best understand discourse problems.

Whatever type of error is involved, the teacher will have to make a selection of those errors needing to be corrected and will then need to find an appropriate way of doing so.

Structural errors may be of one or two basic types. They may be "mistakes"—that is, slips that the learner has theoretically the competence to correct independently. Or they may be errors which are beyond the existing grammatical competence of the learner. Most errors will probably be of the former type. The teacher therefore must distinguish between mistake and error and act appropriately. Clearly it will be wasting everybody's time if a mistake is dealt with by means of a long grammatical explanation.

We might also wish to classify structural (and, for that matter, vocabulary and pronunciation) errors according to their communicative significance. The teacher can try to judge the extent to which a particular error impedes communication and thereby judge whether to correct it or not. The learners too can be encouraged to make such judgments for themselves.

Certain structural and vocabulary errors will, at least with less advanced classes, bring up the question of the use of structures which the teacher may feel are too advanced or obscure to be appropriate for the class at this stage. In any case, and with any level of class, time limits will also impose a need for selection.

In most situations we would expect the teacher to concentrate on those errors which have the most communicative significance—those which are most likely to get in the way of effective communication. An exception might have to be made with examination classes where grammar is a criterion of significance. We would also expect teachers to deal with mistakes (i.e., problems which are already within the learner's structural competence), rather than with errors which the learner could not be expected to correct independently. In my own survey of teacher correction in simulation both these tendencies were confirmed, emphasizing the fact that teachers see simulations as primarily relevant to communicative teaching and of relatively little use in teaching new structures, although very valuable in their revision. An additional sobering tendency was also shown. Certain errors are difficult to correct succinctly and therefore go uncorrected. These are errors which require either a very long quotation in order for there to be sufficient context for their correction, or a sophisticated explanation which the teacher does not have available.

The way in which correction is approached will clearly vary. If, as is frequently the case, the teacher feels that the learners could correct the error themselves, the teacher may simply quote the error and ask them to correct it. In many cases, teachers working with monolingual classes deal with errors which they feel arise from first language interference by quoting in the first language and asking the students to translate. If the error does arise from interference, the fact that the use of translation highlights this for all may help to avoid its repetition.

Vocabulary correction generally poses fewer problems, whether or not the item involved is one the learners have already met. Teachers' corrections of vocabulary are best dealt with pragmatically. The value of any item to the particular group of students should be rapidly assessed. The teacher can then decide whether or not the correction of a particular item will be of help to the learners in the future or whether it is, at least at the moment, too obscure to waste a lot of time on.

Pronunciation, on the other hand, is a more problematic area. Mispronunciation of individual words can be effectively handled in debriefing, but probably most pronunciation problems will not be in this area. Problems of rhythm and intonation are more difficult to handle in debriefing (unless they are merely at the word level) because, like discourse errors, they require the manipulation of large quantities of text for their exposition. The tape recorder may be useful in such cases. Mispronunciation of individual items may also be limited by effective briefing.

Three approaches to debriefing

In the previous section I have been concerned principally with the what and why of language debriefing. I should now like to consider the how and when.

Leaving aside those aspects of debriefing which require significant learner participation and which are best carried out immediately after the simulation, the teacher can also decide when to carry out the debriefing. First, the teacher can collect and collate the errors and go over them with the class as soon as the simulation has ended. Second, the teacher can collect and collate in the same way but debrief in a subsequent session with the same group. Third, the teacher can consolidate a delayed debriefing with a rerun of the same (or a similar) simulation. The effectiveness of the different approaches is obviously difficult to establish experimentally, but most teachers would probably agree that these three approaches, as described in more detail below, are among the most useful.

The first approach can probably be considered the classic, and its use has been implicit in much of the preceding discussion. After the participant-centered debriefing has concluded, the teacher takes over, runs through those errors which seem to be the most important, either eliciting correction from participants or giving it him or herself with appropriate explanation and exemplification. In some cases, exercises may be improvised to ensure that participants have understood and are able to apply what they have learned.

Such an approach is not, however, the only one possible. An alternative is for the teacher to make no immediate corrective debriefing, or perhaps to limit correction to a few straightforward vocabulary problems. Then, outside the classroom, the teacher analyzes the kinds of error that have taken place and integrates a correction of these into a subsequent class—perhaps, indeed, as part of the briefing to another simulation.

There are a number of good reasons for delaying this part of the language debriefing in this way. First, the teacher has the chance to analyze the errors and to develop strategies for dealing with them at leisure rather than having to operate on the spur of the moment. Second, after the excitement of participating in the simulation, the learners may not be in the best frame of mind for assimilating language debriefing. They are more likely to feel in need of a break and a cup of coffee immediately after the simulation, and they will be in a more receptive frame of mind later. On the other hand, they may expect an immediate language debriefing (even if they are not very receptive to it) so a certain amount of straightforward vocabulary correction may well be appropriate immediately.

A further advantage of postponing the greater part of the language debriefing to a later date is that the teacher will be in a better position to develop some form of synthesis of the errors which took place and integrate this into a later class. The object of this class will be to reinforce the acquisition of the language areas highlighted in the original simulation and examined in the synthesis.

This approach to debriefing integrates very effectively with a third possibility. This is to consolidate the original debriefing with a repetition of the original simulation or with the running of a similar one.

Suppose that the original simulation reveals problems both of behavior and of language and that these have been looked at in debriefing. For these to be effectively consolidated, the most valuable approach would be to have these same difficulties arise in another simulation so that the participants can experiment with handling them more effectively. Such difficulties are clearly likely to arise again if the simulation used is the same as, or resembles, the original.

In some cases, it may prove fairly easy to modify the original simulation a little before rerunning it. This has the advantage of giving the participants the possibility of coming to different conclusions, and the simulation retains the attraction of novelty. For example, it is often possible to modify a business simulation simply by changing a few figures. The simulation will retain the same basic form, but some of the decisions reached may be different. This is particularly the case, for example, in computer-assisted simulations where either one or two variables can be modified, or where a random factor dictates that in any event no two simulations will follow exactly the same course. Variety can also be introduced by having some of the participants change roles. In any event, no good, flexible simulation will ever run twice in exactly the same way.

Whether or not modifications have been made, it will frequently be appropriate to rerun the simulation. The language and behavior inputs which the participants have received as a result of debriefing introduce new factors into the simulation and will modify the way in which it develops a second time around. In addition, it may well prove an advantage that the participants have a better idea of how the simulation may develop before starting; they may have more time available to concentrate on language and be able to put into practice points which came up in the language debriefing.

All the above suggests some kind of ideal debriefing scenario. It is well to bear this in mind as an ideal, even if it is not used in every case.

The simulation is followed immediately by a behavior debriefing, in which the principal participants are the learners themselves. This is followed by a language debriefing which includes an examination of those things which the participants would like to have said but which they did not have the capacity to say during the simulation. This first debriefing phase concludes with a brief teacher-led examination of some vocabulary problems. There is then a break until the group meets again at a subsequent class, during which time the teacher has had a chance to examine the errors noted and to work out a strategy for dealing with them. This debriefing also stands as a briefing session for a second simulation, which is similar to the first, and which is designed to consolidate the acquisition of the problem areas brought to light in the first simulation and dealt with in the debriefing. In this way an entire course program can be centered on simulations, the debriefing of one also serving as briefing for its successor.

Conclusion

The reader will conclude from the above that for a simulation to have any real *use* in the language classroom, both briefing and debriefing must be adequate. The simulation will have been chosen in the context of the language development of the class, so language briefing (other than vocabulary) will probably not occupy a very large amount of time. Behavior briefing, the information necessary for the carrying out of the simulation is likely to be more time-consuming and will need careful preparation.

Debriefing, and indeed briefing, should generally be organized so as to involve participants as much as possible in the process, especially in the case of behavior debriefing. And whatever approach is finally adopted for this, postsimulation strategies which enable consolidation to take place are perhaps the most important considerations in the whole process of using simulations in language learning.

Chapter 5

Simulation/game design and adaptation

Martha Graves Cummings and Rhona B. Genzel
Rochester Institute of Technology

Theoretically, simulation/game design is a creative process in which the designer moves from language, desired outcomes, and objectives to the finished simulation. This is a three-stage procedure. First, game criteria and the need for the exercise are determined. Second, the basic game idea, including content, format, and structure, is decided upon. Third, materials are developed, tested, and modified to meet design criteria.

However, in simulation/game choice and modification, the designers examine a finished product to determine if their objectives can be met, even partially. When evaluating nonforeign second language learning designs which concentrate primarily on situation, language evaluators must also consider the additional dimensions of language and culture, both central components of the language learning simulation/game. By applying the principles of game design, language instructors can modify games to meet learning objectives and target group needs.

In practice, however, the game design comes from playing around with ideas and combinations, experimenting through trial and error, and reshaping things as one goes along. The elements which follow are only to provide a framework for the design process. As one begins, one quickly learns that design does not always proceed logically. It is a mad combination of the logical and illogical, the creative and the predictable.

Determining game criteria

The first, and often most difficult, step in game design is deciding upon game criteria. One may begin by asking, "What do I want my students to know, to do, or to learn?" An example of a general objective is: "I want my students to become more comfortable when visiting restaurants or to be more at ease in business situations, such as negotiating a contract."

Specific objectives are refined from these general objectives; they are the backbone of the game's design and should be stated concretely and concisely. Specific objectives usually draw in other secondary objectives. They might include "I want my students to know how to give their orders in fast food restaurants" or "I want students to know how to ask about foods or send food back in restaurants." By examining these educational objectives, the designer can isolate those areas which lend themselves to a simulation experience.

At this point, it is crucial to consider the effect of language behavior as an additional game component. Although situational simulation/games, by their nature, generate language, we should keep in mind the specific language behaviors, usages, and vocabularies we wish to emphasize and design situations in which they can be used in a realistic context. Special consideration should be given to level of difficulty, idiomatic usage, inflection, register, and correctness of expression. For example, Genzel and Cummings (1986) developed four simulation/games to accompany text material. Each of these simulations focuses on different situations that students are likely to encounter outside the classroom. For instance, after studying introductions, small talk, and ordering in a restaurant, students play a simulation/game based on an American nightclub. They dance, order from a menu, and make conversation. Here the purpose of the game is for students to use language in a real context.

Once the objectives are clarified, one must consider the target group. It is necessary to determine not only who will be using the simulation but also their level, previous experience, and needs. This will facilitate development of appropriate game situations and materials and ensure that the situations do not require more advanced language than the students have acquired, although most simulations can be used at different levels.

Before proceeding, however, the designer should research existing games. One may find an available game which meets the instructional criteria or can be modified or used as a basis for a new simulation. Research provides an excellent starting point for creativity and the opportunity for mutual sharing.

Developing the basic game idea

Creativity is needed when developing the basic game idea. Here the designer chooses game content, format, and structure appropriate to the learning objectives. The design may be directed toward cognitive learning or the development of affective or broad-based skills applicable in many areas, or a combination of these.

Depending upon objectives and needs of the target population, a simulation can be three-dimensional/interactive, computer-assisted, or individually paced and directed. The main criteria are that the simulation be realistic, interactive, and challenging to players. For example, a simulation of a school party or dance would be an excellent format for helping students gain confidence and skill in making social introductions and conversation. A computerized simulation based on case studies may be a good choice for teaching problem-solving or managerial techniques. The instant responsiveness and branching options of programming provide the student with immediate feedback on decisions.

Game design need not be solely the realm of the instructor. Based on a common format, frame games provide the opportunity for instructors and students to modify game contents or to design their own simulations. The frame structure can be loaded with different content and complexity and thus change the level of the game. Using archetypal situations, students can develop games which address their interests, concerns, or needs. Because they perceive objectives, needs, and situations from a different viewpoint, students often produce games which are both stimulating and relevant.

After format and content, the designer chooses the game structure. One must decide what the players must do, the order of play, and how situations are to be dealt with. Visualization of the simulation, including interaction patterns, organization, and possible stumbling blocks, is facilitated by plotting the sequence of action. Flow charts, especially those with movable parts, allow the designer to observe the game sequence. This visual dimension often reveals omissions or necessary changes and more clearly indicates interaction and language patterns which must be considered. For example, in a restaurant simulation, a player would need to receive a menu, ask about certain dishes, order, and receive the food before s/he could complain about the quality of the meal.

By carefully examining language interaction, one realizes what vocabulary and social skills must be taught to students before they can play the game successfully. In addition, the instructor can assess the level of difficulty of the exercise and determine if it suits students' needs and abilities. Through analysis of game components, the designer can delete, add, or modify structure and contents to achieve a relevant, consistent simulation.

Creating game materials

After deciding upon game format, structure, and contents, one then creates game materials. Activities and supporting materials may involve all levels of learning, from recognition to synthesis, from repetition of information to argumentation and persuasion. A crucial point, however, is that the activities should reflect a realistic situation and be based on game objectives and class instruction.

Materials should be designed to create a variety of realistic actions or interactions involving all players, and to encourage individual and group involvement on several levels of learning. For example, one should not construct activities in which two people are interacting while the rest of the group watches, unless those watching are involved in a planned evaluation of the interaction.

Creative design and use of materials encourage participation and, if desired, competition. For example, including tasks with varying difficulty levels allows students who are less fluent or confident to participate in the simulation. Chance factors controlled by the facilitator may be built in to equalize play in groups of unequal ability. Having players themselves evaluate interactions and indicate whether an activity is completed correctly increases motivation and players' language awareness. This feature, especially when incorporated into the discussion following the simulation, can be an excellent springboard for additional instruction and exchange of ideas.

When developing materials, one must also consider the impact of the use of *roles* within the game. Not only must facilitators be familiar and comfortable with all the roles, but students also must have the necessary background and expertise to play their assigned roles correctly and confidently. This may involve preteaching or discussion in detail of game materials before the simulation begins. Players do best when their roles are clear and appropriate for their level and background.

Cultural factors of the target group, including gestures, body language, and attitudes toward touching, authority, religion, and male/female roles, must also be addressed. This requires tact, sensitivity, and creativity. For instance, a simulation where a player is required to order an alcoholic beverage would offend a Moslem student. However, a simulation which allows the player to refuse a drink and encourages him or her to use pretaught language for refusing politely would be an acceptable and useful alternative.

Assigning *points* for activities has interesting repercussions. First, assigning points to different exercises may encourage some students to attempt more challenging activities, or to choose those the designer wishes to emphasize for pedagogical purposes. For example, a higher value could be placed on an activity involving synthesis than upon one requiring recognition or repetition. Point assignment can also create competition either between individuals or between groups. This can encourage team consensus and effort or individual thought and development.

Props can be simple or elaborate, depending upon game purpose and financial and time constraints. Simple signs may be used to label places or items; however, the more realistic the setting, the more enthusiastic the student response. For example, in the simulation/game GOING TO A NIGHTCLUB facilitators may choose either to transform the classroom into a nightclub by using table decorations and taped music or merely to re-arrange furniture and use signs to represent the dance floor, table area, and reception area.

A central aim of game design is to make the simulation usable by someone other than the designer and clear to the players. Therefore, *directions* should include the following:

1. Objectives for the game.
2. Complete directions for players' and facilitators' roles (if needed).
3. Game setup instructions, including placement of props and materials required and their use.
4. Play instructions, including rules, interaction patterns, action sequences, time limits, and other special cautions or directions for players and facilitators.
5. Procedure for aftergame feedback and discussion.

Adequate time must be provided before the game to let players know what they must do during the game and to rehearse the game with facilitators. Allowing participants to ask questions beforehand stimulates interest in the simulation, increases player confidence, and increases the level of participation.

Testing and revising

Before putting the game into actual use, the prototype game must be given an intensive trial run. This means actually playing the game complete with directions, props, and actual playing materials, and feedback session. The game should be played with peers or students who will provide constructive feedback. These evaluators can contribute ideas and point out problems that may have been overlooked. This is also an excellent way to recruit future facilitators and game designers.

Special attention also should be given to the aftergame discussion, because this is where much of the learning from the simulation takes place. Rather than superficial treatment of "what happened," the questions should challenge students by probing into deeper cognitive, affective, and interactive phases of game play. After the trial run, players may be asked to contribute questions which they feel are germane to game and learning objectives or which will provide a forum for students to discuss experiences or language concerns. (See Chapter 4 for ideas about debriefing.)

Choosing and modifying games

Choosing and modifying an existing game requires examining a finished product to determine if one's learning objectives can be met, even
partially, by the game. When seeking a game for target language use, one
should consider games designed explicitly for language learning, as well
as games not designed explicitly for language learning. Although the latter
do not concentrate explicitly on language behavior per se, they are often
better designed and emphasize different concept areas and skills not usually covered in pure language games. If these games can be modified to
include specific language aspects, the result is usually highly satisfactory.

One area of concern, however, in game adoption and modification is
level of language and difficulty. Therefore, it is crucial to pay particular
attention not only to game activities and objectives but also to phraseology,
interaction patterns, and social skills, as well as level of language difficulty.
With different loading or other modification, simulation games, especially
frame games, can be repeated or run at different levels. Modification may
include rewording of materials, preteaching necessary skills, or adding or
changing specific information, directions, or activities to facilitate play.

Conclusion

In conclusion, game design is a creative and often circuitous process
in which one moves, through experimentation and refinement, from language and objectives to a finished product. Game choice involves the con-
scientious evaluation of a finished product to determine if the game can
be used as is or modified to meet one's learning objectives. In either process,
the instructors, through their own creativity, produce a unique instructional tool which will aid students in language use and acquisition as they
gain confidence in the target language.

Questions and activities

1. For those who have never participated in or conducted a simulation/game: Read the chapters in this section very briefly. Then get hold of some colleagues, and try out one of the games in Section F, or one of those to be found in one of the collections listed in Chapter 24.
2. For those who have participated in (but not conducted) a simulation/game: Read the chapters in this section and then think back to a few simulation/games in which you were a participant. Make a list of things which you think the game organizer might have done better or more effectively (in a column on the left) and then specify briefly (in the right-hand column) the ways in which those things might have been done better or more effectively. Now conduct a few games with students (perhaps along with a colleague or two as coorganizers).
3. For those who have already conducted (and probably participated in) a simulation/game: Take a couple of specific simulation/game sessions you have conducted and relate them to the comments made in this section. To do this you may wish to produce a list of topics (in a column on the left), then relate each topic to particular comments and advice provided in the chapters (in a middle column), and finally making brief notes (in the right-hand column) of how these comments and advice might help in future sessions you plan to run.
4. List five possible problems in developing and conducting simulation/games. Note down the solutions proposed in the chapters and add any solutions of your own (if possible, by brainstorming with colleagues).
5. In what ways can you prepare yourself to conduct simulation? Which of these appears to be the most practical for you? Why? Choose one of these ways and carry it out. Write up your experience in summary or note form.
6. How does the structure of a simulation affect its message? Explain in terms of convergent and divergent models. What other terms might be used? Why?
7. What are the functions of briefing and debriefing, and how do these two phases relate to the main part of the simulation? What problems might arise in briefing and debriefing? How might they be solved?

73

8. Note down three or four institutional and other constraints that may be encountered when using simulation. How might such constraints be dealt with? Take part in WE'RE NOT GOING TO USE SIMULATION—a game designed by one of our leading gamers, Ken Jones. It is found in Jones (1982).

9. What are the main steps proposed in the design process outlined in Chapter 5? If you have ever designed a simulation/game, how does your experience differ from that described in Chapter 5? To explore the design process further you might like to take part in the game in Chapter 23.

Specific applications

Introduction

The application of simulation/gaming to specific areas

Outside of foreign/second language learning, simulation has been used in a huge range of subject areas, and for a wide variety of purposes. For example, in literacy training, in business, in international relations, or in geography, and for communication skills training, for counseling, for negotiation, or for cultural awareness. It is indeed one of the most powerful features of simulation/gaming that it can be used with equal effectiveness for a very wide variety of applications. As Noel et al. (1987) say: "It is difficult to imagine a more polyglot area of kindred scholarly activities than simulation. It reflects a coming together of a rather amazing variety of intellectual traditions."

The sheer quantity and variety of simulation/games in a whole range of subject areas can be almost bewildering, and language teachers have hardly begun to tap this rich source of material. This section of the book thus discusses the ways in which simulation/gaming is ideally suited for more specialized language areas, just as it is already widely used in many specialist nonlanguage areas. The eight chapters in this section consider specific applications of simulation/gaming in language learning. Such applications range from learning to learn, through developing specific language skills, testing, using languages for specific purposes (LSP), to teacher training.

Simulation/gaming is particularly useful in the development of particular skills. As we saw in Chapter 1 and in Section B, one of these skill areas is, of course, communicating in a new language. Achieving communicative competence can, however, also be enhanced by developing other related skills, especially those involved in *learning to learn* another language (see Chapter 7). Simulation/gaming can help here, too, and thus contribute indirectly to learning to communicate in another language.

But learning to learn is also important in teacher training, and since the main goal of this book itself is to contribute to the professional development of teachers (as is the aim of a vast number of other books on language instruction practices, applied linguistics, and the like), the first chapter in this section looks at the way simulation/gaming can contribute to language *teacher training*. Many other books tend to concentrate on the content, as opposed to the process and context, of teacher training. In education generally, simulation/gaming has proved to be a particularly valuable and effective technique in the process of teacher training or development. However, simulation/gaming does not yet seem to be widely used for the training of language teachers. It is therefore important to look at this topic at some length, particularly since the use of simulation/gaming for the training of teachers (e.g., for syllabus design) *also* provides teachers with indirect training in simulation/gaming techniques themselves. Chapter 6, by Marion Geddes, Gill Sturtridge, Rebecca Oxford, and Hana Raz, presents a rationale for using simulation/games in language teacher training. The authors describe how simulation/gaming can be used as an integral part of language teacher training and walk us through a number of different types of exercises that can be used with trainee teachers.

In a similar vein, Chapter 7, by Jim Fernandes, Gail Ellis, and Barbara Sinclair, looks at the way in which simulation/gaming may help language learners to develop certain additional or helping skills useful in their pursuit of learning the target language. *Learner training* is becoming a major area of interest in education generally and in simulation/gaming circles in particular. It goes by a number of terms, such as "learning to learn," "learner training," or "strategy training," depending on what particular aspect is emphasized. Simulation/gaming was one of the first educational methodologies to recognize explicitly the importance of learning by doing (experiental learning) and of encouraging the learning of learning skills, and thereby to take the learning process explicitly into account. This is hardly surprising because a central concern of gamers is learning—rather than teaching. Gamers wish to overcome some of the limitations imposed by more traditional teaching techniques, and to enable learners to develop various skills to enhance their learning. In this chapter, the authors provide us with a survey of a few of the areas in which learner training can be fostered by simulation/gaming, such as developing ways of planning and organizing language work (metacognitive strategies) and gaining an awareness of the principles of verbal communication. Specific examples of exercises illustrate the usefulness of simulation/gaming in helping to "educate" learners about various aspects involved in learning another language.

Chapter 8, by Rebecca Oxford and David Crookall, concentrates more specifically on one key aspect of helping students to become better learners. This aspect is *learning strategies*, which are actions or steps taken by learners to enhance their own learning (to be contrasted with instructional or teaching strategies—i.e., the actions that teachers employ to help their students learn). As we show in this chapter, there is a close correspondence between certain characteristics of simulation/gaming and the aims of many learning strategies. We outline some of the ways in which simulation/gaming may encourage language learners to develop and use beneficial strategies.

From learning to learn, we move to learning a language. Chapters 9 and 10 concern themselves with the general language applications of simulation/gaming for enhancing reading and writing skills and for testing, while Chapters 11, 12, and 13 concentrate on languages for specific purposes (science, business, and international studies).

Most language teachers tend to view the use of simulation/gaming as a means of encouraging naturalistic *oral* language use. Indeed, most simulation/games, especially those published for foreign/second language learning, tend to encourage the spoken forms of the language, although certain amounts of reading are required as provided by the initial simulation/game documents. In Chapter 9, Robin Scarcella and Susan Stern redress the misunderstanding that simulation/gaming is useful only for oral communication, and show how simulation/gaming can be used to great effect for the two skills of *reading* and *writing*, as well as for instruction in the related area of literature.

Testing language skills is a complex process, partly because of the complexity of language use itself and partly because of the problems associated with assessing language in a testing situation as though it were not a test. In other words, the introduction of testing schedules into a language-using context usually produces a wholly unnatural situation. The problems of the actual measuring of language level are compounded by the effect testing has on the way students use language to be tested—in other words, the test may not actually fully achieve its aim of measuring students' nontest competence. A key issue here is how to create language testing situations which correspond to more natural and authentic language contexts, in much the same way that pedagogic practices often attempt to give learners the opportunity of practicing naturalistically. Simulation/gaming is a particularly efficient way of reducing the "testing effect," as well as of creating situations in which the language to be tested is used in a more natural way. Indeed, one component of the Oral Proficiency Interview (ACTFL/ETS/ILR) includes a "situation," which often takes the form of a small role-play. In Chapter 10, Andrew Littlejohn examines the advantages of using simulation/gaming as a testing device and illustrates how this is done.

The three chapters (11 to 13) on using simulation/gaming in learning *languages for specific purposes* (LSP) cover a broad range of specialties. The notion of content-based language learning is central to this. The importance of subject matter and content as a context for language learning was probably given its first major impetus by the Bullock Report (Bullock Committee, 1975) in Britain. Since then the idea has blossomed in the area of language learning. As Mohan (1986) says:

Any educational approach that considers language learning alone and ignores the learning of subject matter is inadequate. . . . Yet much educational thinking treats language learning and content learning separately. And this is surprising, since education is fundamentally a process which occurs through the use of language. Language is the major medium of instruction and learning.

Three chapters in this section embody this idea and provide examples of the ways in which simulation/gaming is particularly well qualified to integrate content and language learning, particularly in the LSP sphere. As Tom Hutchinson and Chris Sawyer-Lauçanno point out (Chapter 11), there has been a notable neglect of simulation/gaming in LSP circles, despite its obvious and powerful advantages. The authors provide a concise and convincing account of the ways in which simulation/gaming can contribute to the learning of a range of language and communication skills needed by students of *science and technology*. This is followed by a similarly inspired chapter (12) by Mike Brammer and Chris Sawyer-Lauçanno, but one which concentrates on language skills used by those in *management, commerce, and industry*. Chapter 13, by David Crookall, looks briefly at the integration of languages and *international studies*, and describes one particular simulation/game, ICONS.

Chapter 6

Teacher training

Rationale and nine designs

Marion Geddes
Freelance Teacher Trainer

Gill Sturtridge
University of Reading

Rebecca L. Oxford
University of Alabama

Hana Raz
Haifa University

Communicative language learning has many important classroom implications, not only for students but also for their teachers. Training of language teachers must be reoriented so as to support and enhance the beneficial changes caused by the communicative approach. In this chapter we discuss implications of the communicative approach for teacher training. We also present nine innovative, simulation-based designs for training teachers of second or foreign languages.

Implications of the communicative approach

Some of the conclusions we drew in the late 1960s and the 1970s from discussions and arguments about language teaching and learning now seem self-evident. Indeed, we sometimes wonder why it took us so long to realize the implications of the fact that "knowing a language" is not simply a question of knowing grammatical rules and lexical items; it is also knowledge of how these rules of construction are affected by rules of use in communication. We are now armed with new syllabuses and with materials and ideas for activities that teachers can use in the classroom to help their learners communicate in the target language. We also have available a considerable literature providing both empirical and theoretical support for the communicative approach to language teaching (see, e.g., Widdowson, 1979; Littlewood, 1981, 1984; Richards & Rodgers, 1986; Oxford et al., 1989).

Changes in roles and responsibilities

Another legacy of the late 1960s and the 1970s is the influence that psychologists such as Carl Rogers (1969) have had on our perception of the teacher's role. Many teachers have moved from an image of themselves as imparters of knowledge and instructors to see themselves as facilitators of learning (K. Jones, 1988), giving students greater independence and responsibility for learning and doing their best to adapt to differences in learners' styles, strategies, and personalities. In the last two decades, the center-stage role of the teacher has inexorably given way to a primary focus on the *learner*. Language learners are encouraged to find answers and develop skills for themselves, with direct help from their peers and with facilitation by the teacher.

We are beginning to recognize that language learners play a key role in shaping their own learning in accordance with the axiom "The mind is an instrument to be developed, not a receptacle to be filled." Language learners are discovering that they must "learn how to learn." The process of learning how to learn pushes students to take responsibility for learning, identify their preferred learning style (e.g., global vs. analytic), and tap the strength of that learning style. This process also helps learners to develop the skills of planning, arranging, and evaluating their own learning, to notice the specific strategies or behaviors (such as imagery, repetition, and naturalistic practice) they use in language learning to expand their strategy repertoire if necessary, and to use errors as a vehicle for further progress. Language teachers need to be trained to help students learn how to learn (Holec, 1981; Crookall, 1983a; Wenden & Rubin, 1987; Oxford, 1990b).

Affective and social domains

If language teachers are to help learners cope with their own feelings, have positive attitudes toward learning, and work cooperatively with other people, teachers themselves must be trained in these important affective and social areas. Concern for the affective aspects of language learning has been growing as a response to the urgings of psychologists like Rogers and language instruction theorists like Krashen (1982) and Brown (1987). Language teachers frequently face reluctant learners and problem situations. They need help in dealing with a variety of underachievers; with fearful, frustrated, aggressive, or apathetic students; and with those whose low self-concept leads to a lack of willingness to make an effort. Language learning—particularly when it involves speaking the target language in the presence of others—can be extremely anxiety-provoking, as noted in a wealth of research summarized by Horwitz (1990) and Horwitz and Young (1990). Under such circumstances, no amount of expertise in methodology alone is sufficient. Methodology must be coupled with an awareness of the psychodynamic factors found in the classroom. Teachers do not teach "material" but instead teach people, whose attitudes, beliefs, and feelings must be considered (Gardner, 1985). Greater focus on learners' affective side has changed the climate of the classroom in dramatic and positive ways.

Classroom climate is also altered by changing the social structure of the classroom through cooperative learning (group work), which is often viewed as an essential part of the communicative approach (see Gunderson & Johnson, 1980; Gaies, 1985; Oxford et al., 1989). In cooperative learning, the communication shifts from the hierarchical, teacher-to-student mode to the networked, student-to-student format. Cooperative learning typically involves working in pairs or small groups on a language task, such as interviewing each other, creating and performing a skit, designing a magazine in the target language, or working on a jigsaw reading exercise. Cooperative learning typically makes the classroom atmosphere far more relaxed and enjoyable and much less threatening.

The affective and social elements seem to be more central to the learning of languages than to the learning of any other skill or content area. Therefore, teacher training which explicitly deals with these elements is not a frill but an urgent necessity.

Interdisciplinarity

In today's rapidly changing world, the human knowledge base is increasing exponentially, and the intertwining of disciplines is becoming commonplace. Language learning, like many other fields, has been caught up in the wave of interdisciplinary momentum. Interdisciplinarity has allowed language learning to step off of its pristine academic perch and mingle with other disciplines, thus producing communication-oriented instruction in language for special purposes (LSP), such as science, technology, and business. It is easy to see how LSP courses merge specific disciplines with language learning. In a broader sense, language learning touches on and cuts across all disciplines, because language itself is basic to communication in every field and because people often learn new languages so that they can pursue studies in one or more disciplines.

Language instruction has been influenced in still other ways by interdisciplinarity. Language teachers are involving their students in role-plays, games, simulations, and structured exercises drawn from a wide range of fields outside of language learning per se. Authentic target-language materials like advertisements, menus, travel brochures, and TV shows—real-life materials that were not originally designed for language teaching—are put to use in the language classroom. Teachers need training in order to understand and exploit fully the interdisciplinarity of language learning.

So there is no doubt that language teaching methodology and our attitudes to education and learning have altered significantly over the last 15 to 20 years. We have briefly mentioned how the communicative approach has changed the demands placed on the training of language teachers. Let us now look more closely at the process of teacher training.

The training of language teachers

Teacher training is a broad concept. We use the term to cover the training, education, and the development of beginning teachers as well as teachers who are well along in their careers. Teacher training which occurs before the teacher takes his or her first teaching job is known as "preservice training," while teacher training which occurs later can be viewed as "in-service training." In the rest of this chapter, "trainee" refers to any teacher who is a recipient of either in-service or preservice teacher training. "Trainer" designates the person or team that designs and provides the teacher training. These terms do not imply that the trainee is passive and the trainer is active; both trainee and trainer are totally active in the training process, and each learns from the other. Just as a teacher is a facilitator of student learning, so a trainer is a facilitator of the trainee's learning.

Teacher training does not provide just a set of classroom gimmicks; nor is it a turnkey operation in which a simple move instantly unlocks all the secrets of teaching and learning. On the contrary, teacher training is a long-term, incremental process that involves looking at the emotional, cognitive, and social aspects of learning and teaching. It requires immersion in a variety of materials, experiences, and tasks that help trainees themselves to learn how to learn. Trainees consciously develop their learning-to-learn skills through peer interaction and sharing, through putting themselves in other people's shoes, and through experience and doing. Simultaneously, trainees clarify their personal beliefs and attitudes concerning the roles of teacher and student.

No philosopher's stone

The communicative approach is by nature eclectic, drawing on a variety of specific techniques and methods. These techniques and methods are used in many different ways, but they all reflect the underlying principle that students should learn to use language for the purpose of communication rather than merely for academic dissection and analysis. Partly because of the eclecticism of the communicative approach, few (if any) trainers believe we have found the Holy Grail or the philosopher's stone of language teaching methodology. It seems reasonable to consider present techniques and methods as being in a continual state of development as we incorporate new ideas and research from other disciplines, such as educational and social psychology, counseling, and management science.

As trainers, we certainly have a responsibility to help trainees develop their classroom skills and craft. We need to offer training that will give trainees the knowledge, skills, and insights necessary to devise and employ a communicative approach in their teaching. But we must also produce teachers who can adapt to change and creatively draw upon various disciplines in their new insights about language teaching. We must develop teachers who "have the comfortable expectation that it will be continuously necessary to incorporate new and challenging learnings about ever-changing situations" (Rogers, 1969). Teacher training therefore must involve experiences that will help these individuals continue to develop as teachers throughout their careers.

Elements essential to teacher training

Trainees can far more easily help their students to work cooperatively, to learn how to learn, to enjoy language learning in a relaxed atmosphere, and to develop language skills by using wide-ranging, authentic materials *if they themselves have had such experiences*. Teacher training techniques and the whole training process are as important as methodological content.

Put simply, it is counterproductive to lecture about group work in a teacher training course; training must itself provide ample opportunity to experience group work. It is unrealistic to hope that language teachers will help students sharpen their learning-to-learn strategies unless they themselves have had training in learning how to learn. It is unfair to expect language teachers to develop a caring, nonthreatening classroom climate if they have not experienced such a climate in their own teacher training program, especially with their trainers. And it is foolish to believe that language teachers will be able to convey to students the need for active involvement with authentic materials drawn from many disciplines and sources unless in their teacher training program they have sampled a wide range of exciting, cross-disciplinary activities and materials.

Bad training and its effects

The need for these elements—cooperation among trainees, learning-to-learn training, a caring atmosphere, and rich use of authentic materials from many disciplines—is dramatically underscored by an actual training program where for the most part these aspects have been virtually absent: an MA program for training ESL teachers at a major U.S. university. Disastrous results have occurred because the trainers fail to offer even a watered-down version of the necessary elements. A relaxed and caring environment turns out to be antithetical to the principles of the trainers, one of whom proudly announces, "If my students [the trainees] hate me, it means I'm doing a good job," and "We don't need any students here; we get along better without them." Humiliation of trainees has been commonplace in the program: For instance, a trainee was unfairly and publicly accused of cheating because she did well on an examination; another trainee was literally screamed at for accepting a summer ESL teaching job without the trainer's permission. Cooperation among trainees does not occur because it is encouraged by the trainers, but instead happens furtively and in self-defense. The highly theoretical program fails, moreover, to offer adequate practical, practice-what-you-teach training in learning how to learn and in using authentic materials drawn from multiple sources. The only practical advice that trainees receive relates to maintaining the teacher's traditional image of authority—for example, "To be a good teacher, you have to dress well" and "Don't ever let your students call you by your first name."

The effects of poor training can reverberate through time. In addition to harming the trainees themselves, such training has a long-term danger: The trainees may, in their professional careers, tend to repeat the same behaviors and attitudes with their own students. It is difficult to unlearn negative messages.

Research on teacher training

In recent years the value of a number of teacher training techniques has been carefully considered, especially lecturing (Bligh, 1972) and group work (Rudduck, 1978). In addition, simulation techniques are also being researched for their contribution to teacher training. One form of simulation, known as microteaching, requires that trainees teach small segments or highly specific skills, instead of teaching for an entire class period. In microteaching, the "learners" are generally the other trainees. Wallace

(1979) reported on the first stage of a three-year research project on the use of microteaching in EFL and ESL teacher training, and the results testify to the value of this type of simulation in developing trainees' classroom skills.

How simulations can help in teacher training

In teacher training, the term "simulation" covers a range of techniques, such as role-play, microteaching, case study, and gaming. These techniques can be very useful for the training of language teachers. Let us explore the ways in which simulation can enrich teacher training.

We said earlier that trainees need to learn how to learn. No doubt learning-to-learn skills are to some extent part of a "born" teacher, but such skills can—and often need to be—more finely honed through training. At the same time, trainees' attitudes concerning classroom roles and responsibilities should be examined. Experience, rather than didactic lecturing, is the best teacher in terms of strengthening skills and exploring attitudes.

Two kinds of experience

Two kinds of experience exist—real-life experience and simulated experience. *Real-life experience* is the everyday experience of daily life, including serious and difficult problems, intertwined relationships, and a high cost if mistakes are made. Real-life experience is not always practicable during teacher training. It may be too complex for one person to experience; too expensive in terms of money, time, distance; or too risky for the self-confidence of a young (or even a not-so-young) trainee. *Simulated experience*, unlike real-life experience, can offer a safe practice ground, where failures and mistakes have no long-term ramifications or deleterious side effects. Significant aspects of the simulated experience can be isolated, and prompt feedback can be given. Through simulation, trainees can have vicarious experience of classroom circumstances and problems they might not otherwise encounter during their training. Participation in a simulation can provide valuable "grist for the mill," allowing for close but objective analysis of classroom situations and issues.

In our work as trainers we have used a variety of simulation designs. Some focus on different ways of learning (e.g., learning by doing, learning from peers). Others focus on the learning of specific skills, such as decision making, and on heightening self-awareness of learning strategies and attitudes. The design of a simulation determines the activity that takes place and structures the experience of the trainees.

Examples of simulations for language teacher training

The following discussion presents nine examples of simulation as applied in different ways to the training of language teachers. These examples include (1) a role-play about the use of language laboratories, (2) a role-play of an innovative young teacher in a conservative school, (3) a three-way role-play involving power structures, (4) a role-play about syllabus design, (5) a set of minisimulations involving trainee-generated events, (6) role-plays about events described by the trainer, (7) microteaching with role-play, (8) strategy awareness games, and (9) a simulation about materials development.[1]

The first three examples are illustrated by diagrams showing the interaction patterns. For each of the remaining six examples, readers can work out for themselves—in their minds or on paper—the interaction patterns that might occur. Even better, readers can try out some or all of these simulations in actual teacher training courses. All of the simulations here are useful for training language teachers, but a number are generic enough to be used for training teachers in many other fields as well.

Each of the following simulations has been used in actual teacher training courses, programs, or workshops. Although no simulation is included which seeks to train participants in the use of simulation for language instruction purposes, the experience itself often inspires trainees to experiment with the use of simulation in their own language classes. The simulations here may provide an opportunity for English language practice, especially for nonnative speakers, but this is not their primary function; these simulations are designed to train language teachers, not to teach language itself.

The trainer must of course use simulation in such a way as to ensure that the desired objectives of a given training group are met. These examples may therefore be adapted for particular circumstances.

Example 1. Role-play about the use of language laboratories

This simulation is known as the CANBIAN EDUCATIONAL AID PROJECT (Figure 6.1). The simulation was designed and used as a review at the end of a course on the use of language laboratories. It has two objectives, one overt, the other covert. The overt objective is to discuss the merits and selection of a variety of hardware for use in language labora-

[1]Examples 1–4 were written by Marion Geddes and Gill Sturtridge, Examples 5–7 by Hana Raz, and Examples 8–9 by Rebecca Oxford. The authors thank David Crookall for his helpful suggestions. For further examples, particularly related to training teachers about language learning anxiety, see Crookall and Oxford (1990).

Figure 6.1   CANBIAN AID PROJECT.

tories. The covert objective is to expose trainees to the experience of participating in a simulation, so that they can discuss both the value and dangers of using simulation in the language classroom.

All the trainees share common information about the background of the problem. This is given through reading and listening texts. The trainees are then divided into groups, with a minimum of six people in each group and a maximum of eight. Each group has the same task and the same set of roles. Each trainee is given a role-card describing his or her job, personality, and attitudes to the problem and to other members of the group. Before coming to the discussion table, the trainees prepare their role separately. All the groups then discuss the problem, but the groups will differ in how they interpret both the role and the problem.

During the feedback session that follows with the trainer and all the groups together, this variety becomes apparent and can be appropriately exploited. In our experience, most groups bring up and discuss the very points that we would have made in a much more trainer-directed session. A summary of the discussion can then by typed out and distributed to the trainees.

Example 2. Role-play of an innovative teacher in a conservative school

This simulation, entitled GALANTHIA (Figure 6.2), was based on a real problem—that of a newly qualified teacher attempting to inject new ideas into the curriculum of a rather conservative school. The objective of the simulation is to examine the attitudes, beliefs, and behavior of teachers in a conflict-ridden situation.

A young teacher in her first job tries to put into practice what she has learned in teacher training college about group work and communicative activities. She is faced with angry complaints from an older (male) colleague, whom her class has disturbed in an adjacent room. He believes that her methods will lead to a breakdown in discipline and a failure of the pupils to pass their exams. The head of the English language department receives letters from both teachers and decides to call a faculty meeting to discuss the problem. The easygoing sports teacher, who also teaches English, attends the meeting too.

Figure 6.2   GALANTHIA.

The trainees divide into four groups, and each group takes responsibility for the role of one of the teachers. Everyone is given information about the school (pupil intake, family backgrounds and attitudes, the role of English in the community, the English syllabus, and so on). The group with the role of the department head has copies of letters written by the younger teacher and her older colleague. The groups responsible for these two teachers have their respective letters. The group playing the sports teacher does not see the letters but knows that the older teacher has discussed his problem with the sports teacher.

Each group discusses what "their teacher" will say and do at the meeting. When all groups are ready, they select one of their number to represent their role at the meeting. Thus, four participants have the faculty meeting in front of the rest of their teams. Though only one member of each group takes an active part in the discussion, all the others are able to observe the interaction and to consider how their representative is presenting their role. The structure of the simulation gives participants practice in the skills of observing and analyzing. After the confrontation, observers and role-players join in the debriefing session and discuss what they observed and how they analyzed it and reacted. The discussion brings to the surface interesting differences arising from interpretations of the active role-players and of the members of their groups. They have all watched the same interaction but have perceived it in a variety of ways.

Example 3. Three-way role-play involving power structures

This simulation, known as THREE BY THREE (Figure 6.3), was adapted for language teacher training from the TRIAD TEACHER TRAINING EXERCISE. It has been used with various groups, including students at the Institute of Education at the University of London who had just finished their first teaching practice in ESL classes of immigrant children.

The objective of THREE BY THREE is to develop trainees' self-awareness and observation skills. Participants work in threes, A, B, and C. They take turns being the observer and taking on two active roles in each round.

In Round 1, A is the student and is given a role-card describing the situation as well as his or her age and expectations. A is given no indication of how to react or what to say. B is the teacher who has called the student, A, to discuss weaknesses in A's work. C observes the meeting, which lasts 7 to 10 minutes before the school bell rings. C takes notes, following the guidelines given on an observation sheet. After this there is an immediate feedback session among the three, usually led by C.

At this point participants move to Round 2. This time A is the observer. C takes on the teacher's role, but in this confrontation the teacher is faced by B, who has a new role as the head of the English language department

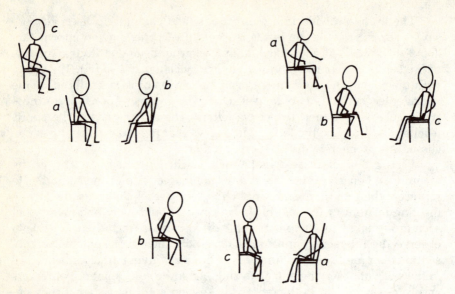

Figure 6.3   THREE BY THREE.

and who is critical of C's work. Again the confrontation lasts about 7 to 10 minutes, and there is a short feedback session.

In Round 3, *B* is the observer, while *A* takes on the role of the head of the English language department. This is now a subordinate role as *A* confronts *C*, who is now in the role of the head of the school.

The use of this triad structure enables all the participants to experience being in authoritative and subordinate roles as well as being a detached observer. The simulation ends with a debriefing in which all the threes come together to exchange experiences and observations.

Example 4. Role-play about syllabus design

A simulation called ILLYRIA was designed for experienced language teachers who are following a short course on syllabus design. The simulation helps trainees practice what they have learned so far about designing a syllabus. The structure of the simulation and the nature of the task allow trainees to learn by doing.

In this simulation, participants have to complete a section of the English language syllabus for the first year of a three-year training program in a private language school. There are no role-cards, and participants work as themselves in small groups or in pairs, as they choose. They are given a description of the national and institutional situation for which the syllabus is being prepared, a needs analysis about the students concerned, and a partially completed syllabus based on the needs analysis.

The overt objective is for each group to produce a syllabus, which is presented in poster form for discussion by the whole class. Trainees are also asked to keep a record of the difficulties that arise and the solutions they propose. They are asked to be ready to evaluate the decision-making procedures they have followed. In the debriefing session, it becomes obvious that the procedures—not the syllabuses—are the key topic that trainees are eager to discuss. This is as it should be; in learning of any sort, the process or experience is often more significant than the product.

Example 5. Minisimulations involving trainee-generated events

The minisimulations described here involve participants in describing and solving problems, cast in the form of classroom events taken from trainees' own previous experiences. Examples developed in past training sessions are listed below.

1. The teacher sends a student out for disrupting the class. It turns out afterwards that another student was to blame.[2]
2. A student is told to leave the class, but refuses to go.
3. The teacher has set a date for a test, but there are differences of opinion among the students as to what date was set.
4. Going into the class the morning after a very noisy lesson . . .
5. A teacher is presenting new material to a very heterogeneous class; more advanced students become impatient with weaker ones.
6. A heated argument breaks out between two students over a matter under discussion.
7. A student is doing homework for another subject or preparing for a test on the next lesson. The teacher becomes aware of this behavior.
8. The headmaster (or school principal) has come in to make an announcement. As soon as he or she has left, the students object loudly to the demands that were made.

The trainee who initiates the simulation of a given event describes the event in writing, prepares the role-cards for the incident, and distributes the cards to participants. The initiator usually takes the role of the problematic student or students (in itself an insightful experience), and another participant acts as the teacher who is trying to cope with the situation. Participants are not told how the initiator dealt with the actual experience.

---

[2]Although we encourage teachers not to send students out of the room, many do so. This minisimulation raises the problem and pinpoints some of the dangers of this practice.

The role-play is then enacted. A discussion follows, and other approaches are often enacted and discussed. The trainer helps the trainee realize the psychological and educational implications of the various courses of action. Thus, a simple event may lead to an in-depth analysis of the various factors involved. Trainees become "reflective practitioners" (Schön, 1983), learning from their own experiences and those of their colleagues. Learning via case analysis bridges the gap between professional knowledge and the demands of real-world practice. The trainee becomes aware of the uniqueness of every situation. Owing to the interaction of various factors, there can be no "recipes" in such instances. It all depends . . .

Example 6. Role-play involving trainer-generated events

Role-play often involves events that have been described by the trainer. Such role-play is useful for rehearsing situations that trainees might encounter in their own language classes. Here we will discuss several simulated events: (1) responses of students to their test scores, (2) cheating on tests, (3) teacher-student and teacher-parent feedback process, and (4) other situations.

Student responses to test scores   While discussing testing, it is possible to use a short simulation of the aftermath of a test. The simulation is conducted in groups of four participants. In every group, the following four student role-cards are handed out:

1. You have received 90 percent on the test. You prepared very thoroughly and expected 100 percent but missed it because of a spelling mistake.
2. You didn't prepare and got 75 percent. You are bright. You are satisfied with your score and glad that you didn't waste time on preparing.
3. You failed—again (45 percent). You spent hours preparing for the test.
4. You have received 65 percent on the test. You are a good student, but you didn't have time to prepare, because you worked long hours at your job (or another reason). You feel frustrated.

The groups are instructed to begin the conversation with "What did *you* get?" Very soon it becomes clear that these results carry the message that effort doesn't pay. External factors are blamed, most often the teacher. This simulation is used to illustrate attribution theory (Weiner, 1972) and highlights the possible effects of testing.

Cheating on tests   Another problematic area is that of pupils helping each other on tests, behavior typically viewed as cheating. While student cooperation and mutual help are generally encouraged in many classroom activities, on tests the same behavior is considered dishonest (see also Chapter 10). How should a teacher deal with such behavior during and after a written test? As various alternatives are enacted, trainees come to grips with the problem.

Teacher-student or teacher-parent feedback process   It is very useful to incorporate short role-plays while discussing certain areas, such as providing specific, constructive feedback to individual pupils—one of the basic elements of effective teaching. Participants practice the process in pairs; one takes the role of the teacher, while the other takes the role of the student. After a while they switch, either when the talk has reached an impasse or when the objectives have been achieved. When experiences are later pooled across all the pairs, general guidelines emerge. Similar role-plays are used as preparation for teacher-parent meetings.

Other events   Trainers can create role-plays of many other instructional events. For instance, a simulated session on supervisory feedback has been devised using a triad structure (supervisor, teacher, and observer). The supervisory feedback role-play is rooted in clinical supervision (Goldhammer, 1969), which aims to make the trainee a partner in the analysis of his or her strengths and weaknesses. Innumerable other role-plays can be designed, limited only by the trainer's imagination.

Example 7. Microteaching with role-play

It is advisable to try out some of the simulations above before moving on to microteaching with role-play. The other activities will serve as a useful introduction for trainees and trainer alike. Microteaching with role-play has been described in detail elsewhere (Geddes & Raz, 1979); here we will present the highlights.

In microteaching with role-play, one of the trainees prepares 10 minutes of a lesson (the microlesson) for a designated age group, and other trainees are given specific student roles with explicit personality characteristics, which often differ from the attributes of the trainees. The roles are suggested by the trainees themselves and assigned by the trainer in such a way as to give the trainees the experience of stepping into their students' shoes. Here are some examples of student role-cards:

1. You are somewhat below average in English, but you try very hard. You need continual encouragement from the teachers.
2. You are a very good student, but you like to show off and tend to answer the questions before the others can get a word in.
3. You are an average student, but are not very interested in English

or in school generally. You find it hard to concentrate in class and often daydream.

4. You are a weak student and tend to become frustrated and disturb the class.

The microlesson is conducted and videotaped. After the microlesson, first the "teacher" is asked for comments, and then each "student" in turn describes how he or she felt during the lesson. For instance, participants may discover how boring and lonely it is for weak students when they are ignored by the teacher, how easy it is to get carried away when one is fooling around and getting attention from one's peers, or how annoying it is to listen to repeated explanations long after one has understood the point.

Usually a certain pattern of teaching behavior gradually becomes evident, and participants gently try to help the person playing the teacher to become aware of this pattern; for example, the teacher may have spent too much time on disciplining and may have thereby diminished the students' interest in the lesson. Participants then observe the microlesson on videotape, making additional comments (as supportively as possible) on both the verbal and nonverbal interaction.

This kind of simulation has been carried out with participants from highly diverse cultural backgrounds. Interestingly, simulated student behaviors tolerated by some participants may be unacceptable to others, depending on cultural expectations. However, those participants who take on the role of teacher tend to react consistently, no matter what their background; they strive to be fair, firm, kind, and respectful.

Example 8. Strategy awareness games

Two learning strategy awareness games are the EMBEDDED STRATEGIES GAME (ESG) and the STRATEGY SEARCH GAME (SSG). The games help trainees understand learning strategies (see Chapter 8) and have been used with large groups of ESL and foreign language trainees. Both games require trainees to put themselves in the position of the language learner. Trainees are not required to act out roles; they just have to identify the language learning strategies they would use in each instance.[3]

Two phases are involved in each game. In Phase I, participants work in pairs to identify the greatest number of learning strategies relevant to a given set of specific language learning activities (in the ESG) or language-

[3]As explained by Oxford (1990b), full-blown role-plays are also possible, especially with the SSG. If the trainer wants to use role-play, the SSG situation descriptions serve as role-cards. The ESG and the SSG can also be used with language students (as well as with their language teachers, as shown here) for the purpose of raising strategy awareness.

related situations (in the SSG). During Phase II, each pair of participants compares its results with another couple.

To find appropriate learning strategies, trainees are allowed to use a list of 62 language learning strategies (see Oxford, 1990b; for examples, see Chapter 8) and to list additional strategies of their own. In either game, specific learning strategies are matched with the language activities or situations in which they could beneficially be used.

In the ESG, players work with a list of 48 language activities, each described in a short sentence. Here are some examples:

Breakdown—You're overwhelmed by long words and expressions in the new language, so you break them down into parts.

Peers Without Tears—You stop competing with your fellow students and learn to work together in learning the new language.

Secrets—You keep a journal of your language learning progress and write down new words and expressions.

Breakdown is a clear example of the analysis strategy, *Peers Without Tears* embodies the strategy of cooperating with fellow students, and *Secrets* reflects the diary-writing strategy. For each language activity, at least one strategy is clearly identifiable.

The SSG operates similarly, except that it involves 19 language situations that are much more complex than those found in the ESG. A detailed paragraph describes each situation, including the place, the constraints, and the needs and motivation of the people involved. Situations include, for example, a set of complicated errands that need to be run by an English-speaking student in Austria, the plight of a school-going Pakistani child in England whose family does not speak English, the need for an American to develop survival Spanish when the spouse is transferred to take over a factory in Latin America, and the need for a Hungarian chemist to sharpen his or her English skills sufficiently to write a technical paper in English and present it at an international meeting. Many language learning strategies—often dozens—are potentially relevant to any given situation in the SSG.

After each exercise, trainees take part in a debriefing during which they discuss questions such as which learning strategies they found to be generally helpful for a large number of language learning needs, and how the game altered their understanding of language learning strategies.

Example 9. Simulation about materials development

A simulation about materials development is entitled CO-MADE, meaning COoperative MAterials DEvelopment. This simulation was devised while its creator was a visiting professor for one semester at a large U.S. university, and it served as the backbone of one of his MA ESL teacher training courses. In CO-MADE, trainees are divided into several groups, each one playing a different role—client and consultant. Therefore, every trainee has the opportunity to work with others to establish the language training needs and requirements (as a client) and also has the chance to develop language training materials (as a consultant).

All decisions are accomplished cooperatively, so the simulation is an exercise in group dynamics and decision making, as well as in the development of language training materials. Every group develops its own identity, title, and characteristics. Each of the consultant groups spends several months conducting a needs analysis, designing syllabuses, and producing instructional materials to meet its clients' needs. Consultants formally present the materials to their clients, and the clients, in turn, evaluate the materials according to their stated requirements. Revision of the materials is carried out on the basis of client feedback. In the initial run of the simulation, trainees rapidly became involved with the simulation, took their group's identity very seriously, and developed some truly excellent language teaching materials.[1]

Conclusion

In the nine simulations for language teacher training discussed above, their structure, not the trainer, provides the trainees' experience. This is not to say that the trainer has no role. On the contrary, the value of the debriefing at the end of these simulations depends on the managerial, listening, and counseling skills of the trainer conducting it. Yet during the main part of the simulation itself the trainer is intentionally nondirective, a characteristic that is helpful as a model to be followed by trainees in their own language classrooms.

Simulation is being used in the training of many people in the helping professions (doctors, nurses, counselors, social workers) and should certainly be increasingly incorporated into the training of language teachers. When the training atmosphere is supportive, simulation enables us to enact and analyze problem situations in all their complexity, to highlight the interconnectedness of variables, and to try out alternative solutions. The experience of seeing the situation through another person's eyes as we take on a different role is revealing and valuable in fostering empathy. Simulation also provides a kind of "psychological innoculation" (Spielberger, 1972); trainees feel that such rehearsals make similar situations in the

---

[1]For more information on CO-MADE, see Crookall (1990).

language classroom less threatening. Their reactions to the simulation experience are usually very positive.

Microteaching simulations are becoming an integral part of language teacher training programs. They are far more valuable than mere peer teaching, which focuses exclusively on methods and techniques. Microteaching forces trainees to conduct lessons from which they must be able to deviate so as to fit the needs of the "learners." At the same time, microteaching helps trainees to attend to the psychodynamic level of classroom life, to "what happens inside and between folks" (Stevick, 1976).

Simulations, often developed jointly by trainees and their trainers on the basis of real-life experiences and familiar situations, seem particularly effective in promoting language teachers' professional growth. Simulations as a training device have much to offer. A variety of designs can be used to explore group dynamics, to gain experience in a low-risk environment, to expand and sharpen learning-to-learn skills, to practice decision making, to examine attitudes, and to review and consolidate information. Trainees' experiences with simulation in teacher training also help them initiate such activities in their language classes.

Chapter 7

Learner training

Learning how to learn

James Fernandes
University of Hawaii

Gail Ellis
British Council

Barbara Sinclair
British Council

Adults returning to a class to learn a new language (and indeed secondary school and university learners) are often faced with a variety of barriers to learning, ranging from psychological difficulties to unawareness of language. Demotivation and unsuccessful learning may also occur if learners have been trapped in previous learning patterns which are not compatible with their individual cognitive styles. Furthermore, there may be resistance to role-plays and simulations if the learner is not properly briefed about their value as language learning activities.

Traditional learner roles

In their everyday lives adults are required to live independently, make choices and decisions regarding their lives, accept responsibility, and learn to do things by themselves. However, language learners in the classroom often tend to revert to the traditional role of the pupil who expects to be told what to do, with which materials, and when to stop. Attitudes and factors which account for this behavior and which affect the learning process may include some of the following:

1. *Overdependence on the teacher.* Students may have come from a past learning situation which concentrated on learning grammar, structures, or simple drills to meet hypothetical "survival situations" and not on learning language as a means of communication and for conveying meaning. According to Hawkins (1984), this type of learning contributes little to language awareness or to offering help in "learning how to learn." As a result, some learners have become teacher-dependent and often feel that it is the teacher alone who is responsible for any learning and progress that takes place. A critical situation arises when learners actually believe the teacher will learn the language for them. This may often be the case for adults whose only previous foreign or second language (L2) experience has been secondary school years ago.

2. *Linguistic prejudice* and parochialism. This is the attitude that the target language is inferior to one's own.

3. *Inhibitions* about communicating in an unfamiliar language. In other words, learners may feel insecure about a real or imagined lack of vocabulary, reflecting little awareness of, or confidence in, using the range of communication strategies at their disposal, such as paraphrasing, word coinage, or circumlocution (Frohlich & Paribakht, 1984). There may also be a fear of losing face in front of peers when trying to use the target language, especially among adults in in-company courses where a professional hierarchy is already established.

4. A *mismatch* between a learner's expectations of how learning "should" take place and current methodologies. For example, because of past learning experiences, many find a communicative approach unfamiliar and difficult to come to terms with, and they do not understand the reasons for, and the value of, many classroom activities such as group work, role-plays, and simulations. Indeed, many teachers themselves do not understand the value of such activities, or are frightened of letting go of control of the class and taking on a less central role.

Adult learners, then, often embark on, or return to, the language learning process ill-prepared; they possess little awareness of language and of the processes involved in language learning and may therefore lack the essential learning tools. They often set themselves aims that are difficult to achieve. Consequently, they become frustrated and demotivated when they are confronted with the reality of the complex nature of the language learning task. In short, they do not have the means to set themselves objectives that are realistic or to assess them in terms of feasibility.

Aims of learner training

Learner training (LT) can be defined as a situation in which the teacher plays an instrumental role in helping the student to become a more successful language learner; it aims to help learners overcome some of the above difficulties. In other words, the teacher's usual role, that of teaching the target language, is expanded to include helping the learners learn how to learn (Wenden, 1985). The teacher plays a crucial role in this process as guide or facilitator, especially in the initial stages. LT involves training in three areas: psychological preparation, methodological preparation, and practice in self-direction (Dickinson & Carver, 1980).

The area of *psychological preparation* is large, and it includes helping the learner to develop an awareness of language, to overcome linguistic prejudice and inhibitions, and to develop self-confidence and motivation to communicate in the target language. *Methodological preparation* includes learning about the metalanguage of language description and teaching, and about the techniques of language learning. *Practice in self-direction* aims to encourage learners to take on personal responsibility for their own learning (Holec, 1979). All three areas include activities which aim to help the learners identify the learning strategies most suited to their own preferences and cognitive styles, and to become more aware of how language works to convey meaning.

The strategies and techniques employed by successful language learners, as far as these can be generalized, provide useful guidelines for devising learner training activities such as pair work, quizzes, communication games, role-plays, and simulations, in which learners are motivated to communicate, are made aware of how language is used for communication, and become actively involved in the learning process (see, e.g., Crookall, 1983a). Learner training can consist of both preliminary LT activities, perhaps more suitable for short, intensive courses where time is limited, and LT activities which are integrated into the usual language classes as an ongoing process. These are more suitable for courses of a longer duration.

LT activities which focus on developing *metacognitive strategies* (O'Malley et al. 1985) (e.g., processes whereby learners think about the nature of learning and regulate it—plan, monitor, and evaluate) are best done separately from the usual language work. This can involve them in communicative activities in the target language, but it can also be done in the first language (L1), depending on the linguistic level of the learners. LT activities which aim to develop *cognitive strategies* (O'Malley et al., 1985) (steps or mental operations used in learning or problem-solving that require direct analysis, transformation, or synthesis of learning materials in order to obtain, store, retrieve, and use knowledge) are best integrated into the usual language class. For example, a listening skills class can expand learners' awareness of the language—the discovery that English is a stress-timed language, that stressed words convey meaning, and that these are therefore the words to concentrate on when listening for gist. There are many different ways of implementing LT in the classroom, and the choice will depend on the course structure, the syllabus, and the students' level of awareness upon joining the course. However, to be successful, LT needs to be carried out systematically. Ellis and Sinclair (1985) have developed a three-phase model of LT which includes both preliminary LT activities in its induction and ongoing LT activities for skills training. LT may include some interesting and worthwhile LT simulation activities, such as the following:

1. A simulation in the L1 as preparation for simulations in the target language or, more specifically, to overcome the potential barriers which learners who are unfamiliar with this kind of activity can face—namely, (a) feeling embarrassed about acting out roles, (b) not understanding the potential of simulations as communication practice activities. Moreover, possibly the greatest stress of all, that of operating in a new language, has been removed so that learners can come to terms with the procedures involved in taking part in simulations. In addition, a postsimulation discussion bridges the gap between L1 and L2 simulations by encouraging learners to analyze aspects such as how they felt during the L1 simulation, communication skills and strategies that might have been developed, and the areas they need to concentrate on in order to transfer these to a similar simulation in the L2.

2. Multilingual games, such as EVERYBODY'S A LINGUIST, which is a confidence-boosting activity. Students think of languages they know quite well and languages they know just a few words of and independently record a few words of up to six different languages on a cassette recorder. Once each student has completed this task, the class comes together and identifies the languages and becomes aware of the fact that they are more linguistically capable and knowledgeable than they may have first assumed.

3. Discussion games or simulations on learning. For example, students can make short in-class documentaries (e.g., radio or TV programs) to simulate the way they have learned languages in the past (e.g., at secondary school or on trips abroad). This can lead to a discussion and exchange of ideas about the roles of learner and teacher as well as alternative learning strategies.

4. A simulation where students create a language teaching broadcast (e.g., on TV or radio for learners of the target language). This involves them in discussion on methodology, choice of materials, scheduling, and, indeed, what they consider to be the best way to learn a new language.

5. Another activity is to consider some of the ways messages are sent and received—in other words, to consider different forms of communication such as communication by animals and human communication with and without words (signals and signs, symbols, and made-up languages). The MICROLANGUAGE LAB is a simulation based on the latter which involves having small groups of students invent rudimentary "languages." It is one way of implementing learner training in the classroom in a concentrated form and includes training in the three areas of psychological preparation, methodological preparation, and self-direction practice described above. Insight into patterns has been shown to be a key element in aptitude for language learning and acquisition and encourages learners to compare their emerging insights in the made-up language with their intuitions about their mother tongue and to develop positive, open attitudes toward other target languages (Hawkins, 1984). This simulation, therefore, helps students learn about broad principles of language and verbal communication. It can also develop sensitivity to the power and influence of language and provide insights into the relationships among language, thought, and culture (Juleus, 1966; Fernandes, 1983b).

We will expand our explanation of the MICROLANGUAGE LAB below.

The MICROLANGUAGE LAB

The MICROLANGUAGE LAB has been employed with a variety of college students in the United States to teach principles of verbal communication and to encourage positive attitudes toward the study of language and communication. The majority of LABS have been composed of native English speakers, although a number of groups have included students with varying native tongues.

A teacher using the MICROLANGUAGE LAB as an initial learner training exercise should precede the activity itself with a brief rationale for the communicative approach and for the function of simulations within it. The practicality of the method, the personal insights which develop from immersion in the learning experience, and the efficiency of learning in a situation where one is wholly involved are all reasons in favor of the communicative approach. With this preface, the MICROLANGUAGE LAB can be introduced as an opportunity to become accustomed to the approach and at the same time to learn about language in general.

The LAB consists of three units, each requiring about one hour to perform. Students work in small groups (of about five people), although mediation of the learning experience can be conducted with the class as a whole.

Instructions for beginning the LAB are simply to "create your own language." Students should think of their group as a cultural unit in need of a common mode of communication. To facilitate this "microcultural" point of view, they might be asked to limit their "world" to the classroom or to another particular context or environment. Groups can begin by choosing some sounds to serve as the building blocks for their languages and then developing a lexicon by linking the sounds together into words with assigned meanings. If the MICROLANGUAGE groups are limited to a particular context, some interesting terms quickly arise as the group confronts more abstract concepts. Juleus (1966), for example, reports how one group whose cultural "world" was limited to the classroom invented a word for God which translated as "teacher-in-ceiling."

As students build vocabularies for their new languages, they are learning about two important characteristics of language: arbitrariness and conventionality. The fact that one set of sounds would serve as well as another to represent the same concept provides an immediate demonstration of arbitrariness. At the same time, group members obviously must come to agreement on the meanings they assign their words; otherwise the words would signify nothing. Thus, the socially conventional nature of language becomes apparent. By experiencing firsthand the arbitrary and conventional characteristics of their budding "languages," students begin to learn to overcome linguistic prejudice. One's own language is not necessarily superior to another, simply different: While the "language" of the *classroom culture* group may be more elegant in describing academic activities, the language of the *tennis-court culture* may be more efficient for discussing sports, just as an Eskimo language would surpass English in a conversation about the characteristics of snow.

During the second unit of the LAB, groups focus on the grammar or syntax of their "languages." In this stage students need encouragement to be creative, to break free from the habits imposed by their own tongue. Often, for example, the groups will unconsciously follow the word order of their native language and must have this convention pointed out to them. As the MICROLANGUAGE creators struggle with the difficulty of escaping from the syntactic bonds of their native languages, they realize what many have always taken for granted: that the way they think about the world is influenced by the way in which their language uses words to categorize perceptions and strings those words together into sentences. In this way, students develop new insights and appreciation for what a grammar really is: a formula for structuring thought.

The third unit of the MICROLANGUAGE LAB involves putting the finishing touches on the "language" and using it for communication. Groups may be asked to perform short skits for the rest of the class or simply to have conversations in their "languages." By this time the activity of the group will have gone a long way toward remedying problems of reticence or timidity about speaking in a strange language. In the first place, the task-focused communication in a small group helps break the ice and puts learners at ease with each other. Second, the apparent whimsicality of creating a group "language" instills a sense of playfulness which allows learners to express themselves more freely. Just as the infant's instinct for play and babbling leads to the acquisition of language, so the playful creation of a "nonsense" language helps open students psychologically to the learning of a second or foreign language.

Mediation of the learning process

An important aspect of the MICROLANGUAGE LAB is the instructor's mediation of the learning process. Students need to be helped to articulate what they are experiencing in order for learning about both language and the language-learning process to become conscious and complete. For example, the concepts of conventionality and arbitrariness of language can be raised in discussing the process the groups went through in developing their own vocabulary and grammar. Likewise, probing questions from the teacher may be required to prompt the realization that different languages have different ways of categorizing and arranging perceptions.

Depending on the particular characteristics of the languages invented in class, further observations about the nature of language and communication can be drawn out in discussions: Comparison of shared features of the invented languages might lead to consideration of language universals. The creation of a gestural language may inspire discussion of concepts such as iconicity or the image-reflecting quality of some symbols, the origins of language, and the relationship between language and nonverbal communication.

As Juleus (1983) points out, the MICROLANGUAGE LAB also encourages learning about group processes: "Anyone who has taught a course on language knows that many of the issues dealt with are social and political rather than linguistic. Group work soon makes that clear." By asking the groups how decisions about their invented languages are made or how grammatical "correctness" is determined, the teacher encourages learning about some of the social issues related to language.

In mediating the learning process, the teacher can also build logical bridges to the target language: What is the target language's term for that word the group just invented? What kind of environmental or cultural factors have influenced the evolution of the target language? How does the grammar of the target language indicate tense or number? This type of questioning will help relate the insights learners gain to the methodology of language learning and will arouse curiosity about the specific target language.

Conclusion

The MICROLANGUAGE LAB is just one example of learner training, but it does illustrate the utility of such training in foreign language learning. By inspiring interest in, and appreciation for, language and encouraging learners to express themselves in another "language," the LAB helps overcome psychological barriers to language learning. At the same time, it introduces learners to some of the methodology of, in this case, the communicative approach to language learning. Finally, by putting students, as small groups, in charge of their own learning, it helps create a sense of responsibility and self-direction. However the teacher chooses to address learning training, whether as a preliminary activity to language learning or as an ongoing process, attention to the areas of psychological preparation, methodological preparation, and practice in self-direction will facilitate the process of language learning and acquisition. For other examples of exercises for learner training, see Ellis and Sinclair (1989).

Chapter 8

Learning strategies

Making language learning more effective through simulation/gaming

Rebecca L. Oxford and David Crookall
University of Alabama

Learning strategies are operations used by the learner to aid the acquisition, storage, or retrieval of information (Rigney, 1978). Extending this definition and applying it to language learning, we can say that language learning strategies are actions or behaviors which learners use to make language learning more effective, efficient, and enjoyable.

Readers might argue that since language learning strategies are student-generated actions, such strategies are unrelated to, and unaffected by, language teaching strategies—that is, instructional techniques or methods used by the teacher. However, we contend that simulation/gaming (as well as other communicative, active language teaching strategies) can implicitly encourage and stimulate students to adopt a wide range of useful language learning strategies. In so doing, simulation/gaming promotes student initiative, motivation, self-direction, and skill.

In this chapter we will outline some useful language learning strategies and show how simulations and games, because of their active and interactive nature, tacitly encourage learners to use a variety of these strategies. We will then provide some concrete examples. Finally, we will explain how language teachers can use simulation/gaming to provide their students with overt, explicit training in the use of appropriate language learning strategies.

Strategies used by good language learners

Much research exists on good language learning strategies and the characteristics of good language learners. Rubin (1975) suggested that the good language learner is a willing and accurate guesser; has a strong, persevering drive to communicate; is often uninhibited and willing to make mistakes in order to learn or communicate; focuses on form by looking for patterns, classifying, and analyzing; takes advantage of all practice opportunities; monitors his or her own speech and the speech of others; and pays attention to meaning. In a slightly more technical vein, Rubin (1981, 1987) identified good strategies which contribute—either directly or indirectly—to language learning success. *Direct* strategies include clarification and verification, guessing or inductive inferencing, deductive reasoning, practice, memorization, and monitoring of errors. *Indirect* strategies include such things as creating practice opportunities and using tricks like circumlocution when the precise expression is not known.

Naiman et al. (1975) identified six strategies used by good language learners: selecting language situations that allow one's preferences to be used, actively being involved in language learning, seeing language as both a rule system and a communication tool, extending and revising one's understanding of the language, learning to think in the language, and addressing the affective demands of language learning. It was found that, in addition to using such strategies, good language learners showed other advantageous characteristics. They were immersed in the culture of the target language or had a great deal of contact with native speakers; demonstrated high motivation and an inherent interest in languages; benefited from good teachers, a stimulating learning environment, and positive parental influence; and possessed certain helpful personality traits.

Finally, Oxford (1989b, 1990a, 1990b) synthesized and significantly expanded earlier lists[1] of language learning strategies, resulting in comprehensive list of six broad strategy groups and 62 strategies:

1. *Metacognitive* strategies (e.g., paying attention, planning for language tasks, self-evaluating, self-monitoring, arranging the learning environment).
2. *Affective* strategies (e.g., anxiety reduction, self-encouragement, emotional self-awareness).
3. *Social* strategies (e.g., asking questions, cooperating with others, becoming culturally aware).
4. *Memory* strategies (e.g., grouping, imagery, sound, movement, structured reviewing).
5. *Cognitive* strategies for understanding and producing the new language (e.g., practicing naturalistically, reasoning deductively, contrastive analysis, summarizing).
6. *Compensation* strategies for overcoming knowledge limitations (e.g., guessing meanings intelligently, using synonyms or other production tricks to express oneself).

[1]Including lists by Stern (1983), O'Malley et al. (1985), and Ramirez (1986).

The first three strategy groups (metacognitive, affective, and social) concern general management of learning, and the last three (memory, cognitive, and compensation) directly involve the new language in various ways. Cultural and ethnic background, personality, sex, language learning purpose, and other factors affect the degree to which learners use any single strategy, but all six categories of strategies are important to successful language learning (see Oxford & Crookall, 1988a, 1988b, 1989a; Oxford & Ehrman, 1989; Oxford & Nyikos, 1989; Oxford, 1989b, 1990a, 1990b; Oxford et al., 1989).

How simulation/games encourage good strategies

Language teachers are increasingly turning to simulation/gaming for several reasons—and all of these reasons tie in with language learning strategies. One of the main reasons for the increasing popularity of simulation/gaming in language learning is that simulation/gaming embodies the communicative approach, the goal of which is to develop communicative competence. Simulation/gaming provides active involvement of the whole person (intellectual, physical, social, and emotional) and uses all four language skills (listening, reading, speaking, and writing). This involvement is enhanced because learners often view simulation/gaming as a "real" and meaningful communication situation in its own right, not just as an academic exercise. Active, communicative involvement is a central element in all language learning strategies, particularly strategies like practicing naturalistically. Involvement often means direct interaction with others, entailing a whole range of social learning strategies (e.g., asking questions for clarification/verification, asking for correction, cooperating with peers).

A second reason for the increasing popularity of simulation/gaming for language learning is that it changes the roles and relations of learners and teachers in a positive way, encouraging learners to take a more active role in their own learning process. This has two effects. First, it gives learners much more opportunity to communicate in the target language, because they do not always have to speak to and through the teacher, and second, it places more responsibility on learners to direct their own learning. Both of these aspects—creating and taking advantage of practice opportunities and becoming more responsible for one's own learning—are at the heart of language learning strategies, especially those which come under the heading of metacognitive strategies.

Third, simulation/gaming provides large quantities of input, which can be understood because of the meaningful and engaging context of the activity. This input is at the discourse level—i.e., above the level of single words or isolated sentences; it is connected, contextualized speech embodying all sorts of language functions. Krashen (1982) has demonstrated the importance of large amounts of such authentic input. One of the key language learning strategies is practicing naturalistically—that is, using the target language in realistic situations with large amounts of meaningful input. The input provided by simulation/games also stimulates use of other important strategies, such as memory strategies (used not just to enter new information into memory but also to recall it quickly when needed) and compensation strategies like guessing meanings from context.

Fourth, simulation/gaming allows attention to be given to language form as well as to content. The essence of the communicative approach, embodied in many simulation/games, is to invite learners to become their own judge of appropriateness (using language forms appropriate to the circumstances of use). In some situations, certain forms are clearly more appropriate than others, but in many cases there may be several equally appropriate forms from which the learner must choose. Practice with forms is an important language learning strategy which is fostered by simulation/gaming.

If, however, mistakes *are* made in either form or meaning, the consequences of error are low (see Chapter 1), the fifth advantage of simulation/gaming for language learning. This means that any communication gaffes made during the simulation/game, while real and meaningful during the activity itself, will not have any serious effects in the world outside; thus, the language learner can more freely take risks and make mistakes. Because of the freedom to practice the target language without a cramping fear of punishment or criticism, simulation/gaming has additional affective advantages, such as reduction of anxiety, increase in positive feelings, and improved self-confidence. Willingness to take risks, reducing anxiety, encouraging positive feelings, and gaining self-confidence are also goals of affective language learning strategies, and thus simulation/gaming helps learners practice such strategies in a natural, unforced way.

A sixth advantage of simulation/gaming is that participants are encouraged to communicate even when their knowledge and competence in the language is less than they would wish. Compensation strategies come into play when learners continue communicating even when they do not know the precise target language expression. As mentioned earlier, compensation strategies include guessing meanings of unknown words or phrases, and this is often required during simulation/games, as it is in the outside world. Compensation strategies also include using synonyms, gestures, and circumlocutions to get the meaning across in a conversation. Simulation/gaming, because of its tolerance for errors, helps learners develop self-confidence to take risks and to use compensation strategies; at the same time, the realistic time pressures of simulation/gaming encourage learners to use the target language rapidly, thus making compensation strategies a necessity rather than a luxury.

Seventh, some culturally realistic simulation/games help the learner to identify more closely with the target culture. An important group of social language learning strategies involves developing empathy with others (through gaining cultural awareness and becoming aware of the thoughts and feelings of others); so simulation/gaming again advances the cause of language learning strategies.

Eighth, simulation/games encourage adolescents and adults to once again play with symbols. Playing takes language learning away from the traditional academic world and into the realm of pleasure and enjoyment, the same realm in which people learn their native language as a child. While there are, of course, differences in the ways adults and children learn languages, simulation/gaming nevertheless brings back a touch of the old, long-forgotten magic of discovery. Pleasure, enjoyment, discovery—these are also aims of *all* language learning strategies.[2]

We have outlined eight reasons for the increasing popularity of simulation/games for language learning. These reasons also reflect ways in which simulation/games encourage the use of an amazingly wide array of helpful language learning strategies.

Some examples

To help you understand more concretely how simulation/gaming stimulates the use of good language learning strategies, we will provide three examples.

ICONS

This simulation involves the use of computers and telecommunications systems to exchange messages between teams situated in different places around the world. The simulation recreates a world of international relations, in which each team represents a country (e.g., Argentina or France) and messages are written in different languages (e.g., the team in Argentina transmits its messages in Spanish). For a more complete description, see Chapter 13.

Observing ICONS sessions close up, we saw pride and enthusiasm in the learners, as well as a wide assortment of language learning strategies. Social strategies are necessary because ICONS is a cooperative learning effort. Students who receive the incoming messages in foreign languages (without the benefit of an allied translation subteam) must use a whole set of cognitive and compensation strategies to aid in reading comprehension.

[2]For further discussion on this aspect, see Saunders and Crookall (1985).

Metacognitive strategies such as planning for a language task, paying attention, and self-monitoring are evident. ICONS is a powerful and exciting means of developing skills in foreign languages, negotiation, and decision making. It implicitly encourages self-direction and autonomy through the use of language learning strategies.

NO RECUERDO

This simulation (English name: "Don't Remember") is based on videodisk technology. Real-world data are used and combined with fictional elements. The learner communicates with protagonists in an attempt to revive lost memories. For more details, see Chapter 15.

This simulation, like other high-technology simulations of similar quality, encourages the use of many language learning strategies. In NO RECUERDO, participants are entertained and motivated by interaction with various characters and exploration of diverse locales. In addition, the nature of the material challenges learners to rely on themselves and especially to call upon their own cognitive strategies, such as reasoning deductively, transferring information from the native language to the target language, analyzing expressions, analyzing contrastively, recombining, and practicing naturalistically. Metacognitive strategies such as paying attention, self-monitoring, and self-evaluating are likely to be tapped by NO RECUERDO. Because of the requirement to "communicate" interactively with the two (artificially intelligent) protagonists via computer, certain compensation strategies, such as using a circumlocution or synonym and selecting the topic, are involved, and compensation strategies for guessing intelligently are often used for getting the meaning. Affective strategies might be used to cope with the fast-moving stimuli of the videodisk. If NO RECUERDO is used in small peer groups for cooperative learning, use of social strategies would be unavoidable. This simulation illustrates how computer-assisted instruction, especially when enhanced by interactive videodisk capabilities, can be an exciting, strategy-rich means of language learning.

SPEAKING FACES

The set of games that SPEAKING FACES comprises involves dealing in a variety of ways with packs of 96 cards, each card containing a photograph of a face.[3] Many kinds of faces are included: young, old, plain,

---

[3]Maria Matheidesz (1987) of Budapest has developed a set of games commercially published under the name "96," but more popularly known as SPEAKING FACES. For a review, see Oxford and Crookall (1989).

attractive, sad, happy, tired, animated. The photographs are professional quality, multiethnic, and very interesting, and when used in communicative language games, they seem to come alive. The learners' self-generated, creative descriptions of the people represented by these faces (their identities, ages, occupations, emotions, desires, family, social relationships, educational background, and so on) form the basis of many of the communicative games in the SPEAKING FACES set. Not all 96 cards are used for every activity; the number depends on the activity.

People's faces can be endlessly interesting, providing many clues about, and triggering reactions to, such human characteristics as emotion, occupation, age, education, experience, and relationships. When faces are used within the context of a game, they can stimulate a relatively high degree of free communication and imagination, thus encouraging the use of a wide range of strategies. For example, cognitive strategies such as practicing naturalistically and recombining are clearly evident, along with memory strategies such as grouping and associating/elaborating and compensation strategies such as guessing intelligently, topic selection, and using a circumlocution or synonym. The games also motivate the use of social strategies for cooperative learning, and they help learners relax and have fun (with affective strategies like using laughter). In addition, the imagery of the cards, as well as that sparked off in the participants' minds by the cards, helps develop the learning strategy of using imagery.

Implicit versus explicit strategy training

We have just presented three examples of simulation/games and have demonstrated how they *implicitly* encourage the use of a myriad of language learning strategies. All language learners, through the process of participating in simulation/games, will get practice with a range of language learning strategies. More alert and more motivated students will be able to take greater conscious advantage of these strategies than will less alert and less motivated students. The simulation/games described above, while implicitly fostering language learning strategies, do not provide explicit or overt training in the use of learning strategies.

In contrast to implicit encouragement of strategies, *explicit* strategy training attempts to make language learning strategies a conscious, integral part of the repertoire of all language learners. Therefore, we suggest that in addition to using simulation/gaming to provide implicit practice with good language learning strategies, teachers should also offer explicit strategy training to increase their learners' skills in strategy use.

By using simulation/gaming, not only for language learning per se but also to conduct explicit training in the effective use of strategies, teachers will be able to provide their students with tools enabling them to make language learning more effective in general, not only through simulation/ games, but also by other means. Thus, a combination of simulation/games and explicit strategy training can be seen as a particularly effective way of interdependently developing both language skills and strategies.

Explicit strategy training shows learners why and how to do the following: (1) use new learning strategies, (2) evaluate the effectiveness of different strategies, and (3) decide when it is appropriate to transfer a particular strategy to a new situation or task. In this way the strategies are explicitly pointed out, demonstrated, practiced, applied, and evaluated in different language tasks. Strategy training should be related to regular language activities.

There are three ways in which explicit strategy training can be provided through, or linked with, simulation/gaming. *Option 1* is to run a simulation/ game, then provide explicit strategy training, and rerun the simulation/ game so that learners can have a chance to practice the language learning strategies in a more informed, more overtly conscious way. *Options 2 and 3* both involve a strategy training game—that is, a game which is designed with the clear purpose of providing explicit strategy training—but these two options differ in terms of the specificity of the training. In Option 2, participants play a game which raises their overall awareness of language learning strategies in general and gives them an understanding of the vast range and power of strategies in different language learning situations. Examples of such games are THE EMBEDDED STRATEGIES GAME and THE STRATEGY SEARCH GAME, described briefly (as a teacher training exercise) in Chapter 6. In contrast to the general strategy awareness games in Option 2, Option 3 involves playing a game which provides an opportunity to develop, practice, and examine highly specific strategies, such as memory strategies. An example is MEMORY TRICKS. Option 3-type games can be run first in the native tongue and then rerun (perhaps with a variation) in the new language. Of course, combinations of the three options may be built into a language and strategy training program.

A number of steps can identified for conducting explicit strategy training using simulation/gaming.[4]

1. Identify the basic conditions (e.g., the needs of the learners, the amount of time available, the most useful kinds of learning strategies to train).
2. Choose the strategies for training (based on factors in Step 1 above).
3. Determine how to integrate strategy training and simulation/games (i.e., which types of training and games are to be employed; note options above).

[4]For further details on learning strategies, strategy training, and some strategy games, see Oxford (1990b) and Oxford et al. (1989). For more linkages between strategies and simulation/gaming, see Oxford and Crookall (1988b) and Oxford (1989a).

4. Consider motivational and attitudinal issues. If these are negative, perhaps use simulation/games to help make changes before embarking on strategy training.
5. Prepare the simulation/game materials.
6. Run the simulation/game.
7. Evaluate the outcomes.
8. Revise the simulation/game if necessary; return to Step 1 to recycle the process. Such a strategy training process can be carried out by any teacher who wants to help students take greater charge of their own language learning.

Conclusion

In this chapter we have described helpful language learning strategies, shown how such strategies are *implicitly* encouraged by simulation/gaming, and provided some concrete examples. We have also outlined how simulation/gaming can be used in various ways to provide more *explicit* strategy training. Simulation/gaming, even without overt strategy training, is a powerful tool for making language learners more active, self-directed, and proficient, but simulation/gaming linked with explicit strategy training can speed up that process for all language learners.

Chapter 9

Reading, writing, and literature

Integrating language skills

Robin Scarcella and Susan L. Stern
University of California, Irvine

The importance of integrating the "four language skills"—speaking, listening, reading, and writing—has long been recognized. Unfortunately, however, relatively few pedagogues have suggested ways to integrate these skills successfully in language instruction (for a notable exception, see, for instance, Swain, 1984). Even fewer pedagogues have suggested activities which both integrate the four skill areas and are consistent with second language research (see, however, Stern, 1985, 1987). To help bridge these gaps, this chapter describes some specific simulation activities which are consistent with recent research and can be used to integrate reading, writing, and literature. While the activities we suggest include speaking and listening tasks, we focus here on reading and writing.

In recent years, reading and writing research has resulted in breakthroughs which have, directly or indirectly, affected language teaching. For example, reading research has identified some of the characteristics of good readers; good readers are said to (1) understand what they are reading—by using *contextual* cues (Smith, 1986), (2) read *extensively* (Krashen, 1983), and (3) *enjoy* reading (Smith, 1982). In line with this, writing research has identified the characteristics of good writers: They (1) *read* extensively, (2) *actively* engage themselves in writing tasks, (3) write to *communicate* (Brice-Heath, 1983), and (4) *believe* that they are capable of communicating effectively (Smith, 1973).

Simulation activities for integrating reading and writing

Overall, the research suggests that activities which integrate reading and writing should involve meaningful, interesting texts, genuine communication, and active student involvement. In addition, such activities should foster self-confidence in using the target language. We suggest that the activities below do just this.

Letter writing

Littlejohn and Hicks (1986) suggest a variety of letter-writing activities which can be used to create genuine writing tasks for language students. For example: reacting to newspaper articles (in letters to editors; seeking advice in letters to columnists who answer personal letters and give personal advice); asking for information (in letters to travel agencies and apartment managers); complaining (in letters to hospitals, stores, telephone companies, or the Better Business Bureau); and inviting others to parties (in letters to friends and colleagues). In an exercise suggested by Swain (1984), students are asked to write notes. The directions are as follows:

> In this exercise, we are asking you to write a note to other young people your age. The style should therefore be informal.
>   Imagine the following situation: you have been in Louisbourg for several weeks now and you would like to visit Halifax next weekend. You decide to post a note in French in the cafeteria in order to find someone who can drive you to Halifax at that time. In your note, mention that you will share expenses for the trip and that you have a driver's license. Leave your telephone number to indicate where you can easily meet. Don't forget that you are writing to someone *your own age*. (Swain, 1984.)

Such situations can simulate real-life situations that are relevant and interesting to specific groups of students. As Littlejohn and Hicks point out, many teachers ask students to complete very artificial writing tasks. Simulation activities provide more genuine writing tasks. (For a detailed description of an excellent letter-writing simulation activity, see Littlejohn & Hicks, 1986.)

Resumés

Simulation activities need not be limited to letter writing. Swain (1984), for example, suggests a simulation activity in which students might write resumés. In this activity, students are asked to choose between two sources of summer employment, one in Sudbury and another in Louisbourg. A booklet is given to the students which contains information about each position—for example, the job qualifications being sought for each job, the nature of each job, remuneration, working and leisure time. Having chosen between Sudbury and Louisbourg, the students then write resumés in which they describe their qualifications. A panel of students then chooses the best applicants for the jobs.

Dialog journals

Dialog journals have become increasingly popular in ESL writing classes. In these dialogs, native speakers are paired with nonnative speakers, and all communicate their thoughts and feelings in journal form. (For a more detailed description, refer to Kreeft, 1984.) David Crookall (personal communication) suggests that, if journal writers are willing, the journals could be submitted to a panel of editors who have to decide which ones are to be published. They then exercise their editorial perogatives, type out the journal entries on a word processor, and then get these entries "published" by the school printers, and, who knows, even a real publisher might be interested. This simulation might possibly lead to the real thing—only in the form of a school or class-produced publication. Such a long-term simulation would involve the teacher as an editorial advisor.

Values clarification exercises

In values clarification exercises, students are asked to discuss life situations which "call for thought, opinion-making and action" (Simon et al., 1972). While these exercises are often used to develop speaking and listening skills, many of them can be used to develop reading and writing skills as well. For example, we have found that "the trip to another planet to form a new civilization" particularly lends itself to writing instruction. In this exercise, students pretend that they are going to form a new civilization and only have room in the spaceship to bring certain items. They must decide what items to bring. Students are given literature concerning possible life on other planets. We ask the students to form panels to draw up a report to submit to the government, the president, the CIA, and other entities. Their proposals are then read by these groups, who ultimately decide what items will be brought.

From simulation to the real world

It should also be mentioned that simulations may lead to real-life activities. For example, in the simulation tasks suggested by Swain (1984), students are given a list of government offices that offer, or organize, special programs for the summer employment of youth. This list encourages interested students to write for more information. Similarly, Crookall (1986b) suggests that students should be encouraged to submit short stories to the BBC. These may have begun, and have been developed, through simulation and drama activities.

Literature-based simulation activities for integrating reading and writing

Drama-inspired writing activities can also come out of the reading of plays, short stories, novels, and sometimes even poetry. They involve the student's stepping into the consciousness of a character and writing about that character's attitudes and feelings. Each of these activities can be coordinated with an oral presentation, either by preceding it and providing a basis for it or by following it, in which case a simulation role-play activity would be the inspiration for a writing assignment. These activities include dramatic monologs, dramatic dialogs, and character histories. (See Stern, 1985, 1990 for a more complete description of these activities.)

Dramatic monolog

In the dramatic monolog, the student selects one of the characters from the literary work and, taking into consideration that character's feelings, emotions, ideas, and style of speech, assumes the role of that character and writes about a particular situation, issue, or character depicted in the work. For example, the student might consider (1) how that character feels about an event or another character, (2) what the character's value judgments are in regard to an issue raised in the work, (3) why the character thinks something happened or somebody acted the way he or she did, and (4) what the character hopes is going to happen, or how he or she hopes the conflict will be resolved.

For Robert Browning's poem "My Last Duchess," for example, a student assuming the role of the duke could explain whether or not a husband or wife should express or demonstrate love for his or her spouse and, if so, how; or the student playing the duke could express his disapproval of the way in which the duchess had responded to the compliments and kind gestures of others and/or describe how he expects his new wife to act. For Shirley Jackson's short story "The Lottery," the students in turn could assume the role of one of the characters from the work and express an opinion about the lottery in general, as an institution, and about how they feel that it had been handled that year. Arthur Miller's play *Death of a*

Salesman offers numerous topics for monologs. To name just a few: Willy, the protagonist, could describe his feelings about the rude and callous way his employer had treated him, and in particular how he feels about being fired after all the years that he has worked for the company. His son Biff could explain exactly what he meant when he told Willy, "Pop, I'm a dime a dozen, and so are you," or when he said that his father had had all of the wrong dreams.

Dramatic dialog

The dramatic dialog is similar to the dramatic monolog, except that it takes the form of a conversation between two of the characters of the story, play, or poem. The instructor or the students select a particular situation or issue raised in the work, and the students write a dialog about it between two of the characters, taking into consideration once again the characters' feelings, emotions, ideas, and style of speech. For example, for Robert Frost's poem "Mending Walls," a dramatic dialog could be written between the speaker of the poem and his neighbor in which the former tries to convince the latter that the wall is not necessary and should be taken down. For *Death of a Salesman*, a dialog could be written between Willy and Biff in which Biff tries to persuade his father to forget about being a salesman at this point in his life, and to devote himself to doing what he likes best—working with his hands. Perhaps Willy could even start his own little business doing this. Another dialog could be written between Biff and his younger brother, Happy, in which Biff tries to discern if Willy's dream, which Happy had adopted for himself, is really the dream that *he* wants to fullfil or if he is only trying to make his father happy.

A variation of the dramatic dialog as described above would be for the dialog to be between one of the characters and the student. This would allow students to express their personal feelings with the character and sympathize, debate, offer advice, as the case may be. For example, for the short story "The Lottery," a dialog could be written between Old Man Warner and the student, in which the student tries to convince him why the lottery in the town should be abolished.

Character histories

Writing character histories, an activity suggested by Via (1976), may be considered a variation of the dramatic monolog. The students take the role of one of the characters and, applying their imagination to what is actually presented about that character in the work, write in first person about the past history of that character—where he or she had been and what he or she had been doing before entering the scene onstage. Via intended this activity to complement the study of plays, for very little background information is generally given about the characters in the stage directions. But it can just as successfully be used with short stories and novels.

Conclusion

The simulation activities we have suggested here call for additional empirical research which examines their usefulness in language instruction. However, these activities are consistent with existing second language research and serve to integrate various skill areas. As Swain points out, such integration is essential in communicative language teaching.

Chapter 10

Testing

The use of simulation/games as a language testing device

Andrew Littlejohn
University of Lancaster

Despite claims made by their designers, present-day "communicative tests" frequently require learners to carry out tasks that bear little relation to normal language use. The use of simulations as a testing device is therefore an important development since it should be possible to replicate the situations in which learners will have to use the language. Replication gives a more direct insight into how the learner actually performs in the target situation and allows us to view not only the language *product* but also the *process* by which that language emerged. A full example is given of how a simulation can be used to test writing skills and the ways in which the results can be assessed.

Communicative tests

Recent thought in language teaching theory and methodology has stressed the view that classroom procedures should mirror the nature of communication. Thus, we have seen the development of communicative, task-based activities which aim to provide opportunities for learners to engage in unrehearsed, purpose-oriented use of the foreign language. Concurrently, attempts to specify more clearly the situations in which the learner will need the target language have also enabled the design of materials and activities which aim to replicate the settings and tasks which the learner is likely to encounter.

This widening of the concerns of language education has suggested a parallel widening of the nature of language tests. According to Carroll (1982), we should thus "incorporate into our test settings as many features as can economically be employed of the settings we are testing for." Communicative tests will not, therefore, be characterized by "the all-too-well-known test formats . . . with their endless multiple choice items to send even the most active to sleep or into a semi-hynoptic trance." Rather, communicative tests will be "purposive, interactive, contextualized, authentic, human and in themselves worthwhile."

Most people would readily acknowledge that the design of a test that did indeed meet Carroll's description would be extremely useful in language testing. In reality, however, such a test is yet to be developed. In attempting to provide authenticity of task and language content, most communicative tests generally require the testees to carry out tasks such as filling in forms, writing letters, making lists, or ploting information on a chart—normally making use of some written, verbal, or graphic material. These task types are held to replicate the way in which the language is used in real life. Yet there are problems with this approach—as the extract from a test, designed following Carroll's guidelines, indicates (see Figure 10.1).

In order to complete the first task, the testees are asked to imagine that they are Aisha explaining to her teacher what happened. The testees learn nothing more about Aisha than her name and date of birth, and their writing has no direct bearing on any further situation with Aisha. One wonders, therefore, to what extent the task can be said to be "contextualized." The testees do know, however, that whatever they write will not actually be read to discover the message that it contains; rather, they know that the only reaction that they will get is the teacher's mark. (In fact, once they have written the explanation, they have to forget they are Aisha as they read about her in the next section.) The task does not, in other words, reflect any real-life communicative goal. It is indeed true that what the testees write "depends crucially on what is said or written" (Carroll, 1981) to them, but it is interesting to note that the first task actually involves *writing* what Aisha would *say*. This is the job of a playwright, not the way most of us use language in real life. Normally, the way we express ourselves is affected by the skill we are using, as the well-established distinction between spoken and written language demonstrates. In this task, however, the examinees are asked to write while imagining that they are someone else speaking—a rather strange request.

These points are not meant merely as a criticism of this particular test but are relevant to many of the task types used in communicative tests at present. The problem, it seems, stems from a basic fact about tests. This is that they are designed to sort out individuals. Cooperation between individuals is thus "cheating." This means that while communicative classroom activities may capitalize on students working together, communicative tests would seem to be prevented from doing so. The interpersonal element thus has to be provided through an imaginary character like Aisha,

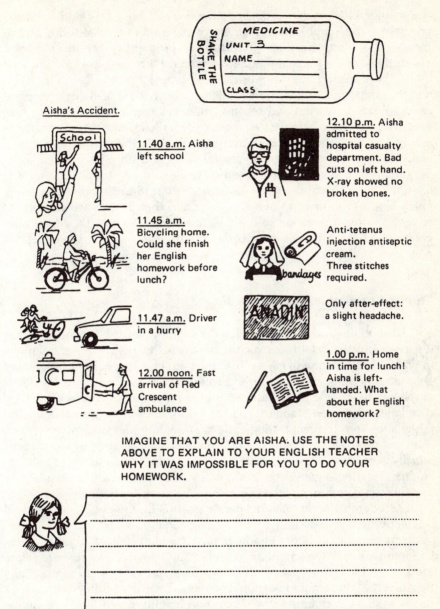

Figure 10.1   Aisha's accident.

whose very creation jeopardizes authenticity of both task and language processes. The role of the examiners then becomes one of trying to put themselves in the shoes of the imaginary recipient of the message and assess how far the testee's writing would have achieved its objective, had it been produced in the real world.

In an attempt to get around this problem, some of the more recent examinations in foreign and second languages require the testees to take part in a role-play or discussion, usually with the examiner but sometimes in a group, with the examiner observing. To date, the technique has generally been used in the testing of oral skills and on a very small scale. Candidates are not normally asked to work toward producing anything together, and the activity rarely lasts more than 15 to 20 minutes, usually much less. Yet the nature of simulations and their role in bringing about communicative interaction in the classroom suggests that they may hold great potential for the design of communicative tests, a point to which we now turn.

The use of simulations for testing

The potential value of simulations as a communicative language testing device lies in the extent to which it is possible to replicate the situations in which the student will need to use the target language. Replication may give us something close to a *direct* insight into the abilities of the student in relation to specific tasks, rather than the *indirect* assessments offered by correlations between standardized tests and student performance in the target situation. Indirect testing aims to show how the student *might* perform in a given situation; the use of simulations will show how the student *actually* performs. This distinction is particularly relevant in relation to language testing. Since successful performance in interactive simulations depends on communication taking place between individuals, the ability of the student to accomplish a specific goal using the new language will be clearly demonstrated.

Any simulation offers windows onto the participants' abilities in relation to two interdependent areas: *product* and *process*. *Product* here refers to the actual language produced by the participants. In some simulations this may be the communication between participants that the activity necessitates—for example, the discussion leading up to the decision of, say, whether or not to build a new road. In other simulations, the product may be some piece of work that the participants are required to produce together—for example, a 10-minute news broadcast or a set of business recommendations. *Process*, however, refers to how the participants approached the task. In terms of organization, this may include how efficiently they made use of their time, took account of changing information, and adapted to new situations as they arose. In terms of language, this may include how far the participants displayed self-correction and sensitivity to the factors that affect the appropriateness of utterances.

Evaluation of the product of a simulation presents no new problem. This is the skill and craft of the professional language teacher who may employ objective measures or subjective assessments, based on experience, to evaluate the language produced. In fact, insofar as the simulation will make readily apparent how far communication actually takes place between participants, the task of assessing language in relation to the accomplishment of a communicative purpose will be made so much the easier. The real challenge in using simulations as a testing device is of a different kind. This is to find ways in which the process of the simulation can be meaningfully evaluated and in which the contributions of the individual participants to both process and product can be separated from the group as a whole while preserving the interactive nature of the simulation.

Techniques for assessment

It would be extremely difficult—if not impossible—to devise objective measures of the sum value of a student's participation in a simulation. Taking account of both process and product means that the simulation must be seen as a whole, preventing itemized analysis and percentage marks. A basic technique used, therefore, has been to construct an educated description of the skills that the participants are likely to need in the simulation and then use this description as a guide to forming a subjective assessment of the student's abilities. To enable a reasoned assessment, two observers are present and the results are discussed and argued through after the simulation has been carried out.

Typically, an observer's guide sheet can be drawn up using three basic sections, with other sections being added for specific simulations. The three basic sections are language, content, and process. *Language* here covers the broad range of factors that are the teacher's traditional concern. Depending on the simulation, this may be accuracy in spelling, punctuation, pronunciation, grammar, and vocabulary, as well as appropriateness of register and politeness/informality. *Content*, however, involves factors that are not often seen as the direct concern of the language teacher. Here, the observer will pay attention to the accuracy of the information given by the participant and whether the participant actually attempts to perform certain acts with the language such that the simulation drives rather than drifts toward a conclusion. If, for example, the simulation involves two companies arranging a deal, then one would expect a motivated solution to involve the participants in key language acts, such as giving specific information, explaining, suggesting, persuading, and checking that interlocutors have understood. In the present argument presented here, both language and content are aspects of *product*. *Process*, as outlined earlier, relates to how the participants go about the task. Factors for consideration here may include speed of response, evidence of self-correction, grasp of key points in the course of the simulation, ability to discern which information is irrelevant, and use of reference texts supplied when the need is apparent.

The simulation itself must be designed so as to contain the potental for using, within a reasonable time limit, the abilities to be tested. This makes the technique particularly suitable for students of language for special purposes (LSP), where the target language situation can be more easily identified. This also means that, in practice, few published simulations can be used—intended as most are for general audiences—so it is normally necessary to tailor-make one. A tailor-made simulation does, however, have the advantage that the assessment guide-sheet can be drawn up with a deeper understanding of the demands that will be placed on the students.

Example of an assessment guide sheet

The guide sheet presented in Figure 10.2 was drawn up for use with AN EXPORT ORDER, specifically designed for intermediate students of commercial correspondence in English. The basic situation in the simulation concerns a company, Abdul Rahman Construction Establishment (ARC), which is attempting to buy window frames from one of two suppliers—Dolmovan Glassworks (DG) and Jombory Frames (JF). The participants can only communicate with each other in writing, through letters or telexes, in order to make a deal. During the course of the simulation, new information is introduced (such as a strike in a supplier's factory or a currency devaluation), causing the participants to reassess the information that they have, make new decisions, and quickly act upon them in writing. (For a complete description of the simulation and the rationale behind its development, see Littlejohn & Hicks, 1986.)

For the purposes of this simulation, a fourth section is added to the guide sheet, *Format*, relating to the layout and conventions of business correspondence. The observers make notes during and after the simulation on the guide sheet and, if it is appropriate to the purposes of the test (Figure 10.2), add a grade for each section and an overall impression grade. The notes form the basis of an observer's discussion of the simulation and lead to either a description of the participants' performance or a final letter grade, or both.

Participants, physically separated from each other, are divided into groups of three, each person in each group representing one of the three companies. The maximum number of students that may be tested at any one time is between 15 and 18, given the demands placed on the observers.

AN EXPORT ORDER: ASSESSMENT GUIDE SHEET   Group _____

Names: ARC _____ DG _____ JF _____

Enter your remarks in the space provided.

1 *Format of the letters:* layout, salutations, close, date, paragraph-   Grade
   ing, addresses
   ARC: ☐

   DG: ☐

   JF: ☐

2 *Language:* spelling, grammar, punctuation, vocabulary, formal
   business tone, abbreviations and short, clear telexes
   ARC: ☐

   DG: ☐

   JF: ☐

3 *Content:*
   ARC: number of frames required, dates for delivery, payment   ☐
   method, placing, cancelling and confirming orders.

   DG & JF: prices, discounts, dates, payment details, persuading,
   accepting order, apologizing, resume delivery.

   DG: ☐

   JF: ☐

4 *Process:*
   ARC: self-correction, dictionary use, speed, identifying cheap-   ☐
   est supplier, implication of delay, taking decisions

   DG: self-correction, dictionary use, speed, of response   ☐

   JF: self-correction, dictionary use, speed, of response   ☐

   _____

Overall impression grades   ARC _____ DG _____ JF _____

Average of section grades   ARC _____ DG _____ JF _____

Observer _____   Date _____

Figure 10.2   Assessment guide sheet.

This may seem uneconomical in comparison with the mass testing offered by a multiple-choice approach, but it is not unrealistic given the teacher-student ratios commonly found in LSP courses. To provide a deeper insight into *process*, participants are required to submit all draft work in addition to their final versions. The simulation runs for approximately two hours. Dictionaries are supplied.

Using the results

As discussed earlier, one of the principal benefits of using simulations as a testing device is that they demonstrate, in behavorial terms, the student's capacity to operate in something close to the target language setting. This therefore offers a flexibility not provided by conventional pen-and-paper tests, since the results of the simulation may be expressed either as a specification of what the student can and cannot do or as a letter grade, depending on the purposes of the test. If, for example, the test is being administered for diagnostic purposes, then a specification of abilities (rather than a grade) will aid in the design of a suitable course (see Figure 10.3). Similarly, as a progress test, the technique will reveal student achievement and enable ongoing modification of the course in the light of this. For the purposes of promotion to other courses within an institution, or to satisfy the demands of a sponsor of a course, the results may be translated into a letter grade. In this case, the testing institution should devise a banding system, similar to that proposed by Carroll (1980), specifying the level and abilities that each grade represents.

The example of AN EXPORT ORDER in Figure 10.2 illustrates how a simulation may be used to test writing as an interactive skill. Potentially, however, the technique may be adapted to test other skills. In terms of speaking skills, for example, simulations may be devised which replicate a decision-making meeting relevant to the target language situation of the participants (e.g., for civil engineers, a discussion over the siting of a building). Similarly, for students of a language for academic purposes, seminars, requiring reading, and/or listening to a lecture may be replicated. In each case, however, it will be necessary to devise a simulation which provides differentiated tasks for each participant and a means whereby the language product and—if possible—process may be examined after the simulation has ended. Clearly, video and audio recording may prove valuable here.

Conclusion

The argument put forward here has been that present communicative (and noncommunicative) tests do not require testees to demonstrate their

COMMERCIAL CORRESPONDENCE

Report on: *Daniel Carrillo*

At present, Mr. Carrillo's work displays little familiarity with the basic conventions of business correspondence and standard letter phrases. His grammatical
control is generally accurate with occasional slips which he should be able to
correct, were he to reread his work carefully.

His spelling is weak and he makes no attempt to use a dictionary. He is able
to identify the essential information in most routine commercial correspondence
and construct a meaningful reply.

Recommendations for training
    —letter layout and conventions
    —standardized business phrases
    —extensive practice in proof-reading his own work
    —dictionary skills

Figure 10.3   An example of a participant description.

abilities in relation to the demands of the target language situation. By
providing a setting for the kind of purposive, interactive tasks that typify
normal language use, simulations may prove a valuable development in
testing approaches. Perhaps then we may begin to feel confident that our
tests present a valid and honest assessment of the abilities of the language
learner. For further examples, the reader is referred to Littlejohn (1988).

Chapter 11

Science and technology

Specific purpose language training

Tom Hutchinson
University of Lancaster

Christopher Sawyer-Lauçanno
Massachusetts Institute of Technology

Simulation is not a technique that springs readily to mind when considering the teaching of technical English. Most of the emphasis in English for science and technology (EST) has been on handling the language of written texts. This is, however, very largely the result of historical factors in the development of English for special purposes (ESP), and it does not truly reflect the language needs of the scientific and technological world at large. In this chapter we will first explore why simulations are currently little used in EST and then consider ways in which they can be effectively employed.

Simulation and EST pedagogy

There are at least four reasons why simulation is not a common technique in EST. First, many EST programs have been designed in response to a *need to read* texts that are available only in English. Translation cannot keep pace with the vast amount of literature that the world of science and technology produces, with the result that large numbers of students and professionals around the world need to be able to read English in order to study their specialist subject or to keep up with developments in their field. Some of the most influential ideas in EST have sprung from projects set up to deal with this need—for example Trimble, Selinker, and Lackstrom's work in the United States, Ewer's work in Chile (see, e.g., Swales, 1985), the UMESP project in Malaysia (see ELT Documents 107). The emphasis has been on developing reading skills, and this has tended to give the impression that technical English is mainly concerned with written texts. As a result, social interaction techniques such as simulation have played little part in EST orthodoxy.

Second, one of the abiding problems in EST is the specific nature of the *content knowledge* involved. Teachers frequently feel inadequate to handle the content knowledge effectively. The tendency, therefore, is to avoid creative or interactive situations, where the demands on content knowledge are higher. Written text dealt with in a traditional text analysis way are a safer option for the insecure EST teacher than the creative unpredictability of the simulation. The lack of interactive techniques in EST may also reflect the typical prejudices of the humanities-trained language teacher toward the sciences, which are seen as uncreative, unimaginative, and almost unsociable activities. Simulation thus seems to have little place in these subject areas.

Third, shortage of *time* is a feature of EST courses. Simulations are often time-consuming both to design and to run, and may be avoided for this reason, too. Fourth, EST learners are overwhelmingly adults who have already completed a standard education. A creative methodology which shows no readily *measurable returns* may conflict strongly with the view of teaching and learning which the learners have acquired in their previous educational experience. Simulation can arouse initial adverse reactions among students, and teachers may not consider the technique that could be used to avoid this.

Thus, there are a number of reasons why simulation has generally played little part in orthodox EST. However, if we examine these reasons more closely, they can be seen to have little substance.

First, we can tackle the problem on the basis of the nature of technical communication. It is a false assumption to think of technical English as operating predominantly through the written medium. This is a distortion that has arisen because of the particular needs of the situation where influential work on EST has been carried out. In reality, technical communication is neither more nor less oral than any other area of communication. This emphasis on the written medium can cause considerable problems for language learners. Students who have learned their English through written texts often experience great difficulty in English-medium situations, where they need to talk about technical matters in a range of different registers from formal presentation to informal chats with peers in, for example, project work. This is also a problem for many people in the world of business, such as engineers at conferences who can read or even present conference papers but cannot participate in the informal discussions that go on outside the lecture hall. In brief, technical communication is as socially interactive as any other kind of communication and should, therefore, be amenable to the same methodological techniques as are found in other forms of language teaching. Simulations are widely used in science and technology, so why not EST?

We might also counter the apparent assumption in EST that the choice of methodology must parallel the procedures of the target situation. Even if in the target situation the learners will not need to *use* the language in a social setting, they might still *learn* the language more effectively through the use of a socially interactive methodology. Techniques such as simulation provide a greater *variety* of classroom activity, a more meaningful context, and a greater level of learner *involvement*, thus contributing to the effectiveness of the learning process. It is important to keep the perceived needs of the learners in mind, of course. They may react against activities that they see as irrelevant to their target needs. But simulation is a very flexible medium. The content of the simulation can be varied to match the needs of the learners, by adjusting the amount of reading, listening, writing, or speaking involved. Simulation can require a great deal of reading and writing. Herbolich (1985), for example, describes a simulation in which the learners had to design and build a box kite, explaining the research and design in the form of a project.

Thus, from both a linguistic and a pedagogic point of view, there is no justification for the lack of attention that has generally been accorded to simulation in EST. Simulation can provide an effective learning context for EST as readily as for any other form of language teaching.

EST simulation types

In designing simulations for use in technical language learning, a variety of factors must be considered. First, the simulation must mirror the relevant system to an extent that is commensurate both with the study objective and with "playability." Second, the simulation must be designed so that interactive communication is a natural component without detracting from the technical or scientific component. Third, the informational content must not be so overwhelming as to intimidate the participants (and the teacher), or so simple as to bore them. Fourth, the simulation must respect the learners' perceptions of their language needs. (A full discussion on simulation design is found in Chapter 5.)

Translating these general criteria into LSP terms, we can say that an ideal language-based simulation must allow the participants the opportunity to manipulate a specific range of vocabulary in a specific context for a specific set of purposes. Despite the emphasis on specificity, it should not be thought that each simulation requires a separate design. In fact, many simulations used for technical language training purposes can be of the "frame-game" type; i.e., the structure or procedures are the same from one time to the next, but the subject matter and level of expertise vary with the specific aim and linguistic abilities of the participants. Examples of common LSP frame games include the following:

1.   *Structured role-plays*, in which students manipulate specific vocabulary and grammatical structures in a variety of contexts.
2.   *Free-form role-plays*, in which students solve a specific problem and in the process manipulate acquired and new vocabulary and grammatical structures.
3.   *Realia-aided role-plays* (structured or free form), in which students use realia to lend greater realism to the role-play.
4.   *Model building*, in which students physically construct an object from a model kit while manipulating the specific vocabulary and grammar required by the task at hand.
5.   *Computerized simulation*, in which students use a microcomputer as an adjunct data bank for gathering and/or processing information, or in some cases, completely interactively: as another player.

Although we have classified them separately, it should be stressed that these various types of frame games can often be profitably used in conjunction with one another: Role-plays can be combined with computer-aided simulations, model building with role-plays, etc. It should also be noted that realia-aided role-plays and model building often overlap in their actual execution; the differences lie in the intent of the simulation. With a model-building simulation the aim is to teach language within the context of assembly or construction; a realia-aided role-play, on the other hand, may include assembly, but the focus is generally on interactive communication in which the object(s) represented by the prop(s) serve only to aid that communication by providing an element of concreteness or realism.

The reasons for using realia are directly related to technical communication itself: Technical language is very often linked to performing an operation, describing a process, or conveying information about a particular object. LSP in industrial settings, in particular, can usefully include the physical objects that form the basis of the communication. The language of mechanical assembly, for instance, is far more easily and effectively generated when the simulation uses the objects, or models of the objects, actually being assembled (see Hutchinson, 1978). Even very basic technical operations, such as "pushing," "pulling," "turning," "opening," "closing," "lifting," and "removing," are more readily understood when they are performed physically rather than when they are simply described (or even worse, left as abstract grammatical forms).

In more formal terms we can see that the use of realia creates less of a gap between the simulation and the object system being simulated because it removes the element of abstraction that can frequently accompany technical discourse. It should be noted, though, that realia should not be construed as a component separate from the simulation, but rather as an integral part of it. Many simulations, in fact, are built on realia or physical objects that represent some "real-world" reality.

Simulation examples

In order to understand more fully the relationship involving frame games, realia, and technical language learning, a couple of examples will be useful.

> *Example 1:* A group of technicians with rudimentary language skills are to be sent overseas to receive specialized instruction in installing the company's new product line.
>
> Object System: Installation/assembly vocabulary and grammar
>
> Appropriate Simulations: Structured role-plays (with and without realia); model building

This example shows how specialized content knowledge can be inserted into a couple of different frames. Into the structured role-play frame, for instance, we might load a vocabulary and grammar consisting of a number of imperative verb forms, a few adjectives (colors, shapes, and sizes), and a fairly large number of nouns. Typical sentence structures would consist of utterances such as "twist the nut," "turn the screw," "pull out the black knob," "push in the small, round knob." The use of the actual objects would obviously greatly facilitate learning. The actual simulation would consist of one student telling another student to perform a specific task using the new vocabulary and grammar. The student would then act out or (if realia is used physically) perform the task.

The simulation could also provide the basis for a writing assignment. Here, groups of students would write simple assembly instructions for another group; after correction, this group would then be required to build the model according to the instructions. Although this could be turned into an extremely sophisticated assignment, it does not have to be. Simply by limiting the number of pieces and/or steps required to assemble the model, the instructor can ensure that the language level needed to perform the simulation does not exceed the capabilities of the students.

> *Example 2:* A group of technicians with intermediate to higher-intermediate language skills are to be sent overseas to act as technical support personnel. In the host country they will be required to interact with a variety of individuals, both in their own subsidiary company and in client companies.

Object System: Technical instruction/technical trouble-shooting/prob-
lem solving/general communication

Appropriate Simulations: Some structured role-plays; a number of free-
form role-plays; realia-aided role-plays, often in conjunction with model
building; possibly computerized simulations

Given the broader learning objectives and the increased linguistic abilities of this group of students, a great deal more flexibility exists within
the syllabus. At the same time, only a limited number of frames need be
used; the content and learning goals, however, can easily be changed in
order to tailor the simulation to the specific needs and abilities of the
students.

The simulations appropriate for this group encompass all of the basic
types characterized earlier, but the skills that need to be acquired cannot
be limited to technical language. To be sure, this is an important aspect of
the target training, but as technical support personnel these technicians
will also be expected to communicate effectively in a variety of situations.
As a result, the simulations must have as their aim social communication
about both technical and nontechnical matters.

How, then, will the simulations be constructed? Structured role-plays
can be used to reinforce grammatical structures and vocabulary as well as
allowing the students to practice new patterns. Although it is difficult to
pin down specific topics, the role-plays could include situations such as
these: asking for and receiving information (both technical and nontechnical), mechanism and process descriptions, scheduling appointments and
events, reporting difficulties, and a variety of topical conversations. Realia
could, of course, be easily integrated into the mechanism and process
descriptions, but none of the other situations require any additional materials or groups.

Free-form role-plays would be used to promote socially interactive
communication through both technical and nontechnical problem solving.
Here, depending on the group, a variety of subjects could be used, ranging
from management/personnel problems to discussing and recommending
solutions to technical problems. Some of these role-plays could also be
profitably enriched with the use of a computer programmed with a variety
of technical and statistical data related to the simulation. In these cases,
the computer would serve as a tool for verification of the best approach to
solving a technical problem. Although the use of a computer for calculation
does not advance LSP per se, the resulting discussion between participants
can often greatly enhance the simulation's possibilities. (For discussion of
computerized simulations, see Chapters 14–16.)

Realia-aided role-plays would take the form of "hands-on" exercises.
The technicians would use actual products, physical models, or computer-
designed models, within simulations structured so that the students are

able to practice the full range of language skills required to train others in the installation, repair, and replacement of the company's product. The simulations could include active listening/response exercises as well as the more general one-way communication tasks of giving precise instructions, describing objects, and demonstrating specific methods and/or solutions.

It is obvious that all of these simulation types can quite easily be adapted to specific language and technical goals. And, at a fairly advanced level, it is also useful pedagogically to employ greater variety in the simulations, including a combination of frame games, or a series of simulations increasing either in language skill or in content, or both.

A model-building simulation, for instance, can be used as an active listening, speaking, and writing exercise, even though its primary aim might be to increase familiarity with the language of mechanical assembly. As mentioned earlier, all of these simulations could employ a computer either as a calculating tool or as an integral part of the model-building and designing process. In some cases, and with some educational software, it can be used in a completely interactive manner, sending, receiving, and processing both technical and linguistic messages.

In combining frame games, the goal should be to add another dimension to the simulation. Caution is advised, however, because both horizontal and vertical loading takes place when two or more frame games are fitted together. The use of a computer, for example, adds an extra, and often very sophisticated, task to the burden of language learning. At the same time, too much emphasis on manipulating the technical or technological realia can sometimes detract from the language acquisition goal. The best rule is to introduce the extralinguistic elements in such a fashion that they are linked to the specific language task.

Conclusion

Traditionally, simulations have been little used in EST, largely because of the emphasis on reading skills. We have argued that such a state of affairs is not justifiable from either a linguistic or a pedagogic viewpoint. Simulations should be seen as a valid and effective technique in EST, and we have shown some ways in which this can be achieved.

Chapter 12

Business and industry

Specific purpose language training

Michael Brammer
Manufacture Michelin

Christopher Sawyer-Lauçanno
Massachusetts Institute of Technology

In this chapter we discuss the use and suitability of activities based on simulation in business and industrial language training programs. We describe the realities of language training in industry and then deal with the aspects of teacher approach, linguistic constraints, native and nonnative speaker differences, and the meeting of trainees' needs.

Different types of simulation are then discussed, and particular attention is paid to the use of case studies as simulations. Throughout the chapter we emphasize practical rather than theoretical problems and underline the need for a blend of relevant subject matter and linguistic tasks accessible to the language learner if the simulation is to be successful.

Industrial setting

In order to appreciate the ways in which simulation-based language learning activities may be used in the context of business and industrial language training, it is necessary to describe briefly the organization and objectives of such training programs.

Over the past two decades several accounts of language training organization in industry have been published. Jupp and Hodlin (1975) give a thorough description of industrial language training methodology with immigrant workers in England. Freudenstein et al. (1981) analyze language training problems in German industry. More recently, Lavery (1985) and Kerridge (1985) describe their programs at 3M Germany and ESSO France, respectively. All emphasize the specific context of industrial language training and how objectives are always set in collaboration with technical training managers and personnel department staff.

The organization of language training programs will depend on a number of factors, such as the professional objectives as specified by management, the linguistic needs of the trainees, the length of the program, the trainees' aptitude for language learning, the language to be studied, and the level of attainment to be achieved. After an initial needs analysis and thorough testing of the trainee's proficiency in the target language, a training program is worked out taking the above points into account.

The fundamental difference between pre- and postexperience language training cannot be overemphasized. Postexperience trainees are learning for immediate and tangible professional reasons and often have a job to do at the same time. Although age, status within the company, previous training, and future objectives will differ greatly, the major goal remains that of developing practical competency in the target language. The materials and methods must be chosen, therefore, in order to enable the trainees to master specific communication skills in a limited amount of time. Simulations often function ideally in this regard because they involve the trainees in using and manipulating the language in a "real-world" frame. This increases familiarity not only with the target language but also with a range of business and cultural practices.

Use of simulation

Literally hundreds of business games are currently available (see Horn & Cleaves, 1980, for an extensive compilation and categorization), but they are generally of two main types. The older and most widely used are the *functionally integrated games* in which an entire company within a specific industry is simulated. In contrast, *functional games* focus on a particular business practice. While the effectiveness in imparting business concepts of functionally integrated versus functional games has yet to be determined, both types appear to be useful and applicable to LSP learning.

Of the functionally integrated games, the older UCLA GAME (in various models), the HARVARD BUSINESS SCHOOL GAME, and the CARNEGIE TECH MANAGEMENT GAME have all been used quite effectively with both native and nonnative speakers. Of the newer games, the BUSINESS MANAGEMENT LABORATORY, although quite complex, and the games of intermediate complexity, such as the EXECUTIVE GAME and MANAGER, are quite suitable for LSP gamers. Of the functional games, MARKETING STRATEGY, for marketing, FINGAME, for finance, and the MULTINATIONAL MANAGEMENT GAME, for international business, are all appropriate for use in a variety of business language training programs. For an excellent evaluation of these games and many others, see Wolfe (1985).

Native/nonnative speaker differences

The ultimate aim for native speakers of any business simulation is to provide students with the opportunity to encounter, identify, understand, and solve actual business problems. With nonnative speakers there is an *additional* objective of increasing competency in the target language and culture. Simulations designed for native speakers can clearly be used profitably with nonnative speakers; however, it may be necessary to provide additional supports for the simulation, particularly for students at less than an intermediate level of linguistic expertise. An example will best illustrate what we mean.

A very common type of functionally integrated management game used in educational, operational, and/or research environments involves some type of decision making in which gain must be measured against risk. One typical management game, for instance, involves the participants in developing and evaluating a variety of marketing strategies for increasing sales of an existing product. At the outset, all the participants are given a corporate profile consisting of a brief description of the company—its capital, resources, size, manufacturing lines, existing market share, department or division structure, and a financial statement. Next, the participants are assigned roles, with the organizer taking the role of CEO and the participants the roles of department executives in the finance, marketing, and personnel departments. Each group is then given additional information specifically pertinent to its role. The finance group, for example, receives detailed financial summaries, balance sheets, sales and earnings projections, and past growth summaries; the marketing group, information on the product, competition, list of trade shows, target media with advertising insert statistics; the personnel group, employee salaries and guidelines, employee expertise, organizational charts, hiring projections. The participants will then separately consider this information using the data in addition to their real-world knowledge to initiate a preliminary strategy. The finance groups will be responsible for making an initial allocation of resources, the marketing group for preparing a detailed budget based on their new marketing formulations, and the personnel group for allocating human resources including projected hiring. The groups then hold a meeting to work out their differences.

During the group meeting, the participants forming each group will present their ideas and argue their positions. The organizer may arbitrate disputes, but generally that role is one of an observer. Once a consensus is reached, each group will return to its individual meeting area to finalize the strategy. The final task is to present a combined approach to the CEO, who represents the board of directors. At this point, the CEO/organizer may accept, ask for modifications, or reject the plan. Modifications, if not extensive, can usually be worked out on the spot. If the objections of the CEO are substantial, however, or if the plan is rejected outright, the game recycles until a new strategy is developed and presented. If the simulation makes use of computers, the participants would employ them as accessories: to verify quantifiable data and to perform sophisticated calculations.

With native speakers, the entire focus, on the part of both the instructor and the students, is on making the best decision and on the process involved in making that decision. With language learners, solving the problem is only *one* of the goals, for the entire simulation process represents an important learning experience. Reading and listening comprehension are acutely involved in simply understanding all aspects of the simulation and the assigned role. The discussion of the problem and its possible solutions provides an excellent opportunity for developing a whole range of language and cultural skills, mainly speaking and listening, and to a lesser extent, reading. Many instructors also encourage their students to write up the results or explain their decisions.

If this game were to be utilized with intermediate to advanced language learners, it might be necessary to provide additional pre- or postsimulation exercises in dealing with grammar and vocabulary, and the organizer would no doubt have to take on an additional role during the game as a language advisor. It is important to note, though, that the simulation itself remains basically unchanged. Additional time may need to be allocated, of course, for actual language instruction, and the organizer may need to create supplementary materials and/or do additional preparation, but the game does not require either simplification or modification.

Pedagogical approach

In all types of simulation activities the approach is learner-centered. The instructor will provide the source material, advise on its exploitation, and explain the rules of the game, but the work done in the classroom will essentially be left to the trainees' initiative.

During the course of the simulation with language trainees the instructor will often need to suggest, encourage, and correct. Some participants may well get their message across and thus may be said to have "communicated," but the verb tenses may be wrong and the pronunciation sloppy or even incomprehensible to the native speaker having absolutely no knowledge of the trainee's mother tongue.

The instructor has three ways of tackling the problem of language error correction: ongoing correction, note taking and postactivity evaluation, and preactivity language exercises. All three should be used to obtain the most satisfactory results, although each has its drawbacks. Correction during the simulation can easily disrupt the activity. Postactivity evaluation sometimes gives the trainee the impression that we are more interested in the "look where you went wrong" aspects, unless it is counterbalanced by highlighting what the trainee did in fact manage to do correctly. Preventive language exercises are potentially unlimited, and the instructor has the responsibility for selecting the most important points given the nature of the activity and the language level of the participants. As stressed by Brammer and Macmillan (1982), such exercises are nevertheless a very important aspect of simulation exercises with language students.

Matching the simulation to the needs of trainees

In order for a simulation to be effective it must accurately represent its targeted object system (the real world). In turn, the object system being modeled must interest and be accessible to the students. Too often simulations fail because the interests of the participants are not accurately met by the simulation. In assessing student participation in relation to the simulation, a designer/instructor must keep in mind two basic factors. First, the simulation must be linguistically appropriate—i.e., not demand linguistic competency beyond the actual level of the students' abilities—and second, the simulation must represent a desired real-world goal for the trainees.

In discussing the use by language learners of simulations designed for native speakers, we noted that many of these simulations can indeed be profitably adapted for use in the language classroom. It is evident, however, that the management game described earlier demands a linguistic competency far beyond that of low-level students. Even if the students were capable of doing the analyses and even solving the problem because of their sophisticated knowledge of business practices, the simulation would do little to improve their language abilities. On the other hand, games such as the PRISONERS' DILEMMA, also a common management game, can be used very successfully with even low-level language students.

Appropriateness must always be a function of both linguistic and professional knowledge. Although a low-level language class may require simulations that are more structured than those for an advanced class, in LSP learning this simply means that the activity must be more closely tailored to the actual needs of the students.

An example of "tailoring" is one in which language learners are given simulations that mirror as closely as possible situations they are expected to encounter. A group of businesspeople, for instance, who are being prepared to go abroad and conduct routine business in a new language can profit from the use of simulations in which the focus is on practical survival skills. Examples include "arrival in the foreign country," "ordering food," and "introductions." For more linguistically accomplished trainees, simulations could revolve around meeting foreign executives, presentations, negotiating, and generally conducting conversations specifically related to the main focus of the firm's business. The buyer-seller negotiation is a very common example. The more familiar a situation is in the mother tongue, the more confident one feels about handling that situation in the target language, on both a professional and a linguistic level.

Types of simulations

Simulations in business and industrial language training programs generally attempt to reflect the actual world of business, usually with specific emphasis on a particular management topic. In-house programs are usually centered around the firm's main international business. Despite the specific emphasis of the simulation, the types do not always differ greatly from those used in other language learning situations.

Probably the most common type or component of simulation involves some sort of role-playing. With fairly low-level classes (250 to 300 hours of previous instruction for the average adult beginner), the role-play tends to be somewhat structured, with an emphasis on practice of certain learned patterns. This does not mean that the model should be the printed page. In fact, students should be encouraged to go beyond the textbook patterns and structures, so long as mistakes which hinder communication do not become the major feature of the exploration. Typical situations include assigning one student the role of a businessperson from Company X who needs to find out some specific information from someone at Company Y, and possibly to accomplish some task (e.g., make a business agreement or appointment).

Case studies as simulations

Case studies, still widely utilized in business education, are not, in and of themselves, simulations. Indeed, many gaming proponents have seen cases in opposition to games (see, e.g., Wolfe & Guth, 1975). For at least two decades, however, others have attempted to show how cases can become simulations (see, e.g., Cohen & Rhenman, 1984; Sawyer-Lauçanno, 1984, 1986). The key factor in transforming a case from a static assignment into a dynamic simulation depends entirely on the trainer's method. If the trainer organizes the case study activity as a participatory role-playing exercise, the result is an active and highly effective simulation, usually at a fraction of the cost of purchasing a management game.

As a simulation, a case study works like this: A situation that a company has actually encountered is presented through a series of documents. Most case studies begin with a background of the company(ies) involved and information regarding the particular problem awaiting solution. Accompanying the background is a series of exhibits containing financial and statistical information, memos, letters, and reports. Occasionally, case studies also include a dialog between key personnel in order to convey qualitative aspects of the problem. Through analysis and discussion of the situation, now sometimes done with the help of a microcomputer, students can arrive at a solution to the dilemma.

As a language learning device, the case study method has a number of advantages. First, it fosters active communication since students must work together, discussing, arguing, and analyzing the problem, in order to arrive at a solution. Second, because students are continually required to present ideas and defend positions, the case method promotes thinking in the target language. Third, the written case materials, because they contain actual business documents, serve as tools for building and reinforcing vocabulary and sentence structure. Finally, the case study method reorients the classroom so that the primary responsibility is placed on the trainee. This most often results in a dynamic, self-motivating learning situation.

An example

Many case study and role-play activities for language learning are available on the market, and most international companies with language training facilities have developed their own subject-specific simulations. In the manufacturing industries, a common scenario revolves around the launching of a new product.

The research and development department of an imaginary company has, at great expense, come up with a revolutionary new product X. The problem is how, when, and where to market the product. Participants form groups representing R and D, production, sales and marketing, personnel, the consumers, etc., and work with statistical and technical data to solve problems such as deadlines, competition, production line obstacles, and possible staff redundancies due to increased automation.

The imaginary company and product may bear an astonishing resemblance to a real company and product well known to the participants. In this case we may expect a greater personal interest and involvement. Technical vocabulary will correspond directly to the professional and linguistic needs of the trainees. On the other hand, simulations having no *specific* connection with a real company's activities have proved to be of equal interest. There are probably two reasons for this. First, involvement in such simulation activities requires a good command of the language in question, and, at this level of linguistic competency, technical terms specific to the participants' professional activity tend not to be a problem. Second, language learning in industry should be made as enjoyable as possible for the trainee in order to achieve the best results. Many trainees welcome a change of subject matter, so long as the general context is related to their professional activity.

Conclusion

In this chapter we have tried to give a clear, honest account of how simulations are used in business and industrial language training departments. We have emphasized the specific context, objectives, and constraints, the native and nonnative speaker differences, and the need for all simulation activities to be of professional interest to the participants, although we do not necessarily have to take this to extremes by simulating the offices and workshops in which they work. Finally, given the linguistic problems of language trainees, we have pointed out that loosely structured simulations can be used only with high-level language learners, and that in many cases simulations not explicitly designed for language learning can be adapted and used as language learning activities.

Chapter 13

International relations
Specific purpose language training

David Crookall
University of Alabama

This chapter provides a glimpse of the use of international relations simulation/gaming for the purposes of language learning and looks in a little detail at two types of simulation/games, one of which provides for the full integration of international studies and language instruction via computer networking.

Language, international relations, simulation/gaming

Language is the primary means whereby international communication takes place. Much of that language is not the mother tongue of the people concerned. Most diplomats, officials, company representatives, conference delegates, students, tourists, and even spies find at some time or another in their travels that they have to use a language which they did not learn as a child. This puts such communication at the peril of misunderstandings, since people tend, especially in times of tension, to interpret ambiguous phrasing in a negative way. Many contracts have been lost as a result of these linguistic hiccups, and even wars have started because of crosslanguage mistranslation. Much is at stake in international relations—for example, pride, identity, prosperity, even lives. Some disputes arise out of pure subscription to dogma, as illustrated by Jonathan Swift's tale about the dispute between the big-endians and little-endians. The role of language in reinforcing and crystallizing such disputes is widely documented.

But this also puts a great responsibility on those whose task it is to provide language training for people at the key interfaces in international relations, whether these be the decision makers themselves or their interpreters. It is difficult in any specialist area to provide language instruction unaccompanied by training in the closely related skills of decision making, negotiation, and problem solving, not to mention any understanding of the underlying issues. Learning to communicate in another language with others goes hand in hand with learning to negotiate, cooperate, and understand.

International relations cover a very wide spectrum of areas and activities (as reflected in the above list of travelers), and it is perhaps in these areas that simulation/gaming finds one of its most welcome homes. That is, simulation/gaming has proved invaluable as a training tool both in the various aspects of international relations and in the communication skills needed for those aspects.[1]

It is not possible here to cover all aspects, so I shall confine myself to what might be termed high-level or summit-level international political and institutional encounters. Examples are meetings held by such organizations as the European Council of Ministers, the United Nations, and the Commonwealth, or high-level dealings involving heads of state or ministers. Many simulation/games have been designed which encapsulate the essence of such meetings and dealings, but most of them assume all players are equally competent in one common language. However, this does not preclude their use as a language training medium; on the contrary, as other chapters in this book show, simulation/gaming (in whatever field) can be used to great advantage in language learning.

Many simulation/games involving various aspects of, and situations in, international relations have been designed. They may be relatively simple in structure (but often complex in development and outcomes) or involve a whole array of interconnections among issues, stakes, power relations, resources, ideologies, and interpersonal skills. Many of these can be used to good effect in the language classroom. It is wise to use a simple simulation first, so that students also learn about what it is like to participate in such simulations, before moving on to the more complex ones. International relations simulations can last from an hour to a month or more. Some of them are general, dealing with wider issues such as power relations; some of them are more specific and/or technical.

Let us now look at two examples of language learning through international relations simulation/gaming. In the first, a monolingual group of French students use English as a foreign language; in the second, several groups of students situated in different parts of the world use several languages.

[1]The father of international political gaming is considered to be Harold Guetzkow. He was the author of the famous INTER-NATION SIMULATION (one of the first human-machine simulations concerned with international relations). For further discussion see, e.g., Guetzkow et al. (1963), Clarke (1978), Ward (1985), and Hughes (1988).

A glimpse of the action

The photographs in Chapter 1 were taken during a simulation (using English as a foreign language in France) based on a real-world problem which arose some years ago about sugar surpluses resulting from the Common Agricultural Policy (CAP) of the European Community. Teams represented the various European countries, and the meetings represented those of the Council of Ministers, with additional input from the European Commission, the African, Caribbean, and Pacific (ACP) sugar producers, and European sugar manufacturers. The general issues were complicated by technical considerations, such as monetary compensatory amounts (MCAs) and other European regulations (e.g., on such technical things as "grubbing up"). The simulation/game documents consisted of some 50 pages of background information, specific country profiles, and technical texts. These were handed out to students some three weeks before the session. During that period, they spent considerable amounts of time both in and out of class reading the documents and doing their own research. The simulation/game itself took a full day, 10 hours in all, and it would have continued the next day had it not been Sunday and the university closed. Smart clothing was encouraged in order to help in the initial creation of a working atmosphere—one African student (representing the ACP countries) actually turned up wearing his traditional costume.

Interactions and negotiations were essentially of two types, illustrated in the photographs. As in the real Council of Ministers' encounters, much was decided during informal corridor meetings, and most of the time during the simulation consisted of teams engaging in informal negotiations. From time to time, a plenary formal meeting of the Council was held, where formal agreements were made.

Throughout the whole day, the students spoke most of the time in their target language, English. This kind of activity can be exhausting (for both participant and organizer), and toward the end of the day, a number of students were clearly succumbing to this fatigue and lapsing more than usual into their native French. I then decided to stop the game, to clarify this situation. Should students continue to the bitter end in English, or should they finish on a high note and use French to allow them to concentrate fully on the issues and decisions without the handicap of having to handle these in another language? (After all, it is rather unnatural to expect a bunch of native French speakers to speak to each other in English. How many French people in the street do you find speaking in English?) So, to decide what to do, we agreed that students should express their thoughts on the matter (some in French, some in English), and one even suggested we finish the day in Latin! The students voted to continue in English. Despite the obvious fatigue and because the students themselves had made the decision, the day ended in English. We then went to a restaurant—where we spoke French.

That is just one example among many of using international relations simulation for learning one single language. But what about learning several languages? After all, international relations involve several languages.

Toward global multilingual communication

In monolingual classes—i.e., where all students have the same mother tongue and are learning the same new language—it does not seem generally possible to use international relations (or indeed any) simulation/games to teach several languages at once. However, two cases do arise in which several languages can be used in the same international relations simulation/game used for the purposes of learning another language (as well as other related skills; see above).

The first case is where we have a multilingual class, the members of which may wish to learn different languages. Let us take the hypothetical example of a class of 16 students from Britain, France, Germany, and Spain (4 from each country), and assume that all the students wish to improve their communication skills in the three other languages (e.g., the English speakers learn French, German, and Spanish). An international relations simulation/game for language learning can easily be designed to accommodate those wishes. Let us call our hypothetical game INTELANG. It might be based on informal European agricultural negotiations, on a fishing dispute, or on trade. The countries represented in INTELANG would, hardly surprisingly, be Britain, France, Germany, and Spain, and communication would take place among all four countries.

But then, how do we allocate country roles to our students? Two arrangements seem possible. In the first, students represent the country of their own language; for example, English-speaking students will form a team representing Britain, French-speaking students represent France, and so on. In the second, we have a sort of goulash—mixed language teams, where one student from each language forms a team; for example, the team representing Britain will comprise an English, a French, a German, and a Spanish student. The other three teams would be composed likewise.

It would not be difficult to imagine many differences in the varieties of communication skills and language learning opportunities and pitfalls that would arise from two such differing configurations. It might be added, in passing, that this illustrates how the allocation of roles can sometimes be an important factor in running simulation/game sessions. It would require too much space, however, to pursue such matters, however intriguing they appear.

Instead, we also need to look at the message-sending system. Obviously, communication within teams is going to be largely oral (apart from making notes, drafting documents, and the like). But what about communication between teams? Again, two possibilities seem plausible. Either members of different teams are allowed to meet, in which case they will conduct almost all their communications orally, or else they are not allowed to do so, or may not even be *able* to do so (because, perhaps, they are located in different places). In this case, they will have to communicate in writing.

Let us take the second possibility, where teams can communicate only in writing. Let us also recall our two types of teams—monolingual (the same native tongue for all members) and mixed (different native tongues for members). Let us consider, on the one hand, how INTELANG would operate with monolingual teams. In such a simulation, the team representing Britain will send its messages to the French team, who will deal with those messages in what for them is a foreign (or second) language. In turn, the British will receive messages in French as a foreign (or second) language from the French team. But these teams will also be getting messages in the other two languages as well; for example, the French team will be getting messages, not only in English, but also in German and Spanish. This means that each team will have to read and understand messages which are in foreign languages. Reading in a foreign or second language is a vital part of learning the language, and since the messages were sent by native speakers, the readers will also be reading authentic text. This communication scheme, of course, also reflects what happens in international relations in the real world. Countries usually send their communiques, texts, contracts, and the like in their own language. It is then the recipient country which takes responsibility for translating and understanding incoming messages, and, as we all know, this has led in the past to unfortunate events.

If, on the other hand, INTELANG were operated with multilingual (i.e., mixed) teams, the incoming messages would be read by a native speaker. For example, a French member of the team representing Britain would have little (or much less) difficulty in understanding the incoming French messages (presumably sent from the team representing France). The other (non-French) members of the team representing Britain would consider it most appropriate that the French speaker deal with incoming French messages. But then, that French speaker still has to convey the essence, at least, of the incoming French message.

Now let us go back to the previous case of a multilingual class. Although there may be many multilingual classes around the world, the students in them do not generally wish to learn the language(s) of the other members in their class. With a few notable exceptions, such students usually wish to learn the language of the country in which the class is being held, which often fails—unfortunately and paradoxically—to contain any native speakers, save the teacher, of that language. A typical example would be the ESL class in the UK or the United States.

ICONS

So what do we do to get students together who wish to learn each other's languages? How do we get native-speaking students to help teach their own language to other students? The answer is fairly simple. We take several language classes from different parts of the world, build a simulation not dissimilar to INTELANG, and let the students communicate with each other via electronic technology. This would involve not only the old workhorse personal or home computer (fitted with a word processor and some form of communications software) but also telecommunications networks (known in the jargon as value-added data packet switching networks).

Now, if that seems a bit farfetched, perhaps a short description of one simulation which actually does this might whet your appetite. The simulation we shall look at is called ICONS (International Communication and Negotiation Simulation), and in it teams may be in different parts of the same building or they may be situated in different places around the globe. The general term that gamers use for this kind of simulation, in which teams are linked via computers, is simply "network gaming."

The methodology of political (or international relations) network gaming was pioneered by Bob Noel in the late 1960s and early 1970s. Since those times, computer technology has improved by leaps and bounds, with the result that it is now a very simple process to get two machines to "talk to each other" around the world. Bob Noel's initial design was later taken over by Jon Wilkenfeld, and then with Dick Brecht it was developed to integrate a language component. If we think back to our INTERLANG simulation, it should be easy to see how some of the situations hypothesized above can be brought to life. Instead of requiring a single class of British, French, German, and Spanish students who want to learn at least one of the other languages, we can now have several classes situated in different parts of the world participating in an international relations simulation, and learning languages from each other in the process.

For example, a class or team actually situated in France will represent France, a class in Argentina will represent that country, and so on. The teams will send their messages in their own mother tongue, but these messages will, for the recipients, be incoming target-language messages. Also (as in the mixed language INTELANG example), the teams may contain native speakers of target languages. If teams contain native speakers, they will also help the foreign language learners and, in turn, get additional practice in their own second language. That is precisely what happens in ICONS.

But what might an actual simulation look like? What will be the kind of issues students will examine, the sort of problems they will attempt to solve, the nature of the negotiations they will engage in, and the type of situations or crises they will contend with? Students taking part in ICONS will generally be given a scenario which paints a picture of the simulation world and which outlines the issues, dilemmas, problems, and/or crises which have been part of, or have just arisen in, that world. One such scenario, written by Bob Noel, is called the MUF Crisis, MUF meaning "materials unaccounted for," in the arcane jargon of the nuclear establishment. The introduction to that scenario will provide a good idea of what is involved.

> This is a diplomatic exercise, not a wargame. Although it deals with nuclear weapons, its focus is meant to be political, not military. The exercise is set in the contemporary Middle East and involves actual nations. The situation is purely hypothetical, however. Nonetheless, it poses problems which have great relevance for the nations of that region today. For our purposes, this setting offers interesting possibilities for diplomatic interactions. The principal country teams in the exercise are: Iraq, Israel, Saudi Arabia, the Soviet Union, Syria and the United States. The matrix of conflicting and cooperative interests among these six nations constitutes a rich field on which some of the international political effects of nuclear proliferation may be played through. (Noel, 1987)

It is clear here that language will play a vital role in such a situation, and problems associated with communicating in several nonnative languages will arise. Although major languages, such as French or Spanish, may not be represented above, bringing in such languages is simply a matter either of including countries that would legitimately be involved (e.g., France), or of changing the locality or topic of the simulation setting. Once students have begun the simulation, they will become totally immersed in the language; indeed, they will forget they are learning the language and will move toward that much-desired but less-often-attained state where they are unknowingly learning it through *using* it in a very real and meaningful situation. Printed descriptions of ICONS cannot capture the sense of excitement and involvement of participants, and it is this involvement which encourages students to use language to communicate.

Further extracts from the MUF Crisis scenario will build a clearer picture of what may be involved in political network gaming.

> This scenario makes no projections. The initial state of affairs is assumed to be just as it is today in the Middle East and in the world generally. . . .
> There is one development, however. In an article which appeared in an authoritative Western newspaper yesterday it was reported that Western intelligence sources strongly suspect that several atomic bombs

may have found their way into the clandestine arms market. . . . The article reported that the source of the weapons is not known, but they are not believed to be military items stolen from one of the nuclear powers. This means that the so-called "back yard bomb," long feared by experts, may have become a reality.

. . . This stunning announcement has precipitated a crisis in the Middle Eastern capitals and in Washington and Moscow. It is precisely this kind of event that could ignite the Middle East and spread from there to a global conflagration. (Noel, 1987)

This the kind of situation which can catch the imagination of students, not only of those specializing and needing special-purpose language skills in political science, but also of those following more general language courses. The above scenario paints a crisis situation (and it is often used in what is termed "crisis gaming"), but noncrisis situations are equally possible and just as involving. Innumerable situations based on international relations can be elaborated. They can involve real countries (as above) or they can use imaginary countries, usually reflecting essential aspects of real ones.[2]

Conclusion

Because of the realistic nature of the political negotiations that take place in such simulations, students quickly develop a wide range of language skills. Also, as messages are received from native speakers in other countries, students are exposed to large quantities of authentic language input.

The use of international relations simulation/games can provide students with a particularly motivating and involving environment for language learning and communication skills development. When such simulation/games explicitly build in structures and procedures whereby foreign and second languages are allowed to play their natural role, they can then become an especially potent medium both for developing language and communication skills and for integrating language, substantive areas and issues, and other important cognitive and human relations skills.

The use of international relations simulation/games for language learning seems to be a little-used resource. I hope that this chapter will encourage language teachers to explore the rich opportunities that such simulations offer to language students.

[2]For further information on ICONS, the reader is referred to Brecht et al. (1984), Crookall and Wilkenfeld (1985, 1986), Noel et al. (1987), and Crookall et al. (1988).

Questions and activities

1. Write down a list of about a dozen specific applications of simulation/gaming in foreign and second language learning. Classify these into groups, and add a few more applications. Compare your list with lists by colleagues.
2. What is meant by "learning to learn" skills? Why are such skills important?
3. In what ways does learning to learn apply to teacher training? How does the communicative approach influence teacher training? What implications do your answers have for the use of simulation/gaming?
4. How can simulation/gaming be used for teacher training? Draw a table, with teacher training topics down the right-hand side and types of simulation/game exercises across the top. In the intersecting boxes, give examples or short descriptions of simulation/games that might be used.
5. What are learning strategies, and what is learner training? Make a list of the skills and strategies you already encourage your students to adopt. How might you be able to use simulation/gaming to help develop those skills and strategies in your students?
6. In what ways can writing and reading skills in another language be enhanced by simulation/gaming?
7. How does simulation/gaming apply to language testing? What types of tests are most suited to simulation/gaming? Take two or three of the tests you already use and explore ways in which they might be incorporated within simulation/games.
8. How can simulation/gaming aid learning languages for special purposes? Draw up a list of specific ways in which this can be done. Compare your list with lists made by colleagues. Combine and summarize all the lists in a diagram or chart.

Using computers

Introduction

Computerized language learning simulations

Over the last few years, computer technology and simulation techniques have been increasingly combined to produce a highly motivating and very effective medium for learning. Some of the most interesting educational software includes simulation, and a number of the best simulations contain a computerized element. There has been a new discovery of simulation through the computer. In foreign and second language education, teachers are beginning to follow suit.

Many computer-assisted language learning (CALL) programs remain drill-based or computer-oriented, and they are valuable in that they provide instant feedback and are tireless. However, computers cannot replicate social interaction, in which language is used as a means of communication, but they can be used to assist various forms of simulation. Some computerized simulations are thus ideal vehicles for language instruction, for they can replicate social situations and thus encourage participants to relate communicatively to each other as human beings. Language ceases to be treated as an unapplied object of study and becomes a means for communicating with others within a socially meaningful context.

The three chapters in this section provide a glimpse of the wealth of ideas in, and applications of, CALL simulation in foreign and second language learning. Chapter 14, by David Crookall, Doug Coleman, and Ed Versluis, raises some issues which should be borne in mind in dealing with this medium for learning, and outlines a few parameters which may be taken into account in any discussion on computerized simulation, whether in language learning or in any other subject area that involves learning about human processes. In Chapter 15, John Higgins and Doug Morgenstern look at the problem of reality in simulation (a theme taken up again in Chapter 20, in Section E). They also consider some of the main parameters involved in computerized simulation (e.g., plausibility, time, process, and parsing) and give us some interesting examples. Doug Coleman, in Chapter 16, looks at an area of growing interest in computerized simulation, particularly for language learning. This is computerized conversational simulation, in which the computer takes the part of a conversational partner. Such simulations have shown great potential in language learning, for they allow the learner to engage in simulated conversation, albeit of a simple and highly constrained kind, and yet to receive feedback on the all-important aspects of accuracy and appropriateness. The use of computers is also discussed briefly in Chapter 13 (in the previous section). The views expressed across the chapters in this section often coincide, but they also differ, and this should lead to some healthy debate.

Simulations and computers have had a mutually beneficial effect on each other, both in language learning and in many other areas. There is little doubt that the advent of the microcomputer has conferred a greater legitimacy upon, and promoted a more widespread use of, simulation. By a similar token, simulation has undoubtedly come to the rescue of computer use in the classroom.

Chapter 14

Computerized language learning simulation

Form and content

David Crookall
University of Alabama

D. Wells Coleman
University of Toledo

Edward B. Versluis
Southern Oregon State College

Two developments have recently caught the imagination of language teachers: computers and simulations. When these two are combined, we have a potentially very powerful methodology. This chapter looks at a number of issues related to, and characteristics of, computerized simulations and discusses their application in computer-assisted language learning (CALL).

Backdrop

Almost all books on CALL mention simulation, even if only briefly—a situation which contrasts with other books on language learning. Although many teachers employ role-play and it is discussed in many books, it seems that the term "simulation" is more often discovered through familiarity with computers. And many CALL courseware designers have been inspired by simulation/gaming methodology.

It is thus worth making a few points on computerized simulation as a backdrop to this and the other two chapters in this section. Both computers and simulations, being essentially content-free, have proved useful in almost every discipline. Computerized simulations come in many forms, from weather or chemistry simulations (in which the role of the human participant is restricted to entering initial starting variable values) to those in which the people participating have full control over simulation events and interact with each other rather than with the computer (this will be discussed in more detail later). Here we wish to touch on various issues raised by the use of computer technology in simulation/gaming, especially those which relate to the perceived relations between computer technology and simulation/gaming methodology and to the implications of such perceptions on the ways we can harness the power of computerized simulation for the development of communication skills among humans whose native tongues are dissimilar.

Although computerized simulation (as opposed to other types of courseware) is generally seen as having great potential in language learning, the way computerized simulation is referred to in some CALL books gives one the impression that simulation is an entirely computer-related phenomenon. This is manifestly not the case. The instructional use of simulation/gaming was widespread long before computers were invented. But computers and simulation/gaming have been associated ever since computers came onto the scene; indeed, it was a major game theorist, Jon Von Neumann, who designed one of the first modern computers. And many valid and powerful simulation/games continue to be designed and used without having recourse to computer technology of any kind.

One example, among many, of this failure to see simulation/gaming as possessing a tradition, or even a kind of "philosophy," of its own, independently from computers, is to be found in a book on CALL containing a section entitled "Simulation and Other New Instructional Applications," a title which is doubly misleading. First, simulation is not "new," at least not in the sense that the authors seem to intimate (i.e., new like CALL). Second, simulation/gaming is not special to computers or to CALL. Most simulations are manual exercises (i.e., operate without computers), and the best simulations in which a computer is used are usually built primarily as simulations, not as computer software. It is the simulation which counts, not the computer. Some authors, though, do hit the nail on the head, though probably bending it a little in the process, when they make pronouncements to the effect that simulations can "brighten up language courses." One wonders, however, what value they do place upon simulation methodology if it is indeed seen as merely a means to "brighten up" a course. A few books on CALL, while extolling the benefits of computerized simulation for language learning, devote only a paragraph or two to it, which makes it well-nigh impossible either to mention the simulation/gaming tradition and its basic underlying philosophy or to explore some of the special features associated with computerized simulation (in language learning or in any field). Simulation can do far more than brighten up a class, as the chapters in this volume amply attest; indeed, a whole course can be based on a series of simulations as their main instructional medium.

Although some of the major applications of computerized simulation for language learning have been identified in a number of CALL books (such as to encourage real communication between learners or to bridge the gap between the classroom and the work situation, e.g., in LSP courses), various questions in that literature reflect certain misbegotten assumptions about these things. A question like "What types of computer programs are best?" reveals an unhealthy overemphasis on the computer and a dangerous neglect of the learner and the learning process. Other questions must also be asked, such as "In what different *ways* can specific computerized simulations be *used* or *adapted* for this or that *purpose*?" and "What sort of environment do we wish to encourage by this or that type of use?"

The modern microcomputer was enthusiastically hailed as a solution to many of the teaching problems of the time, the operative word being "teaching." We now realize that earlier CALL programs showed little imagination and tended to promote rote learning in a sort of programmed instruction sequence (a somewhat euphemistic name for this is "tutoring programs"). Recently, however, a more enlightened attitude has developed, in which the main focus is placed upon the learner and the learning process. For many years simulation/gaming has recognized this; indeed, the basic philosophy of simulation/gaming is that teachers cannot learn for their students, that the teacher is only a facilitator of learning, and that firsthand experience, active involvement, and enjoyment underlie all effective learning. And these assumptions (or beliefs) are no less true in language learning. A simulation, by creating a rich and challenging environment, provides that experience and allows participants to become actively involved. A computer does not by itself provide such an environment; what it may do, though, is to simplify or enhance simulation procedures (e.g., by carrying out complex calculations or offering easy access to information). As Oppenheimer and Winer (1988) point out, the computer, by helping to make certain boring and time-consuming procedures transparent, allows participants to concentrate on the main objectives, concepts, and processes without getting bogged down in complex and abstract equations.

The computer has the major advantage of removing the teacher from center stage in the classroom and of at least dampening his or her potentially negative feedback to students. At first the computer seemed to provide "the answer," because it was ideally suited to manipulating some of the variables and complexity inherent in many simulations. The initial enthusiasm over computers, however, has been tempered by a sense of realism and by the realization that it is not the computer, even with all its software finery (e.g., graphics, sound), which enhances learning. The luster of new fads wears off; now people want "better" courseware.

We have begun to realize that many factors simply cannot be satis-

factorily computerized, especially those involved in the social and interactional dimensions of language behavior, at least not without adopting
some form of simulation. Simulation software (or "simware") has come to
be recognized as one of the most sophisticated kinds of courseware and
as possessing the greatest potential for the development of certain human
skills, including communication in another language, especially when the
computerized simulation is designed not from the computer end but from
the model and learning end. Again, it is not the computer which has
brought about new educational practices, but rather it has allowed them
to develop; likewise it is less the computer part and more the simulation
component of a computerized simulation which embodies such thinking.

The focus on computers may be due to the educational philosophy
behind the use of simulation, or it may reflect a perception of computerized
simulations as being entirely computer phenomena, or it may have something to do with the fact that a computer is a concrete object, whereas a
simulation is an activity and thus much less palpable. Perhaps some types
of simulation require too great a change in student-teacher relationships
and are therefore felt as threatening by some teachers, especially those
who cannot see that a student fully engaged in a task is less of a threat
than one who is forced by dint of the marks/grades carrot to grind through
dull drill tutorials. Perhaps, too, teachers are disconcerted because some
computerized simulations, especially the more recent ones, are open-ended;
that is, they provide no right answer. One objective of education should
be to give students an opportunity to develop a tolerance for ambiguity,
to say without worry, "I don't know, and that's okay." This is particularly
relevant in language learning, where learners have to grapple with often
fluid aspects of behavior shaped by social convention and the negotiation
of realities and meanings. Whatever the reasons, it is safe to say that
teachers are often more worried about these problems than students, and
that the proper use of simulation often requires a more radical shift in
teacher and administrator attitudes than does the use of computers.

Computer people perhaps tend to think of simulation as something
new and wonderful, while simulation people tend to consider the computer
as simply one tool in a range of game paraphernalia, along with such items
as dice and boards. Thus, gamers tend to ask, "Is a computer necessary?
Would the simulation be just as easy to run and just as effective in achieving
its purposes without a computer?" Computer people must by definition
use a computer, and when they discover simulation, often through some
computerized simulation, they may see it as a way to show off the computer
and the programming.

The danger is that there will be less concern with the simulation than
with the computer; there is far more to a computerized simulation than
the simware or gameware. A successful computerized simulation requires
the expertise of both simulation specialists and computer experts. However, given that a simulation is usually based on some conceptualization

of reality (i.e., some form of model), it is the general simulation design which should determine the role of the computer, rather than the other way around. The simulation characteristics should be paramount, and the computer configuration should follow from these. Technology serves substance, and that relationship proves to be a potentially very rich language learning resource.[1]

Synergism

Computerized simulations constitute a peculiar breed of language learning aid. In fact, when properly conceived and implemented, they can provide interesting examples of synergism, the cooperation of both the computer and simulation producing effects which are somehow greater than the effects of either computers or simulations taken separately. Indeed, some of the most interesting educational software is in the form of simulation, while simulation designers have recognized the usefulness of computers in some simulation designs. Many types of simulation are ideally suited to the computer, and the computer is often an ideal medium for simulation (see, e.g., Kay, 1984). We may better form an understanding of computerized simulation's potential if we begin by considering the non-simulation "powers" of computers. The computer is a flexible tool for handling and processing information. Beyond that fact, the computer does not itself determine the purpose or manner of its use—it is content-free.

What a computer does, then, is really a question of what people do with it, and yet we are still impressed by the computer's power to manipulate data. Indeed, more than any other creation, the computer seems to be able to mimic certain attributes of our own minds. Harnessing this capacity involves carefully defining what tasks the computer should perform. What we have yet to explore fully is just how varied are the tasks which the computer is capable of performing. Simulations can be used to define computer tasks and, in turn, to take new forms as the computer is applied to them. The computer (and a piece of software) can itself simulate certain phenomena, but it can also be used to handle or process data within a larger simulation—although such a distinction may not have much widespread practical implication for computerized language simulation until artificial intelligence (AI) and natural language processing (NLP) have been considerably developed. Indeed, advancements to date in the application of both AI and NLP to foreign and second language applications have probably been much overrated.

It is useful to remember that simulation existed long before computers came onto the scene. But since their earliest days, computers have been

---

[1]For further discussions on some of these issues see Crookall (1988a, 1988b), from which some of the above ideas and phrasing have been taken. See also Watson and Crookall (1987).

used as a component in simulation. And it is probably true to say that simulation has contributed more to the innovation of educational software than computers have revolutionized simulation. Since the ENIAC computer of the 1940s, a wide variety of computerized simulations have been generated of many different types of systems, ranging from business systems to airplanes in flight, from chess games to fantasy adventure worlds. Gamers consider computers as an aid in their simulation design; programmers consider simulation as a particularly powerful software paradigm. In a computerized simulation, the *raison d'être* of the package is the simulation, not the computer.

Varieties of computerized simulation

The wide variety of computerized simulation is a starting point to any meaningful discussion. We also need to look at what happens during participation. Above all, we should avoid talking about computerized simulations as if they could all be described in the same terms, and as if they all possessed the same format, procedures, and relations. In a sense, of course, they do all possess the same essential characteristics: (1) They can be considered as representations of essential aspects of referent systems; (2) during participation, they may take on a reality of their own; and (3) they make use of computers.

Educational variables

Beyond this lowest level there is, however, tremendous variation in their configuration. A distinction may be made between educational and noneducational applications. Yet this is not necessarily the best place to start; simulations devised for research purposes may often lead to educational applications, or the other way around (e.g., G. W. Holden, 1988; Oppenheimer & Winer, 1988). Simulations of economic or global systems devised for analysis or forecasting can often be used directly for teaching and can give rise to versions employing hypothetical or actual historical data and used in wider educational or training contexts, such as management training, environmental studies, and political decision making (e.g., G. W. Holden, 1988; Hughes, 1988; Schrodt, 1988; Scott, 1988). Such adaptations of social science simulations are gradually finding their way into the language classroom. When such simulations are text-based (presenting text in the target language, rather than relying primarily on computer graphics, for example), they provide a unique kind of feedback regarding students' reading comprehension. One example (created as a historical simulation, but often used for ESL/EFL CALL) is OREGON TRAIL, in which the player adopts the role of "the head of a family of five with $700, a wagon, and a dream of reaching Oregon City in five or six months" (Expeditions, 1986).

Educational context and aim also influence many of the other variables, especially at the design and application stages; yet these are not inherent in the simulation or the language material to be learned. The age, the numbers, and the motivation level of learners are all factors bearing on the design of computerized simulations. The age of students has obvious enough consequences. Whether the computer is to be used by one student or by a group is, however, an issue to be determined by what language skills and objectives the designer chooses, and in turn by how much the designer intends the simulation to provoke discussion between students (a question explored in greater depth below). Student discussion can be as "simple" and intense as two students debating over which choice to select (e.g., "Yes/No," or how many items to buy) or as complex and far-ranging as a class working for days on alternative responses to some problem or complex situation arising in the simulation (see, e.g., ICONS, described in Chapter 13).

Motivation can be raised both by relevance to student interests and by simulation design options; the rapid sequencing of choices is only the crudest of these, whereas encouraging student interaction can make the difference between a simulation which is educationally rewarding and one which holds little interest for the language learner. Only recently have in-depth analyses of such discourse begun to appear, however. For example, discourse among groups of learners using GRAND VILLE, a CALL text-based simulation for learners of French as a target language, was recorded as part of the Dusseldorf CALL Project. Wolff (1988) and Legenhausen (1988) analyzed the corpus for structure/coherence devices and use of code-switching strategies, respectively.[2]

Content

Another source of variation is content or subject matter. Many simulations are purpose-built for specific curricular elements in particular subject areas, and limit themselves to very specialized domains of knowledge. A well-known example of this type of program is SOPHIE, which simulates faults in an electronic circuit and acts as a tutor in troubleshooting techniques. SOPHIE's creators purposely did not generalize its design. Instead, they took advantage of the relatively high degree of predictability in student-computer interactions within a narrow domain (electronic circuit troubleshooting)—especially in designing SOPHIE's natural language component (Brown et al., 1982).

Other simulations, however, are less easy to classify. They may have been constructed as content-free packages, often referred to as "frame

---

[2]Other studies in this area include Sharrock and Watson (1985), Watson and Sharrock (1985), and K. Jones (1986).

games." These allow data from a wide range of subject areas to be loaded (or inserted) into the frame. Other computerized simulations, although designed for one specific area, may be used, with little (or even no) structural alteration, in a completely different area. This, it should be noted, is due to the simulation model rather than the computer program. The program merely embodies a preconceived (noncomputer) model of the referent system. However, not any model will allow any content to be loaded onto it. For example, many business simulation/games are based on highly circumscribed contents, and their structure is not easily adapted to other content areas, although the ways in which they are used may correspond to principles governing use elsewhere.

Computer variables

Another set of variables—the so-called machine-dependent variables —is related to the computer itself: the language used (e.g., BASIC, PASCAL), the type of program (e.g., structured, data base), the type and capacity of computer (e.g., Acorn BBC, IBM PC), screen presentation (e.g., graphics, text, color), and so on. These are variables which should ideally be determined, not by a "computer-for-computer's-sake ideology" but quite simply by what it is we wish the simulation to achieve in terms of learning outcomes. That is, the computer is subordinate to the simulation; objectives define technology.

Unfortunately, this is rarely the case. The field is rampant with what Papert (1980) refers to as "QWERTY phenomena"—features that have stuck, perhaps out of a "this-is-the-way-it's-always-been-done" mentality, even long after superior alternatives have appeared. This problem appears to be particularly engrained in educational technology—a field where one would, on the contrary, expect new ideas to be especially welcome. With regard to CALL simulations, the use of BASIC as the most frequent programming language is a case in point. Most dialects of BASIC, lacking true subroutines (e.g., procedures called by name), make it relatively difficult to design structured and clearly defined procedures for a task-oriented simulation.[3] Most BASIC dialects are also totally unsuited to the construction of parsers for the analysis or "understanding" of natural language input from the learner. Thus, some simulations written in BASIC tend to

[3]A notable exception to this is, of course, BBC BASIC. This allows procedures and functions to be called by name, with the passing of arguments and variables, and allowing "local" variables to be defined. It also has a large range of loop structures (e.g., FOR NEXT, WHILE WEND, REPEAT UNTIL). The result is that long and complex programs can be written without using any GOTOs or GOSUBs. BBC BASIC is also the fastest dialect available, and it allows assembler and BASIC code to be mixed in the same program. BBC BASIC, currently at version V, is used on the Acorn BBC, Master, and Archimedes machines, and it can also be obtained for the IBM and MacIntosh computers. The nearest equivalent in the USA is QuickBASIC.

allow only multiple-choice-type responses and tend to have a complex branching structure not unlike that of Crowderian (programmed instruction) drills. BASIC is still the programming language most frequently packaged with newly sold microcomputers and is typically still the first (and often the only) language learned by fledgling microcomputer programmers, especially in educational fields. Since more attractive alternatives exist and are readily available, one can only think that market forces, social norms, educational inertia, or a combination of these lie behind the manufacturers' and vendors' resistance to change, and CALL simulation programmers' reluctance to learn a different language. For further discussions, see Martin (1988).

Computer memory limitations are another factor, but one that is often much overrated. Higgins's (1987) "artificially *un*intelligent" CALL programs, some of which are simple simulations, attest to the fact that when the goal is to foster group discussion, "unintelligent" programs with very limited capabilities can serve the purpose admirably. There are many simulations in which the computer merely calculates and produces a set of figures at the end of each round (e.g., the archetypal business game) or in which the computer serves as a data transmission system or as a sophisticated typewriter. These simulations are, nonetheless, excellent for encouraging interaction among students and the communicative use of language.

Compatibility (or frequent relative lack of it) between computer systems is another factor, especially with regard to display screen and graphics formats. This kind of incompatibility has often led CALL simulation designers to shy away from the use of the most sophisticated graphics their machines have to offer. Computer graphics, as a result, are all too often mere high-tech window dressing rather than a critical component of the simulation. This is unfortunate, since computer graphics have the potential to add a richness to the simulated environment that can build a greater sense of reality into the simulation experience. Here, of course, videodisk technology can contribute much (see, e.g., Chapter 15).

At various points above, we have referred to interactions between the computer and participants and among the participants themselves. We have also hinted at the influence or control that participants and computers may exercise over what happens as the simulation unfolds. These two variables prove to be very useful in our discussion, and it is to these that we now turn.

Control and interaction

Probably one of the most useful approaches to computerized simulation, especially those in education and language learning, is to analyze its use in terms of the activity generated in a given situation. This means considering a computerized simulation, not as a generalized phenomenon and subject to blanket statements about the learning package or even about the software, but above all as a particular and unique personal experience. This reflects the distinction that Widdowson (1979) has drawn between language usage and use. It also reflects the nature of simulation—to wit, that each time a simulation package (or simulator) is used, a different situation and experience is generated. A simulator has a certain potential; it is the way it is used which determines whether this or that aspect of its potential is realized.[4]

Here we shall look at the quantity and quality of two dimensions in the use of computerized simulation. These two dimensions or variables are control and interaction, or, more precisely, the amount and type of control that the participants and the computer have over simulation events and outcomes, and the amount and type of interaction patterns generated between participants themselves and between participants and the computer. The quality and quantity of each dimension are not infinitely variable for each simulation or each use. Nevertheless, control tends to be fairly closely determined at the design stage, since it is built more firmly into the underlying model, and thus into the computer program. Interaction, on the other hand, depends more on the way the simulation is used, and can therefore vary more from use to use. This is particularly relevant to the use of computerized simulation for learning another language, whether or not the simulation has been designed specifically for such a purpose.

The *control* dimension describes the extent to which the software and the running of the game allow participants to control the evolution of simulation events. This may be illustrated by a continuum, running from maximum to minimum control by the participant(s), or from control by the participants to control by the computer (see Figure 14.1). A computerized simulation at position X would indicate that the greatest control of what happens remains in the hands of the participants themselves. Position Z indicates that control is exercised mainly by the computer. In position Y, control is shared fairly evenly.

The *interaction* dimension is concerned with the extent to which the simulation program facilitates interaction between participants. This can be represented by a similar diagram (Figure 14.2). A computerized simulation may vary along this axis depending very much on how it is used in any one instance. Some types of use generate much greater interaction between participants (position A) themselves than between these and the computer. In other uses, the interactions between the computer and the participants may predominate (position C).

---

[4]The basic idea here is taken from Crookall et al. (1987).

Control by _____ X _____ Y _____ Z _____ Control by
participants   computer

Figure 14.1   The control dimension.

Interaction   Interaction between
between _____ A _____ B _____ C _____ computer and
participants   participants

Figure 14.2   The interaction dimension.

Other variables, mentioned above, determine how it is used. For example, a game designed to practice certain language forms will tend to encourage high computer-student interaction and low interparticipant communication. An example of this is TERRI, in which the student "converses" with the computer by ordering it to move objects around. This type of use does not, of course, exclude discussion between two or three students sitting at the keyboard, but the main activity remains screen-oriented. On the other hand, if the objectives are to practice and explore the communication patterns—say, at a board meeting—then the computerized simulation should encourage interactions at position A.

We shall now briefly review these two dimensions and provide a few examples of how they may be used and for what purposes in the language classroom.

Control

At the extreme computer-control end of this continuum are simulations of the type where the user is essentially a passive observer. Thus, an animated demonstration of a human heart or an internal combustion engine may unfold on the screen while the users watch, their only element of control being to repeat the performance by rerunning the program. Further along this continuum, users may have the facility of interrupting the program to obtain a freeze-frame effect or of deciding what starting parameters to use.

At the other end of the continuum are simulation programs which require constant user input in order to progress. Examples of this type are adventure games, which progress by responding to decisions made by the user at regular intervals. The "microworlds" simulated by adventure games were originally fantasy domains (haunted caves, Dracula's castle); however, the applicability of this technique to simulation of real-world domains is now becoming widely recognized (for a discussion, see, e.g., Hart, 1987). Many computerized simulations for language learning tend to fall somewhere between these two extremes, and to be located in more recognizably human worlds—for example, LONDON ADVENTURE (which also incorporates time elements).

Another type of simulation requiring constant input to progress is the flight simulator, and its cousin space invaders. This type often includes real-time graphic representations of their simulated world on the computer screen. This type of program will continue to run for a short while if user control stops, but only by adopting a default of input values. A lack of user input is often interpreted as a decision to maintain the current progression, which can result in catastrophe (e.g., a crash), thus terminating the game.

Interaction

At the low end of the interaction continuum are those programs which require constant single-user operation. Examples of this are some flight simulators and most arcade games. Their real-time running nature and high speed of situation-change require users to fix their concentration on the screen, and give no time for consultation between decisions. At the other end of the continuum are programs which require input from a number of users, either playing different roles in an organization of different characters moving through the same "microworld." Between these extremes are many simulations formally requiring one player but which, usually by having a move-based mode of progression (i.e., changes of state are initiated by new decisions being taken), can be effectively used by a group who may interact between decision-making points. In these cases, decisions may be the outcomes of group discussion or consultation.

Our two continua (of control and interaction) can be combined to form a computerized simulation grid with two axes (see Figure 14.3). The four quadrants characterize in a rough-and-ready manner the opportunities which simulations offer for different types of use.

Content and primary/secondary simulations

The above dimensions do not tell us anything specific about what the simulation is about, what it is supposed represent, or what realities it may generate. For this we have to look at content. The content of a computerized simulation is also a variable that has implications for the way a simulation is used and perceived by its users. One of the aims of a simulation is to attempt to represent part of the "real world" so that participants can gain

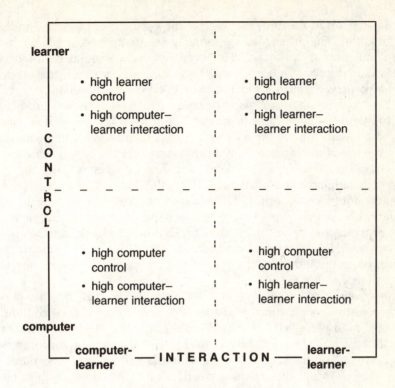

learner

- high learner control
- high computer– learner interaction

- high learner control
- high learner– learner interaction

CONTROL

- high computer control
- high computer– learner interaction

- high computer control
- high learner– learner interaction

computer

computer-learner —— **INTERACTION** —— **learner-learner**

Figure 14.3   The control/interaction grid.

experience of certain aspects of that real world. One of its main uses in the language classroom will be to recreate social situations in which students are encouraged to use language spontaneously. The "communicativeness" of this language will depend very largely *not* on how faithfully or minutely the situation created reflects the relevant features in a real-world situation, but on how realistically and credibly the students perceive that it does so. To this extent, the language used by students may be considered authentic (or at least approaching authenticity) and communicative, rather than form-focused like the language of classroom drill.

If, for example, the content is the English language, it is embedded in simulated social situations, whose construction affects the authenticity of the language. The importance of the simulated social situations in this context raises the old question of the balance between various elements in language learning—for example, vocabulary, discourse structure, and social skills. To help clarify the issue of content, it is useful to consider the notion of primary and secondary simulations. When the simulated situation carefully models a culturally rich interaction, the more linguistic aspects play a greater role in the understanding of the significance of each element in the situation. The primacy of the language content, then, qualifies this sort of simulation as "primary." However, when the simulated situation involves shared cultural norms, more typical of human social interaction than of a particular culture's practices, the vocabulary, grammatical form, and other "purely language" aspects tend to be treated as secondary—hence the term "secondary simulation." The foreign or second language learner deals with the situation in such a case mainly in terms of his or her knowledge of human social interaction, not in terms of a specific language or culture. This suggests a kind of duality between socially appropriate use of language and other more linguistic skills.

That is not to say that primary simulations are necessarily superior to secondary simulations. Preferences between the two depend upon the pedagogical biases of people using the simulations. Of course, a preference for social interaction of the sort found in secondary simulations for language learning has implications for the role of the computer, an issue we will take up shortly.

Primary simulations deserve one last observation, that they are particularly sensitive to variations in the level of abstraction of their content. One simple example is WILLIAM THE CONQUEROR, which presents the user with those variables William had to consider in achieving his mastery over the English opposition. While not a simulation designed specifically for language learning, this example clearly shows the direct relation between content, like the number of soldiers available at any given time, and the simulated events, like the Battle of Hastings. Variables like numbers are pretty abstract when compared with the reactions of simulated audiences to particular language choices. This contrast can be seen in a second example, FRENCH ON THE RUN. Here the learner assumes the role of an RAF pilot shot down in World War II France. The attempt to pass as French, in order to escape the Germans and their agents, immerses the student in the French language. Since the simulated problem to be solved primarily involves the mastery of French, this a good example of a primary computerized simulation for language learning and an example of how easily primary simulations can deal with quite specific materials.

Computer intrusiveness

Whether the language content is presented in a primary or secondary simulation, there remains the issue of how intrusive the computer is in the presentation of that content. One solution is simply to confine the computer to an occasional source of data or number cruncher, in what above we called a "computer-assisted simulation." This control of the computer can be motivated by preferences in content. As one article stresses,

"It seems important . . . that particular care is taken to ensure that simulations which involve the use of computers do not over-simplify or, worse, ignore group processes, interpersonal communication and social skills" (Coote et al., 1985). Or as another admonishes, "The use of the microcomputer is most effective when it is integrated with the work of the class and where it complements other classroom activities. The benefits are most obvious where it inspires other classroom activities" (SED, 1987). However, these views carry an implicit restriction, which is based on the conception that the computer's most important role is that of a readily accessed repository of information. Of course, the computer can be conceived of as a manipulator of information as well, a capacity which enables it to imitate, in fact, all sorts of things.

And perhaps the most interesting thing a computer can imitate is a human being. This capacity was "discovered" by Joseph Weizenbaum, whose DOCTOR program provoked a response that convinced him that "people were conversing with the computer as if it were a person who could appropriately and usefully be addressed in intimate terms." This was for Weizenbaum a "delusion," about which he and others after him have had reservations.[5]

But, delusion or not, even the temporary perception of the computer as a humanlike entity is due to some of the humanizing material routinely put into computer programs. For example, when a program responds to a student's choice with "Yes, do go on," or "No, please try again," the program acts in a way that no other nonhuman entity does. Books, the cherished offsprings of our minds, are in that respect passive. Other creatures and devices in the world may respond to our choices, but rarely in words. And the more polite the wording of the programmed response, the more the computer imitates a polite (i.e., feeling) human being.

Since a minimal imitation of human traits is apparently unavoidable, and a richer imitation is possible, we should consider whether the resulting illusion can be exploited on behalf of language learning. If a student's errors in language use could be detected while they were being made, a gentle nudge might be put into the program to elicit an immediate correction. Such a nudge could take the form of a cautionary comment, like "She may be offended if you refer to her simply as your 'old auntie.' " The question of how obliquely the computer might respond to student errors warrants further discussion. Three points seem relevant here.

First, there seems to be an assumption that detecting student errors and producing an immediate correction is a good thing; this is an assumption that is widespread in the CALL literature in general, and probably stems from the simplistic (and dehumanizing) behaviorist theories of feedback and reinforcement. Recent research seems unable to show a clear

[5]For further discussions on this, see Chapter 15.

benefit to almost any sort of error correction in language learning, except in a few restricted areas—for instance, when the correction actually results in new input and/or reprocessing of the previous output (e.g., in the correction of certain types of errors in compositions), or in those cases when conscious awareness of specific potential errors plays a strong role during production (see, e.g., Krashen, 1982).

Second, as argued by Coleman (1988a), error detection/correction is actually a more ambitious goal than a limited form of "understanding" by the computer. Error detection requires a flawless performance; the software cannot be allowed to slip up, or it will sometimes scold the learner when nothing is wrong. Understanding by the computer can be hit-or-miss, so long as it is "hit" most of the time. The real "misses" are the ones where the program's capacity to understand has been exceeded. In such a case, it can inform the learner of its failure to understand and can often also provide an oblique suggestion via modeling (Underwood, 1984). This sort of suggestion, however, cannot be equated with a "correction," because the computer is not assigning blame, or rather cause, in the communication failure to the learner. Obviously, this hit-or-miss sort of understanding requires far less artificial intelligence than the flawless mechanical tutor that provides error detection and correction.

Finally, when the computer is in authority and is continually correcting errors, it is like a game organizer who interferes too much. There is always a temptation for the teacher to butt in and take on the all-too-common (and all-too-easy) role of controller, and the temptation also exists to design a CALL simulation program that does the same. And as K. Jones (1982) has rightly warned, this can destroy the reality of the simulation for its participants. In sum, most direct forms of error correction imply an authoritarian teacher-learner relationship which is incompatible with learning, and learning to learn, via simulation.

The first of the above issues arises from a rather arcane and misinformed applied linguistics perspective; the second is a practical issue to do with implementation; the third arises from perspectives on simulation design and philosophy. But all point in the same direction: All argue against constant direct and overt error correction per se in CALL simulation programs.

But however and whenever correction is implemented, the pseudo-human agent created by a computer illusion should be more of a gentle and friendly sidekick than a diabolical electrofiend. Whatever the limits of personality design for sidekicks of this sort, they all have in common one thing. Each of them replaces an awareness of the computer-as-machine with an awareness of an active human intelligence (the simulation designer's own). This pseudohumanizing effect can be a considerable enhancement to the simulation if the content of the comments engages the learner's attention with the language tasks at hand. Of course, imitated human intelligence can be utterly wasted, even distracting from the simulation itself, if its comments are restricted to the mechanical tasks which simply advance the learner through the simulation.

Authoring

Whether one is designing or choosing a CALL simulation, there are clearly several varied and oddly interdependent elements to consider. The level and number of learners, the balance between linguistic and social aspects, and the choice of computer-as-information-source versus computer-as-sidekick make the computerized simulation an intriguingly problematic tool. Yet nowhere do all of these issues come together in so challenging a fashion as in the context of an authoring program. Authoring programs can be simple or complex, but they all offer the possibility of tailoring special computerized simulations for quite specific language learning situations.

Both the powers of and the problems with authoring programs can be demonstrated if we examine one rather complex example, the driver program for AUNT SADIE'S GIFT (see Ryberg & Versluis, 1987). AUNT SADIE'S GIFT is a computerized simulation designed to teach audience awareness in an imaginary thank-you letter situation. The simulation has the learner assume the role of Sadie's nephew, now the recipient of a 6-foot-long rattlesnake, sent as a Christmas present by his well-intentioned aunt. Tactfully and graciously expressing thanks within the bounds of truthfulness is the problem that occupies the entire letter the nephew must write, and is one which is especially difficult to accomplish in another language.

The experience of writing the letter can be completed in less than an hour by a single 18-year-old student. This can be qualified as a primary simulation because of the concentration on Aunt Sadie's probable response to each sentence selected. The constant feedback from a sometimes sarcastic computer sidekick replaces "authentic" social interaction. All of this is mounted on a driver program—that is, an authoring program so constructed that any simulation obeying the same constraints can simply be entered from the keyboard by someone with no knowledge of computer programming.

In fact, two other letter-writing simulations, BUCCANEER BILLY'S BAD BARGAIN (a complaint letter simulation) and MORTAL REMAINS (a request letter simulation) are already being mounted on this program. The interesting question is, what would a simulation for language learners look like?

Consider A DEATH IN THE FAMILY, an admittedly fairly speculative program to assist in the learning of another language. The initial problem is posed in a letter (in that language) to the learner, informing him or her that a relative has died in the country where that language is spoken. Responding to the surviving relatives, in the appropriate vocabulary, mindful of the relevant social and moral values of that culture in this situation, would be quite a challenge. Beyond just the right words, the right expressions of sympathy, grief, and family feeling would be required. Other areas are not difficult to imagine—for instance, business letters or applying to study in a foreign university.

For the time being, such computerized simulations have yet to be written. However, when they are written, they and others like them will reveal new and powerful patterns, uses, and choices for computerized language simulations.

Conclusion

This chapter has sought to look at some of the relationships that obtain between simulation/gaming, computers, and language learning, particularly as regards their form and content. It highlights such dimensions as the patterns of control and interaction that are generated between participants and computerized simulation and among participants themselves. Despite the possibilities for new developments, language learners and learning to communicate in a new language must remain the prime focus of these exercises.

Chapter 15

Simulations on computers

Elements and examples

John J. Higgins
University of Bristol

Douglas Morgenstern
Massachusetts Institute of Technology

Simulation is not life. Participating in a simulated decathlon competition on a microcomputer is not the same as training for and competing in that event on the sports field. In fact, the differences are ludicrously great: a finger waggling in place of whole body coordination and effort, a few bars of "Chariots of Fire" in place of the real elation of qualifying or winning, and the 10 events complete in 15 minutes or so rather than in two days.

So great is the discrepancy that, when one plays this particular program (DALEY THOMSON'S DECATHLON), one can be affected by a feeling of guilt that one is not doing something more outdoors and healthy. Certainly this is how an outsider is likely to see it, since the solitary keyboarder is almost a symbol of social withdrawal and of self-destruction. But to what extent does playing a computer simulation *replace* the real-life activity it represents? In an airline pilot's training the answer is "a great deal," for the very good reason that it is cheaper and yet close enough to its real-life counterpart. In the case of the decathlon simulation, time spent on it is clearly providing no effective training for the running track, but there is no need to assume that the result is morally reprehensible. The same complaint could be made against romantic fiction—namely, that reading it uses up time which could otherwise be spent kissing—but not many people would recommend the abolition of reading on those grounds.

Ownership via creation of facts

The first author has used the DECATHLON program with EFL classes. Some students play through the events, while others keep note of what happens in order to write (simulated) news reports of the (simulated) sporting achievements. The "athletes," of course, have the right to complain to the editors if they feel that the reports undervalue their achievements or contain errors. The most successful of them can be interviewed, possibly in front of video cameras. There is a great deal of useful language practice to be mined by a well-prepared teacher from this set of contexts: a variety of tenses, *if*-clauses, comparatives, superlatives, and indirect speech. The main benefit that the computer brings to the practice is the "ownership" generated by the creation of facts by the students.

In an earlier book (Higgins & Johns, 1984), a similar use of a simulation to stimulate writing was reported. Using a simplified management game called THE BLEEPER, students first played through several years of trading, and then received a printout of figures and graphs describing their performance as managers, which was to be embodied into a company report. The fact that the students were writing up the history of their own performance turned out to be highly motivating.

Class management

In a recent account of the use of a well-known computer simulation called YELLOW RIVER KINGDOM, G. Jones (1986), draws attention to the computer's limitations as a simulator of communication: Groups working collaboratively did not discuss their strategy in well-formed dialog but tended rather to bark numbers at each other. In order to turn the activity into an opportunity for overt language practice, the teacher in charge has to set it up as a role-play and make sure that only one member of the group, functioning as a messenger for the rest, operates the keyboard. What is obvious from Jones's article is that the introduction of a computer in no way relieves the teacher of the responsibility for lesson planning and good class management.

Plausibility

The computer's ability to "create facts" rests on its speed in doing complex arithmetic and the way in which it allows randomness to be incorporated plausibly into a complex scenario. In a political simulation, for instance, the machine is able to react to the user's decisions—for example, by producing election figures—in a way which reflects both the predictability and the randomness that would be found in reality. It can also generate disasters at appropriate points in the game. Knowing, as we do, how capable a micro is of elaborate processing, we may accept the results it generates rather too unquestioningly; the fact that the machine could process all the relevant formulae to calculate demand for a product does not mean that it has been given all the correct formulae to work on. There are simulations which have been thrown together by computer buffs without the benefit of advice from a subject expert.

The use of time

All computer simulations are what can be called "intervention models"—i.e., representations of processes in which the user may intervene to change some of the variables affecting the process. The way in which the user intervenes can be time-bound or time-free, which leads to a division of simulations into those which are time-based and those which are move-based. With the former, events are generated at a pace dictated by the machine, and the user may fail simply by not reacting or by reacting too slowly. All arcade games belong to this category, as does the DECATHLON simulation. Move-based simulations are typically business simulations or strategy games in which decisions are made and the consequences calculated; the machine does nothing while it waits for the decision to be input. Most adventure games fall into this category. Becoming more common, however, are time-limited activities which are a blend of time-based and move-based. In those activities there is time for discussion and negotiation before making a decision, but only a limited amount, and the passage of time is often made audible or visible in the form of a screen clock or countdown. The British Council's recently published FAST FOOD trading simulation is of this type.

Process and goal

Another possible classification of simulations is into process simulations and goal-oriented simulations. The latter in particular are often labeled "games" since there is a clear distinction between success and failure: Either one slays the dragon and returns with the princess and the money, or one perishes. There is a great temptation to dress goal-oriented activities in the plot accoutrements of medieval fantasy, though little work has yet been done on whether this meets the needs or wants of a language learner. In reaction, the British Council team has written LONDON ADVENTURE, which covers a foreign visitor's final day in London, a shopping excursion involving changing money, visiting suitable zones to buy different presents, and reaching Heathrow in time for the check-in.

Parsing

The way in which decisions are communicated to the machine can be by joystick movement or arrow key, as in most arcade games, by menu selection, or through language. If the last of these is used, then the machine must be equipped with some form, however rudimentary, of language understanding. Adventure games, for instance, are usually equipped to parse two-word sentences in which the first element is treated as "verb" and the second as "noun." This allows a fairly simple matching procedure to be used, covering a vocabulary of 50 to 100 items. Even with a parser as primitive as this, there is still some language learning benefit to be obtained from exploring the machine's linguistic limits. There can also be frustration when it becomes clear that the most obvious commands in a given situation will not work. Ultimately, using language to communicate with the machine and to conduct a simulation will demand the development of bigger and better parsers, so that something closer to a sensible conversation can occur, and a great deal of development work on these lines is now taking place on both sides of the Atlantic.

British examples

Researchers at the University of Essex, for example, are investigating the application of natural language processing to EFL programs in novel ways (Cook & Fass, 1986). Vivian Cook's ESCAPE FROM UTOPIA is a blend of an adventure scenario with a number of conversation emulators, advanced forms of the ELIZA parser. When the students enter any of the buildings, such as the hotel, the police station, or the cafe, they have to conduct conversations, trying hard not to make any mistakes, such as failing to be polite, which will raise their "suspicion index." At Lancaster University an attempt is being made to build limited-domain parsing into logic puzzles. In a program tentatively called TIGLET, the learner has to offer food to a hungry tiger and work out on what principles the animal is accepting some kinds of food and refusing others. As well as having a vocabulary of several hundred words for food, the program can distinguish offers from other kinds of questions and can sort out the countable/uncountable/plural distinctions, giving an appropriate response in nearly every case.

An American experiment

A project seeking to combine artificial intelligence (AI) capabilities and computer-involved language learning is being undertaken at the Massachusetts Institute of Technology. The Athena Language Learning Project is part of a large-scale five-year experiment involving MIT, IBM, and Digital Equipment Corporation. Experimental software prototypes for French, German, Russian, Spanish, and ESL are being designed to run on networked microcomputers expected to be universally available by the end of the decade. Most of these prototypes are communication-based programs which offer "microworlds" for learners to explore. One of them is called NO RECUERDO (I Don't Remember), described next (see also Chapter 8).

Technical features

NO RECUERDO is designed for intermediate-level Spanish learners. The simulation is enhanced by access to visual and auditory material stored on videodisk. Output consists of still photos and short video and film segments, presented in flexible combination with audio (including voice-over) and text overlay; access to glossing and a note-pad screen window is also planned. There is an emphasis on processing user input. The initial version uses pattern-matching of the user's typed input; however, AI researchers are also working on a truly intelligent system to process the input. Such a capability is feasible only because the input is already reduced by topic predictability and the limited lexical and syntactical range of the L2 learner.

Interactive fiction

NO RECUERDO has classic simulation features—experiential learning, problem solving, reliance on strategic thinking—but it also belongs to another genre, that of interactive fiction. The user can observe and "interact" with characters that inhabit a quasi-fictional world of mystery, romance, and science fiction against a background of authentic locales and events. One route through the program involves helping a South American scientist, who is an amnesia victim, remember and reconstruct events involving an illicit entanglement, a kidnapping, and a potentially catastrophic experiment in genetic engineering. Before reaching these core memories, the user must keep the character talking about peripheral topics such as the weather, sports, and food. During these interchanges, words and subtopics trigger gateways to more sensitive areas. The access to information is designed so that the user becomes aware of the intentions of the inter-locutor, thereby discovering and practicing discourse strategies. Also, fail-ure of the AI module to understand input will be masked by natural discourse patterning; for instance, the character will ask, "Did you mean . . . ?"

Multiple perspectives

The fictional basis of NO RECUERDO permits confrontation of a prob-lem central to simulation in general:

> The manipulation of information and misinformation and creating a fertile ground for differential constructions of reality on the part of the players still seems a useful strategy. Most games remain relatively sim-ple in that they do not provide any opportunity for the multiple realities that characterise everyday life to emerge even during play. (Greenblat & Gagnon, 1979)

NO RECUERDO attempts to present multiple perspectives: Characters "remember" different and even contradictory versions of events and of other characters' behavior. The program user experiences these memories as reality, especially when they are presented as filmed segments. Program users thus have differing perspectives, a condition which allows for infor-mation gaps (and "interpretation gaps") to stimulate in-class discussion and role-play.

Issues

Insofar as NO RECUERDO is art, its devices are clearly derivative of certain Hispanic American novels of the 1960s and of Kurosawa's 1951 film *Rashomon*. But here artifice must serve pedagogical ends within an inter-active computer environment. Since these are largely uncharted waters, it is not surprising that the experiment, even in its design stage, raises many questions and even doubts:

1. What are the merits of the exploratory mode (inspired by the computer language LOGO) preferred in NO RECUERDO and the other proto-types? Most other programs are presentation-centered; i.e., the user reacts rather than initiates.
2. What are the dynamics of the relationship among the following ele-ments: the individual program user, other program users during non-computer interaction, the hardware, the software (the program and stored audio and visual material), the linguistic and cultural target knowledge and skills? Examples of issues:

a. Typed input (since there is no voice recognition) results in various output combinations of text, audio, and visuals.

b. Some output is "canned" (prerecorded); other output (text) is created during the interaction.

c. The illusion of immersion in the fictional world and the empathy with a character will have to be maintained during a move-based interaction which can be interrupted for glossing and other help functions.

3. How does this particular learning format benefit from a blend of content elements (adventure and fantasy; practical, tourist-type situations; actual socioeconomic realities)?

Conclusion

This chapter has discussed some key elements in computerized simulations, such as reality, ownership, class management, plausibility, time use, process and goal, and parsing. Some British examples have been offered here. One American experiment, NO RECUERDO, has been analyzed in terms of its technical features, interactive fictional aspects, multiple perspectives, and other issues.

Chapter 16

Conversing with the computer

Environment, structure, and reality

D. Wells Coleman
University of Toledo

The purpose of this chapter is twofold. First, I will outline the major features of learner-computer conversational simulations. Second, I will in the process attempt to show that such simulations are not only feasible, but potentially of significant value for foreign and second language learning.

To bring into clearer focus the topic under discussion, I will begin by presenting a segment of a sample conversation between a language learner and a computer program called RELATIONS (Coleman, 1988a).

> **Learner:** is pat mendez boy?
> **RELATIONS:** Hmm . . . a boy? Yes. Next question?
> **Learner:** is grown up man?
> **RELATIONS:** I do not understand completely. I beg your pardon?
> **Learner:** is he grownup?
> **RELATIONS:** Hmm . . . a grown-up? No. Next question?
> **Learner:** is tom mendez brother in-law ed wilson?
> **RELATIONS:** The brother-in-law of Ed Wilson? No. Next question?
> **Learner:** is gene mendez bob wilson's brother in-law?
> **RELATIONS:** No. Anyway, Bob Wilson is only a boy. Next question?

The learner has been provided with a paper which contains (1) a family tree diagram with only two names filled in and (2) a list of names of 21 people. The first two names on the list, which are lightly crossed out, are the two names which have been written on the diagram. The learner has also been given the task of completing the family tree diagram by asking the computer "yes"/"no" questions about how the different people are related.

K. Jones's (1982) definition of a simulation is a very useful one, if not the most precise. He identifies the required elements of a simulation as (1) a simulated environment, (2) structure, and (3) reality of function. In the three sections of this chapter which follow, I will relate the elements of Jones's definition to the major features of learner-computer conversational simulations such as the one above.

Environment

Immediately, the circularity of defining "simulation" in terms of a "simulated environment" leaps out. But it seems quite clear from Jones's (1982) work as a whole that he intends the simulated environment to be a representation of a "real-world" environment (or a hypothetical "real-world" environment). In this sense, his definition incorporates what Crookall et al. (1987) call the "representational" perspective of simulation (but not only this perspective—see below). In a conversational simulation, the simulated environment is provided by the computer, as in TERRI (Coleman, 1985), for example. TERRI presents an animated image on the computer's display screen. A room containing several simple objects is pictured. In response to student commands (couched in English imperatives), TERRI moves these objects around the room in real time. Conversational simulations may be supplemented with printed materials (e.g., RELATIONS), but they are inherently what Crookall et al. (1986) call "computer-based simulations" (CBSs).

It is necessary for such programs to maintain simultaneously two representations of the environment. The obvious one is the *external* one the language learner sees on the display screen or accompanying documents. But the computer cannot read the documents and cannot see an animated image. For the computer, the simulation author (a computer programmer) must provide an *internal* representation: abstract data structures and programming language instructions for accessing or altering the information in these data structures. This internal representation is never seen by the language learner. The simulation author provides things like animated images and printed documents as a "bridge" that allows the learner to enter the simulated environment. This duality of simulated environments is one feature which distinguishes learner-computer conversational simulations from other types of simulations.

Structure

The structure of a simulation is created by rules. Rules may be "imported" by participants or may be explicit in the design of the simulation

(Crookall et al., 1987). The explicit rules of a conversational simulation are influenced by several factors.

One factor is the scope of the simulated environment. Within a highly restricted simulated environment, a program can provide a very "realistic" conversational simulation while possessing only very low-level artificial intelligence (AI) capabilities. RELATIONS is a good example of this. It "knows," for example, that Bob Wilson is not an adult and therefore cannot be married, and in turn cannot have a brother-in-law. (See the sample conversation, above.) Restricting the simulated environment also narrows the conversational domain in thematic terms. This can greatly reduce the amount of vocabulary which is to be handled by the program's parser. For example, Higgins's (1987) TIGLET has a vocabulary of only about 300 words. TERRI and RELATIONS each have vocabularies of less than 100 words.

Conversational simulations tend to be oriented toward the achievement of some specific goal. This is a factor which limits the range of language functions the learner needs to employ and, in turn, the range of utterance types needed to express them. For example, learner inputs to TERRI are always, in purely functional terms, instructions to move objects (with the exceptions of the commands *quit, check,* and *help*—see Coleman, 1985). This in itself does not *require* the use of the imperative form (e.g., "Put the black box on the clear one"). The same general function can be expressed via other utterance types (e.g., "Would you please put the black box on the clear one?"). It does, however, narrow the possibilities, excluding certain forms (like "Where is the black box?" "This is a clear box," and so on).

Two factors may justify further narrowing the range of utterance types to be handled. Pedagogical considerations (which, it should be remembered, are really a matter of language teaching rather than language learning) can play a part. An author may design a conversational simulation with the explicit purpose of providing practice in a specific grammatical structure or set of structures. In addition, narrowing the range of utterance types may increase the challenge to the learner and thereby improve the "playability" of a simulation. For example, if learners could ask RELATIONS, "Who is John Smith's daughter?" the problem-solving aspects of the simulation would dissolve. Restricting learners to "yes"/"no" questions encourages them to develop *strategies* for guessing how one person might be related to another (the most obvious being based on surname and gender). As an even more extreme case, imagine a version of the game TWENTY QUESTIONS in which a player was permitted to ask, "Who or what are you thinking about?"

The goal-oriented, problem-solving nature of conversational simulations has another effect. Their AI and parsing capabilities are inevitably quite limited (most conversational simulations, primarily for reasons of cost, are implemented on microcomputers). For this reason, they are unable to deal with radical changes in the topic of a learner-computer dialogue. This sets computerized conversational simulations apart from other types of simulations and simulation-like activities (e.g., the "scenarios" of Di Pietro, 1987) and from "real" (nonsimulation) interpersonal discourse (Di Pietro, 1984).

Conversational simulations involve learner-computer interaction via a keyboard and display screen, rather than the participant-participant interaction of many simulations (Crookall et al. 1986). This usually precludes the interruptions and negotiation of conversational control that characterize most real dialog (Higgins, 1982). Learner-computer dialog tends to be "move-based" (Higgins & Morgenstern, Chapter 15, this volume) and involve artificially strict turn-taking.

The end result is thus a highly structured learner-computer interaction resembling real dialog in certain ways but not in others.

Reality

Jones's (1982) "reality of function" incorporates the participant's view of a simulation: the "reality" perspective of Crookall et al. (1987). Within a conversational simulation's highly structured dialog about a restricted environment, a computer program can appear to understand language and produce it meaningfully. Small-scale natural language processing (SNLP) is sufficient to maintain a plausible dialog and thereby support the learner's "reality" perspective of the simulation event.

SNLP applications deal with only a small subset of a language. Their vocabularies are small, ranging from perhaps a few dozen to a few hundred items. Only a small number of syntactic forms are taken into account, and the semantic rules for the interpretation of these structures are kept as simple as possible (see Coleman, 1988a, for a discussion of a specific case).

Such limitations might on first examination appear insurmountable but are much less a problem than they seem. The computer program does not need to be a flawless communicator any more than does a human participant in a real dialog. For example, in the segment of dialog between a learner and RELATIONS (above), there is the following exchange:

> **Learner:** is pat mendez boy?
> **RELATIONS:** Hmm . . . a boy? Yes. Next question?

It is entirely plausible (given a larger context) that the learner intends to ask something like "Is (he) Pat Mendez(') boy?" RELATIONS (albeit arbitrarily) selects the interpretation "Is Pat Mendez a boy?" In this example, neither interpretation is necessarily "better." One of them is "right" in the sense that it matches the learner's intention. But it really doesn't matter if

RELATIONS chooses the "wrong" interpretation, because a human speaker-listener might do the same in the same situation. What is important is that RELATIONS makes its interpretation explicit somehow. It does this via modeling—i.e., "Hmm . . . a boy?" Another more explicit option open to the program would be to ask, "Do you mean. . . ?" (Higgins & Morgenstern, Chapter 15, this volume). Even "I don't understand" is a valid response by the computer, if it does not crop up too often.

Contrast this situation with that of tutorial CALL programs which attempt solely to diagnose the learner's grammatical errors. Such programs must "know" what the learner intends, or they cannot guarantee a correct identification of the learner's errors. And they *must* guarantee a correct analysis (via a syntax-only parse), since tutorial programs do not have the option of responding, "I don't know if you're right or wrong." Still, there are times when the program cannot determine the precise nature of a learner's grammatical error (as in the above case), so it is a certainty that such tutorials will sometimes make false diagnoses and thereby misinform the learner.

Many writers in the field of CALL seem to regard conversational simulations as more "advanced" (in terms of software technology) than tutorials which diagnose grammatical errors—and place the former "out of reach" of the current state of the art. The basis for this conclusion is that grammatical error-diagnosing tutorials (supposedly) require parsers that perform only syntactic analysis, while conversational simulations require parsers for syntactic *and* semantic analysis. Authors of tutorials are the first to admit that they haven't perfected their syntax-only parsers. So, they argue, it will be a long time before parsers for syntactic *and* semantic analysis are perfected. The key word here is "perfected." Authors of error-diagnosing tutorials need "perfect" parsers, because anything less leads to incorrect error diagnosis and misinformation to the learner. On the other hand, authors of conversational simulations do not need to create programs that can engage in "perfect" linguistic communication, because there is no such thing. And they have two kinds of analysis available (syntactic and semantic), while authors of error-diagnosing tutorials have only one (syntactic). As I have argued elsewhere in detail (Coleman, 1988b), conversational simulations actually have *more modest* parsing requirements than error-diagnosing tutorials. As programs like RELATIONS demonstrate, providing the learner with a "reality" perspective (Jones's, 1982, "reality of function") is achievable with existing SNLP techniques.

So far in this section, I have focused almost entirely on the program's interpretation of learner input—i.e., on parsing. But a dialog must have two sides, and the other is represented by the computer's responses. As the excerpt from RELATIONS (at the beginning of this chapter) shows, the language of these responses need not be terribly varied or structurally complex. The responses must *not*, however, contain grammatical judgments of learner input. There is the question of whether this can be done reliably, of course. There is also the question of what effects highly negative judgments will have on the learner's self-esteem and motivation. But there is another very serious objection to such judgmental responses *in a simulation*. They destroy the learner's "reality" perspective. When the computer repeatedly steps out of the role of "conversant" and into the role of "teacher," it is like a clear message to the learner: "You are putting on a performance for me, and I am keeping score." The version of TERRI described in Coleman (1985) is occasionally guilty of this, sometimes offering comments like "You have an unclear noun phrase." RELATIONS, on the other hand, uses modeling (as suggested by Underwood, 1984) without damaging the reality of the simulation. Thus, a caveat is in order. While the "reality" perspective is achievable in a conversational simulation, it can be easily destroyed by judgmental responses from the computer.

Conclusion

Conversational simulations, like "exploratory" CALL programs in general (Higgins, 1987) and computer-aided simulations (Crookall et al. 1986), represent a use of the computer that is more compatible with currently accepted "communicative" approaches to language learning than are tutorials. Unlike quiz-structure tutorials, they do not perform "right"/"wrong" evaluation of student input but, instead, simulate meaningful communication. In addition, an adequate level of parsing is more achievable in conversational simulations than in syntactic error-checking tutorials; without 100 percent accuracy in parsing, error-checking programs will make incorrect diagnoses at least some of the time. Conversational simulations do not require "perfect" parsing, and they have more information available (syntactic and semantic) to use for the parse in any case.

Questions and activities

1. What different types of computerized simulations are discussed in this section? Compare the classification systems proposed in Chapters 14, 15, and 16. Write down the main classification criteria used in each chapter. What points do they have in common? How do they differ? Are these differences a matter of terminology, or do they denote different underlying characteristics, or do they reflect different perspectives on computerized simulation? Draw a table which compares and highlights the similarities and differences.
2. What different roles does the computer play in the computerized simulations described in the three chapters in this section (and in other computerized simulations you know or have read about, e.g., in ICONS, Chapter 13)? How do learners relate to these roles?
3. What are the different uses of computerized simulation? Draw a table which lists the different uses down the side. List the different games mentioned and several that you know yourself across the top. Mark with "*" the major uses, and with "x" the minor uses.
4. What are the main issues in designing and using computerized simulation for language learning? How is the usual simulation philosophy reflected in computerized simulations? How is reality handled in computerized simulations? How can conversation be simulated by computers?

Background

Introduction
Theoretical aspects of simulation/ gaming and language learning

The chapters in this section all present background readings on a variety of more theoretical concerns related to the use of simulation/gaming in foreign and second language education. We say "more" theoretical concerns because, although each chapter presents its ideas and arguments within a theoretical framework, the practical implications are not far from the surface, and are indeed often easily discernible. Simulation/gaming comprises more than just running exercises, for it poses and implies a number of issues which invite debate and reflection, as many of the chapters in the previous sections will already have intimated. By tackling such issues, however, we should also become more skilled at running simulation/games and at situating them within a wider language learning context. Such discussion also helps us to understand the advantages of simulation/ gaming and to be more aware of the potential pitfalls. The discussion too will suggest guidelines for research into the more practical pursuits of simulation/gaming.

The set of chapters in this section covers many of the major issues related to the use of simulation/gaming in language instruction. This is not to say that the coverage is comprehensive; it means that some important questions are raised, and tentative answers are suggested. Obviously, in such a short space as permitted by the section, not all the issues can be covered, nor can they be dealt with in great depth. However, since all the topics covered are directly relevant to language teachers, these chapters do provide a valuable starting point and indicate some of the avenues interested readers should pursue.

It is vital to become aware of such topics as the relationships involving culture, communication, and simulation/gaming (Chapter 17) or the nature of reality construction during play (Chapter 20) if we are to go beyond the idea of simulation/gaming as merely another type of language practice exercise, and to see this methodology as providing opportunities for the creation of rich learning environments, where people (rather than students) may not only learn to communicate with others in another language but may, through language, also discover more about themselves, others, and the world. As Greenblat (1989) aptly puts it, "people with different backgrounds, values, or communication styles may be brought together, and through simulation tasks, may develop greater understandings of one another."

We are lucky here to have chapters also written by people from fields outside language instruction, for such people can provide new insight into many of the issues and can articulate new perspectives on them from the outside, as it were. Language education is increasingly drawing upon the resources and ideas of other disciplines, and people from other disciplines here contribute much to our thinking about language instruction in general and the use of simulation and gaming in particular. We have people working in the areas of communications studies, social psychology, ethnomethodology, and ethics.

Chapter 17, by Brent Ruben and Linda Lederman, provides a broad backdrop and outlines the major links among four central notions: simulation/gaming, culture, communication, and language learning. Such a wide-ranging discussion provides us with a valuable introduction to their interrelations and to the importance of the wider aspects of culture and communication offered by the use of simulation/gaming in language learning. Some of the elements in this chapter are elaborated upon in the subsequent chapters.

The next three chapters should probably be read together. All three deal with considerations pertaining to the actual learning of the target language. Bob Gardner and Richard Lalonde (Chapter 18) examine them from a social psychological angle, Robin Scarcella and David Crookall (Chapter 19) tackle them from an applied linguistics and acquisition stance, while Rod Watson and Wes Sharrock (Chapter 20) look at them from the perspective of ethnomethodology.

Chapter 18 deals with an area of vital concern in language learning. Certain social psychological dimensions, such as motivation and attitudes, are now widely recognized as being crucial dimensions in learning another language. This chapter presents some original ideas on how we may conceptualize language classroom activity, and considers how simulation/gaming may have a positive social psychological effect on the process of learning another language.

Chapter 19 looks more broadly at the ways in which simulation/gaming may be considered to help in the acquisition of a new language. They inquire into the ways in which simulation/gaming helps increase comprehensible input, active involvement, positive affect, schemata elaboration, appropriate use of strategies, cultural understanding, and general enjoyment.

Chapter 20 constitutes an invaluable contribution, not only to simulation/gaming but also to language education. The perspective of ethno-methodology as a research tradition has been conspicuous by its absence in language education and in simulation/gaming. Whether this is due to the interests of (mainstream) ethnomethodologists, whether it is because language and simulation/gaming practitioners and researchers have shied away from it, or whether some other reason is to be invoked is difficult to ascertain—and is in any case beyond the scope of this book. Things are, however, beginning to improve. In recent years, ethnomethodology (as well as its derivative, conversation(al) analysis) has begun to show interest in simulation/gaming as a legitimate object of study, and it is noteworthy that much of this interest has focused on the use of the methodology in language education, thereby also throwing light on the language learning process. Here the authors look at an all-too-neglected aspect of participation in foreign language simulation/gaming—to wit, how participants negotiate and sustain their game realities, and how these are managed in another language. It is through such processes that language is ultimately acquired.

The last chapter in this section (21), by Bob Vernon, goes beyond all these aspects and considers an area which (like ethnomethodology) has received too scanty attention not only in simulation/gaming but also in language education. This concerns ethics. The author looks at some of the important and often overlooked, even evaded, ethical problems that may arise in running simulation/games. His discussion, moreover, is as relevant to education generally and to teacher training as it is to actual language learning.

The chapters in this section, although concentrating on what are often branded as theoretical or even irrelevant concerns, do nevertheless have profound practical implications. This is due, at least in part, to the fact that simulation/gaming is and remains an essentially practical pursuit, with theoretical underpinnings. Practical activity may be better understood and made more effective if theoretical considerations are brought to bear. As the saying goes, there's nothing so practical as a good theory.

Chapter 17

Communication, culture, and language

Interactive simulations

Brent Ruben and Linda C. Lederman
Rutgers University

Communication between people is a complex process. When the people who are attempting to engage in that process come from different cultures, the communication becomes even more complex. People learn much about the communication process through everyday experience in a cultural context. Of all the tools of communication acquired through active participation in a culture, none is more significant to the human experience than language. One can learn a second language in a classroom, but that learning is often quite limited. Much of the flavor of when and how to use the language, the differences—often subtle—between words which are synonyms denotatively but convey different connotations, are learned in everyday social interaction as the language is used.

Much the same is true for nonverbal cues: appearance, dress, facial expressions, gestures, the use of space, body positions, and the meaning of time. What is the appropriate distance between individuals during casual conversation, or the proper attire for a given social event? In each such instance, the appropriate communicative behavior is defined by one's culture.

To the extent that much human communication is culture-bound, teaching about communication involves teaching about culture and its relationship to communication. One meaningful way to introduce the study of these concepts and their relationship is by using interactive simulations. To the extent that the processes inherent in communication and culture are learned in life through interactions with others, interactive simulations, which create or recreate social situations, are a potentially powerful tool in the study of communication and culture. This chapter will examine the nature of communication and culture and will discuss the role of interactive simulation for instruction relative to these concepts.

Communication

Communication as an area of specialized study has a multidisciplinary heritage involving scholars from such apparently diverse areas of study as language and linguistics, journalism and mass media, rhetoric and speech, nonverbal behavior, organizational behavior, symbolic interaction, psychology, sociology, and the sociology of knowledge, to name but a few. Classicists in the field trace their view of communication to ancient times and the writings of Aristotle, Socrates, Cicero, and other significant thinkers, modeling communication on the classical notion of the five canons of oratory (Murphy, 1972). In this century, the early perspective has been expanded substantially through the work of individuals such as Lasswell (1948), Shannon and Weaver (1949), Newcomb (1953), Wiener (1954), Westley and MacLean (1957), Schramm (1954, 1966), Berlo (1960), Katz and Lazarsfeld (1960), Miller (1965), and others. Models in the last 50 years have evolved a theory of human communication which focuses on the ongoing dynamic processes by which messages in various codes are shaped and encoded and then transmitted through a variety of channels from which they are received, decoded, and interpreted.

One particularly useful approach to the study of communication is drawn from general systems theory. The communication systems approach goes beyond a concern with particular components of the process (e.g., sender, message, channel, receiver), directing attention to the functions served by the interaction of these parts acting in concert with one another (Ruben, 1972, 1975, 1984). Rather than maintaining a strict concern with particular message-initiation transmission-reception sequences, as have other models, a systems perspective defines communication as the process whereby symbols are created, transmitted, interpreted, and intersubjectified, thereby constituting one of the two basic life processes of humans (Miller, 1965; Thayer, 1968; Ruben, 1972, 1975, 1984).

The systems perspective focuses on the continual, cyclical, transactional signal- and symbol-using processes by which living systems (individuals, groups, societies) informationally maintain themselves in their environment. As opposed to having a primary concern with antecedent stimuli and consequent effects, a communication systems approach focuses on identifying and explaining mutually causal relationships between interactants (e.g., spirals, do-loops, infinite regressions) as they occur in a range of human information and communication-related phenomena.

The approach provides some interesting ways of conceiving of human behavior in relation to information. Communication is defined as the process by which environmental data are transformed into information for use by living systems (Ruben, 1984). Through this process, systems are initiated, grow, evolve, prosper, or deteriorate. One level is that of the individual with its receptor-conductor-effector systems which permit it to behave appropriately toward other individuals and the physical environment. Another level is the social communication from individual to individual, and generation to generation, through reproduction and development that supplies the continuity of participants over time (Lawson, 1963; Ruben, 1984).

Culture and language

Just as there are many approaches to *communication*, so, too, can *culture* be viewed in a variety of ways. For purposes here, *culture* will be defined as the complex combination of the common symbols, knowledge, information-processing patterns, rules, life-styles, and attitudes and values which link and give a social identity to a particular group of people at a particular time (Ruben, 1984).

The symbols of a society are perhaps the most visible signs of the process. Of these, spoken and written language are the most pervasive. Verbal and nonverbal symbol systems link individuals to one another, provide a basis for a common identity, and create a medium for interaction and negotiation among members.

There are also many other significant symbols—heroes and heroines, leaders, monuments, buildings, flags, songs, and places that have important symbolic value for the citizens. To Americans, George Washington, Martin Luther King, "The Star Spangled Banner," and the Statue of Liberty have important symbolic significance. Shared communication patterns, orientations toward religion, politics, sex roles, courtship, childrearing, race, and other facets of social life also become a part of the culture of any society.

Communication and culture

There is an intimate relationship between communication and culture. As much as it is accurate to say that culture is defined, shaped, transmitted, and learned through communication, the reverse is equally correct. Culture is the by-product of human communicative activity. The verbal and nonverbal patterns that individuals develop are largely the result of having adapted in particular ways to the demands and opportunities presented by the cultures of our various social systems. In effect, then, there is a reciprocally influencing relationship between human communication and culture. Through communication we shape cultures, and, in turn, cultures shape communication rules and patterns (Hall, 1959; Ruben, 1984).

Most of what characterizes a culture is taken for granted by, or invisible to, the individuals it envelopes, as is the air which surrounds them; culture is so subtle and pervasive that it simply goes unnoticed. Residents of the United States, for example, simply take the English language for granted as they do the characteristic two- or three-pump handshake greeting, the intermittent eye glances, and the 2½ to 4 feet separating us from others in casual conversation, all of which are characteristic of our particular culture. In a similar way, people have come to accept their subcultures without much thought about them; the romantic glances and expressive touch between intimates, and the conventions of dress and jargon in various groups and organizations, become "natural" and "automatic" behaviors to the persons involved.

Communication, culture, and simulation

The subtlety of culture, the pervasiveness of communication, and the intricate and dynamic relationship between the two is difficult to model and hard to teach with traditional methods. Definitions and relationships can be articulated informationally in a lecture or a book, or by a similar means, but what is missed in this is the sense of how one participates in, shapes, and in turn is shaped by the process. Interactive simulation is an instructional method that allows for learning about communication and culture through direct and actual experience. Simulations are most often defined in the literature as operating models of reality or some aspect thereof. Even those who argue for systematic assessment of the effectiveness of simulations (Lederman & Ruben, 1984) base that framework for assessment on the assumption that they are operating models of reality. Yet simulation may in fact be more than a model of reality. It might also be depicted as an operating reality in and of itself, and this way of thinking would hold equally true for all simulated participatory activities (Lederman, 1983).

The basis for this reconceptualization of simulations derives from a comparison between interactive, participatory simulations and other types of models. Unlike mathematic models of the marketplace or clay models of houses, interactive, participatory simulations are composed of the same materials (people, behaviors, structures) as their real-world counterparts. And like their real-world counterparts, once created and set into motion, they take on a life of their own.

By reconceptualizing simulations as "operating realities," we place great value on the actual behavioral dynamics as they unfold, and upon their implications. If one treats simulations as *real* experiences, participants can be provided with *real* insights into those experiences and the implications of them for the other realities in which they interact in the world outside the structured experience (Lederman, 1983).

The more complex the theoretical base into which one wishes to initiate the learner, the more complex the simulation of it needs to be. Simulations and games for instruction in communication and culture require a fair degree of complexity, particularly when utilizing a communication systems theory perspective; such simulations need to be structured so that communication functions in a processlike fashion by operating on individual, group, organizational, and societal levels providing for reciprocally causal relationships within and between those levels of analysis. Perhaps more important, the simulation model must take into account the symbolic nature of human information-transforming processes.

A simulation, for example, of a communication system in which the scout bee searches out and conveys information to hive-mates as to the location of food or suitable places to construct a hive would be process-oriented, complex, and involving reciprocally causal communicative relationships (Frisch, 1950). Such relationships, however, involve *signals* as opposed to *symbols*. The scout bees as senders or initiators of messages create and transmit their messages through a "waggle dance" which elicits highly predictable responses among recipients. Both the sender's capacity to send such messages and the recipient's capacity to decode them are consequences of genetic programming and so involve no learned interpretative processes. There is a fundamental distinction between these sorts of signals and socially defined symbols which are the essence of the interpretative process and those which mark human communication. Thus, for bees there are no questions as to what the dance "means," or concerns regarding how it got to mean what it did. There are no questions as to the impact of culture on the communication process, or of communication on the development of culture. There are no classes where bees are taught how to initiate or interpret messages.

The example of the communication among bees provides a contrast to a human communication transaction. In human communication, questions of meaning, interpretation, and social definition are central. Unlike lower animals of other species, humans must *learn* their culture—their symbol systems and the significance attached to the situations, people, and things to which those symbols refer.

From this perspective, three critical criteria emerge as necessary to simulations of human communication. The first criterion is *structural*: An environment is required in which all of the necessary elements of the process of transformation of information are included (e.g., information, people, media, or networks).

The second criterion is *functional*: The environment must be operationally consistent with the model or notion of communication systems. Since the elements of a communication system are *people, information, media,* and *the environment* itself, each of these needs to be accounted for functionally. Thus, the simulation must provide a means for participants (*people*) to create and deal with information so as to provide an understanding of its nature, its generation/creation/discovery (related but differing possibilities for where and how information arises), its acquisition, its transmission, and the range of possibilities for its utilization. It must also provide opportunities in which participants generate, create, select, and act upon *information* in a manner reflective of their own unique information-creating/interpreting styles. This means that people and their roles in relation to information and to one another is a necessary point of focus in the simulation.

Furthermore, the simulation must take into account any and all mechanisms, human and technical, which can or do function as pathways (*media*) through which that information flows, and must provide opportunities for analysis of the effects of the interrelationships among media, information (messages), and people in relation to each. Finally, the simulation should provide an *environment* complex enough to replicate pertinent "real-world" reality and reality processes. In this way, the environment and its structure provide a set of infinite possibilities for exploring and focusing on the relationships involving people, information, and the networks between them.

The third criterion is *pragmatic*: The parts that constitute the whole as depicted above must be put in motion in some way so that the desired processes and dynamics occur, and some mechanism must exist for observing the workings of all of these phenomena. That is, something must be set in motion and things must occur as a result of that initiation. The resultant actions need to have some observable process that can be used as manifestation of the initial states and the relationships between those initial states, and the eventual outcomes.

When the simulation is to incorporate experience with culture along with communication, there is an additional consideration. Lederman and Ruben (1984) label this element, "reliability." Reliability in relation to a simulation manifests itself in either *product* or *process* reliability. Product reliability refers to the capacity of the simulation to produce *consistent outcomes*; process reliability to the production of *consistent dynamics*. Depending upon the culture and/or cultural aspects to be incorporated in the simulation, it needs either to provide product or to process reliability.

An overview of the communication/culture learning process

In the next section, we will turn to a more specific discussion of the use of simulation for communication and cultural instruction. Before exploring these issues, it is useful to consider briefly the central question upon which the validity of communication and cultural instruction ultimately depends: How do people learn about culture and communication?

Clearly, this question could be the topic of many volumes; it is therefore important to provide an overview of certain basic elements in the communication and culture learning process which are important as a foundation in thinking about designing, using, and evaluating simulations.

When people become aware of the existence and nature of their cultures and subcultures, it generally happens in one of two ways. The first is when someone within the subculture or culture violates cultural patterns and standards. Consider the customary handshake greeting as an illustration. Few people think much about handshakes unless their expectations about them are violated. If, for instance when two persons meet for the first time, one of them takes hold of the other's hand with a very limp or exceptionally overpowering grip, the other person is likely to take note. Even more dramatic is the response when an individual continues to pump the hand five, six, or even seven times, and only then reluctantly lets go —a pattern that may be quite typical in some cultures, but not in the American one. There are instances or patterns which are appropriate in some cultures but stand out as inappropriate in others. Another example is the often observed behavior in international meetings, where one person "chases" another around the room, one person wishing to remain "close," the other to keep his/her distance.

The second way in which one can be alerted to the presence and impact of one's culture is when one encounters someone from another culture or subculture and observes unique behaviors. To the Arab, men kissing one another on the cheek as a greeting goes unnoticed, while this same behavior startles and often upsets the European. And the Japanese habit of closing the eyes when concentrating on a question may be quite traumatic to the Canadian businessperson who has no idea how to interpret the action.

Adjusting to a culture or subculture is a learning, mapping, rule-internalizing process through which people adapt to the symbolic and social realities created by the relationships, groups, organizations, and society of which they are members (Ruben, 1984). For the most part one absorbs cultures—becomes American, Swiss, Tanzanian—with virtually no effort or awareness that it is happening. Even less obviously, people adapt to and absorb the subcultures of relationships, groups, and organizations in which they become involved. We become "a corporate person," "a salesman," "a Protestant," or "a female," with very little effort on our part, as we "take on" the subcultural conventions of gender, friends, family, ethnic group, profession, and society. Most of the learning is natural and inevitable. People *learn* to speak their native language; they are never *taught it*. But cultural adaptation also involves persuasion or "social pressure," as with the education provided by family, church, and school aimed at providing the knowledge, values, and rules which others deem necessary.

Because adaptation to human cultures and subcultures is more or less automatic, it is often a difficult and stressful matter to readjust to others.

The dynamics of cultural adjustment are a doubled-edged sword. On the one hand, they are the sources of considerable stress and strain. On the other hand, they are also opportunities for personal growth and learning about the impact of culture and communication.

Culture-specific and culture-generic simulations

In broad terms, there are two types of simulations of communication and culture: (1) simulations designed to provide *culture-specific* learning and (2) simulations designed to foster *culture-generic* learning.

Specific simulations

Many simulations have the goal of teaching learners one or more of the elements of a particular culture. One can design role-play simulations, for instance, in which participants use their knowledge of the verbal and nonverbal communication and culture codes of a particular society to accomplish a given task. The purpose of such a simulation would be to teach *particular* verbal and nonverbal communication patterns as they operate in particular contexts in Mexico or Spain. As such, the activity is an example of a culture-specific simulation. However, with a similar goal of imparting information about a particular culture, one could design sophisticated structures serving a variety of functions. Cultural-specific simulations can be designed to enhance instruction in language, gestures, facial expressions, use of space and time, and customs for virtually any culture. Generally speaking, instructional methods of this sort are most productively used to reinforce or augment more traditional methods of instruction.

Generic simulations

Another quite different, but equally relevant, use of simulation is for more general learning about the nature of culture and communication and their relationship to one another. Whereas culture-specific simulations strive to foster learning about *particular* cultures, generic simulations encourage learning about the processes underlying the development and change of *all* cultures.

A simulation designed to replicate the process through which common verbal and nonverbal symbols develop among a collectivity of individuals would be an example of a culture-generic simulation; so would an activity which sought to provide participants with firsthand experience with the dynamics of cultural adaptation.

Figure 17.1   Types of culture simulations.

While we have discussed culture-specific and generic simulations as two distinct types of activities, the two are perhaps better thought of as end points on a continuum (see Figure 17.1). As indicated, some simulations one might design quite clearly exemplify one or the other of these extremes. Many others fall somewhere on the continuum between them, some emphasizing specifics about verbal and nonverbal communication within a particular culture, others the more general processes of culture creation, adaptation, and change.

A number of simulations dealing with culture fall near the midpoint on the continuum, seeking to demonstrate contrasts between the verbal and nonverbal behaviors of particular types of cultures or between sub-cultures within a single culture (e.g., BAFA BAFA, HYPOTHETICA, AGI-TAINIA, MEDITANIA, SOLIDANIA, or LOBU-ABU). Yet, more generally, such simulations may also seek to foster learning about the nature of culture, the way it emerges and changes, the role of communication in these processes, and the nature and problems of cross-cultural communication (Ruben & Budd, 1975; Ruben, 1979, 1980).

Conclusion

The central question in the use of simulations for instruction in communication and culture is: What is the goal? The answer to that question provides the basis upon which one designs, selects, uses, or evaluates any simulation. The discussion and framework provided in this chapter suggest a number of issues that must be taken into account in arriving at the answer: What is meant by communication? How is the relationship between the two conceptualized? Is the concern primarily with language, the verbal codes of communication? Or is emphasis to be placed on the nonverbal codes—appearance, gestures, facial expressions, touch, the use of space and time? Or both? Has ample consideration been given to the appropriate structural, functional, and pragmatic characteristics? And, finally, is the learning goal culture-specific or generic?

Chapter 18

Social psychological considerations

Robert C. Gardner
University of Western Ontario

Richard Lalonde
York University

First language acquisition parallels socialization. In the process of growing up, children discover that to make their needs or wants known to parents, guardians, or peers, language is a powerful tool, and here begins the unending concern with communication. Often words, phrases, pronunciations, and the like are acquired without any conscious awareness on the part of the individual, and somewhere along the way, language becomes part of children's sense of identity. Language becomes linked with questions such as "Who am I?", and part of the answer is, for example, "I am English" or "I am French." Such answers have cultural and national implications, but, more important, they also demonstrate a symbiosis of self and language.

Because of the bond between self and language, second or foreign language learning will involve not only the acquisition of a new symbolic system but also the modification of the self-concept to some extent. This general orientation underlies much of the research involved with the role of social psychological variables in second or foreign language learning, and a theoretical model has been proposed to integrate and explain the results obtained in this research (Gardner, 1981). The socioeducational model of such language learning hypothesizes that affective and cognitive characteristics interact differentially with formal and informal language acquisition contexts to produce both linguistic and nonlinguistic outcomes. A major construct of this model is the integrative motive, characterized as "a high level of drive on the part of the individual to acquire the language of a valued second language community in order to facilitate communication with that group" (Gardner, 1981).

Recent investigations have made use of causal modeling techniques to test operational formulations of this model (for a review and an analysis see Gardner, 1985). This causal model proposes that two classes of attitudes, Integrativeness and Attitudes Toward the Learning Situation, "cause" motivation, and that motivation and language aptitude influence the relative degree of proficiency that individuals achieve in the other language. This model is an individual difference model that makes no statement concerning the effects of teaching strategies, classroom environment, or the like on language proficiency. It is concerned with explaining individual differences within a given classroom environment, and in this context it argues that language aptitude and motivation play distinct roles. Language aptitude is believed to be important because it provides the cognitive foundation on which new language material can be built. Motivation, on the other hand, is considered to play a role in that it influences how active the individual will be in attempting to learn the language.

Extensions of this model have considered the potential role of personality variables (Lalonde & Gardner, 1984), and other causal modeling studies (Clément & Kruidenier, 1985) have considered the role of self-confidence along with attitudinal/motivational characteristics. Although the structure of these models differ somewhat, it remains that attitudinal/motivational variables and language aptitude are found to play important roles in second or foreign language acquisition.

By stressing the sociocultural aspects of language acquisition, this model appears to ignore a basic fact—namely, that in many contexts a target language is a school subject, and many students are not consciously concerned with losing their sense of ethnic identity by learning some features of the language. The intent of this chapter, however, is to show that because of the link between language and identity, factors like the integrative motive and language aptitude can be shown to be implicated in various aspects of language learning regardless of the approximation to real language use.

Levels of simulation

The focus of this book is on simulation in the language classroom. As considered in this chapter, simulation is taken to mean "a working representation of reality" (van Ments, 1980), and various language learning contexts can be seen to reflect different levels of simulation. We have chosen to direct attention to four levels of simulation that represent increasing approximations to real language use or development, though there is no intention to suggest that any given context does not draw on features from each level. These levels include (1) extremely artificial learning environments, (2) traditional classroom environments, (3) language classrooms employing role-playing and dramatic techniques, and (4) immersion programs.

Extremely artificial learning environments

Such environments rarely exist in and of themselves as a language training strategy, yet there are aspects of language programs that are somewhat artificial. If students are instructed to learn a vocabulary list by pairing words in the new language with words in the old, or when they are required, for example, to master drills or answer tape-recorded questions, these can be viewed as instances of low-level simulation of language activity. There is no real communication involved, so that none of the truly social aspects of language behavior are present.

Very little research has investigated the role of integrative motivation and language aptitude in truly artificial contexts. The one study that has been conducted indicates that the generalizations derived from the socioeducational model are applicable even in artificial contexts. The paired-associate learning paradigm is perhaps the most basic learning procedure, and it is used in many studies of verbal learning to simulate more complex processes. Gardner, Lalonde, and Moorcroft (1985) used this paradigm to study the effects of aptitude, integrative motivation, and mode of presentation (visual vs. aural) on the rate of learning 25 French/English vocabulary noun pairs. The pairs were presented in a different random order for six trials using an anticipation procedure in which the English word was presented, followed by a 7-second interval during which subjects gave the French equivalent before it was presented. The results of this study indicated that, whereas subjects knew very few of the words on trial 1, high-aptitude subjects learned faster than low-aptitude subjects, and highly integratively motivated subjects learned faster than those who were low. Moreover, the rate of learning was more rapid under visual presentation than under aural presentation. Other results demonstrated that subjects' perceptions of their effort and interest on each trial were influenced by their level of integrative motivation and by the mode of presentation, but not by language aptitude.

Such results suggest that, even in a highly artificial environment where the simulation of any true social language behavior is minimal, cognitive and affective variables are operative in a manner that is consistent with the socioeducational model. In its simplest form, actual learning was shown to be mediated by language aptitude and integrative motivation, and integrative motivation (but not language aptitude) was shown to effect motivational differences operating in this context.

Traditional classroom environments

The traditional classroom environment encompasses a varied set of language teaching strategies (for a review, see Stern, 1983), but a major characteristic of this environment is that the language is taught as a school subject. The topic of the class is the target language, but the language of instruction is, by and large, the first language. As a consequence, most of the meaningful communication in the classroom takes place in the dominant language, and relatively little takes place in the new language. The traditional classroom environment, therefore, represents a relatively low level of simulation of the truly communicative aspects of the other language. Breen (1983) explores the many social facets of the traditional foreign language class, clearly showing how it has a culture of its own. Throughout his discussion, however, it is clear that "one of the conventions assumed to be honoured by participants in the culture of a language class is the willingness and capacity to suspend belief, to participate in simulated communication *within* class-room specific interaction."

This type of program has been the one most extensively investigated from the point of view of the socioeducational model. The typical research approach is to factor-analyze attitudinal/motivational indices, along with measures of language aptitude or intelligence (in most cases) and target language achievement. Such studies have been conducted in many different cultural and linguistic contexts by a number of researchers. Gardner (1985) has summarized much of this literature, which has investigated English-speaking Canadians learning French, French-speaking Canadians learning English, American students learning French and Spanish, Finnish students learning English, and children in Belize learning English. The general conclusions arising from these studies is that language aptitude and attitudinal/motivational characteristics are two relatively independent factors related to proficiency in the target language. As might be expected, however, the relative strength of these relationships varies somewhat from one context to another.

Many of these studies have suggested that a form of situational anxiety also plays an important role in this process. At least one researcher (Clément, 1980) proposed that self-confidence with the other language develops from an integrative motive and prior experiences with the other language community. Using causal modeling techniques, Lalonde and Gardner (1984) demonstrated, furthermore, that high levels of motivation tend to "cause" reduced levels of anxiety and thus greater self-confidence with the language. In addition to being related to measures of target language achievement, attitudinal/motivational variables have also been linked with persistence in language study and active participation in the language classroom (see Gardner, 1985), suggesting that they have a wide-ranging influence in this context.

Role-playing and dramatic techniques

Role-playing and dramatic techniques are generally used by teachers to bolster the learner's motivation (Wright, 1979; Stern, 1980; K. Jones, 1982). In such settings, students are required to express their thoughts, feelings, or intentions, so that the focus of their attention is not on learning but rather on communication. These techniques, therefore, exemplify simulation strategies that foster language development. Although no research has been conducted that looks at the role of language aptitude and/or integrative motivation in such settings, it seems reasonable to assume that they would mediate the level of achievement developed. Clearly, other research does indicate that related social psychological variables are involved.

It has been observed, for example, that role-playing techniques reduce anxiety associated with communicating in a new language (e.g., Jones, 1982), presumably in part because the teaching role is reduced. Social comparison theory (Festinger, 1954) would suggest that this occurs because comparisons of abilities are operating at a more comfortable level. Individuals tend to compare their abilities with those of others, and in more traditional language courses the focus of comparison is often the more able language teacher. In role-playing, however, the focus of comparison is on peers, and thus the differences in ability will tend to be reduced, resulting in less anxiety.

A second consequence of role-playing is that it can encourage (or even create) a sense of self-confidence to the extent that the participants become so involved in the simulation that their self-consciousness is reduced. Since many role-playing tasks are loosely structured, the course of events is often self-directed. The self-directed nature of role-playing and the immediate feedback in terms of content promote self-confidence, which may not be acquired readily in more traditional language programs. From an empirical perspective, Clément (1980) and Lalonde and Gardner (1984) have demonstrated that self-confidence is an important determinant of language proficiency. It follows, therefore, that methods that can promote self-confidence will serve to enhance second language performance.

One other feature of role-playing is that it permits the development of the nonverbal component of language. Participants can experiment with movement and facial expressions in a dramatic situation and thus may learn some of the subtleties which often distinguish one language from another. These secondary features of language become even more salient when video is introduced (Wright, 1980b). When students are given the opportunity to observe themselves in a new language, they acquire the sense that language is more than the simple use of words; it embodies actions that may express ethnicity and culture. It is reasonable to assume, moreover, that it would also make attitudinal/motivational variables more salient.

Immersion programs

Immersion programs differ in length from short-term programs of five or six weeks' duration to long-term programs involving an academic year or more. They also differ in terms of implementation, some beginning when the child is very young, and others starting in more advanced grades (Tucker, 1974). Such programs are used here as examples of the highest level of simulation, though some may not agree that they are even simulations. To a considerable extent, the immersion program is more than a "working representation of reality"; it is reality. Students in these programs are required to work and interact in the target language. Substantive courses like geography or arithmetic are taught in the other language, and even extracurricular activities focus on communication in the other language. Nonetheless, since at least one purpose of such programs is to promote proficiency in another language, they can be viewed as simulations of more socially oriented communication.

Relatively few studies have examined the role of affective and cognitive variables on target language achievement in immersion programs, but those that have suggest that these variables are influential even in this context. One study, for example, conducted by Tucker et al. (1976), investigated the role of such variables in three types of programs (early immersion, late immersion, and a traditional language program). They found that different variables interacted with the different programs to predict achievement in different language skills. One finding they obtained, which is particularly relevant to the present discussion, was that attitudinal/motivational variables contributed significantly to prediction of all indices of language proficiency.

Students in immersion programs obviously develop higher levels of proficiency in the other language than students studying the language in a regular curriculum (Swain & Lapkin, 1982). There is even some indication that participation in such programs results in attitude change, particularly among young students (Lambert & Tucker, 1972). In reviewing studies of both short-term and long-term immersion programs, Gardner (1985) concludes, however, that it would appear that "changes in social attitudes assessed at the time may be greatest where the programmes involve novel experiences of rather brief duration" (p. 106). Long-term programs may nonetheless have long-term consequences, as demonstrated by Cziko et al. (1980). These researchers investigated graduates of the St. Lambert program (which was an elementary school program) many years later as they were finishing high school. In comparison with a control group, these students expressed more self-confidence and satisfaction with their proficiency in the second language, and more favorable attitudes toward the target language community.

Conclusion

As this brief review indicates, attitudinal/motivational variables and language aptitude appear to be implicated in second or foreign language acquisition regardless of how closely the particular context comes to approaching the truly communicational use of language. It remains to be determined whether or not teachers can actually instill such predispositions, but, if this is the case, many exciting possibilities arise. A new role for the researcher could then be to determine the characteristics of simulation methods that nurture positive attitudes and motivation such that teachers may work them into their teaching strategies. Because of the link between language and self-identity, the learning of another language requires adjustments on the part of the individual. Simulation might provide an environment that will facilitate such adjustments!

Acknowledgments

Preparation of this chapter was facilitated by a research grant from the Social Sciences and Humanities Research Council of Canada to the senior author, and a postdoctoral fellowship, also from SSHRCC, to the junior author.

Chapter 19

Simulation/gaming and language acquisition

Robin Scarcella
University of California, Irvine

David Crookall
University of Alabama

Many educators have recognized the value of simulation and gaming activities in language instruction. However, despite intuition as to their value, no comprehensive rationale for using simulation/gaming in foreign and second language learning has yet been developed. This chapter, therefore, presents a brief rationale for the use of simulation/gaming in language learning, first by reviewing some of the relevant research and then by discussing ways in which simulation may encourage the development of specific skills.

Factors affecting language acquisition

Current research provides us with some of the clues to understanding how simulation may facilitate second or foreign language acquisition. This research investigates factors which have been shown to help successful language learning, including comprehensible input, active involvement with this input, and positive affect.

Comprehensible input

One theory proposes that learners acquire language when they are exposed to large quantities of "comprehensible input" (Krashen, 1980a, 1980b, 1981, 1982). Input is thought to be comprehensible when it is near the learner's current proficiency level, and it is hypothesized to be optimum when it is just a little beyond the learner's current proficiency level. "The best input is the input that we naturally give people when we talk to them so that they can understand" (Krashen, 1982). In line with work on speech accommodation theory (see, e.g., Giles & Smith, 1979), and when the situation is characterized by a communicative and cooperative climate, speakers tend to provide their conversational partners with comprehensible input. When their partners fail to understand them, speakers may simplify their language; for example, they slow down, change the topic to one which can be more readily understood, repeat, use simpler sentences, or check to make sure that their partners are following. (For a review of the literature on simplified input, see, e.g., Gass & Madden, 1985.) Research on communication patterns in second/foreign language simulation already provides us with insight into some of the ways in which simplification and accommodation take place (see Sharrock & Watson, 1985; K. Jones, 1986).

If, as the theory suggests, natural language results in comprehensible input, then simulation presents a major advantage because, by encouraging genuine communication, it provides students with large quantities of such input. Moreover, because simulation is a socially bounded activity and the consequence (for the outside, nonsimulation, world) of making errors is relatively low, participants are under less pressure to produce complex language, than they may well be in many natural or "real-world" situations. The relatively safe environment provided by simulation allows participants to use and repeat simpler language, as well as to examine their errors.

The theory also suggests that the best input for beginners may come from other language learners, since this input is often likely to be just above the beginner's current level (Krashen, 1980b). Later, when the students reach a more advanced stage, it is suggested that more optimum input might be provided by native speakers who are sympathetic to the linguistic and cultural backgrounds of nonnative speakers and who thus simplify their own language. If this is true, simulation should be an ideal tool for providing language students with optimum input, since they can be given sufficiently simplified and comprehensible models of input from native speakers and even more simplified models of input from their peers.

Active involvement

A number of research reports have demonstrated that exposure to input is insufficient; that is, even when learners are exposed to large quantities of input, this alone does not result in optimum language learning. For example, Swain and Lapkin (1982) suggest that learners who begin exposure to French at very young ages do not acquire French with nativelike proficiency despite the large quantities of input they receive. As Long (1983) points out, learners may be exposed to input but not necessarily pay attention to it. The research on simulation (see, e.g., Greenblat, 1975; Orbach, 1979, Bredemeier & Greenblat, 1981) shows that it generates high levels of motivation and involvement. Simulation, by inherently generating motivation and involvement, in one sense helps draw attention to input. As we shall see, though, it also helps the language learner to concentrate on communicating meaning—in other words, to become a motivated language user.

Grimshaw and Holden (1976) propose a slightly different explanation of why learners may not acquire language despite exposure to large quantities of input. They suggest that this phenomenon may be explained by the notion "functional economy." Learners put their efforts into activities which appear to them to be the most essential. When learners have arrived at the stage of being able to communicate minimally or sufficiently with others and to negotiate their social relations with relative effectiveness, they then begin to expand their learning horizons and put their efforts to other objectives. Because certain situations requiring higher communicative challenge or complexity may be relatively rare, many students will not feel the necessity of learning the more difficult skills required in such situations; they may perceive other activities to be more attractive or urgent.

One important characteristic of simulation is its capacity to allow a wide range of complex and varied communication patterns and social relations to develop. In addition, simulation allows the topic or issues under discussion to be dealt with at a variety of levels of complexity, thereby allowing participants to continue to be attracted to learning. Simulation therefore tends to raise the level at which "enough has been learned"—in Grimshaw and Holden's terms, it helps to increase the level of functional economy. Because it is inherently motivating, simulation may encourage learners to be more willing to continue expending energy on language learning—or rather, on activities which encourage the learning of language.

One effective way of encouraging students to attend to the input is to provide opportunities for them to become actively involved with it. Stevick (1976) calls this "charging" the input. As noted above, research on simulation suggests that participation in simulation generates high levels of involvement, and it thus helps to charge the input because it involves students in worthwhile, absorbing interaction. Such involvement tends to encourage students to forget they are learning the new language, and simply to use the language in a socially and personally meaningful and intellectually interesting situation. In this way, linguistic abilities are stretched and language use begins to resemble ordinary language use outside the classroom. As Brumfit (1984) points out, when learners are put into situations in which they communicate purposefully and spontaneously, they develop their abilities to use the language creatively and appropriately. Simulation is a way of providing learners with a reasonably natural context in which they may be allowed (rather than cajoled) to communicate, and thus of deploying their own idiosyncratic creativity, both socially and lin-guistically. The natural context of immediate feedback provides them with clues or indices about the appropriateness and effectiveness of their com-munication.

Positive affect

Research has identified another factor which appears essential for suc-cessful language acquisition; this is "positive affect." Schumann (1975, 1978) has long talked about the importance of affect (the learner's desires, feelings, and attitudes) in facilitating second language development. Sim-ilarly, Gardner and Lambert (1972), Gardner (1985), and others reason that a process involving some form and degree of reidentification underlies the long-term motivation needed to master an additional language. Yet others, such as Krashen (1982) and Dulay and Burt (1978), argue that low-anxiety situations (which Gardner, 1985, suggests operate through motivation) are conducive to language development. Many simulation contexts have the potential of creating a supportive, low-anxiety environment which fosters positive affect since, in simulation, students have the opportunity to try out new behaviors in a relatively safe environment. It may also be that this environment encourages elaboration of new behaviors.

Specific aspects of language development

Having discussed some of the factors which appear to facilitate lan-guage acquisition, we would like to consider more specific skills involved in language development.

Reading

In the last few years, researchers have pointed out the importance of schemata in teaching students to read. According to Carrell (1984), readers relate meaning to schemata which result from cultural expectations and prior experience. When their expectations and experiences are the same as the writer's, reading is facilitated. When their expectations and expe-riences are different, their reading may be impaired. Some simulations give students new experiences and encourage an openness to see things in a new light, thus altering their existing schemata.

In addition to increasing the learners' target language experiences, simulations may also provide learners with exposure to a wide range of genres (such as letters, documents, and telegrams) to which students are not often sufficiently exposed in the language classroom. Also, as a result of involvement in the simulation task, learners may become better motivated to read.[1]

Writing

Simulation is especially helpful in teaching writing. First, it provides students with situations in which writing occurs naturally. As Littlejohn and Hicks (1986) point out, in many classrooms students are asked to write about topics in a vacuum. It is extremely difficult to make anyone *want* to write under such conditions. In contrast with these rather dull writing exercises, simulation tasks provide students with opportunities to write about interesting, relevant, and motivating experiences. Second, simulation helps students overcome writer's block by producing a "high degree of student involvement rarely found in ESL writing activities" (Littlejohn & Hicks, 1986). Third, simulation can be particularly helpful in the brainstorming and revising stages of the writing process. It provides students with opportunities to *see* their ideas in action and to *observe* the consequences of their ideas and the alternatives.[2]

Verbal interaction skills

In the mid-1960s notions of linguistic competence were expanded. Linguistics became concerned with language appropriateness (that is, how people vary their language according to the situational context, e.g., Halliday et al., 1970), rules for conversation (such as openings and closings, e.g., Sacks et al., 1974; Schegloff, 1987; agreement and contiguity, e.g., Sacks, 1987), speech acts (such as apologies and complaints, e.g., Austin, 1962; Searle, 1969), and communication strategies (which enable speakers to stretch their ability to communicate competently, e.g., Tarone, 1981). Hymes (1972) used the expression "communicative competence" to describe a person's ability to communicate appropriately. Underlying this ability are the rules and principles governing what to say to whom and in what manner.

Canale and Swain's (1980) framework expands upon that of Hymes. In their view, communicative competence minimally involves four areas of knowledge and skills. These include (1) grammatical competence, which

[1]For further discussion on the use of games and simulations to encourage reading, see Chapter 9, this volume, and also Crookall and Watson (1985) and Lonergan and Crookall (1986).

[2]For an example of simulation/games which involves writing, see Littlejohn (1988).

reflects knowledge of the linguistic code itself and includes knowledge of vocabulary and word formation; (2) sociolinguistic competence, which "addresses the extent to which utterances are produced and understood appropriately" (Swain, 1984) and includes knowledge of speech acts such as the apology and the refusal; (3) discourse competence, which involves mastery of how to combine grammatical forms and meanings to achieve a unified or written text in different genres such as "narrative, argumentative essay, scientific report or business letter" (Swain, 1984); and (4) strategic competence, which "refers to the mastery of the communication strategies that may be called into action either to enhance the effectiveness of communication or to compensate for breakdowns in communication" (Swain, 1984). See also Omaggio (1986) for application of this framework in developing foreign language proficiency.

Researchers such as d'Anglejan (1978), Henzl (1979), Holmes and Brown (1976), and others have discussed the limitations of the language classroom in developing communicative competence. They have pointed out that only in the classroom does one speaker (the teacher) normally control the entire conversation, determining, for example, who will speak (and who will not), what will be spoken about (and what will not), and even how long the conversation will last and when it will end. In addition, as Delamont (1976), Long and Sato (1983), Stubbs (1976), and others have also noted, only in the classroom are conversational participants so frequently asked display or "test" questions, which call for answers demonstrating knowledge. In the language class this usually means answers about grammatical features. Genuine communication is frequently absent. Students are often exposed to one predominant register, usually teacher talk. They fail to learn different registers, such as the casual talk between friends or argumentation in a work setting.

A varied repertoire of registers is important in all classrooms, but it is particularly so in language classrooms. In a geography classroom the matter being learned is not language, but in a language classroom the subject matter is the very same as the medium through which it is being taught. In a language classroom, teacher talk is the primary model which students encounter in learning their subject matter. Because the figurehead is the teacher, such a model becomes particularly powerful, and if the model does not reflect the full range of types to be found in the outside world, students are less likely to gain a full picture of how language is used in the "outside" world.

Simulation can compensate for the limitations of the traditional teacher-centered language classroom by relocating the locus of conversational control and allowing other language models to be introduced and experienced. Indeed, simulation can go some way toward "declassrooming" the classroom, as Sharrock and Watson (1985) put it. It can provide students with a whole range of conversational models between a variety of speakers (e.g., doctor/patient, boss/employee, lawyer/client) in a variety of speech situations. In addition, it can expose students to a variety of speech acts not normally found in teacher-centered classes, such as apologies, excuses, promises, threats, and compliments. It can also teach students rules of conversation. In some classes, simulation may provide students with opportunities to observe and/or interact with native speakers in extended discourse. It can also be used to develop communication strategies, such as miming, paraphrasing, and circumlocuting. These strategies can be used to stretch the learners' linguistic proficiency and can enable them to acquire language on their own long after the language class has ended. (For further discussion on these aspects, see Cunningsworth & Horner, 1985.)

Simulation can also be used to help students overcome communication difficulties. When speakers rely on the conversational features of their first language to communicate in another language, serious communication breakdowns may occur. In a series of papers, Gumperz (1978, 1982) documents these breakdowns. He discusses how Punjabi and Pakistani Indian speakers, when interacting with British professionals, constantly use the word "no" as a pause filler, in a similar fashion to the way it is used in their native language. Unfortunately, this results in negative stereotyping, whereby the British perceive the Punjabi and Pakistani speakers as hostile and negative.[3]

The advantage of simulation for learning about such problems derives, at least in part, from two basic features. First, simulation may allow such breakdowns and possible resulting hostility to be accepted more easily as part of a learning process and thus to be examined more dispassionately (especially in the debriefing phase). This is possible because participants know that errors in a simulation *can* be made, indeed are even encouraged, for the purpose of learning, and that the consequences of such errors do not go beyond the simulation. Related to this is the second feature. This is that simulation allows new behaviors to be "tried on"; it allows participants to experience new types of interaction patterns and customs and then to stand back and examine them more objectively. Simulation can thus be used to display, experience, and experiment with differences in communication style and to discuss the consequences of negative stereotyping. This in turn helps students overcome communication difficulties (see Scarcella, 1990a).

Culture and nonverbal behavior

Simulation can also help students acquire and internalize cultural norms. Language and culture are intertwined. It is difficult to teach one fully

---

[3]For interesting discussions of communication breakdowns, see, e.g., Phillips (1972), Gumperz & Tannen (1979), Scollon and Scollon (1983), and Weeks (1983).

without the other. Simulation can be used to teach a variety of culturally sensitive areas, such as greeting, tipping, apologizing, cheating, and self-presentation.

Nonverbal behavior is critically important in face-to-face interaction. Simulation can be used to teach, and to allow students to practice, aspects of nonverbal communication. Through simulation, students are not only exposed to a wide variety of gestures, they are also exposed to the finer features of nonverbal behavior that accompany discourse; for example, they learn that, in English, glancing away from one's interlocutor is a cue that one does not want to take the next turn of talk, and that downward head nods indicate the completion of talk.

Conclusion

Clearly, research and theory concerning the development of second and foreign language are only in the initial stages. Further study will undoubtedly provide a richer, broader understanding of language acquisition. It is our contention that such study will confirm the intuitions of many teachers and students—namely, that simulation is indeed a particularly powerful and enjoyable way of fostering language acquisition.

We have outlined in this chapter a number of reasons to believe that simulation/gaming can encourage improved language acquisition. These reasons include comprehensible input, active involvement, positive affect, reshaping and expanding schemata, communication strategies, and cultural understanding. Underlying these, though, is perhaps something even more fundamental—having fun while learning. So, perhaps "before anything else, we would like the students in our classrooms to become excited about and to enjoy learning, including learning a new language" (Enright & McCloskey, 1988). Despite the current paucity of research into some of the above reasons and the general effectiveness of simulation in language learning, one thing we can be sure of is that many simulations are delightfully enjoyable and learners have a lot of fun. This in itself makes learning more effective and may well be enough to warrant its use, for fun and enjoyment can do wonders in the language classroom, both for learners and for teachers!

Chapter 20

Realities in simulation/ gaming

D. R. Watson and W. W. Sharrock
Manchester University

One is always aware that to introduce the word "reality" into discussions is normally to invite many difficulties and confusions. In this case, however, we are sure that we are warranted in giving this troublesome expression a central place and are hopeful that we may contribute to the clarification of some of those difficulties that have come to attend it. In connection with the examination of gaming and simulation exercises, it seems to us that focusing on issues of "reality production" is not merely right but unavoidable, precisely because the issue of relationship to reality is live and central to the exercises themselves. What we will do in this brief chapter is to sketch in some sociological issues, outline a possible response to those, and indicate the direction in which that response might be taken in respect to the study of games and simulations. We should perhaps add that our comments are from outside and upon the world of gaming and simulation: We seek, from the standpoint of sociology, to describe and analyze what people are doing in staging simulations and games and are not ourselves directly concerned with challenging or justifying their use, or with assessing or improving their efficacy as teaching instruments.[1]

We regard it as important, in thinking about social activities, to try to draw people's attention toward things with which they are familiar and about which they may be satisfied that they know all there is to know. We have no intention of suggesting that they are perhaps erroneous in such a supposition, but we want to try to point out to them that their very familiarity with them may be such as to blunt their awareness of them, and that when they come to reflect on things that they do, they may just

---

[1]In this respect our position differs somewhat from that adopted by Heap (1971). His paper occasionally tends to alternate considerations derived from the "practical attitude" with those derived from the "theoretical attitude."

overlook and leave out of account the very things that they would, in a less reflective mode, be depending upon for the conduct of their affairs.

The kind of idea we have in mind is that of, for example, "the social construction of reality," an idea which many seem to think deeply disturbs our conception of what reality is. Some think that this is for the better, and that it will replace unjustifiable absolutist beliefs with a much healthier relativism. Others accept that the consequence of taking the idea of social construction of reality seriously would indeed mean giving up absolutist beliefs but think that this would also involve giving up much else that we treasure (in particular, our attachment to our science) and would, in any case, be simply a mistake.

The reader can now see why introduction of the term "reality" can engender the difficulties we warned about, because it can draw us into the complicated, long-running, and so-far-unresolved controversies about the objectivity or otherwise of reality. We want, however, to pitch our arguments in such a way that they take us, not into these controversies, but away from them. Rather than beginning with the supposition that the idea of reality as a social construction is a conception which subverts or negates our usual suppositions, we might want to suggest that it is one which, instead, can and should serve to draw out our usual suppositions. Far from pointing us to things of which we have been hitherto unaware, it serves to provide a forceful reminder of things with which we are familiar, and which affect our conduct and the social settings produced through that conduct including the settings we call "games" and "simulations."

The consideration of gaming and simulation exercises provides an excellent opportunity for the elucidation of this point (and of our "usual presuppositions") precisely because it is a feature of the introducing, contriving, and conduct of many such exercises that considerations as to the reality of what is going on in the exercise and how that relates to the reality of real-world situations are intrinsically important to their organization.

Our remarks are confined, in what follows, to the use of gaming and simulation in pedagogic work, and we would note that a base for the consideration of their role there is often in terms of the objective of introducing "real-world" factors into the classroom. It happens that the classroom has for some reason come to be conceived as an "unreal world" and that it is unreal by comparison with other situations, paradigmatically those of work and practice. Contrasts between the real and the unreal in this connection are characteristically intended (as we read them) to point to the possession or lack of seriousness, consequentiality, and practicality in the two areas, respectively. Insofar as pedagogy is putatively engaged in preparing people for life and action outside the classroom, then it has been seen, for some time, as a problematical fact about the classroom that it is an unreal environment by contrast with that for which its activities are intended as preparation. The extent of the "unreality" of the classroom situation is something which can be very forcefully impressed upon those who move from it into the "real world" of practice, so much so that Miriam Wagenschein was moved, many years ago, to describe the transition experienced by those moving from teacher training into teaching as a "reality shock."

Thus, the first service of our approach is to enable us to see that it is putatively a task for the teaching profession, and certainly the actual task of many of its practitioners, to reorganize pedagogic practice in order to move the classroom situation closer to reality (though we might add that the measures which they conceive as achieving that are various and may well be at odds with one another). Insofar as the general point about talk of a social construction of reality is concerned, we hope that even these brief remarks show that there is nothing amiss or unlikely in suggesting that people are engaged in organizing and reorganizing action in order to set up, to produce, situations which have "the accent of reality" (an expression which we take from Alfred Schütz). Whether events which take place within a classroom and the situations which they produce there will be adjudged real or more like real life will depend upon what people *do*, and it is in that sense that we talk of their constructing (or, as we would prefer, "producing") reality.

As we indicated, there are different ways in which the classroom world may be found to deviate from reality. We do not want to suggest that it is the educator's problem solely to find ways of bringing classroom situations into line with reality, for it is also the educator's problem to determine how, in the first instance, the classroom world is *relevantly* an unreal one. Where solutions will be sought will depend on where the problem is perceived to lie.

One strand which we have noticed in pedagogic attempts to deal with the unreality of the classroom situation is by what we have called "de-classrooming." At least a partial answer to the problem, as far as some are concerned, is to reorganize classroom activities such that they are less like the traditional situation. They seek an in-classroom solution to the problem, the measures that they take being implemented within the classroom itself but through a restructuring of the activities housed there so that they depart from conceptions of the traditional classroom. These involve two particularly important aspects: (1) restructuring relations between teacher and pupil and (2) reconstructing the relevances of the educative task.

The traditional relationship of teacher and pupil has fallen into disrepute in many circles (though there may be moves to rehabilitate its standing currently afoot), and the corresponding traditional arrangement of the classroom ecology with the teacher talking to seated pupils falls into equal disrepute as the method of implementing and sustaining that relationship. This traditional relationship is in disrepute, partly because it sustains an authoritarian relationship where these are, themselves, increasingly disapproved, but also because it is seen to be incompatible with effective learning and with the transmission of the kind of knowledge and skill that is to be imparted through it.

What goes on in the classroom is further conceived to involve the discharge of responsibilities to the society at large, and educators are called upon not merely to relay new information but to adapt to changes in the nature of knowledge available in society and to meet the identified needs of society in terms of providing an appropriate output (whatever that may be determined to be). In that respect, educators are called upon to change their conceptions of what are suitable matters for inclusion within a curriculum, what are suitable topics for instruction in classrooms, and therefore what activities may be suitably located in the classroom. For example, the extension of gaming and simulation promotes the notion of play as an activity suitable to classrooms rather than just to the schoolyard.

Thus, the adoption of gaming and simulation is continuous with other ways of restructuring the classroom to make it less like the traditional classroom, to employ teaching methods which (for example) place the onus on the students to do things for themselves and to discover what they need to know, where guidance displaces instructions, and where the purpose is (sometimes) to enable the acquisition of skills that could not be acquired in the "traditional" setting (i.e., the natural conversational skills, for speaking a new language). On the other hand, gaming and simulation exercises may (alternatively or simultaneously) be designed to make the classroom *more like* some real-world environment, as in the case of the provision of situations in which second language learners are placed in situations in which they must attempt natural conversational use of the language in ways that would not be possible in the framework of a teacher-pupil relationship.

We want, though, to emphasize the extent to which, in these situations, the relationship to "reality" is complex and problematical for parties and is oriented to as such: what real-world linguistic behavior requires is *not* something that is readily and definitely specified, which would mean that persons contriving games and simulations are seeking to determine both (1) what real-worldly behavior is like and (2) whether adequate—for the purposes of learning—approximations to this can be produced within the classroom environment.

Further, we would point out that the problems as to how reality is to be found within the game/simulation situation is not solved outside the game/simulation itself. We want to draw attention, finally, to the way in which the participants in the game are given the task of finding out how to play it, of determining just in what ways and with what effort they are to seek to manage the relationship between "it's only a game" and "we are supposed to be in a real situation." Thus, one can see that players are, in mastering a game, feeling their way toward some relationship between these by looking at the uneases and uncertainties and the way in which these relate to the participants' conceptions of (and uncertainties about) how people might behave in corresponding real situations, and that these matters are also much affected by what one can do in a situation which is, after all, located in a classroom.

Let us now proceed to unpack further some of these aspects of "reality-construction." As we shall see, these aspects are far more complex than a simple simulation-reality dichotomy. We must not ask whether any given simulation maps or reflects some real-world situation, but instead we should ask how, and to what extent, do students and other parties to the simulation *treat* it as simulating reality? What are their practices in changing the "constitutive accent" so that the simulation is collaboratively taken by participants as realistic-for-all-practical purposes? Obversely, what are participants' practices in jointly sustaining an understanding that this simulation is not realistic or real-worldly? What is the communicative work which contributes to both the suspending and the sustaining of disbelief in simulations and games?[2]

The above set of analytic questions shifts the problem away from the usual issue of the extent to which various simulations and games mirror reality. The problem is moved to comprise a treatment of simulations and games in terms of participants' sustaining of game realities. The problem treats games and simulations as bounded frames of reference for participants' practices and as settings inhabited, so to speak, by these participants with their various involvements—settings with their own social organization, their own terms and definitions.

In turn, this line of approach focuses our analytic attention on the communicative/interactional competences deployed by participants—competences which are not game-specific but which form their generic cultural and interpretive competences. Consequently, as Heap (1971)[3] notes, any culturally competent member of society is potentially a competent game/simulation player. As Heap puts it, "similar types of interpretive procedures are required to understand both 'finite provinces of meaning,' as Alfred Schütz calls them."

A corollary of this position is that it shifts the focus onto other realities than the one(s) purportedly mirrored in the game, as we shall see. For example, participants bring to the simulation/game a variety of real-world identities, capacities, and understandings of what "typical" actions typically mean in everyday life, and in one form or another these realities may come to be woven into the texture of the game—not necessarily in a sub-

---

[2]The beginnings of an empirical analysis based on these questions are offered by the present authors elsewhere (Sharrock & Watson, 1985).

[3]Here the notion of culture denotes a corpus of procedural knowledge—i.e., of society members (interpretive) procedures for making sense of social settings, conduct, etc.

versive way, since game realities may on occasion usefully trade on these imported realities. Participants' orientations to the simulation/game frame of reference—a crucial topic for analytic scrutiny—may well trade on these imported identities in a whole range of currently unexplicated ways.

Another imported feature of games and simulations is conceived by Heap (1971) as, following Garfinkel's conception, a basic, external role, where basic rules constitute participants' commonsense devices for producing and displaying conduct recognizable to others (using the same rules) as examples of game conduct. The game rule which is instanced by Heap is that of "treat the (game-simulation) situation as if it were real" (our insertion in parentheses). For Heap, this is a rule which, strictly speaking, is external to the game/simulation setting. The ability to do this is, again, a feature of participants' competence—competence which is always operative in simulations and games, albeit tacitly so. It is our task to make explicit these taken-for-granted schemes of interpretation, so that they can be subjected to detailed analytic inspection.

This analytic approach, moreover, points us firmly in the direction of looking at the actual occurrence of games and simulations. The analysis of games and simulations must be firmly empirical; the same game or simulation may take on very different realizations on each occasion on which it is transacted. Games and simulations are, in other words, "contingent accomplishments" achieved and sustained through, and across, whole arrays of contingencies which by definition vary from occasion to occasion. Indeed, whether, in participants' or pedagogic terms, they succeed cannot be guaranteed in advance of any specific occasion. Each occasion of playing is, in Garfinkel's phrase, "another first time."

Consequently, any approach to the playing of games or simulations had better avoid ex cathedra generalizations and had better start much more modestly in examining these events in an instance-by-instance way, in as much detail as possible. The comments we have cautiously made above are derived from our initial inspections of video-recorded data and of transcripts thereof, and it is this order of data (what Mehan calls "retrievable data") which is required. If we want a detailed, finely tuned analysis of changes in constitutive accent among simulation- and game-players, then this order of data is *de rigeur*.

There is a tendency among those involved in devising, conducting, improving, assessing, and otherwise commenting upon games and simulations to rely upon their past experience and participant/nonparticipant observations in that sphere. However, past experience, however extensive, tends by its very nature to gloss over many of the salient details of simulation and gaming; we are thinking here of matters such as the details of what was said and the sequences involved, the nonverbal communication, the proxemics (spatial distribution of the group), and so on. At best, those transacting games and simulations will recollect such matters, if at all, in a very general and ad hoc way which necessarily edits out the texture of the events recalled. Moreover, the recollections and experience of the person who is running the game or simulations are "located" recollections and experiences; the students involved in the game may have very different recollections from their standpoint and practical interests.

Audio and video recording and transcription allow us to retrieve the interactional or social organizational details of specific occasions of simulations and details. Such recording and transcription allow us to focus on the organization of the verbal, kinesic, and proxemic transacting of the game by all concerned. We no longer need to rely for our theorizing and analysis on ad hoc recollections from particular standpoints and set of interests—recollections based on participants' tacitly accepted, unexplicated commonsense understandings and taken-for-granted models of gaming and simulation. Not only will these understandings and models be quite possibly empirically misleading, for analytic purposes, but also they do not provide adequate constraints on what can be said by the analysts about simulations and games. Recollected versions can be all too expedient for the analysts, tempting them into purpose-built, self-confirming anecdotal supporting "evidence" for their claims. Recording and transcription also allows the reader to assess the adequacy of the gamer's/simulator's claims with regard to retrievable data and allows claims to be checked in detail against a corpus of multiple instances of the same activity (e.g., starting or closing down games), and also allows simulators and gamers to avoid designing their claims (and, indeed, their recollections) in terms of the orthodox and conventional—albeit untested—conceptions prevalent in the field.[4] In short, the insistence on retrievable data avoids a variety of pitfalls inherent in the experience-based approach.

In another, highly prefatory, approach to simulation and gaming, based on video data, we noted several complications in the switches in constitutive accent/the accent of reality. The complications in some respects attested to what Schütz termed the paramountcy of the "natural attitude" of everyday life as opposed to the attitude adopted by, say, players within a "game reality." We found, in our empirical observations, a complex mix between the two attitudes, a mix that was socially displayed in the interpersonal communication within and around the game (e.g., in pregame talk).

An example of this mix was the players' orientation to gender. Although the roles given in the simulation/game were not as such oriented to, or based on, gender, passes were made (and rejected) by the male to the female players. Other examples were the establishing and displaying of what Goffman (1962) calls "role-distance." Various devices, such as

---

[4]On retrievable data, see Atkinson and Heritage (1984), especially the introduction and the chapter by Sacks (1984); on retrievable data in the sphere of education see Mehan (1978, 1979).

byplay, joking, and irony, could be used to establish distance from roles allocated within the game and from the game frame of reference. Moreover, since this was a game conducted in an English-as-a-foreign-language course, role distance could be achieved through utterances made in French, the native language of the players. Since English was the official language of the game, the utterances in French were hearable as asides and as nongame talk. The French language was, after all, the medium of these students' everyday life, and using French preserved some features of the attitude of everyday life across the relevances of the game. On the other hand, players could and did use their everyday commonsense knowledge of types of persons in playing the various game roles, and on occasion played them straight—i.e., with displayed seriousness and commitment.

These brief examples bear various relations to the playing of the game. Many of these phenomena might be seen as preserving the paramountcy of the attitude of everyday life in a manner which detracts from the bona fide playing of the game/simulation. Other of the devices may be seen as supportive of, and, perhaps, even essential to, the playing of the game/simulation; these were contextually occasioned matters. What was evident, though, was that the devices through which everyday life *and* game-playing attitudes were displayed were very much features of the transaction of the game and were intricately and inextricably interwoven with each other. Players' orientation to these realities (as displayed to and for each other and therefore recorded on video) is a highly complex matter in two senses: (1) In practical terms, it *may* (not *must*) present management problems for them in transacting the game/simulation. (2) Analytic problems for researchers arise. Unraveling these complexities analytically requires great care and is not possible without retrievable data. On top (and, partly, because) of these complexities, there are the ways in which players (not to mention directors/controllers/teachers and observers) may continuously monitor and assess various features of the game or simulation as realistic, authentic, contrived, phony, embarrassing, and so on.

We have argued that conceptions of reality are not all of a piece, but that this is so not because different people may have different conceptions of reality (though in some connections they may have). Rather, it is because people can recognize that there are different ways in which things can be real, can find themselves called upon to make things "realistic" and find that there are different and perhaps conflicting requirements thereby imposed upon their activities, presenting them with the task of managing those demands. They may do this by switching the accent of reality around, as in gaming, by, for instance, alternating between recognizing that it is only a game and taking the terms of the game as providing a reality within which, for now, they operate.

Chapter 21

Ethical issues

Robert V. Vernon
University of Michigan

Any classroom situation can produce a nightmare. Students can learn falsehoods; coercion can take place; cruel and unusual dynamics can arise. In this chapter, I describe some of the inherent problems which games can produce and provide basic guidelines for thwarting them. As both a designer and a user, I take the position that gaming is a powerful and invaluable teaching medium, but that sensitive vigilance is necessary.

A nightmare

Join me in a brief nightmare. Imagine that you especially enjoy teaching Framish Studies because the language is so expressive and the people of Framistan are modest, generous, and enlightened. You taught your favorite Introduction to the Framish Language course last semester. The class was made up of many different and enthusiastic students. One of the highlights was a game called FRAMISH VILLA. It was highly recommended by a trusted colleague and you had been pleased with the results. The students' evaluations of the game were exceptionally good, and you were delighted that it had modeled basic Framish customs so well.

This morning you saw a few of your old students and struck up a conversation. You asked what they thought of Framish life and culture. You were astounded. Each was convinced that the Framish are parochial, mean, cheap, and dull. To your amazement you discovered that they formed these firm conclusions directly from playing FRAMISH VILLA! You retreated to your office and called up your colleague. She too was shocked. You are both seasoned teachers and have been using simulations and games for years. You agree that the game is cleverly constructed, has been well received by students, is easily run, and mirrors the essentials of Framish life in a balanced way. Your colleague has used the game reliably for a long time. The designer is a reputable Framish scholar and gifted game creator. Yet the students formed awful conclusions based on the game.

Extreme? Not really. This story happened to a colleague of mine not long ago. All teaching media have their darker sides. Powerful lecturers can incite riots, and a few occasionally get stoned in the process. Our simulations and games, hopefully less lethal, can still pose serious ethical problems. Students can draw very false conclusions. People can be needlessly coerced and embarrassed. Harassment between students is not unknown. Grading a student's ability through simulation participation can be suspect. These and other side effects can produce disasters which are unwarranted and unfair. What can be done?

Ethical dilemmas

Marshall (1975), Orbach (1979), and Greenblat (1980) have described ethical dilemmas in the design and use of simulations and games. Other colleagues such as Duke (1974), Stadsklev (1974), and Shirts (1976) have discussed problems in a variety of contexts. Yet there are few hard-and-fast rules. We all have unique gaming styles. What works well for you may not work for me at all. The diversity of simulations and games is extreme. Structured experiences range from the very literal to the highly abstract. We use games in a wide variety of contexts and with many different audiences. Given these fundamental characteristics, it may be helpful to discuss general questions rather than list specific answers.

My first point is a simple but vital one. Simulations and games often teach *far* beyond their specifically designed objectives. What people actually learn by playing simulations and games is theoretically and empirically difficult to determine (Bredemeier & Greenblat, 1981). Other technologies have their hazards as well, as those of us who make the mistake of reading our own students' lecture notes quickly find out. But interactive technologies can be quite slippery. We need to remember that games present multiple dimensions. Cognitive, affective, *and* behavioral learnings take place simultaneously in many gamed experiences. Some learnings, invariably those never listed in the game's "objectives section," can be very detrimental. In our Framish horror story the game may have been cognitively accurate, but the feelings and behaviors generated during play may have seriously affected the final impressions made on the students. The reality is that covert and unanticipated messages can always be present, even in well-developed and reliable materials. While skillful debriefing will curb some of this, there are finite limits to what can be accomplished. It is always possible that spurious learnings will pass unnoticed. At the very least, it is helpful to ask what a game *may* be teaching beyond its specifically designed concepts. Potential adverse conclusions can be addressed at several points in the gaming process. Chapters 2 through 5 touch on these aspects and offer some specific suggestions.

The degree to which reality is abstracted may also invite unwanted consequences. Experiential learning tools can be classified along a spectrum which runs from detailed simulated environments to highly abstract games (Greenblat & Duke, 1981). Some simulations are almost baroque in reproducing literal gestalts right down to physically working telephones. As one progresses away from the literal toward the abstract, the chances of drawing ambiguous or false conclusions increases. Perhaps some of the transactions in FRAMISH VILLA were too symbolic and were never fully understood. Highly metaphoric games such as TALKING ROCKS and BAFA BAFA can be easily misinterpreted. The general issue becomes how to discover if players are reaching false conclusions and what steps can be taken to protect against this. Stadsklev's (1974) insight that debriefing is the place where actual learning occurs becomes paramount. Practical guidelines are provided in Chapter 4.

Our Framish class was made up of "many different and enthusiastic students." One common danger is to see only the group and overlook the nature of each individual's experience. Unless one is teaching Framish in a monastery, the reality is that all the participants depart with their own separate understanding, never again to be a part of the same group that shared the experience. It becomes very important to consider the potential impact a game may have on each individual within the class. This is certainly difficult because we generally know so little about our students prior to their taking the course. Traditional classroom conditioning has usually taught them to reveal as little of themselves as possible. Sensitivity to two issues is called for.

First, not everyone likes to play simulations and games. The research of Pratt et al. (1980) indicates that personality variables highly color the students' receptivity to games. Orbach (1979) discusses this problem extensively and concludes that certain types of students find simulations and games very uncomfortable and that playing alternatives should be available for them. Bereft of familiar routines and trusted transactions, fearful students can be made very insecure and feel undermined in gamed situations. The inherent problems of self-revelation and potential embarrassment become obvious. Perhaps the FRAMISH VILLA players we met this morning were a subset of these particular students. They may have compensated by individually or collectively discounting the game. Vigilance for unintentional violation of the individual becomes important.

These problems are far more common in simulations and games as compared with more passive teaching approaches because of the large degree of involvement most games produce. We need to address the general issue of how coercion and deception enter into a gamed situation and what preventive steps are called for. Greenblat's (1980) concern for individual coercion by groups, especially in competitive experiences, is most salient. Petranek's (1985) misgivings about "innocent deception" is highly articulate. The potential for psychological mayhem cannot be overlooked or underestimated, even with trusted materials.

Allied with this is a second phenomenon, which is not well understood. Some people learn quite a bit from simulations and games but others may not gain much at all. Cognitive styles can seriously effect what a student may be able to learn from a game (Bredemeier & Greenblat, 1981). Students who prefer experiential or experimental learning events may be at a distinct advantage over those who prefer learning in a more passive way. A crucial question is: Who will learn from this experience and who may not? It is often tempting to default on this issue and select a game for some specific category of students without considering others.

If we reflect for a moment that games can communicate undesired learning effects, that the degree of shared reality can be less than optimal, that some students do not value games, and that some people may not learn much from them, then a final nasty issue presents itself. The ability to play well may not be linked to the appropriate academic talent (Bredemeier & Greenblat, 1981). Games can be most beguiling. We see students enjoying themselves and learning many concepts we deem important. But this can be a veneer. Underneath it may lie very intense feelings of anxiety, stress, and competition. Students who enjoy playing educational games and seemingly are good at it may not be the students with the best mastery of the course materials (Allan Feldt, interview). Is grading fair under these circumstances?

Some solutions

All of these factors can produce unwanted and unfair consequences. How can we guard against them? The basic sequence of selecting, introducing, running, debriefing, and resolving simulations and games offers a process for preventing some of these outcomes. Selection affords us the opportunity to speculate on many of the factors I've discussed. Many ethical problems can be intuitively examined at this stage, and awareness of potential conflicts can prevent some problems at the outset. Our acquired professional judgment and wisdom can be immensely helpful. Harassment, stereotyping, and other adverse outcomes from role-playing can be contractually negotiated between participants when the game is introduced. Hidden agendas and other potentially backfiring surprises can be forewarned without revealing the specific contents. Many of the structural elements, such as scenarios, roles, and transactions, can be modified during the selection and introduction phases.

Attention to individual and group dynamics during the actual play is necessary beyond the level of simply keeping the event running. Norms for competition and cooperation can be discussed in advance and reiterated.

One can interrupt most games if countermeasures become necessary. Modifying roles and transactions during the game is often possible without seriously detracting from the action. Incomplete, spurious, and ambiguous learning problems are certainly best addressed during debriefing, but calling players' attention to false dynamics during the event can make the final resolution easier. Carefully directed papers or similar end-event activities give us an excellent chance to evaluate the individuals' understanding of the subject which is independent from their participation skills. In summary, each step in the process offers an opportunity to anticipate and overcome ethical problems.

Conclusions

The FRAMISH VILLA nightmare could have resulted from any of the factors I've discussed and from other factors as well. Some problems can be anticipated but others cannot. We all risk occasional disasters no matter how seasoned we are. The most reliable game can produce undesired results. The most benign group can injure its members. Yet careful attention to potential ethical problems can help eliminate adverse effects. While the dangers are real, we certainly should not abandon gaming. All other teaching media have hazards as well. To omit gaming from our repertoire would be to deprive our students of powerful opportunities to grow and to learn. Games are experimental and can have adverse effects, mishaps, and mistakes. These can be minimized for participants through careful attention on the part of the teacher. Ignoring the risks invites an accidental visit to Framistan.

Questions and activities

1. Draw a conceptual map of the theoretical linkages among simulation/gaming, culture, communication, and language learning. What other links may be made? What light do these interrelations shed upon discussions in other chapters in the book?
2. In what ways may social psychological difficulties of learning another language be reduced by the use of simulation/gaming? In what other ways does simulation/gaming help in learning and acquiring another language? How may an understanding of these ways help teachers use simulation/gaming more effectively in the classroom?
3. What do ethnomethodologists do? How might their work enlighten language teachers? Compare the findings in Chapter 20 with those discussed in other ethnomethodological work (see Anderson, Francis, Sharrock, and Watson in the References). What implications does all this have for classroom practice?
4. What are the key ethical questions in using simulation for language learning and how may they influence our use of this methodology in the language class? And what implications do such ethical questions have for us as a profession more generally?

Sample simulation/games

Materials: The participants' manual (provided below)—1 copy for each participant; a large board (white or black) or flip chart.

Task: Individuals organize themselves into groups, within certain constraints and preferences.

Space: Large open space free of furniture for the game; small group tables for follow-up work.

Audience: Language learners from intermediate to advanced.

Development and overview of the game

The original idea for this game came out of a teacher training workshop held at the British Council, Paris. A group of about 15 English language teachers attended a three-day workshop on the design of simulation for the purposes of teaching English as a foreign language. During this workshop, participants took part in a number of games, and then played the LANGUAGE SIMULATION DESIGN GAME (see Chapter 23).

The rudiments of ISLAND ESCAPE constituted one of three games that came out of that workshop. In the original scenario a volcanic island was about to be destroyed by an eruption. The inhabitants of the island had to cluster themselves into small groups and escape in those groups. Their decisions were based on personal characteristics and on the nature of other islands to which they might escape. The present authors (along with Alan Coote and Danny Saunders) took the basic idea and then changed and developed it substantially. For instance, we added details (e.g., the capacity and number of escape boats), wrote the the present descriptions of the destination islands, wrote a full manual, and compiled a detailed personal background questionnaire.[1]

Notes for game organizers are to be found at the end of the chapter after the game materials, which follow next. We suggest you read through the game materials before going to the notes for organizers. The game materials start here.

[1]For more details about how this game was developed and for an account of how one particular run of it went disastrously wrong (an experience which helped considerably in the design process), readers are referred to Crookall, Oxford et al. (1988).

Introduction

Sample simulation/games

So far in this book you have learned a great deal about how language learning and simulation/gaming are linked and how language learning can be enhanced through simulation/gaming. But no matter how much you have learned from reading the previous sections, there is no way you can fully understand simulation/gaming, or any other experiential learning activity, without actually trying it yourself. Good ways to gain experience include implementing a simulation/game in a language class with your students or trying out a simulation/game with your colleagues in a teacher training course. In order to do either of these, you need complete simulation/games that you can use or adapt. This section therefore provides two such activities, one for students and the other for teachers in training.

The first simulation/game, found in Chapter 22, is called the ISLAND GAME. Adapted from a blueprint originally developed by a group of teachers of English as a foreign language, this game involves leaving an island on which a volcano is about to blow up. Participants must organize themselves into unified, operational groups to prepare for the dangerous escape by sea, and they must decide on their new destinations. Negotiating, planning, arbitrating, decision making, and cooperating are all essential in this game, which can be used as an ice-breaker or as a more serious communication activity. This game can be used successfully in language classes at different levels of proficiency. Encourage, but do not force, students to use the target language as much as possible throughout the activity. Once they get involved, they typically want to use the new language; the impetus should come from them, not from you. For students at beginning and low-intermediate levels, you might want to provide a short list of key vocabulary related to the game, or have them develop a list for themselves. You might also wish to give them a short list of functional phrases. Help students to realize, however, that they do not need to understand every single word that is said and that they can communicate with each other even without an extensive vocabulary or a complete grasp of all relevant grammar points. The focus is on communicating meaning. Chapters 2 and 4 will be particularly useful to you in preparing to run the game.

Chapter 23 describes how to use a teacher training game for discussing and understanding the simulation/game design process. The game found in this chapter is specifically oriented toward language teachers and others who want to explore how simulation/games may be developed and how the components are interrelated. It is also very useful for those who might someday like to take the next step, designing their *own* simulation/games for the language classroom.

Though space does not allow us to include more than these two simulation/games in this section, the following section provides an extensive, annotated list of sources of such activities in almost any field of interest. Be sure to look there for additional activities. When you consider simulation/games, your best approach is to ask yourself some important questions, including the following: What seems most useful to me? What can I use or adapt, no matter what field it comes from? What would my students enjoy? What would be stimulating and fun? What would promote learning? What kinds of language skills do I want to foster, and which simulation/games might help? Which ones might be most useful for students, and which might be best for teacher training?

Identify interesting simulation/games (and supporting works that discuss the process of design, adaptation, and use) and try them out with students and colleagues. Experiment and be creative. Have fun with the experience, and encourage others to have fun, too. Language learning need not be painful and onerous; it can be entertaining and liberating—as well as more effective—when you use simulation/games.

Chapter

The ISLAND GAME

David Crookall and Rebecca L. Oxford
University of Alabama

Most ice-breaking games (in a native or a new language) are exercises, without a great deal of substance. They tend to remain su ficial, and thus participants get to know each other only superficially. two objectives of the ISLAND GAME (also known as ISLAND ESCA are more substantial: first as an extended ice-breaker, second as a collect decision-making activity. Both these help develop a range of commu cation skills in the target language. If ice-breaking is the main goal, tl second objective serves and amplifies the first. The game encourages pa ticipants to reveal certain aspects of themselves, which are then used a the basis for complex, collective decision making. This in turn allows participants to get to know each other more intimately than they might in shorter ice-breaking games.

Outline of the game

Game data

Basic information about the game is as follows:

Basic aims: To provide an extended and nonsuperficial ice-breaking activity and to develop skills in decision making and cooperation.

Time: From 1 to 1½ hours for the main game, plus another 1 to 1½ hours if the follow-up work is done.

Numbers: From 15 to 35. If the group is larger than 35, either two games may be run in parallel (which has the advantage of being able to compare two runs of the game) or more boats and destination islands may be added to the manual.

The ISLAND GAME (also known as ISLAND ESCAPE)

Aims and synopsis

The ISLAND GAME is primarily an ice-breaker, but it is also a game which involves problem solving and decision making under pressure, negotiation and bargaining about detailed issues, and preferences based on complex information. These are skills that can best be learned through active participation and experience. The ISLAND GAME attempts to provide participants with an environment which will allow them to practice and improve these skills, and also to get to know one another better, as well as to have fun.

The scene is an island upon which you, the participants, have been marooned. In order to escape from the island you must make decisions on what information to reveal, what destination you wish to go to, whom you wish to go with, and the like. This involves weighing complex sets of data on the above questions as well as on your own and others' personal profiles. There is no single correct solution to the problem.

The game is in three stages: a preparation stage (where you fill in the attached profiles, and where nobody may talk), the game itself (see below), and the debriefing.

The situation and the problem

You are one of a group of people, until now almost unknown to one another, who have been shipwrecked on an island, called Alderada. Unfortunately, the island is about to be destroyed by a volcanic explosion, not dissimilar to Krakatoa. At the start of play, the projected time of eruption is in 30 minutes to one hour. This means that you have some 30 to 60 minutes to make your decisions before the volcano erupts and engulfs you in its molten lava and suffocating ashes. However, as the exact moment of a volcanic eruption cannot be forecast with certainty, the exact amount of time you have is unknown. As the fatal moment closes in, you will receive updates on the amount of time left before your escape becomes a matter of life and death. Obviously, the closer the time comes, the more accurate the information will be. You will be told which warning is the last.

There are enough lifeboats (salvaged from the shipwrecked vessel) to take everyone away to some safer, distant islands. These islands vary in their geomorphology, climate, flora, and fauna, as well as in whether or not they are inhabited. The range of geographical characteristics is broad enough to suit everyone's taste, and details of these are to be found on the accompanying Island Survey.

Some of the islands are inhabited, and this is also indicated on the Island Survey. However, it is known that the arrival of more than a total of five people on an inhabited island would be considered a threat by the local tribespeople, who are likely to become dangerously hostile. This means that not more than one boat may go to the same island, including uninhabited ones (to be on the safe side just in case tribes have arrived on islands thought to be uninhabited at the time when the Island Survey was drawn up).

The escape boats you have are listed below, but you may find out that some of them are not seaworthy; the game organizer will inform you during the game which ones are not seaworthy. In addition, owing to various factors (e.g., size, food and water rations, number of oars, hull strength), there is a maximum number of people who can safely put to sea in them. Also, and again owing to several factors (e.g., size, maneuverability, navigation constraints), there is also a minimum number of people who must sail in a boat for it to be certain of arriving at its destination. The minimum and maximum number of people who may board the boats are as follows (there is no relationship between the name of the boat and its capacity):

Boat name	Min. capacity	Max.	Boat name	Min. capacity	Max.
a	2	3	e	4	5
b	2	4	f	4	6
c	3	4	g	5	6
d	3	5	h	5	7

In addition to deciding on passengers for the lifeboats—i.e, the crew members for the escape vessels—you must also choose a captain. Her or his rights and responsibilities will be the same as those of any captain on any ship. (Remember too that the captain is always the last to leave a sinking ship.)

You must also remember that once you arrive at your destination island, you will have to remain there for a certain period of time, up to about 10 years. This is because potential rescue ships ply the surrounding waters only at certain intervals. These times are indicated on the Island Survey. In addition, indigenous communities are fearful of subsequent colonization and will not therefore allow people to leave at all from inhabited islands.

Your task, therefore, is to decide who is to leave the island with whom.

The variables you have to take into account in coming to your decision include destination island characteristics and population, boat capacities and requirements, personal preferences, social groupings, and leadership styles. You have to try to ensure that members of each unit escaping from your present island will be able to live together for the time period concerned.

As the lifeboats are being checked for seaworthiness, no one can leave the island until after a certain time to be specified by the game organizer. Also, no one can leave before the group as a whole has come to a consensus on the major decisions to be reached—i.e., who leaves in what boat and goes to what destination island. In arriving at a consensus, there should be broad agreement by everyone on the decisions taken. It will probably be useful for you to draw up a large table (on a blackboard or flip chart) indicating your decisions, so that everyone can see what is being decided. An example table is given below.

Boat name	Destination island	Crew members (captain underlined)
d	Aceber	Sue, Tom, Dick, Harry, <u>Sally</u>
f	Lakorc	name 1, <u>name 2</u>, name 3, etc.
g	etc.	

Before you start discussions, you all should fill in your Profiles. Your final decision on how to subdivide into your escape groups must be a collective one. Attached you will find the following documents:

Island Survey	Providing information on the possible destinations.
Personal Profile	Personal characteristics questionnaire—guidelines on how to use this are to be found at the top of the profile.

Island survey

1. Aceber With a climate midway between temperate and Mediterranean, this island is mostly covered by beautiful rolling hills and lush green valleys. Perfect land for farming is to be found across the entire island, and abundant shoals (schools of fish) swim in the rivers, lakes, and coastal waters. Although the island is heavily populated by warring and cannibal tribes, an ancient legend speaks of a visit by technologically advanced gods arriving by water to unite the tribes.

2. Alda Most of this island is covered by a year-round ice cap, and temperatures on the coast rise above freezing for only about three months in the year. Nobody lives here, but it has adequate resources to support a very small community. Since it is in the middle of a large and wild ocean, ships shelter in the lee about once every six years.

3. Etoc Rugged mountains and spectacular scenery characterize this temperate island, but it also has the occasional earthquake. The mountain streams carry a fair amount of varied and succulent fish. There is plenty of timber in the mountains, but wild and sometimes dangerous animals often roam in the lower foothills. Only smaller parts near the sea are suitable for agriculture, but the soil there is thin and liable to being washed away by flash floods. The island is inhabited by warring tribes, but they are said to leave newcomers in peace.

4. Lakorc A semiarid desert covers most of this island. There is, therefore, very little surface water, but plenty of underground water, for which wells have to be sunk. Palm tress adorn the coastline, but they quickly give way to savanna and then to scrub further inland. Temperatures are warm, except for a couple of months during the summer, when it can be scorching and stifling. Fishing around the island can be dangerous, but it is abundant. The island is uninhabited, and the shipping frequency of nearby sea-lanes is every nine years.

5. Nala Tropical forest covers most of the rolling hills. Fruit trees and other edible plants are abundant, and the game, though dangerous, is plentiful. Travel around or across the island is difficult, and clearing the forest for settlement is more a question of hard work than of engineering difficulty. Were it not for the massive swarms of flies and other disease-carrying insects, this would be an ideal island to build a community. It has been estimated, for example, that the average life expectancy of the normally very peaceful inhabitants is very short (women live only until the age of about 25 years, and men, surprisingly, 5 years longer than that).

6. Reda This is a tiny island, only a few miles square, but it is visited regularly twice a year by a coastguard ship to carry out maintenance on the unattended lighthouse there. It is windswept year-round, which means that only a handful of small bushes grow along the cliffs on the leeward side. The rest of the island resembles the wilder parts of the Scottish Highlands, and is covered in peat, moss, lichens, and heather.

7. Ynad Lots of game live in the savanna plains that cover most of this generally flat island, while in the more sheltered parts various fruit shrubs and vegetables grow. Extremes of temperature, not only from season to season but also from day to day, are made worse by sudden gales and the occasional typhoon. The tribes themselves are peaceful, even hospitable, but are afraid of, even hostile toward, strangers arriving in large groups.

Personal profile

Before you start any discussions with your fellow marooned shipmates, you should fill in this profile. This has two main purposes: (1) It is the basis for you to build a description of yourself before the game starts, and (2) it will serve as a checklist during the game discussions.

In your replies you should be as accurate as you can about yourself. If there are characteristics you do not wish to reveal about yourself, you have a perfect right not to mention them, and likewise you should not put pressure on others to reveal things they wish to remain silent about. Thus, you do not have to fill in every item below, or give great detail under each heading.

Once you have drawn up your profile, you cannot change it during the game. You must also be consistent with this profile during the game.

Sex _____ Age _____ Nationality _____

Family (e.g., status, offspring, siblings, close-knit) _____

_____

Background (e.g., upbringing, education, social class) _____

_____

Employment _____ Political leaning _____

Religion _____ Astrological sign _____

Personality traits (e.g., quiet, humorous, optimistic) _____

_____

Preferences in others (e.g., extrovert, caring) _____

_____

Likes and dislikes _____

Hobbies and interests _____

Practical skills (e.g., gardening) _____

Intellectual skills (e.g., decision making) _____

Survival skills and features (e.g., swimming, foreign languages; and,

e.g., strength, endurance) _____

_____

Personal habits (e.g., always smiling, nose-picking) _____

Other relevant characteristics _____

Your choices. Please write in your preferences for the islands you would like to escape to in ideal conditions.

1st choice _____ 2nd choice _____ 3rd choice _____

Notes for game organizers

Running the game

Hand out the manual, and allow sufficient time for it to be read (usually about 15 to 20 minutes). Participants should read the manual and fill out the personal background sheets without talking to their neighbors. Answer any questions. Emphasize the main points; for example, no one can leave until there is overall consensus and until at least all boats have been checked for seaworthiness (i.e., at least 20 minutes or so into the game); participants do not need to answer all questions in the background questionnaire but should not present an inaccurate picture of themselves. Get everyone to stand up and move around. Announce the start of play. During play, a number of changes can be made (e.g., boats can be declared unseaworthy). Providing enough places exist, this tactic can be used when a group appears to have made a decision "too easily," or to restructure tentative or initial groupings. Also, an island can be declared out of bounds (e.g., it has itself exploded). Periodically, the amount of time left before the volcano explodes should be written up on the board. At a certain point (say, 10 minutes before the end) this should not be altered further. Participants should be told at the outset that such things may happen.

Use of language

As game organizer, it is up to you whether the game documents are in the learners' native language or in the target language. The latter is, of course, far preferable, and if your students are learning a language other than English, then you will have to translate the game materials. You may also wish to provide guidance on how to read (e.g., skimming first time over, and then reading in a little more detail the second time around). It might also be worth designing an exercise or two to help in the reading. For example, draw a table, with the island names across the top and characteristics down the side. Students will then fill this in.

It probably goes without saying, but we shall say it nevertheless, that students should use the target language as much as possible during the game and follow-up activities. Be reluctant, however, to impose penalties, whether they are delivered by you or are part of the game rules, for students not using the target language. Such tactics may not have the desired effect. Students really have to decide for themselves whether to use the new language—you can only encourage, not force. If they use it because you impose it, they will stop the minute your back is turned; if they use it for themselves, because *they* want to, they will use it—and it will be that much more effective.

Debriefing

Organizers will have their own ideas, suited to their particular groups, or for particular purposes, but the following are suggested. Small groups might rank-order the five main factors which led to the decisions about forming their particular small groups and about the escape boats and islands they chose, and then report back to the entire group. (Many of the reasons for forming small groups will be expressed in rational terms, but it should be noted that in many cases the initial factor is personal attraction, with rationalized justifications added later.) Groups may also note down such things as how they felt about their group's decision or the power structure in their group. It is also possible to conduct the debriefing strictly in small groups, to enhance the ice-breaking nature of the game.

Follow-up activities

There are at least two types of activities that may be carried out after the game has ended. One activity is to have each of the small groups develop a society on its new island, complete with a political structure. In their escaping groups, participants can be asked to draw up a set of guidelines, or a sort of constitution, for their new community. The objective of this exercise is to confront players with the implications of the choices they made during the game and to expand the decision making to the next step. Another activity is to list all the elements that might be necessary to survive on the new island (e.g., food, water) and decide how these elements would be obtained and shared among participants.

Conclusion

The ISLAND GAME is an entertaining and stimulating way to get people to use the target language in a relatively nonthreatening setting. It is a helpful ice-breaker if people do not know each other too well. But regardless of any interpersonal familiarity, the game is useful too for practicing a range of skills, such as decision making, bargaining, and cooperation, all of which involve using language.

Chapter 23

Using a game for discussing and understanding simulation design

David Crookall
University of Alabama

Introduction

The game presented here, the LANGUAGE SIMULATION DESIGN GAME (LSDG), aims to help teachers and trainees examine the many features that make up simulation/games or that contribute to the planning and design of a simulation/game. Participants are divided into groups and asked to work on a card arrangement task that leads to the building of a diagram; at the end of this discussion, each group's finished diagram is explained to the other participants, and further ideas on the design process are exchanged. The LSDG is best suited to those who have read Chapter 5 and those who have at least a little experience of simulation/gaming, as participant, organizer, or designer.

Finding out about simulation design

Language simulations and games do not just appear out of thin air; instead, a series of explorations and strategies shape their design or assembly. The logistics of design will clearly vary in an infinite number of ways, simply because of the endless permutations that result from so many factors that can be associated with the modeling of a social world—and most language simulation/games, especially those that aim to encourage communication among people, do model some aspect of a social situation.

Insight into processes of language simulation/game design can be gleaned from a number of sources: articles and books on the design process itself, more general articles about simulation/gaming, simulation/games which have been published or otherwise made public, and, finally, exchanging ideas with colleagues. Examples of the first three sources are to be found elsewhere in this book. The fourth source of insight into simulation design is working with others. The LSDG provides a creative and nondirective discussion framework allowing people to become familiar with simulation/game components and to share their conceptualizations and experiences of simulation/game design.

Objectives and task

Within the broad aims of learning about the components of language simulation/games and of exchanging ideas on the simulation/design process, two sets of objectives may be listed. The first is concerned mainly with learning about simulation/games and about the design process. Participants are encouraged

1. To identify and categorize a number of crucial components and dimensions of language learning simulation/games.
2. To establish links between these components and dimensions, and to build a general, nonlinear picture of the overall design process as related to language learning.
3. To relate these components and dimensions to concrete examples of language learning simulation/games and their uses.
4. To examine the many features that contribute to the planning and design of a language learning simulation/game, and to gain insight into crucial processes of designing simulation/games for language learning.
5. To share their conceptualizations, experiences, and views of language simulation design, and to identify the many similarities and differences in their experiences.

The second set of objectives is intended not so much for learning about simulation/game design but rather for developing a heuristic device to aid in the actual development of some design project. This is most useful in a workshop where a simulation is to be produced. Here participants are encouraged

6. To construct their own framework for giving structure and direction to the design process.
7. To gain an overview and devise a checklist of the elements to be considered in designing a given simulation/game.

The main task involved in playing the LSDG is for participants (in small groups) to use a set of cards which they may arrange in whatever ways they think fit, in order to develop a nonlinear diagram which condenses the essence of the group's thinking about the patterns, interrelationships, and decisions concerning the stages and elements relevant to designing a language learning simulation/game. In short, participants have to build a model of the group's ideas about design.

It should be remembered, though, that it is not so much the finished product (the diagram) which is important in the LSDG, but rather the resultant confrontation of ideas, the ensuing exploration of ideas, experiences, and element relationships, and the inevitable interpersonal communication about the simulation/game design process which are the major outcomes of the LSDG, especially if the first set of objectives is uppermost. If the second set of objectives is important, then the diagram itself is an outcome which becomes a little more prominent, since it will help guide the subsequent design activities.

The game

Game data

The following notes provide basic information about the LANGUAGE SIMULATION DESIGN GAME.

Basic aims:	To explore and help in the process of designing language learning simulation/games.
Time:	From 1 to 3 hours.
Numbers:	Minimum: 3; maximum: any number.
Groups:	Any number; minimum group size: 3; maximum group size: 5.
Materials:	Set of 38 LDSG cards (provided below)—1 set per group; flip chart sheets of paper and felt-tip pens (several colors if possible).
Task:	By using a free-form, nonlinear card arrangement and discussion procedure, to develop a model of the group's ideas about simulation/game design.
Space:	Large tables, one for each group.
Audience:	All language educators who have had at least a little simulation/game design or participation experience.

Overview

The LSDG involves a creative exchange and exploration task requiring cards to be arranged into an overall diagram, which is then presented and explained to other groups. The cards represent variables that are important in, or at least relevant to, designing simulation/games for language learning. The topics on the cards, however, are by no means mandatory, and participants are encouraged to write new cards and throw away or modify existing ones as they see fit. Cards are shuffled, and each group is asked to arrange them into what participants consider to be some meaningful pattern. This is then transferred to paper. There are clearly no right or wrong answers, and it is vital that all participants realize this.

Procedure

Prepare as many sets of cards as groups. Master copies for cards are provided later in the chapter; photocopy these masters, cut them up, and stick them onto cards (e.g., plain playing cards). Divide participants into groups (minimum size, 3; maximum size, 5). Explain the objectives of the game (see above). Explain the task involved (see above). In explaining the task, it might be helpful to sketch a couple of summary diagrams on the board that resemble, in much simplified form, the final diagrams that might be drawn by the participants. For example, Figure 23.1 should provide the main idea.

Explain that any kind of diagram is valid. The main idea is that the diagram should summarize the thinking of the group concerning the language simulation/game design process. The relationships between cards can be indicated by lines and arrows, by grouping the cards into clusters, or by other means. The idea here is that the patterns of cards and their links should reflect in some way the group's thinking about the relationships among the elements/cards. Emphasize that the diagram produced is likely to be (or should be) nonlinear and that all types of diagrams are valid; best/worst and right/ wrong are not applicable. Before play starts, ask if there are any questions. Some questions can be answered on the spot; others may best be left till later; still others may not have an answer. These are things for you to judge as they arise.

Allow sufficient time for play. The larger the group(s), the more time they are likely to need. The amount of time available should be stated clearly before the start of play, and participants occasionally reminded of the deadline. During the initial stages of play, hand around large sheets of paper (e.g., flip chart sheets) to each group, and explain to each group that the sheet is for recording their final diagram. They should not use the sheets until they have finalized their diagrams, because once it has been committed to paper, all flexibility disappears. In transferring their diagrams to flip chart paper, groups should use only the card headings/titles (and not write in all the details from each card).

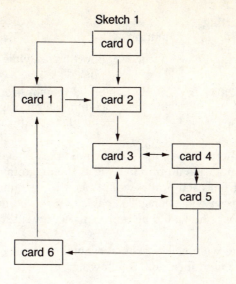

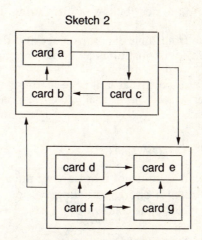

Figure 23.1   Sketches of possible card arrangements.

A sample timetable for a 1½-hour session is suggested as follows:

Step	Starting time	Duration	Task
1	10:00	5 min	Explain game
2	10:05	45 min	Play
3	10:50	10 min	Transfer diagram to sheets

Step	Starting time	Duration	Task
4	11:00	5 min	Short break while sheets are posted
5	11:05	25 min	Spokesperson from each group comments on diagrams produced and answers questions

Alternatively for step 5, it would be possible to have a poster session, where participants walk around looking at the diagrams. In this case, one representative from each group would need to remain with the group's poster to answer any questions. To enable that representative also to look at other diagrams, s/he would be replaced after a while by another person from the group.

If more time were to be made available, extremely useful additional tasks for step 5 might include the following:

1. Groups explore the possibilities of integrating their respective diagrams into one.
2. Groups derive from their diagrams a set of broad-based criteria of what they consider constitutes a "good" language learning simulation/game.
3. Groups look at a particular language learning simulation or game to see whether, at least superficially, it corresponds to those criteria.

Postgame discussion

This is a game that should not require very much debriefing. Step 5 above already constitutes a short debriefing session. Options for more extended debriefing include the following:

1. Mixed group discussions (where new groups are formed by drawing one member from each game group) on topics drawn from any of the tasks suggested above (for stage 5) or on topics of their own or your choosing (e.g., agreeing on a list of things they learned, a list of unfulfilled expectations from the game, and then discussing these).
2. Individual reading (e.g., Chapter 5, Greenblat, 1988; K. Jones, 1985), followed in another session by relating that reading to the game. If participants read different texts, they can pool their knowledge in a discussion format (either in game groups or in new groups, as above under 1) on topics as above.
3. If the LSDG is being used as a prelude to actually designing a language simulation/game, groups may wish to revise their diagrams in the light of other diagrams and of the above discussions.

The idea here will be to draw up for themselves a diagram which constitutes a sort of relational checklist of items and linkages while they design their language simulation/game design. Teachers who have experience with computers or desktop publishing may wish to put their diagram into a printed form.

Group members should not normally have any problems working together, especially if you have grouped them in such a way as to minimize potential problems (often by asking teachers to choose their own groups and with whom they wish to work). If a problem does arise, it is probably better to deal with it right away, rather than leaving it till the end of the game (since this game, contrary to many others, is not essentially about personal relationships). The LSDG is a game in which the game organizer can intervene fairly easily without disrupting the whole game. Such intervention should not, of course, be done in order to settle a genuine substantive and calm argument (as you would not wish to indicate any preference you may have for this or that idea). Any questions about substance (e.g., whether this or that card is more important) should be turned around and participants asked to work out *their* answers for themselves. Questions concerning procedure (i.e., how to play the game) should, of course, be answered as clearly as possible. This may sometimes be tricky, for answers to such questions may sometimes involve making unwitting suggestions as to what kind of diagram might be best.

Other comments

Teachers who know very little about language simulation/game design may not know immediately where to start. This is why the game is recommended for those who have at least participated in a number of different simulation/games, and even more for those who have already tried their hand at designing them. It is also why the LSDG might be done in conjunction with reading the parts of the relevant literature. But it might also be worth playing the LSDG *before* doing any reading; otherwise, participants may simply attempt to replicate the design process recommended in the reading, without thinking things through for themselves. Once they have collectively tackled design problems and issues through the LSDG, participants will find the reading much more relevant, and they will be able to read in a more alert and critical manner.

As mentioned earlier, while you are introducing the game, participants may need to be reminded strongly that the objective of each group is to produce a nonlinear diagram from their discussions. The following remark was made by Don Thatcher, one of our most experienced and respected gamers and designers, after participation in another version of this game.

"Most books that you read on simulation/game design seem to oversimplify everything, and they do come up with a linear thing if they do it in dia- grammatic form. This clearly shows that two separate groups decided that it's not linear at all" (Thatcher, 1987).

This interesting comment supports the idea that diagrams can and often will deviate from linear frameworks conventionally followed by many design theorists. A discrete and irreversible development of simulation/ game design, moving forward through a number of successive stages, appears to be an oversimplified view. Instead, a circular and even tangential network of routes, leaps, and false starts seems to be more accurate.

Be sure to emphasize that each diagram is to summarize the major variables and their interrelations considered by group members to be crucial for designing a language simulation/game. It should also be clearly stressed that there are no "correct" solutions, and that the exercise should be as open-ended as possible.

The idea of asking people to sort cards to aid the learning process is not new. Nevertheless, the use of the technique to assist collective reflection and exchange on the language simulation/game design process has con- siderable advantages. One of these is the flexibility which the technique confers, enabling participants to discard, add, or change cards, as well as to classify them into any clusters and arrange them in any pattern they wish. More important, perhaps, the processes of classifying, arranging, and establishing interrelations inevitably fosters thought, analysis, and informed discussion about design phases, elements, processes, and phi- losophy.

The cards can of course be modified in different ways (e.g., fewer simulation/game cards and more language learning cards), which means that the game can be tailored to suit the needs of any participant group.

This game is concerned principally with communication among gamers on how they design language learning simulation/games. Of equal impor- tance is communicating about this process to nongamers (i.e., to help others see that there is often much more to simulation/game design than meets the eye, and that much research and thought often goes into designing language simulation/games). This, however, goes beyond present bounds, but readers wishing to look into this could do no better than to read an excellent paper by one of our most original and prolific simulation/game designers, Cathy Stein Greenblat (1987).

The LSDG is a simplified and specialized version of the SIMULATION DESIGN GAME (SDG). This latter version does not contain the language cards, while the other cards are more numerous and contain more detail. The SDG has been used in professional workshops in Britain, France, Switzerland, and the United States. For a full account of one session using the SDG, and a complete set of SDG cards, see Crookall, Saunders, and Coote (1987).

Previously constructed diagrams

Some of the diagrams produced during the above-mentioned work-shops are reproduced in Figures 23.2–23.5 and will provide an idea of the sort and range of diagrams that it is possible to generate.

The LSDG cards

The full set of cards to run the LSDG is given in Figure 23.6. They are provided in random order, much as they might be given to participants. The abbreviation "s/g" on the cards stands for simulation/game.

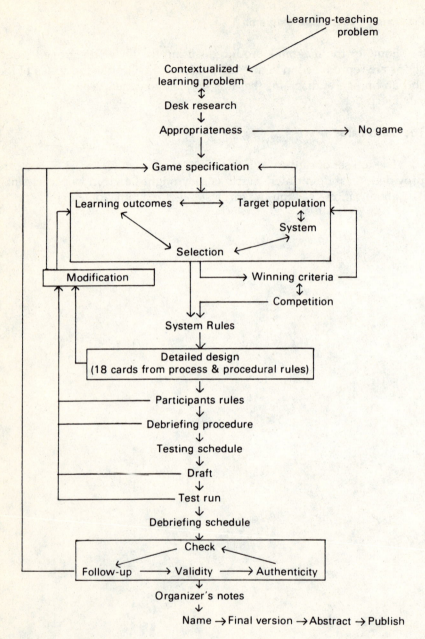

Figure 23.2   Design A.

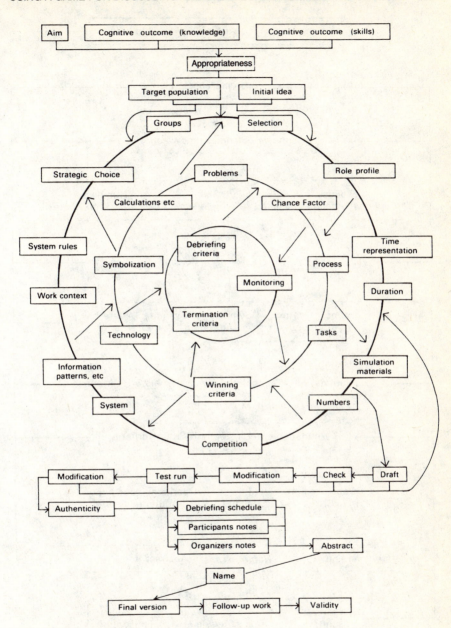

Figure 23.3   Design B.

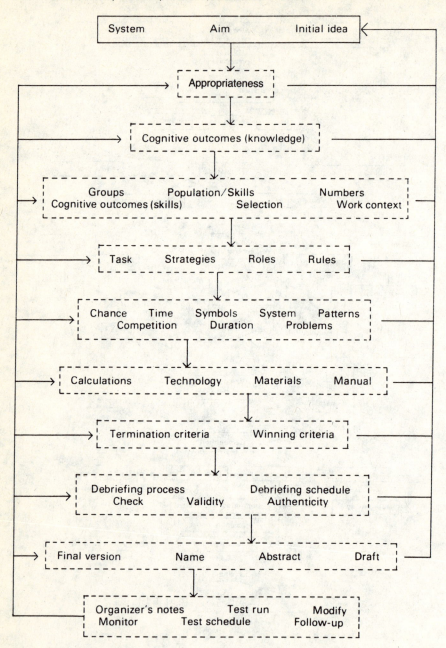

Figure 23.4   Design C.

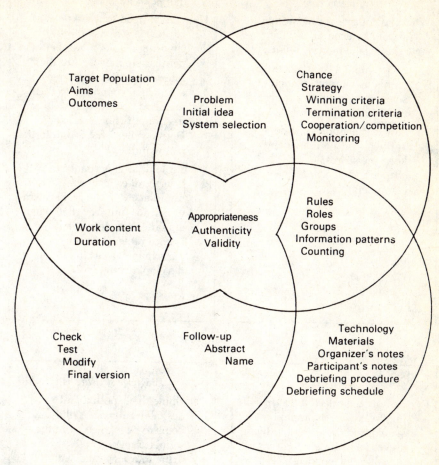

Figure 23.5   Design D.

Calculations

What type of accounting system should be used (if any)?
e.g., chips, fake money, points.

Is an accounting system necessary (either as a representation of some real world system, or for procedural reasons)?

How are calculations to be done, and who is to do them and keep the scores?
e.g., paper and pencil, forms, computers.

Strategic choice and chance factor

How much freedom are participants to have for choosing among a number of permissible moves? Are the role profiles too cramping?
e.g., when compared to their real world counterparts. Is freedom of choice realistic? Does it reflect that found in the real world?

What role (if any) is chance to play? If used, does it reflect randomness in the real system or is it for fun? To what extent are outcomes dependent on chance rather than on participants' skills in developing strategy?

Symbolization

Decide how the selected features of the "real" system are to be symbolized (by using hardware and/or software).
e.g., houses by wooden blocks,
days by minutes,
physical environment by board,
bargaining power by points,
a group of people by one person,
physical constraints, laws and system behaviors by rules,
imponderables by a chance factor

Language skills/items

Determine the expected and desirable language skills and items to be learned from the s/g performance.
e.g., the four language skills
vocabulary
collocation
grammar structures
pronunciation and intonation
register, style, and appropriateness
specific purpose language
study skills

Language exercises

Determine the types of language practice exercises that should precede, be included in, or follow the s/g.

e.g., drills
less controlled exercises
phonological work
supplementary reading
revision of matter already studied
listening to the radio
group work

Language/communication monitoring

Determine how language and communication performance and errors are to be monitored during, and improved and corrected during or after, the s/g performance.

e.g., audio- or videotape recording (for analysis after)
teacher-written notes (during)
peer correction (during/after)
handouts (after)
teacher interruption (during)
predetermined pauses (during)
exercises or lab work (after)

Identify advantages and drawbacks of each for given circumstances.

Learning/training problem and context

What is the nature and scope of the problem, in learning or training terms? Has it been specified in sufficient (or even in too much) detail?

What is the context for which the learning or training problem has been specified?

Omission and censorship card

If you think that there are things left out in this set of cards, that these cards do not cover all the points you wish to consider for a design framework, then write out extra cards to cover these.

If you think that any of the cards in this pack are undesirable, unworkable, illogical, irrelevant, unrealistic, or otherwise intolerable, then please do not hesitate to rewrite cards or simply leave them out.

Target audience and aims

Draft general definition of participants for whom the s/g is intended.

Draft broad statement of educational, training, or research intent.

Does target population definition square with aims and objectives, and with other elements?

Appropriateness/suitability

Determine whether an s/g is an appropriate or suitable technique for the attainment of the aims, objectives, purposes, etc., under consideration, or whether another type of learning activity task or methodology would be more suited.

What criteria are being used to establish such appropriateness or suitability?

Competition

What amount and kind of competition is to be encouraged or allowed in during the s/g performance? (e.g., between: individuals, teams, participants, and goals.)

Is competition a feature of the system being represented and/ or is it introduced for procedural or other purposes?

Is competition desirable or destructive (carrying hidden messages and leading to negative consequences)?

Termination and/or winning criteria

How is the s/g performance to be drawn to a close?

e.g., time limit, announcement of winner, reaching a stated goal, accomplishing a task, solving a problem.

Are there to be (explicit or implicit) winners? If so, what winning criteria are going to be used? (e.g., eliminating others, first to reach stated goal, obtaining highest scores.)

Does the goal of winning carry any hidden negative messages or detract from the game's aims?

Duration and time management

Determine how long the s/g performance is to take, including: length of different stages, preparation time, debriefing time.

How far can institutional constraints be allowed to influence these aspects?

Determine whether the s/g performance can be interrupted and continued later (e.g., once a week for 4 weeks). Can the simulator be modified easily to incorporate this kind of interruption?

Technology

What sorts of technological aids or apparatus are to be used?
e.g., computers, pocket calculators, interactive video disk, radio, telecommunications.

If computers are used, what:
language is to be used?
computer-participant interaction is there to be?
control will participants have over outcomes, as opposed to control by the computer?

Problems and tasks

Determine what specific problem(s) participants have to solve and/ or what specific task(s) they have to accomplish.
e.g., find out "who dunnit," solve the enigma, decide on a budget, find the way out, allocate or balance resources, decide on an action course, come to an agreement, construct a model, buy land, exchange things, hold meetings, write a treaty.

Are tasks and problems germane to the aims of the s/g?

Simulator materials

Determine what kind (and how much) hardware is to be used or designed and produced.
e.g., boards, forms, cards, tape, dice.

How difficult are these to produce and reproduce?

Are they easy to use? Do they serve a useful purpose in s/g procedures? Are they relevant to the aims and objectives of the s/g?

Debriefing and follow-up

What specific debriefing points are to be covered? What types of debriefing procedures are desirable and feasible?

Write notes (or detailed forms) for the organizer and/or participants on main debriefing points and/or procedures.

What kinds of follow-up work (in addition to debriefing) can usefully be done after the s/g is over?

Produce follow-up work materials or guidelines and suggestions.

Testing schedule

Identify criteria to be used during a test run of the draft simulator.
e.g., are there any anomalies?
       are the rules too strict?
       are the instructions clear?
       is competition fairly balanced?
       are profiles "realistic"?
       are roles playable?

What other elements (mentioned on these cards) are relevant to testing the s/g?

Learning outcomes

Determine the expected and desirable learning outcomes:
e.g., knowledge and understanding in subjects, processes, people.
e.g., feelings, attitudes and attitude change, empathy, personal relations, motivation.
e.g., development of skills in making decisions, solving problems, inquiry, cooperating in group work.
e.g., learning-to-learn skills.
e.g., language skills (grammar, communication, appropriateness, fluency, accuracy).

System representation

Identify the features of the real system to be represented.
e.g., committee meeting, foreign culture, international crisis, TV broadcast, job interview, contract negotiations.

Decide how to represent them.
e.g., by: roles (e.g., for professions, institutions, states).
       objects (e.g., for buildings).
       symbols (e.g., for values).
       rules (e.g., for constraints).

How is time to be represented in the s/g? e.g., years by hours.

Rules

Determine procedural rules (i.e., to regulate game processes, and not representing real system constraints).

e.g., "if you throw six, you can have another go," or "you can negotiate only if you are holding hands."

Determine system rules (i.e., representing system procedures and constraints).

e.g., to represent voting, group membership, exchange parameters in the real system.

Authenticity and abstractness

Determine how realistic or authentic and how abstract the simulator should be compared with the real system.

Does a lack of realism or authenticity detract from the simulator's effectiveness in achieving its aims?

Organizer's and participant's notes/guidelines/manual

Produce explanatory notes, guidelines and/or manual for other organizers and for participants.

What items should go in which documents? Organizers and/or participants? Can the game be run by participants?

e.g., how to run the s/g, how to debrief, rules, advice, how to fill out forms, expected learning outcomes, timetable, special points, confidential information, variations, groups, computer operation, numbers, duration, aims.

Draft, test run, and modification

Produce a draft version of the simulator. (Check for such things as anomalies, omissions, contradictions, clarity.)

Carry out a test run or, better, several test runs of the draft simulator. (If possible both the designer(s) and other game organizers should run tests.)

Determine things to be modified in the draft version. (Do any modifications have unforeseen effects?)

Language practice-s/g sequence

Determine the sequencing and interfacing of language practice exercises and s/g performance within an overall plan.

e.g., language practice first and then s/g, or first s/g and then language practice, or combination of these two, or some other format.

Language materials

Produce language practice exercises and materials.

Determine how well they mesh with the s/g itself.

Evaluate and modify exercises and materials.

Test run the exercises and materials, on their own and in relation to s/g in general or to a specific s/g.

Communication

Determine expected and desirable communicative skills development to be encouraged by the s/g performance.

e.g., functional competence
discourse cohesion
illocutionary development
speaker roles
appropriateness
social/personal skills
cross-cultural awareness
register
intonation

Language-s/g order

Determine whether:
1. the s/g is to be designed to develop a predetermined set of language and communication items or units (i.e., first determine the language and then design the s/g to fit the language), or
2. the language and communication items or units will be identified from a finished s/g (i.e., design the s/g and then see what kind of language it generates), or
3. a mixture of these is appropriate.

Language assessment

Determine:

1. if any sort of assessment (test, exam, evaluation) is desirable or necessary.
2. for whom and why such assessment is deemed desirable or necessary.
3. what exactly, if anything, is to be assessed (e.g., human skills, language, grammar, performance, communication, reaction of others, s/g outcomes, interest).
4. what type of procedure, if any, is to be used for assessment.

Learner training

Determine how important it is for learners to have had some previous s/g experience, and for the s/g organizer to know what this is, before participation in the new s/g.

Determine what types of previous s/g experience and/or knowledge learners have and what types they should gain before taking part in the s/g.

Design a learner training scheme to provide learners with this (e.g., trial run of simple s/g).

Numbers and groups

Decide minimum and maximum number of participants for the whole s/g.

Decide:

1. whether or not to have groups.
2. kinds of group configurations (i.e., number and size of groups).
3. how members are to be assigned to groups.
4. whether group memberships are to be flexible or fixed.
5. types of communication cycles and patterns between groups.

Role profile

1. Decide whether or not there will be specified roles.
2. Decide on role types (e.g., individual [Jimmy], social [sister, pilot], institutional [ministry, company]).
3. Decide on how much detail to provide for each profile, from just a name (e.g., developing South American state) to a long detailed and prescriptive narrative.
4. Spell out characteristics associated with each role and write the profile.

Final version

Produce a final version of the simulator.

Is it to be published? In a journal article or book chapter, or as a separate book or kit?

Work context

Think about aspects of work procedure and context. e.g., how team work and institutional support may affect such aspects as the design process, participant perceptions and acceptance, perceptions by other staff, etc.

Information patterns and networks

Determine information timing, density, distribution, flow, retrieval, channels.

e.g., everyone gets same information.

different participants get different information.

combinations of above.

additional inputs of input during s/g.

regulated information networks between participants.

types of misinformation, if any.

value of information (can it be bought? from whom?).

Monitoring

Determine what elements or aspects of the participation are to be monitored and what procedures are to be used for monitoring.

e.g., group cooperation
leadership struggles
use of feedback
communication strategies

e.g., by: video or tape recording
self-reports
observer questionnaires
discussions

Learning or learner training	*Culture learning*
Determine if the s/g is to be used primarily for:	Is the s/g to be culture-specific (i.e., to embody cultural aspects of the target language community), or is it to be relatively culture-independent (i.e., adaptable to a range of cultural contexts)?
1. learning the language and/or culture (e.g., grammar point, negotiation styles, LSP, cross-cultural communication), or	
2. learner training (e.g., learning how to learn, self-direction, learning strategies, basics of language and language learning, group work), or	Are the cultural values embodied in the s/g accurate (e.g., do they avoid stereotypes)?
3. both (equally or mainly one).	How are cultural elements to be incorporated into the s/g (e.g., using authentic materials and based on culturally relevant and appropriate situations)?
Determine whether learners need training, or experience, in s/g's to benefit fully from them.	

Figure 23.6   LSDG cards.

Questions and activities

1. Review a number of simulation/games (see Chapter 24 for sources). Pick out one, or better two, that would be especially useful in your language classes. What are the major differences and similarities with the two in this section? Consider what adaptations, if any (e.g., language, plot, roles) you might like to make to meet the needs of your students. What effect do you think these adaptations will have?
2. Run the simulation/games you have chosen in item 1 above. You might try them out with your teaching colleagues first, or try them directly with your students. Don't worry about perfection the first time, or even later on, for that matter! Some simulation/games can be a flop in one class and an hour or two later with another class be a great success. Such is the uncertainty, and excitement, of the simulation/gaming world.
3. After running each activity (in 2 above), consider the following questions: What elements were the most successful? The least successful? What might be useful to change next time? Why? How effective was the debriefing? What did participants gain from the whole experience? How did they feel about it? What do they think might improve the simulation/game?

Section **G**

Sources and resources

Chapter 24

Learning more about simulation/gaming

David Crookall
University of Alabama

This volume is just the beginning for anyone who wishes to delve fully into the simulation/gaming world. This chapter presents a comprehensive, but not exhaustive, list of sources and resources to enable you to go beyond the discussions presented in this book, to go deeper into the issues raised, and to build on or supplement what you have learned. The sources and resources included here cover associations and periodicals, annotated book lists for further reading, a list of collections of games and simulations relevant or adaptable to language learning, and a list of simulation/game directories. A number of items will, inevitably, have been overlooked; readers who notice omissions are kindly invited to drop me a line (c/o Newbury House/Harper & Row).

Associations and periodicals

Associations and periodicals probably constitute the best sources of recent thinking and practice and of information on new materials and developments. Anyone interested in simulation/gaming should seriously consider joining one of the associations and/or subscribing to one of the periodicals.

Associations

There exist four major simulation associations in the world. They publish their own newsletters and journals (see below), hold their own annual conferences (usually with a reduced rate for members), and provide other services.

ABSEL Association for Business Simulation and Experiential Learning (Information from: Walter Wheatley, College of Business, University of West Florida, Pensacola, FL 32514, USA; or from: Lane Kelley, College of Business Administration, University of Hawaii, Honolulu, HI 96822, USA; or from: Patricia Sanders, Department of Management, Central Connecticut State University, New Britain, CT 06050, USA. Annual conference, usually in the USA, in the spring; proceedings usually published.)

ISAGA International Simulation And Gaming Association (General information from: ISAGA General Secretariat, Jan H G Klabbers, Department of Social Science, State University at Utrecht, PO Box 80.140, 3584 CS Utrecht, The Netherlands. Regional secretaries in various parts of the world [e.g., Eastern Europe, Latin America, North America, Philippines, Africa, Australia]. Membership applications to: Danny Saunders, Department of Behavioural and Communication Studies, Polytechnic of Wales, Pontypridd, Mid Glam CF37 1DL, Wales, UK. Annual conference, in various countries round the world, in the summer; proceedings usually published by Pergamon Press.)

NASAGA North American Simulation And Gaming Association (Information from: NASAGA, 4110 Glencairn, Indianapolis, IN 46226, USA. Annual conference, usually in the USA, in the autumn. The association sponsors the publication of a number of simulations and games, which are then made available at very reasonable cost.)

SAGSET Society for the Advancement of Games and Simulations in Education and Training (Information from and membership applications to: The Secretary, SAGSET, Center for Extension Studies, University of Technology, Loughborough LE11 3TU, Leics, UK. Annual conference, in the UK, in early September; proceedings always published. The association also produces a series of useful resource lists.)

Periodicals

In addition to the above associations, there are three newsletters and two quarterly journals, devoted entirely to simulation/gaming and associated with one or more of the above associations.

ABSEL Newsletter (This can be obtained as part of membership in ABSEL [see address above]. Contains information, news and reviews. Parts of the newsletter are reproduced some months after publication in *Simulation & Gaming* [see below]. The editor is Bob Hornaday, Department of Management, University of North Carolina at Charlotte, Charlotte, NC 28223, USA.)

ISAGA Newsletter (This can be obtained through membership of ISAGA [see address above]. It usually runs to about 20 pages and contains short articles, notes, and announcements from around the world, as well as book and simulation/ game reviews. Parts are later published in *Simulation & Gaming* [see below]. [The 18th volume appeared in 1990.] The editor is David Crookall, Department of English, University of Alabama, Tuscaloosa, AL 35487, USA.)

NASAGA Newsletter (This comes with membership in NASAGA [see address above]. Contains information, news and reviews. Parts of the newsletter are reproduced some months after publication in *Simulation & Gaming* [see below]. The editor is Richard L. Dukes, Department of Sociology, University of Colorado at Colorado Springs, Colorado Springs, CO 80918, USA.)

Simulation & Gaming: An International Journal of Theory, Design, and Research (This is the official journal of ABSEL, ISAGA, and NASAGA and can be obtained either through membership in one of the above associations or by direct subscription to Sage Publications [PO Box 5084, 2111 West Hillcrest Drive, Newbury Park, CA 91320, USA; 29 Banner Street, London EC1Y 8QE, UK]. The journal generally carries four to seven longish articles, usually academic in style. It has book and game reviews, and contains a section of Reports and Communications, as well as a section of news from the three associations. [The 21st volume appeared in 1990.] The editor is David Crookall, Department of English, University of Alabama, Tuscaloosa, AL 35487, USA.)

Simulation/Games for Learning (This is the official SAGSET journal and is obtainable either as part of SAGSET membership or on a separate subscription basis from Kogan Page [120 Pentonville Road, London N1, UK]. The journal typically contains about four short to medium-length major articles per issue, generally of a fairly practical nature. It also has very useful book and game reviews, and contains an abstracts section based on ERIC/ChESS. [The 20th volume appeared in 1990.] The editors are Alan Coote [Department of Management and Legal Studies] and Danny Saunders [Department of Behavioural and Communication Studies], Polytechnic of Wales, Pontypridd, Mid Glam CF37 1DL, Wales, UK.)

In addition to the "dedicated" periodicals above, many other journals regularly publish articles on simulation/gaming. In the nonlanguage field, of particular note is the *Social Science Computer Review* (Duke University Press), while the following language teaching journals should receive a special mention: *English Language Teaching Journal* (Oxford University Press), *Foreign Language Annals* (American Council on the Teaching of Foreign Languages—ACTFL), *Modern English Teacher* (Modern English Publications), *Practical English Teaching* (Mary Glasgow Publications), and *System* (Pergamon Press).

Further reading

In the space between these covers, it was not possible, of course, to cover in detail all aspects of language learning through simulation/gaming. To take just one example among many others, a number of books have concerned themselves exclusively with just the simulation/game *design* process. A single chapter on design, such as the one included in this book, cannot hope to cover all the intricacies of the design process. A similar remark can be made of the other chapters in this book; indeed, it would be possible to write a whole book on the topic covered in each chapter.

The works cited in the chapters of this book are all listed in the References, which therefore include language items and simulation/gaming items as well as more general ones. In addition, the References contain a large number of references to language simulation/gaming not cited in the chapters, but which might be useful to readers. Although the References constitute the most complete bibliography on foreign/second language simulation/gaming to be published to date, it should not be considered as exhaustive.

Simulation/gaming references tend to fall into about seven types:

1. *General works*—these tend to fall into two subcategories. There are the more introductory books, often dealing more with broad aspects of simulation/gaming. Then there are those, often edited volumes, at a more advanced or theoretical level, ranging widely in their coverage of topics or applications, with each chapter addressing a specific subject (sometimes on language learning)—thus, one might find in the same volume a chapter on ice-breaking, one on computerized ecological simulations, and another on political network gaming.

2. *Specialized volumes* focus in their entirety on a fairly well-defined and specific area or application (e.g., science, communication)—these books, however, often contain much that is relevant to other applications or to a more general readership.

3. *Journal articles*—most articles are to be found in the simulation/gaming periodicals, but many are also published in nonsimulation journals (see above).

4. *Simulation/game collections*—a series of games is contained within a single publication, usually a book (often simpler in structure and easier to run than those to be found in type 5 below).

5. *Simulation/game packages*—these contain a single simulation/game (usually a fairly complex one), in book form, in the form of loose-leaf folders or contained in a box.

6. Simulation software or *simware packages*—often, additional printed documents are contained in these.

7. *Directories*—these are books or parts of books containing directories, catalogs, or lists of simulation/games.

No references are provided below to books/packages consisting of just one simulation/game (type 5 above); there are far too many of these to list, and in addition, they would require too much space for a full description of the games. By the same token, no computerized simulation packages are listed (type 6 above). However, information on many of these will be found in the directories section below. Journal articles also are too numerous to list, but these constitute a rich source of discussions on issues and of information on new games; details on simulation/gaming periodicals is given above.

The subsequent sections of this chapter thus contain references to major works on simulation/gaming; i.e., for the most part only books are listed. The lists below are fairly representative of the simulation/gaming field, and they should thus constitute valuable sources of readings for language teachers wishing to explore further some of the topics and areas discussed in this volume.

General works

Many books on simulation/gaming tend to be of a general nature, in the sense that they cover a broad range of concerns. This is due to the fact that simulation/gaming can be applied to such a wide variety of areas. The books may be introductory and deal with more practical concerns (e.g., K. Jones, 1987) or more advanced and theoretical (e.g., Greenblat & Duke, 1981). Some of the more advanced collections sometimes include discussions of a practical nature. The more advanced collections of papers also contain discussions on very specific applications (e.g., management), but they have been included in this section because such collections usually cover a broad spectrum of specific applications and cannot therefore be classified as belonging to any one subject area. Works which do concentrate on a particular area are listed in the next section, entitled "Single-Area Works."

Introductory and more practical works

Abt, C. 1970. *Serious Games.* New York: Viking Press (Looks at the instructional as well as fun aspects of games. Most of the materials discussed in the text are published by the author's company. No references or bibliography.)

Davison, A. & Gordon, P. 1978. *Games and Simulations in Action.* London: Woburn Press (A general overview of games, particularly on the use of drama-based games in secondary schools. Contains a resource list and some complete, ready-to-use games.)

Gillispie, P. H. 1973. *Learning Through Simulation Games.* Paramus, NJ: Paulist Press (An introduction, most of which describes 26 simulation/games [including classics like STARPOWER]. Three complete, ready-to-use games are presented.)

Jaques, D. 1984. *Learning in Groups.* London: Kogan Page; New York: Nichols Publishing (A useful book on the process of learning in groups, much of which is directly relevant to games and simulations.)

Jones, K. 1987. *Simulations: A Handbook for Teachers and Trainers.* (2nd ed.) London: Kogan Page; New York: Nichols Publishing (This is the second edition of this well-known and popular book, originally published in 1980. It has been extensively rewritten to cover the needs and opportunities brought about by major changes in many national education systems, including both the American movement toward more interactive learning and the "English educational revolution," which favor action learning, group work, practical activities, and the assessment of oral as well as written skills. This book provides much very useful and practical advice and guidance on all aspects of choosing, using, designing, running, and assessing simulations. Many examples of simulations at work have been added to help teachers and trainers use simulations effectively.)

Jones, K. 1988. *Interactive Learning Events: A Guide for Facilitators.* London: Kogan Page; New York: Nichols Publishing (This practical text is designed to assist facilitators [teachers, trainers, or instructors who run an interactive learning event] in both the educational and the industrial context. It reflects the growing interest in the use of interactive learning methods such as simulations, role-play, exercises, games, and discussions which encourage more active learner participation. Facilitators are encouraged to look beyond labels such as "simulation" and "role-play," to focus on what actually happens in the course of interactive learning, and then to choose the most appropriate methodology. Practical advice and guidance is given, and potential hazards are pointed out. Debriefing and assessment are also considered.)

Lewis, L. H. (ed.) 1986. *Experiential and Simulation Techniques for Teaching Adults.* San Francisco: Jossey-Bass (A series of introductory essays, covering such considerations as computerized simulation, inductive learning using cases, managerial skills, intercultural relations, philosophical rationale for experiential learning.)

Maidment, R. & Bronstein, R. H. 1973. *Simulation Games Design and Implementation.* Columbus, OH: Charles E. Merrill (A general introduction; contains a complete, ready-to-use game on pollution; one chapter deals with design and use.)

Megarry, J. (ed.) 1977. *Aspects of Simulation and Gaming: An Anthology of SAGSET Journal, Volumes 1–4.* London: Kogan Page; New York: Nichols Publishing (This volume includes some of the articles [which are no longer available] from the early volumes of SAGSET's journal, now entitled *Simulation/Games for Learning* [see above]. Twenty papers cover such topics as communication, effective learning, media, politics, planning, management, and teacher education.)

Milroy, E. 1982. *Role-Play: A Practical Guide.* Aberdeen: Aberdeen University Press (This book has been written for all those involved in the training and development of others, e.g., in teaching youth and community work, community education. The technique of role-play is described in detail, and its validity is evaluated. Advice is given on introducing role-play to people with no experience of it. Ideas are offered for role-play with students of various kinds and for role-play related to various subjects and contexts, from religious education, through conversational skills, to job interviews. There is also a section on scripted role-play.)

Taylor, J. L. & Walford, R. 1978. *Learning and the Simulation Game.* Milton Keynes: Open University Press (A basic primer, an operational handbook, and a reference work all rolled into one. Included are discussions on the evolution and relevance of simulation/games and samples of games [on chemistry, farms, journalism, urban growth, and conservation]. One-third of the book is a directory of games and simulations.)

Thatcher, D. & Robinson, J. 1985. *An Introduction to Games and Simulations in Education.* Fareham, Hampshire: Solent Simulations (80 Miller Drive, Fareham, Hampshire PO16 7LL, England) (This is an excellent introductory handbook, specifically written for newcomers, although seasoned gamers will also find much useful material. A variety of games is described, with notes and hints on using and designing games.)

Thiagarajan, S. & Stolovitch, H. D. 1978. *Instructional Simulation Games.* Englewood Cliffs, NJ: Educational Technology Publications (Suggests ways in which simulation/gaming can be used to achieve objectives, introduce content, integrate new with old knowledge, and evaluate learning. There are in-depth discussions on designing, introducing, playing, and debriefing simulation/games. Illustrative excerpts are provided.)

Thiagarajan, S. 1980. *Experiential Learning Packages.* Englewood Cliffs, NJ: Educational Technology Publications (Concentrates on the practical procedures involved in instructional materials that use the structure of verbalized learning to increase the effectiveness of experiential learning. Topics covered include objectives, curriculum areas, descriptions, and attributes of packages. There is a large section on design, and one on learning outcomes.)

van Ments, M. 1983. *The Effective Use of Role-Play.* London: Kogan Page; New York: Nichols Publishing (Probably the standard work on role-play, which covers all the important topics, such as the concept of role, the advantages and disadvantages of role-play, choosing, designing, running, and debriefing role-play, role-play types, the hidden agenda, and stereotypes, related techniques.)

Wohlking, W. & Gill, P. J. *Role Playing.* Englewood Cliffs, NJ: Educational Technology Publications (This focuses on the training dimensions of role-play. It looks at training objectives and three phases of role-play [warm-up, enactment, debriefing], providing advice on its use. Guidelines are provided for designing role-plays and developing observer guides for use during role-play. Examples of role-play are included.)

More advanced or theoretical references

Boocock, S. E. & Schild, E. O. 1968. *Simulation Games in Learning.* Beverly Hills, CA & London: Sage (Prefaced by James S. Coleman, this book was influential in the late 1960s and early 1970s. It covers many of the important aspects of simulation/games, including theory and rationale, interaction in games, learning effects, game strategies, individual and group effects on enjoyment and learning, competition, participation, decision making. It also covers such topic areas as business, political science, history, and social studies.)

Bruin, K., de Haan, J., Teijken, C. & Veeman, W. (eds.) 1979. *How to Build a Simulation/Game.* Groningen, The Netherlands: Centrale Reproductiedienst der Rijksuniversiteit (The 37 chapters in the two volumes of this work cover a wide range of subjects, and not just game design—for example, group dynamics, health care, affective outcomes, politics, business and management, decision making, computers, urban planning, science, language learning.)

Craig, S. & Martin, A. (eds.) 1986. *Simulations and Games for Capability.* Loughborough: SAGSET (The 18 chapters in this volume revolve around the concept of capability in education and training, and touch on more general aspects of simulation/gaming [e.g., design, communication use in schools, project work], though some deal with more specific applications [e.g., management, language learning, and jigsaw reading].)

Crookall, D., Greenblat, C. S., Coote, A., Klabbers, J. H. G. & Watson, D. R. (eds.) 1987. *Simulation-Gaming in the Late 1980s.* Oxford & New York: Pergamon (The 46 chapters in this volume cover a broad spectrum of applications and issues. Four in-depth papers, in Section 1, tackle topics of central concern to gamers: network gaming and intercultural communication, communicating about simulation design, and problems related to power, reality, and modeling. Section 2 contains a number of papers on various aspects of language and communication, including language learning. Social issues, game design, and research are the concerns of Section 3, while Section 4 focuses on management and business. The last section is concerned with taxonomies and methodologies. Of note are the several papers on ethnomethodological analyses of simulation/ games. There are also a number of papers on computers.)

Crookall, D., Klabbers, J. H. G., Coote, A., Saunders, D., Cecchini, A. & Delle Piane, A. (eds.) 1988. *Simulation-Gaming in Education and Training.* Oxford & New York: Pergamon (The 39 papers in this book are divided into four sections: cultural and social dimensions [e.g., the future of education, debriefing, ice-breakers, national differences in participation, conversational CALL]; management and business [both in Eastern European countries and in the West]; support systems, modeling, and taxonomies; and the Italian perspective on simulation/games. A number of papers deal with computers.)

Duke, R. D. 1974. *Gaming: The Future's Language.* New York: Halstead Press (This classic book, by one of our foremost gamers, has had a major influence on simulation/gaming. It advances the idea that simulation is itself a significant communication form. A variety of communication modes are discussed and linked to the idea of simulation as a language for exploring the world, its realities, and its possible futures. A large part of the book is devoted to game design.)

Dukes, R. L. & Seidner, C. J. (eds.) 1978. *Learning with Simulations and Games.* Beverly Hills, CA & London: Sage (The eight chapters in this anthology discuss and describe many games on a large variety of topics: evaluation of sociology games, mathematics, science, communication, social sciences, urban planning, and political science. Many of the papers originally appeared in previous issues of *Simulation & Games: An International Journal of Theory, Design, and Research.*)

Fitzsimons, A. & Thatcher, D. (eds.) 1987. *Games and Simulations at Work.* Loughborough: SAGSET (This contains 15 chapters organized under the following sections: work-related games and the curriculum, work-focused games in training, games about a world without work, game design, knowledge and skill in business education, and interdisciplinary learning programs.)

Fletcher, J. L. (ed.) 1978. *Human Growth Games: Explorations and Research Prospects.* Beverly Hills, CA & London: Sage (The nine papers in this anthology concentrate on the development of human potential, and consider such topics as self-knowledge, self-directed learning, memory, creativity, and beliefs. The material originally appeared as a special issue of *Simulation & Games: An International Journal of Theory, Design, and Research,* 8:1, March 1977.)

Gibbs, G. I. & Howe, A. (eds.) 1975. *Academic Gaming and Simulation*. London: Kogan Page; New York: Nichols Publishing (This small book contains papers on such topics as science, politics, problems of games, and features of successful games.)

Goldberg, D. & Graber, M. (eds.) 1980. *Simulation/Games in Education, Research and Decision Making / Techniques de Jeux et Simulations pour l'Education, la Recherche et la Prise de Decision*. Geneva: Department of Psychology and Educational Sciences, University of Geneva (The 40 papers in this collection cover a very wide diversity of concerns and topics: manufacturing, domestic finance, game design, economics, urban planning, diplomacy, computers, energy policy, environmental concerns, business, decision making, ethical issues, language learning, war-gaming, learning disability.)

Greenblat, C. S. & Duke, R. D. (eds.) 1975. *Gaming-Simulation: Rationale, Design, and Applications: A Text with Parallel Readings for Social Scientists, Educators, and Community Workers*. Beverly Hills, CA & London: Sage (This classic book has now been rewritten and updated—see next reference.)

Greenblat, C. S. & Duke, R. D. (eds.) 1981. *Principles and Practices of Gaming-Simulation*. Beverly Hills, CA & London: Sage (This is an abridged and revised edition the previously listed volume. Written by two of our foremost gamers, this book has established itself as the major standard work for all those making use of simulation/gaming methodology, and continues to be the main reference in the area. The 20 chapters cover most of the important aspects of simulation/gaming, including problems of learning and communication, basic concepts in simulation/gaming, complexity, design, and construction of games, using games for teaching and training, guidelines on running games, the educational effectiveness of games, group dynamics, games as a tool for research, and applications to various fields [public policy, science and technology, urban planning]. It also contains 25 pages of references, and an index to a few well-known games [e.g., BLOOD MONEY, SIMSOC].)

Hollinshead, B. & Yorke, M. (eds.) 1981. *Simulation and Games: The Real and the Ideal*. London: Kogan Page; New York: Nichols Publishing (This collection of 24 articles covers a wide range of areas: social and public administration, management and business, computers, game design, culture, science and technology, and evaluation.)

Jamieson, I., Miller, A. & Watts, A. G. 1988. *Mirrors of Work: Work Simulations in Schools*. Lewes, East Sussex: Falmer Press; Philadelphia: Taylor & Francis (This book is based extensively on the considerable experience of the British-based School Curriculum Industry Partnership in curriculum development incorporating work simulations. Its discussions are wide-ranging and are applicable to a broad range of concerns. The 14 chapters cover such aspects as concepts and contexts, principles and practice, design, a variety of work-related simulation/game types, running games, debriefing, curriculum integration and evaluation.)

Jaques, D. & Tipper, E. (eds.) 1984. *Learning for the Future with Games and Simulations*. Loughborough: SAGSET (A collection of 24 papers covering a variety of topics, including interpersonal skills, design, organizations, management, city planning, learning processes.)

Klabbers, J. H. G., Scheper, W., Takkenberg, C. & Crookall, D. (eds.) 1989. *Simulation-Gaming: On the Improvement of Competence in Dealing with Complexity,*

Uncertainty and Value Conflicts. Oxford & New York: Pergamon (A collection of papers on a broad range of concerns and issues, including management, environmental planning, decision support systems, education, computers, and methodology.)

Megarry, J. (ed.) 1979. *Human Factors in Games and Simulations*. London: Kogan Page; New York: Nichols Publishing (Some fairly general, as well as a few more specific, aspects of simulation/gaming are dealt with here. The more general topics include group dynamics, debriefing, evaluation, problem-solving strategies, the validity of role-playing, language learning, and tutorial skills, simulation structure, international politics.)

Miller, A. & Crookall, D. (eds.) 1989. *Simulation and Gaming: Pathways to Progress*. Loughborough: SAGSET (A collection of papers on improving understanding and human skills—e.g., political thinking, career development, social attitudes, crisis management, and communication.)

Race, P. & Brook, D. 1980. *Simulation and Gaming for the 1980s*. London: Kogan Page (The 23 papers in this anthology cover a wide spectrum of topics, including case studies, crisis management, health services, modeling, language learning, communication, culture, video, game design, evaluation, economics, and computers.)

Saunders, D., Coote, A. & Crookall, D. (eds.) 1988. *Learning From Experience Through Simulations and Games*. Loughborough: SAGSET (The three sections in this volume cover many aspects of simulation/gaming: general, interpersonal, and business/management perspectives. Topics include debriefing, research, language learning, interpersonal perspectives, learning disability, oral communication, ice-breaking, cross-cultural communication, homelessness, new business ventures, marketing.)

Shubik, M. 1975. *The Uses and Methods of Gaming*. New York & Amsterdam: Elsevier (General coverage of and guide to simulations and games. The first six chapters deal with topics such as definitions, game theory, goals, modeling, computers. Chapters 7 to 11 provide well-annotated guides to information sources and literature guides [including management, economics, political science, international relations].)

Stahl, I. (ed.) 1983. *Operational Gaming: An International Approach*. Oxford & New York: Pergamon (Contains papers on the state of gaming in various countries, the international transfer of games, East-West trade games, and specific areas [environment, management, realism].)

Tansey, P. J. (ed.) 1971. *Educational Aspects of Simulation*. London & New York: McGraw-Hill (A series of background readings which discuss the advantages of simulation/gaming, provides examples of exercises for specific subject areas and teacher training.)

Thorson, E. (ed.) 1979. *Simulation in Higher Education*. Hicksville, NY: Exposition Press (Covers the use of simulation in a wide range of subject areas [liberal arts, chemistry, logic, urban studies, economics, values clarification, geography, history, international relations, psychology]. Also deals with computers and evaluation.)

van Ments, M. & Hearnden, K. (eds.) 1985. *Effective Use of Games and Simulation*. Loughborough: SAGSET (A collection of 20 papers on a range of topics, including competition, management, debriefing, design, literature, conflict, and discrimination, and 4 papers on humanizing the use of computers.)

Single-area works

Many of works listed above contain individual chapters that specialize in a particular area, although overall the works present a broad spectrum of specializations. The works listed below are whole books that tend to specialize in a particular area. These, again, are useful to foreign and second language instruction.

There are two broad area types. The first type involves more specific simulation/game concerns (e.g., design or computerized simulation), while the second type consists of special-purpose areas (e.g., business or science).

Designing simulation/games

Two very good recent books each deal with a broad range of design topics (Greenblat, 1987; Jones, 1985), while useful general surveys will be found in the other books cited below. Discussions on specific aspects of design are also to be found in some of the general works mentioned above (any discussion on design having been mentioned in the annotation).

Abt, C. C. 1976. *Ten Steps in Game Design.* Cambridge, MA: Abt Associates (A very short introduction.)

Bronstein, R. H. & Maidment, R. 1973. *Simulation Games: Design and Implementation.* Charles E. Merrill (A short introduction; also includes discussion on background questions.)

Cruckshank, D. R. 1977. *A First Book of Games and Simulations.* Belmont, CA: Wadsworth (Concentrates on design, in a sort of programmed text sequence.)

Ellington, H., Addinall, E. & Percival, F. 1982. *A Handbook of Game Design.* London: Kogan Page (Discusses different types of game and gives a detailed analysis of the design process of 12 [mainly science] simulations designed by the authors. Types include card, board, simple manual, and computerized games.)

Ellington, H., Addinall, E. & Percival, F. 1984. *Case Studies in Game Design.* London: Kogan Page (An interesting analysis of 12 science games and simulations designed by the authors.)

Glazier, R. 1969. *How to Design Educational Games.* Cambridge, MA: Abt Associates (An early and short introduction.)

Greenblat, C. S. 1988. *Designing Games and Simulations: An Illustrated Handbook.* Newbury Park, CA: Sage (The definitive guide to simulation/game design [for both novice and experienced gamers]. All the steps in the design process are explained with the aid of many illustrations and extended case studies of how different games were designed. Topics include choosing an appropriate game, overview of the design process, setting objectives and parameters, model development, style and form of representation, construction, modification, writing the game organizer's manual. Contains a lengthy list of simulation/games.)

Inbar, M. & Stoll, C. (eds.) 1971. *Simulation and Gaming in the Social Sciences: The Design Process.* New York: Free Press (See annotation below, under "Social Sciences.")

Jones, K. 1985. *Designing Your Own Simulations*. London: Methuen (This is a practical book with plenty of examples and a minimum of theory. It describes what makes a good simulation, suggests ways of getting started, and gives advice on how to make improvements after the first run-through. The author shows that the key to designing successful and lively simulations is flexibility of ideas, and that plausibility and consistency should constantly be kept in mind. His approach is easily adaptable and will also enable pupils to design their own simulations as a classroom activity.)

Pate, G. S. & Parkes, H. A. 1973. *Designing Classroom Simulations*. Belmont, CA: Lear Sieglar (This short book provides guidance on how to design simple simulation/games. Also discusses evaluation.)

Stolovitch, H. D. & Thiagarajan, S. 1980. *Frame Games*. Englewood Cliffs, NJ: Educational Technology Publications (A frame game is a game format or structure which can be loaded with different kinds of content or skills. Although this book is not explicitly and entirely about design, it is listed here because much of it will be valuable to those who wish to design their own games, especially by using well-tried game formats in new settings and with new subject areas. Some of the games are well known [e.g., KIM'S GAME or RUMMY], and the authors show how the latter can be adapted for learning French verbs.)

Computerized simulation

Computers are being used more and more in simulation/gaming, and this is, of course, reflected in the literature on simulation/gaming. The two major journals devoted to simulation/gaming, as well as the more recent simulation/gaming books (see above), thus carry more and more articles on games which employ computer technology. Likewise, the literature on computers increasingly refers to simulation. Many of the educational and academic computing journals carry items on computerized simulation, most notably *MUESLI News* (for CALL) and the *Social Science Computer Review* (in social science and education more generally), both of which are to be recommended. The main simulation volumes on computerized forms of educational simulation/gaming are as follows.

Barton, R. F. 1970. *A Primer on Simulation and Gaming*. Englewood Cliffs, NJ: Prentice-Hall (This short book concentrates on all-computer simulations, mainly in behavioral sciences.)

Crookall, D. (ed.) 1988. *Computerized Simulation in the Social Sciences*. Durham, NC: Duke University Press. (Special issue of *Social Science Computer Review*, 6:1, Spring 1988.) (This special issue contains nine in-depth papers on a wide range of topics in computerized social science simulations, including an authoring system for computerized simulation, cooperation and conflict, precedent-based models, global modeling, economic modeling, research and teaching considerations, psychology, social relations, and social policy.)

Crookall, D. (ed.) 1988. *Simulation/Games and the New Technologies: Applications and*

Problems. Loughborough: SAGSET. (Special issue of *Simulation/Games for Learning*, 18:1, March 1988.) (This special, double-length issue of SAGSET's well-known journal is devoted to discussions on recent developments and problem areas in the use of computer technologies in simulation/gaming. It contains 12 articles on a whole host of topics, including educational technology and simulation, business training, budgetary control, videodisk technology, interviewing skills, police training, computer-assisted language learning, conversational simulation, social relations, PRISONER'S DILEMMA, international relations, urban planning, and spreadsheets.)

Dutton, J. M. & Starbuck, W. A. 1970. *Computer Simulation in Human Behavior*. New York: John Wiley (Provides a picture of the status [in the late 1960s] of computerized simulation of human behavior as a tool for the social and behavioral sciences. Written from a researcher's viewpoint.)

Willis, J., Hovey, L. & Hovey, K. 1987. *Computer Simulations: A Source Book to Learning in an Electronic Environment*. New York: Garland (This book introduces educational simulations, explains how they integrate into the curriculum, outlines theoretical and research aspects, and discusses practical issues of using computerized simulation. Contains detailed reviews of computerized simulation packages. Topics include adventure games, business, problem solving, science, and social studies.)

Foreign/second language learning

In contrast to the number of (1) collections of language learning games (see next section), (2) volumes on simulation outside language learning, and (3) language learning teacher books on other topics (e.g., CALL or acquisition), only very few books actually have as their main focus the use of simulation/gaming in language learning.

Crookall, D. (ed.) 1985. *Simulation Applications in L2 Education and Research*. Oxford & New York: Pergamon. (Special issue of *System*, 13:3.) (Contains 13 papers on a wide range of topics related to language learning simulation/games, including reality construction, research, communication strategies, social psychological effects, teacher training, conversational simulation in CALL, communications technology, international relations, media gaming, specific purpose language.)

ETIC. 1977. *Games, Simulations and Role-Playing*. (ELT Documents, 77/1.) London: English Teaching Information Centre, British Council (The four short papers and one longish essay cover general topics, including specific-purpose language teaching, role-play, drama techniques.)

Jones, K. 1982. *Simulations in Language Teaching*. Cambridge: Cambridge University Press (The main book on the subject until now. Written mainly from the simulation/gaming perspective, this is a practical book for language teachers. Contains a rationale on why simulation/games should be used, help on choosing them and on how to prepare, run, debrief, and assess them. Also looks at simulation/gaming in teacher education. Can usefully be read in conjunction with the present volume. Contains a simulation about the use and usefulness of simulation.)

Livingstone, C. 1983. *Role Playing in Language Learning*. London: Longman (This small book offers guidance on how to prepare for and run role-plays.)

Oxford, R. (ed.) 1989. *Using and Learning Language Through Simulation/Gaming—I*. Newbury Park, CA: Sage. (Special issue of ISAGA News and Notes, in *Simulation & Games*, 20:4.) (Four articles on various aspects of using simulation/ gaming in language instruction.)

Oxford, R. 1989. *Language Learning Strategies: What Every Language Teacher Should Know*. New York: Newbury House / Harper & Row (This not a book about simulation/gaming, but it contains some examples of useful games to heighten general strategy awareness and of gamelike activities for practicing specific language learning strategies.)

Oxford, R. (ed.) 1990. *Using and Learning Language Through Simulation/Gaming—II*. Newbury Park, CA: Sage. (Special issue of Reports and Communications, in *Simulation & Gaming*, 21:1.) (Four articles on various aspects of using simulation/gaming in language instruction.)

Rixon, S. 1981. *How to Use Games in Language Teaching*. London: Macmillan (This small book contains many useful quidelines on using games.)

von Faber, H., Eichheim, H., Heid, M. & Maley, A. (eds.) 1979. *Rollenspiel und Simulation im Fremdsprachenunterricht*. Paris: Goethe-Institut & British Council (Contains 16 papers [in English, French, and German] on a wide range of topics related to language learning simulation/games, including psychological problems, remedial work, authenticity, closed-circuit TV, cross-cultural simulation, creativity, game classification, drama, visuals, teacher training, teaching immigrants.)

Literacy training

Evans, D. R. 1979. *Games and Simulations in Literacy Training*. Amersham, Bucks: Hulton (A practical exposition of the use of "appropriate educational technology" [i.e., games, role-plays] in the teaching of literacy, numeracy, and "social literacy," mainly in the developing world, but of much relevance to industrialized countries. Chapters cover such aspects as the reason for using simulation/games, the nature of literacy games, using games for literacy and numeracy skill development and for literacy training. Includes a short annotated resource list.)

Communication, human skills, values, and leadership

Christopher, E. M. & Smith, L. E. 1987. *Leadership Training Through Gaming: Power, People and Problem-Solving*. London: Kogan Page; New York: Nichols Publishing (By demonstrating the cause-and-effect relationship between leader behavior and follower response, simulation games can teach potential leaders to use power, handle conflicts, and accept responsibility for their actions. Contains many examples of games, many of which can also be used in areas other than leadership training.)

Crookall, D. & Saunders, D. (eds.) 1989. *Communication and Simulation: From Two Fields to One Theme.* Clevedon, Avon & Philadelphia, PA: Multilingual Matters (The fields of communication and simulation have each become well established in their own right. This book examines the increasing interdependence of the two fields and provides insights into how communication and simulation are mutually supportive. The authors discuss how simulation can be a powerful method for helping participants to understand communication, to practice communication skills, and to become better communicators. They also emphasize the value of analyzing the communicational aspects of simulation and show how communication may provide a unifying conceptual framework for simulation. Topics include game identities, discourse rehearsal, language learning, the deaf, conflict, counselor training, discrimination, intergroup communication, organizations, business, women's networks, policy formation, urban planning, media.)

Fletcher, J. L. (ed.) 1978. *Human Growth Games: Explorations and Research Prospects.* Beverly Hills, CA & London: Sage (Contains articles on such topics as transpersonal relations, self-knowledge, self-directed learning, memory, and beliefs. The material originally appeared in *Simulation and Games: An International Journal of Theory, Design, and Research*, 8:1.)

Hawley, R. C. 1975. *Value Exploration Through Role Playing: Practical Strategies for Use in the Classroom.* New York: Hart (Provides help on how to introduce role-playing; contains 21 role-playing scenarios to examine values; provides detailed, step-by-step suggestions on how to use role-play effectively for value analysis.)

Social sciences

Guetzkow, H. (ed.) 1962. *Simulation in Social Science: Readings.* Englewood Cliffs, NJ: Prentice-Hall (A now-classic collection of essays on the use of simulation as a tool for social science research and education, covering such topics as industry, economics, political science, psychology, and sociology.)

Guetzkow, H., Kotler, P. & Schultz, R. L. 1972. *Simulation in Social and Administrative Science: Overviews and Case-Examples.* Englewood Cliffs, NJ: Prentice-Hall (A major report and reference work [over 750 pages], presenting a broad look at simulation [e.g., taxomony of models, purposes, advantages, and disadvantages], 10 case-examples of the use of simulation in the social and administrative sciences, and methodology and theory.)

Inbar, M. & Stoll, C. S. (eds.) 1972. *Simulation and Gaming in Social Science.* New York: Free Press (This book concentrates on how to design simulation/games for teachers and researchers in the social sciences. Describes the evolution of simulation/games and the theoretical bases in the design process. Provides 12 case studies on well-known simulation/games. Includes an annotated bibliography and examples of simulation/games.)

Livingston, S. A. & Stoll, C. S. 1973. *Simulation Games: An Introduction for the Social Studies Teacher.* London: Collier Macmillan; New York: Free Press (This short book was designed to introduce social studies teachers to simulation/gaming, and covers such topics as research, game design, running games. A large part of the book consists of a complete, ready-to-use game on inner-city housing.)

Shaftel, F. R. & Shaftel, G. 1967. *Role Playing for Social Values: Decision Making in the Social Studies*. Englewood Cliffs, NJ: Prentice-Hall (This has become a classic. Discusses theory and rationale, and provides detailed instruction on how to conduct role-playing exercises. Contains extensive materials for use in role-playing.)

Politics and international relations

Brams, S. J. 1975. *Game Theory and Politics*. New York: Free Press (Concerns logical deduction, theoretical constructs, and complex reasoning processes. Chapter 1 focuses on international relations, while the last six concentrate on voting behavior.)

Clarke, M. 1978. *Simulations in the Study of International Relations*. Ormskirk, Lancs: Hesketh (Provides comprehensive coverage of the main topics and issues, including the nature of simulation, rationales for research and teaching, evaluation, objectives, design, control. Five complete, ready-to-use games are provided.)

Coplin, W. D. (ed.) *Simulation in the Study of Politics*. Chicago: Markham (A collection of chapters dealing with international relations, urban affairs, organizational behavior, and elections.)

Guetzkow, H., Alger, C. F., Brody, R. A., Noel, R. C. & Snyder, R. C. 1963. *Simulation in International Relations: Developments for Research and Teaching*. Englewood Cliffs, NJ: Prentice-Hall (A groundbreaking exploration of the human-computer approach to the simulation of the international political-economic system. Describes and analyzes Guetzkow's now-famous INS [Inter-Nation Simulation].)

Ward, M. D. (ed.) 1985. *Theories, Models, and Simulations in International Relations: Essays in Honor of Harold Guetzkow*. Boulder, CO: Westview Press (The 26 chapters in this advanced volume cover many intricate and complex issues—e.g., global modeling, causal analysis in political science, stochastic models in international relations research.)

History

Birt, D. & Nichol, J. 1975. *Games and Simulations in History*. London: Longman (Covers such aspects as the nature of history games, their design, construction, and use. Includes documents for six games, including TRADE & DISCOVERY [in the 16th Century], the RUSSIAN REVOLUTION, and FRONTIER [about the early colonists of British North America].)

Cavanagh, T. K. Undated (circa 1979). *Simulation Gaming in Canadian History*. Sherbrooke: Progressive Publications (An introduction to the area, covering such areas as design, play, debriefing, rationale. Contains an annotated bibliography and six appendices on various topics—e.g., use and design.)

Geography

Cole, J. P. 1976. *Situations in Human Geography*. Oxford: Blackwell.
Dalton, R. et al. *Simulation Games in Geography*. London: Macmillan.
Haigh, J. M. *Geography Games*. Oxford: Blackwell.
Walford, R. 1969. *Games in Geography*. London: Longman; New York: Humanities Press (Introduces the use of, presents a case study of two schools using, and provides a model for developing, simulation/games.)

Health, nursing, and social work

McCaughan, N. & Scott, T. 1978. *Role Play and Simulation Games: Uses in Social Work Education*. London: National Institute for Social Work.
Thatcher, D. & Robinson, J. (eds.) 1984. *Business, Health and Nursing Education*. Loughborough: SAGSET (Ten of the 18 chapters concern the use of simulation/ games in nursing and health education. The other 8 chapters deal with designing and using games and with business games.)
Wolf, M. S. & Duffy, M. 1979. *Simulation/Games as a Teaching Strategy for Nursing Education*. New York: National League of Nursing.

Management, business, industry, and economics

Elgood, C. 1981. *Handbook of Management Games*. Aldershot, Hants: Gower (This is a comprehensive guide to the area. Part One [about half the book] covers many of the main areas, such as models, umpiring, computers, behavior, choosing and conducting a game. Part Two is a directory of British management games.)
Fitzsimons, A. & Thatcher, D. (eds.) 1987. *Games and Simulations at Work*. Loughborough: SAGSET (A collection of 14 papers on various issues related to work [curricula considerations, work-focused games in training, and unemployment] and on game design.)
Gray, L. & Waitt, I. (eds.) 1982. *Simulation in Management and Business Education*. London: Kogan Page; New York: Nichols Publishing (Although this book concentrates on management and business applications of simulation/gaming [including such aspects as education and school management, land administration, business ESP, and world development], it also covers the theory, design, use, and evaluation of games and simulations. Also has a couple of papers on language learning.)
Jamieson et al. (1988). See "General Works," above.
Reid, M. A. & Keys, B. (eds.) 1987. *Training and Management Development Methods* (Vol. 1). Bradford: MCB University Press (A practical resource for trainers, providing examples of training materials as well as suggestions and hints in the use of various methods. The papers in the simulation section cover such topics as management decision making and strategies, organizational problems, time management, appraisal systems, and business gaming. Many of

the articles include ready-to-use exercises, along with practical "tips" for trainers.)

Wolfe, J. (ed.) 1987. *A Practical Guide to Business Gaming.* Newbury Park, CA, & London: Sage. (Special issue of *Simulation & Games: An International Journal of Theory, Design, and Research,* 18:2, June 1987.) (A collection of articles on various aspects of business gaming, touching on such topics as the impact of micro-computers, experiential learning, and total enterprise business games.)

Science and technology

Ellington, H., Addinall, E. & Percival, F. 1981. *Games and Simulations in Science Education.* London: Kogan Page; New York: Nichols Publishing (This provides comprehensive coverage of the area and discusses the following aspects: rationale for the use of science-based simulation/games, card and board games, computerized simulations, selecting, adapting, and using games, game design, evaluation. Some 60 pages of this 200-page book are given over to a detailed directory of science-based simulation/games.)

Collections of simulation/games

There exist a large number of collections of simulation/games, both in the foreign language field and in others. Many of those cited below were designed specifically for learning English as a second or foreign language (ESL/EFL), but they are, of course, readily adapted to other languages. The items written specifically for language learning, especially those containing very simple games and gamelike activities rather than more complex simulation/games, carry very short annotations, since language teachers will find them easier to get hold of than the other items.

In addition to the collections cited below, some ready-to-use games may be found in some of the books mentioned above (e.g., Clarke, 1978; Taylor & Walford, 1978). It should also be pointed out that many of the collections cited below (especially those containing small-scale exercises, mainly designed for language learning) are no substitute for longer, more complex, and often more involving simulation/games. Some of these larger exercises are to be found in some of the collections below (e.g., Jones, 1985, 1986), but the reader should also look to the next section, "Directories."

Baddock, B. 1983. *Press Ahead: A Teachers' Guide to the Use of Newspapers in English Language Teaching.* Oxford: Pergamon (Not a collection as such, but contains many useful ideas for activities.)

Bond, T. 1986. *Games for Social and Life Skills.* London: Hutchinson (A collection of over 80 games which teach a range of communication, social, and life skills [including self-awareness, decision making, trust, goal planning]. Games should be chosen with care.)

Brandes, D. & Phillips, H. 1978. *Gamesters' Handbook: 140 Games for Teachers and Group Leaders*. London: Hutchinson. Brandes, D. 1982. *Gamesters' Handbook Two*. London: Hutchinson (Both these books contain many games for ice-breaking, developing self-awareness, confidence, decision-making skills, trust, assertiveness, and fun. Games from these books should be chosen with caution because some of them are rather artificial and may make people feel awkward rather than relaxed. Many of the games, however, are worth using.)

Byrne, D. & Rixon, S. 1979. *Communication Games*. (ELT Guide 1.) London: British Council & NFER Publishing (A collection of simple communication games adapted or designed specifically for language learning.)

Carrier, M. 1980. *Take 5: Games and Activities for the Language Learner*. Walton-on-Thames: Nelson-Harrap (A useful collection of interesting exercises.)

Chamberlin, A. & Stenberg, K. 1976. *Play and Practice: Graded Games for English Language Teaching*. London: John Murray (Over 90 exercises, some of which are more useful than others.)

Christison, M. A. & Bassano, S. 1981. *Look Who's Talking: A Guide to the Development of Successful Conversation Groups in Intermediate and Advance ESL Classrooms*. Oxford: Pergamon; San Francisco: Alemany Press (A collection of over 50 games and gamelike activities.)

Clark, R. & McDonough, J. 1982. *Imaginary Crimes: Materials for Simulation and Role Playing*. Oxford & New York: Pergamon (Eight language learning simulation/games involve students as counsel for defense or prosecution, defendant, or witness in courtroom-based dramas.)

Crookall, D., Coote, A. & Klabbers, J. H. G. (eds.) 1986. *ISAGA'86 Games Pack: A Collection of Relatively Simple and Ready-to-Use Games*. Toulon, France: Laboratoire de Simulation, Université de Toulon. (Write to: ISAGA General Secretariat, PO Box 80.140, 3508 TC Utrecht, The Netherlands.) (This small booklet contains a number of games which are not generally available from "standard" simulation/game sources.)

Di Pietro, R. J. 1987. *Strategic Interaction: Learning Languages Through Scenarios*. Cambridge: Cambridge University Press (Discusses and presents a number of gamelike, scenario-based activities.)

Dixey, J. & Rinvolucri, M. 1978. *Get Up and Do It!: Sketch and Mime for EFL*. London: Longman (A collection of useful activities for language learning.)

Dorry, G. N. 1966. *Games for Second Language Learning*. New York: McGraw-Hill (A collection of very simple games.)

Dubin, F. & Margol, M. 1977. *It's Time to Talk: Communication Activities for Learning English as a New Language*. Englewood Cliffs, NJ: Prentice-Hall.

Farthing, J. 1981. *Business Mazes*. St. Albans, Herts: Hart-Davis Educational. Farthing, J. 1982. *Out of the In-Tray*. St. Albans, Herts: Hart-Davis Educational. Farthing, J. 1983. *More Mazes*. St. Albans, Herts: Hart-Davis Educational (Based on the techniques of action mazes and in-tray exercises, developed by A. A. Zoll [1966, *Dynamic Management Education*, Addison-Wesley], the activities in these books have been designed specifically for language learning.)

Frank, C. & Rinvolucri, M. 1983. *Grammar in Action: Awareness Activities for Language Learning*. Oxford & New York: Pergamon Press (A collection of games and gamelike activities to practice grammar.)

Genzel, R. B. & Cummings, M. G. 1986. *Culturally Speaking: A Conversation and Culture Text for Learners of English.* New York: Harper & Row (This book contains a number of simple but effective exercises designed to give intermediate and advanced learners of English the tools they need to communicate effectively in everyday cultural situations. Good examples of how simulation/games are woven into other materials and learning activities.)

Hadfield, J. 1985. *Elementary Communication Games: A Collection of Games and Activities for Elementary Students of English.* Walton-on-Thames, Surrey: Thomas Nelson.

Hadfield, J. 1985. *Advanced Communication Games: A Collection of Games* and *Activities for Intermediate and Advanced Students of English.* Walton-on-Thames, Surrey: Thomas Nelson (Each of these two spiral-bound books contains 20 activities, especially designed for language learning. Plenty of monochrome visuals for reproduction.)

Hayworth, F. *The Language of Discussion: Role-Play Exercises for Advanced Learners.* London: Hodder & Staughton (A small collection of [rather artificial and simplistic] role-plays.)

Herbert, D. & Sturtridge, G. 1979. *Simulations.* (ELT Guide 2.) London: British Council & NFER Publishing (Contains four simple simulations designed for language learning [one of which was inspired by Ken Jones's RADIO COVINGHAM, in *Graded Simulations*].)

Holden, S. 1981. *Drama Techniques for Language Learning.* London: Longman (Useful discussion and ideas.)

Hope, J. & McAra, P. 1984. *Games Nurses Play: Experiential Games for Behavioural Science Programmes.* Oxford & New York: Pergamon (A collection of 12 games dealing with many of the social aspects of work in hospitals and health care units. Topics include social hierarchy in a ward, use of formal and informal communications networks, power structures, ingroup and outgroup feelings, prejudice, conflict.)

Hoper, C., Kutzleb, U., Stobbe, A. & Weber, B. 1975. *Awareness Games: Personal Growth Through Group Interaction.* London: St. James Press (Over 100 games are divided into five categories: making contact, communication and group formation, observation and perception, identification and empathy, aggression and self-assertion. Games should be chosen with caution, but many are suitable for the language classroom.)

Hopson, B. & Hough, P. 1973. *Exercises in Personal and Career Development.* Cambridge: Hobsons Press (After an introduction to the subject area of the book, a series of exercises are grouped under the following topics: sensing, feeling, thinking, doing, education, occupation, life.)

Hover, D. 1986. *Think Twice: Communication Activities for Beginner to Intermediate Students.* Cambridge: Cambridge University Press (A collection of 39 gamelike language activities, mainly for pair work.)

Hyman, R. 1977. *Paper, Pencils and Pennies: Games for Learning and Having Fun.* Englewood Cliffs, NJ: Prentice-Hall (Contains ideas for simulation/games, role-plays, and values-clarification exercises that last anywhere from a minute to an hour, that can be used in a variety of settings, and with nothing more than paper, pencils, and coins.)

Jones, K. 1985/86. *Graded Simulations.* London: Longman. (This comprises three volumes of nine simulation/games, ranging from fairly simple to complex simulation/games on a variety of topics: media, wealth and poverty, job interview, urban development, international crisis, courtroom libel cases. All materials are provided, and permission is given to photocopy student handouts. Originally published in 1974, these games have proved to be some of the most enduring and popular ones around, both in general and communication education and for language learning.)

Jones, K. 1987. *Six Simulations.* Oxford: Basil Blackwell (A set of simulation/games similar to *Graded Simulations* [above], except that they were designed more recently.)

Jones, K. 1989. *A Sourcebook of Management Simulations.* London: Kogan Page (Contains all the information, instructions, and documents that trainers will need to run the 10 management simulations described. The range of skills covered includes decision making, strategy, interpersonal communication, planning, evaluation, presentation, and interviewing.)

Jones, L. 1983. *Eight Simulations For Upper-Intermediate and More Advanced Students of English.* Cambridge: Cambridge University Press (Inspired by Ken Jones's *Graded Simulations* [above], this collection has been designed especially for language learners. In addition to the game materials themselves, a number of language practice exercises are also provided. Themes revolve round the media, education, politics, and public meetings.)

Jones, L. & Kimbrough, V. 1987. *Great Ideas: Listening and Speaking Activities for Students of American English.* Cambridge: Cambridge University Press (A collection of simple but effective gamelike activities.)

Klippel, F. 1984. *Keep Talking: Communicative Fluency Activities for Language Teaching.* Cambridge: Cambridge University Press (A collection of over 100 good and well-explained games and gamelike activities.)

Krupar, K. R. 1973. *Communication Games.* New York: Free Press; London: Collier Macmillan (Contains 33 activities on a range of topics, including self-awareness, perception, listening, decision making, problem solving, organizational communication.)

Lamb, M. 1982. *Factions and Fictions: Exercises for Role-Play.* Oxford & New York: Pergamon (A collection of 15 role-plays for language learning, mainly on economic and political topics.)

Laver, M. 1979. *Playing Politics: Seven Games That Bring Out the Politician in All of Us.* Harmondsworth: Penguin (A collection of some often very exciting political games, which need very few materials to set up. Topics include getting your own way, seizing power, making money, reneging on your promises, fighting elections. Well worth trying with language students who have an interest in politics.)

Lee, W. R. 1965. *Language Teaching Games and Contests.* Oxford: Oxford University Press (Contains many useful items, among some rather simplistic ones.)

Lewicki, R. J., Bowen, D. D., Hall, D. T. & Hall, F. S. 1988. *Experiences in Management and Organizational Behavior.* 3rd ed. New York: John Wiley (This contains some 60 exercises on a wide range of topics: interpersonal and group relationships, decision making and problem solving, negotiation and conflict, leadership, power, communication, career roles.)

Lohfert, W. 1983. *Kommunikative Spiele für Deutsch als Fremdsprache.* Munich: Hueber Verlag.

Lynch, M. 1977. *It's Your Choice*. London: Edward Arnold (Contains six fairly simple, but well-designed, role-plays for language learning.)

Macdonald, M. & Rogers-Gordon, S. 1984. *Action Plans: 80 Student-Centered Language Activities*. Rowley, MA: Newbury House (A collection of games and gamelike activities.)

Maier, N. 1975. *The Role Play Technique*. La Jolla, CA: University Associates (Contains material, detailed instructions, and comments for 20 situations, mainly for business and management training.)

Maley, A. & Duff, A. 1975. *Sounds Interesting*. Cambridge: Cambridge University Press. Maley, A. & Duff, A. 1978. *Variations on a Theme*. Cambridge: Cambridge University Press. Maley, A. & Duff, A. 1979. *Sounds Intriguing*. Cambridge: Cambridge University Press (All three books contain varied, interesting, and intriguing activities, aimed at catching the imagination of learners and allowing them to express themselves creatively.)

Maley, A. & Duff, A. 1982. *Drama Techniques in Language Learning: A Resource book of Communication Activities for Language Teachers*. (2nd ed.) Cambridge: Cambridge University Press (This now-classic collection contains over 170 drama-based activities [German edition: *Szenisches Spiel und freies Sprechen im Fremdsprachenunterricht: Grundlagen und Modelle für die Unterrichtspraxis*. Munich: Hueber Verlag].)

Marshall, S. & Williams, N. 1986. *Exercises in Teaching Communication*. London: Kogan Page; New York: Nichols Publishing (Mainly aimed at communications courses [particularly at Polytechnics in the UK], the book contains about 40 exercises, some of which will be of use for language students, especially those who specialize in science, engineering, and business.)

Menne, S. 1975. *Q-Cards: Role-Playing System for Conversational English*. Tenterden, Kent: Paul Norbury (A few [rather artificial, awkward, and simplistic] role-plays.)

Moskowitz, G. 1978. *Caring and Sharing in the Foreign Language Class*. Rowley, MA: Newbury House (A classic book, containing many useful activities.)

Norman, D. Levihn, U. & Hedenquist, J. A. 1986. *Communication Ideas: An Approach with Classroom Activities*. London: Language Teaching Publications (A discussion, followed by a collection of 82 activities of all kinds.)

Page, B. (ed.) 1982–1984. *Communication in French*. Cambridge: Cambridge University Press (A series containing much useful material.)

Pattison, P. 1987. *Developing Communication Skills: A Practical Handbook for Language Teachers, with Examples in English, French and German*. Cambridge: Cambridge University Press (Contains materials and detailed instructions for over 60 games and gamelike activities, as well as a useful discussion about communication practice in the classroom.)

Paulston, C. B., Britton, D., Brunetti, B. & Hoover, J. 1975. *Developing Communicative Competence: Roleplays in English as a Second Language*. Pittsburgh: University Center for International Studies and the English Language Institute, University of Pittsburgh (A collection of 34 very simple role-plays.)

Pfeiffer, J. W. & Jones, J. E. 1969–. *Handbook of Structured Experiences for Human Relations Training*. (Several volumes over several years, starting 1969.) La Jolla, CA: University Associates. Pfeiffer, J. W. & Jones, J. E. 1972–. *Annual Handbook for Group Facilitators*. (Several volumes over several years, starting 1972.) La Jolla, CA: University Associates (Probably the most famous and successful of all the collections of human relations games or "structured experiences" [many of which have inspired games in some language learning and other collections]. The books in both series contain a number of ready-to-use simulation/games and similar exercises. A very wide range of topics is covered, including planning, trust, competition, cooperation, perception, attitudes, group cohesion. Full details are provided on each exercise [e.g., group size, time, step-by-step instructions].)

Porter Ladousse, G. 1987. *Role Play*. Oxford: Oxford University Press (One of the better collections of role-plays designed specifically for language learners. Contains over 50 role-plays, from the simple to the more complex, lasting from 5 minutes to 4 hours and more, on a wide range of topics and situations, for both general and specific purpose language.)

Ramsey, G. 1978. *Play Your Part*. London: Longman (A collection of 10 very simple role-plays for language learning.)

Rinvolucri, M. 1984. *Grammar Games: Cognitive, Affective and Drama Activities for EFL Students*. Cambridge: Cambridge University Press (A collection of a variety of 56 simple but effective games and gamelike activities.)

Rogers, R. 1985. *Six Role Plays*. Oxford: Basil Blackwell (A collection of simple role-plays for language learners. The allocation of roles should be done with care, since roles tend to be very personalized and somewhat behavior-prescriptive. The choice of role-play too needs care—e.g., KIDNAPPED would seem to be an unlikely situation for most language, indeed any, learners. Probably more suitable for younger learners, who may have less difficulty in being a little theatrical.)

Ruben, B. D. 1979. *Human Communication Handbook: Simulations and Games, Volume 2*. Rochelle Park, NJ: Hayden. Ruben, B. D. & Budd, R. W. 1975. *Human Communication Handbook: Simulations and Games*. Rochelle Park, NJ: Hayden (Good collections of experience-based activities [puzzles, group exercises, games and simulations] focusing on personal, social, and mass communication processes. Topics include journalism, English, social studies, mass communication.)

Sawyer-Lauçanno, C. 1987. *Case Studies in International Management*. Englewood Cliffs, NJ: Prentice-Hall (Ten case studies, dealing with international management situations, are tied together by two common themes: their international nature and the prominence of English as a language of worldwide communication. These cases will help students of English to become more fluent in the four skills while learning about the world of business.)

Spaventa, L. (ed.) 1980. *Towards the Creative Teaching of English*. London: Allen & Unwin (A collection of games, gamelike and role-play activities.)

Troyka, L. Q. & Nudelman, J. 1975. *Taking Action: Writing, Reading, Speaking, and Listening Through Simulation Games*. Englewood Cliffs, NJ: Prentice-Hall (Contains simulation/games with a social science setting designed for [first language] English and communication studies. Each simulation/game involves the four language skills. The book also includes an introduction to using simulation/games and a chapter on communication skills.)

Ur, P. 1981. *Discussions That Work*. Cambridge: Cambridge University Press (Well known to language teachers, this book contains many useful games and gamelike activities for language learning.)

Ur, P. 1988. *Grammar Practice Activities: A Practical Guide for Teachers*. Cambridge:

Cambridge University Press. (Contains nearly 200 games and gamelike activities, with guidelines for the design of such activities and for effective classroom presentation. Covers all of the essential structures of English, and many of the activities can be adapted to other languages.)

Walcott, C. (ed.) 1980. *Simple Simulations II: A Collection of Simulation/Games for Political Scientists.* Washington, DC: American Political Science Association (A collection of 24 simulation/games, covering such topics as American politics, public administration and government, the judicial process, political theory, comparative and international politics.)

Watcyn-Jones, P. 1981. *Pair Work: Activities for Effective Communication.* Harmondsworth: Penguin (A collection of language learning games and gamelike activities, using two books [one for each member of a pair].)

Watcyn-Jones, P. 1981. *Act English: A Book of Role-Plays.* Harmondsworth: Penguin (A collection of 24 simple role-plays for language learning.)

Weeks, W. H., Pedersen, P. B. & Brislin, R. W. (eds.) 1979. *A Manual of Structured Experiences for Cross-Cultural Learning.* Yarmouth, ME: Intercultural Press (and the International Society for Intercultural Education, Training and Research) (A collection of 59 exercises on such topics as the dynamics of communication, values clarification, roles, group processes, feelings, attitudes, and intergroup communication.)

Weiss, F. 1983. *Jeux et Activités Communicatives dans la Classe de Langue.* Paris: Hachette (Some useful activities.)

Winn-Bell Olsen, J. E. 1977. *Communication-Starters and Other Activities for the ESL Classroom.* Hayward, CA: Alemany Press (A large collection of games, gamelike and other activities.)

Wright, A., Betteridge, D. & Buckby, M. 1979. *Games for Language Learning.* Cambridge: Cambridge University Press (Details on a many useful games.)

Wynn, M. 1985. *Planning Games.* London: Spon (These are more case studies than simulation/games. Contains seven exercises on various aspects of urban and rural planning.)

Directories

A number of directories, catalogs, and resource lists of books and articles and of simulation/games themselves have been published over the years. Those that carry information on games tend to become out of date fairly quickly simply because many of the smaller games remain available only for a short time. However, games published in books or in book form stay in print for longer periods. The items below will provide readers with ample leads to find games suited to their particular purposes. In addition to the sources below, the periodicals on simulation/gaming (see above) provide much hard-to-come-by information on new publications and games.

Belch, J. 1973. *Contemporary Games.* Vol. 1. Detroit: Gale Research Company (Lists over 900 simulation/games for all educational levels [up to 1972]. Information provided includes brief annotations, cross references, a guide to 74 subject areas, age, grade, producer. Note that many of the games listed will now be out of print or unobtainable.)

Belch, J. 1974. *Contemporary Games.* Vol. 2, Bibliography. Detroit: Gale Research Company (Contains over 2300 bibliographical entries [from 1965 to 1973], most of which are annotated. Categories include general, classroom use, business and management, research, directories, other bibliographies.)

Coppard, L. C. & Goodman, F. L. (eds.) 1979. *Urban Gaming/Simulation: A Handbook for Educators and Trainers.* Ann Arbor: University of Michigan (The first 40 or so pages of this book are given over to discussions on the nature of urban gaming, its growth, design, evaluation, and use, and an annotated bibliography. The last 530 pages constitute a very detailed, evaluative directory of nearly 100 games.)

Elgood, C. 1981. *Handbook of Management Games.* Aldershot, Hants: Gower (About half of this book is a detailed directory of British management games in alphabetical order, but many of them seem to be expensive or unobtainable.)

Gibbs, G. I. (ed.) 1974. *Handbook of Game and Simulation Exercises.* London: Spon (Provides information on almost 2000 games, although many of the games would now be difficult to obtain.)

Horn, R. E. & Cleaves, A. (eds.) 1980. *The Guide to Simulation/Games for Education and Training.* (4th ed.) Beverly Hills, CA: Sage (This is considered to be the definitive directory of simulation/games. The 690 pages of this large-format book provide detailed descriptions and evaluations of over 1200 simulation/games in almost every conceivable area. The first 290 pages are devoted to 24 essays, which either provide comparative evaluations of a number of games on a particular topic [e.g., social studies, business, sex roles] or evaluate a particular game [e.g., SIMSOC]. The games are listed under 32 headings [e.g., ecology, politics, economics, marketing]. Information provided includes grade, number of players, time, packaging, description, cost, producer. Note that some of the games listed will now be out of print or unobtainable.)

SAGSET. Various dates. *Resource lists.* Loughborough: SAGSET (These resource lists contain the most up-to-date publications on available books, articles, and simulation/games. They can be obtained for a modest price through membership of the British-based association SAGSET. New members automatically receive Don Thatcher's *Introduction to Games and Simulations: A Resource List.* Other lists cover such topics as international relations, human relations, language learning, design. Full details from SAGSET [see "Associations," above].)

Stadsklev, R. 1979. *Handbook of Simulation Gaming in Social Education.* (Part 2: Directory of Non-computer Materials). Tuscaloosa, AL: Institute of Higher Education Research and Services, University of Alabama (The 380 pages of this large-format book provide detailed notes on over 700 simulation/games. Subject areas include environment, economics, geography, health, history, political science, psychology, sociology, and teacher training. Information provided includes source, grade, time, number of participants, cost, description. Note that some of the games listed will now be out of print or unobtainable.)

See also Taylor & Walford (1978), above, under "Introductory and More Practical

Works.'' Note that many of the games listed are now out of print or unobtainable.

See also Willis et al. (1987), above, under "Computerized Simulation," for a directory of computerized simulations for education (running mainly on the Apple computer).

Questions and activities

1. From Chapter 24, select at least two books which discuss simulation/gaming, preferably nonlanguage works such as K. Jones (1987, 1988), Greenblat & Duke (1981), Greenblat (1988), or Crookall and Saunders (1989). Read them (or parts of them!). Make a summary of their key points and discuss with other people.
2. Find a collection of language simulation/games such as those listed in Chapter 24. Try out some of these activities with your classes.
3. With your language classes, select some non-language-learning simulation/games (i.e., ones not designed primarily with language learning purposes in mind) from the collections listed in Chapter 24. Consider how these simulation/games can be useful to you and your classes, and in what ways they can be tailored to serve your students' particular interests and language needs. Try out the selected activities, as you did in item 2.
4. Contact one or more of the simulation/gaming associations listed in Chapter 24. Joining one of these associations—and especially attending its annual conferences and reading its publications—will provide rich benefits if you are seeking new ideas for the classroom. Go to a conference or workshop sponsored by the association. Read the association publications. Get to know other members. Consider what you are learning and how this can help you and your students.

References

The following list of references includes a number of foreign and second language simulation/gaming works not cited in the text of this volume. They have been included here for those who wish to explore further the application of simulation/gaming to foreign and second language learning. For an annotated list of works on simulation/gaming, the reader is referred to Chapter 24.

If you learn of any relevant references not mentioned below, please send them to the publisher, who will pass them on to the editors for inclusion in any new edition of this book. Appropriate acknowledgment will be made. Thank you.

Abbott, E. 1984. Tackling two problem questions-forms with a communication game. *World Language English*, 3(2):104–106.

AGITANIA; LOBU LOBU; HYPOTHETICA; MEDITANIA; SOLIDANIA. Ruben, B. D. & Budd, R. W. 1975. In Ruben, B. D. & Budd, R. W. 1975. *Human Communication Handbook: Simulations and Games* (vol. 2). Rochelle Park, NJ: Hayden.

Alatis, J. (Ed.) 1980. *Current Issues in Bilingual Education*. Washington, DC: Georgetown University Press.

Al-Gaylani, G. 1978. Role-simulation and spoken English. *IDELTI Bulletin*, 5:9–11.

Allwright, R. 1976. Language learning through communication practice. *ELT Documents*, 76(1).

Anderson, R. J. 1987. The reality problem in games and simulations. In Crookall, D., Greenblat, C. S., Coote, A., Klabbers, J. H. G. & Watson, D. R. (Eds.) *Simulation-Gaming in the Late 1980s*. Oxford: Pergamon.

APARTMENT SEARCH. 1989. Cambridge, MA: M.I.T.

Atkinson, J. M. & Heritage, J. (Eds.) 1984. *Structures of Social Action: Studies in Conversation Analysis*. Cambridge: Cambridge University Press.

AUNT SADIE'S GIFT. Ryberg, C. & Verluis, E. 1982. Ashland, OR: Southern Oregon State College.

Austin, J. L. 1962. *How to Do Things with Words*. Cambridge, MA: Harvard University Press; Oxford: Oxford University Press.

BAFA BAFA. Shirts, R. G. 1974. La Jolla, CA: Simile II.

Barrows, J. & Zorn, J. 1983. Fifteen concise role plays and how to use them. *English Teaching Forum*, 21(1):23–70.

Beckerman, B. 1970. *Dynamics of Drama*. New York: Knopf.

Belanger, B. 1981. Play in the second language classroom. *Medium*, 6(1):17–22.

Berger, P. L. & Luckmann, T. 1966. *The Social Construction of Reality: A Treatise on the Sociology of Knowledge.* New York: Doubleday; Harmondsworth: Penguin.

Berger, M. & Rinvolucri, M. 1981. *Mazes: A Problem-Solving Reader.* London: Heinemann.

Berlo, D. 1960. *The Process of Communication.* New York: Holt, Rinehart & Winston.

Bertrand, Y. 1974. Simulation et enseignement de langues. *Praxis Neusprachlichen Unterrichts,* 21.

Bertrand, Y. 1978. Quelques problèmes psychologiques du jeu de rôles. *Recherches et Echanges,* 3(1). Reprinted in Von Faber, H., Eichheim, H., Heid, M. & Maley, A. (Eds.) 1979. *Rollenspiel und Simulation im Fremdsprachenunterricht* (Pariser Werkstattgesprach, 1977). Paris: Goethe-Institut & British Council.

BLEEPER, The. Higgins, J. Unpublished. For Newbrain computer.

Bligh, D. A. 1972. *What's the Use of Lectures?* London: Penguin.

Blumer, H. 1972. Symbolic interactionism. In Budd, R. & Ruben, B. (Eds.) *Approaches to Human Communication.* Rochelle Park, NJ: Hayden; New York: Spartan.

Bolitho, R. 1981. Review of Jones (1980). *English Language Teaching Journal,* 36(1).

Bonin, T. N. & Birckbichler, D. W. 1975. Real communication through interview and conversation cards. *Modern Language Journal,* 59.

Boyle, J. 1980. Establishing the right atmosphere for role play. *Modern English Teacher,* 8(1):4–6.

Brand, M. 1983. Developing communicative skills in non-native speakers through dramatic techniques. *Association for Communication Administration Bulletin,* 45:44–60.

Brecht, R. D., Noel, R. C. & Wilkenfeld, J. 1984. Computer simulation in the teaching of foreign language and international relations. *Foreign Language Annals,* 17(6):575–584.

Bredemeier, M. E. & Greenblat, C. S. 1981. The educational effectiveness of simulations and games: A synthesis of findings. *Simulation and Games,* 12(3).

Breen, M. P. 1983. The social context for language learning: A neglected situation? *Second Language Acquisition,* 7:135–158.

Brice-Heath, S. 1982. What no bedtime story means: Narrative skills at home and school. *Language and Society,* 11:49–76.

Brice-Heath, S. 1983. *Ways with Words: Language, Life, and Work in Communities and Classrooms.* Cambridge: Cambridge University Press.

Brims, J. 1981. Role playing for advanced business classes. *Al-Manakh,* 5(2):99–116.

British Council. 1979. *Communication Games in a Language Programme.* London: British Council, English Language Teaching Institute. (Films for Language Teachers No 4; accompanying notes for teacher trainers.)

Brossard, G. 1976. Exemple de simulation. *Français dans le Monde,* 123:31–34.

Brown, H. D. 1987. *Principles of Language Learning and Teaching* (2nd ed). Englewood Cliffs, NJ: Prentice-Hall.

Brown, J., Burton, R. & de Kleer, J. 1982. Pedagogical, natural language and knowledge engineering techniques in SOPHIE I, II and III. In Sleeman, D. & Brown, J. (Eds.) *Intelligent Tutoring Systems.* London: Academic Press.

Bruin, K., DeHaan, J., Teijken, C. & Veeman, W. (Eds.) 1979. *How to Build a Simulation/Game: Proceedings of the 10th ISAGA Conference.* Leeuwarden, Netherlands: ISAGA.

Brumfit, C. 1984. *Communicative Methodology in Language Teaching: The Roles of Fluency and Accuracy.* Cambridge: Cambridge University Press.

Brumfit, C., Phillips, M. & Skehan, P. (Eds.) 1985. *Computers in English Language Teaching*. (ELT Documents, 122.) Oxford: Pergamon.

Brunt, J. 1984. In *Times Educational Supplement*, 26 October 1984.

BUCCANEER BILLY'S BAD BARGAIN. Versluis, E. 1983. Ashland, OR: Southern Oregon State College.

Budd, R. 1989. Simulating academic research: One approach to a study-skills course. *English Language Teaching Journal*, 43(1):30–37.

Budd, R. & Ruben, B. (Eds.) 1972. *Approaches to Human Communication*. Rochelle Park, NJ: Hayden; New York: Spartan.

Bullard, N. 1983. Ideas on group animation. In Holden, S. (Ed.) *Second Selections from Modern English Teacher*. Harlow: Longman.

Bullock Committee. 1975. *A Language for Life*. Report of the Committee of Inquiry appointed by the Secretary of State for Education and Science. London: HMSO.

Burke, E. V., Khoo, R., Boey, L. K., Richards, D. R. & Richards, J. C. (Eds.) 1979. *Guidelines for Communication Activities*. Singapore: SEAMEO Regional Language Centre.

Burke, E. V., Khoo, R., Boey, L. K., Richards, D. R. & Richards, J. C. (Eds.) 1980. *Guidelines for Language Games*. Singapore: SEAMEO Regional Language Centre.

BUSINESS MANAGEMENT LABORATORY, The. Jensen, R. L. & Cherrington, D. J. 1984. Plano, TX: Business Publications.

Button, G. & Lee, J. R. E. *Talk and Social Organisation*. Clevedon: Multilingual Matters.

Butzkamm, W. & Dodson, C. J. 1980. The teaching of communication: From theory to practice. *International Review of Applied Linguistics*, 18(4):289–309.

Byrd, D. R. H. & Clemente-Cabetas, I. 1980. *React, Interact: Situations for Communication*. New York: Regents Publishing Company.

Byrne, D. 1977. Cuecards for interaction. *Modern English Teacher*, 5(3).

Byrne, D. 1983. Cuecards. In Holden, S. (Ed.) *Second Selections from Modern English Teacher*. Harlow: Longman.

Byrne, D. & Rixon, S. 1979. *Communication Games*. (ELT Guide 1.) London: NFER-Nelson for British Council.

Cameron, K., Dodd, S. & Rahtz, S. (Eds.) 1986. *Computers and Modern Language Teaching*. London: Horwood.

Canale, M. & Swain, M. 1980. Theoretical bases of communicative approaches to second language teaching and testing. *Applied Linguistics*, 1:89–112.

CANBIAN EDUCATIONAL AID PROJECT, The. Herbert, D. & Sturtridge, G. 1979. In Herbert, D. & Sturtridge, G. 1979. *Simulations—ELT Guide 2*. London: ELTI & British Council.

Candlin, C. N. & Murphy, D. (Eds.) 1986. *Lancaster Practical Papers in English Language Education*, Vol 7. Oxford: Pergamon.

Care, J. M. 1983. Des "matrices" pour des jeux de rôles. *Français dans le Monde*, 176:75–78.

Carrell, P. 1984. Schema theory and ESL reading: Classroom implications and applications. *Modern Language Journal*, 68(4):332–343.

Carroll, B. 1980. *Testing Communicative Performance*. Oxford: Pergamon.

Carroll, B. 1981. In ELTA/OUP (1981). London Workshop 1981. Beirut, Lebanon: Oxford University Press.

Carroll, B. 1982. How to develop communicative language tests. *World Language English*, 2(1).

Cazden, C., Vera, J. & Hymes, D. (Eds.) 1972. *Functions of Language in the Classroom.* New York: Teachers College Press.

Centre for British Teachers. Undated. *Take Five.* Colchester: Centre for British Teachers.

Chamberlain, A. & Stenberg, K. 1976. *Play and Practice! Graded Games for English Language Teaching.* London: Murray.

Cheery, C. 1957. *On Human Communication.* Cambridge, MA: M.I.T. Press.

Christison, M. A. & Bassano, S. 1981. *Look Who's Talking: A Guide to the Development of Successful Conversation Groups in Intermediate and Advanced ESL Classrooms.* Oxford: Pergamon.

CILT. 1982. *Using Drama, Roleplay Games and Songs in Foreign Language Teaching: Specialized Bibliography.* London: British Council, CILT.

Clark, M. & Handscombe, J. (Eds.) 1983. *On TESOL '82: Pacific Perspectives of Language Learning and Teaching.* Washington, DC: TESOL.

Clark, R. & McDonough, J. 1982. *Imaginary Crimes: Materials for Simulation and Role Playing.* Oxford: Pergamon.

Clarke, M. 1978. *Simulations and the Study of International Relations.* Ormskirk, Lancs: G.W. & A. Hesketh.

Clément, R. 1980. Ethnicity, contact and communicative competence in a second language. In Giles, H., Robinson, W. P. & Smith, P. M. (Eds.) *Language: Social Psychological Perspectives.* Oxford: Pergamon.

Clément, R. & Kruidenier, B. G. 1985. Aptitude, attitude and motivation in second language proficiency: A test of Clement's model. *Journal of Language and Social Psychology,* 4:21–37.

Cohen, K. & Rhenman, E. 1984. The role of management games in education and research. *Management Science,* 7(2):153–158.

Cohen, L., Thomas, J. & Manion, L. (Eds.) 1980. *Educational Research and Development in Britain 1970–1980.* Windsor, Berks: NFER-Nelson.

Coleman, D. W. 1985. TERRI: A CALL lesson simulating conversational interaction. In Crookall, D. (Ed.) *Simulation Applications in L2 Education and Research.* Oxford: Pergamon. (Special issue of *System,* 13(3).)

Coleman, D. W. 1987. Computer-assisted language acquisition: Planting a SEED. In Crookall, D., Greenblat, C. S., Coote, A., Klabbers, J. H. G. & Watson, D. R. (Eds.) *Simulation/Gaming in the Late 1980s.* Oxford: Pergamon.

Coleman, D. W. 1988a. Conversational simulation in computer-assisted language learning: Potential and reality. In Crookall, D. (Ed.) *Simulation/Games and the New Technologies: Applications and Problems.* Loughborough: SAGSET. (Special issue of *Simulation/Games for Learning,* 18(1):77–87.)

Coleman, D. W. 1988b. Simulating conversation with a PARUT. In Crookall, D., Klabbers, J. H. G., Coote, A., Saunders, D., Cecchini, A. & Della Piane, A. (Eds.) *Simulation-Gaming in Education and Training.* Oxford: Pergamon.

CO-MADE (Cooperative Materials Design simulation). Crookall, D. 1989. Unpublished simulation/game.

Condon, C. 1979. Treasure hunts for English practice. *English Language Teaching Journal,* 34:153–155.

Condon, C. 1983. Treasure hunts for English practice. In Oller, J. W. Jr. & Richard-Amato, P. A. (Eds.) *Methods That Work: A Smorgasbord of Ideas for Language Teachers.* Rowley, MA: Newbury House.

Cook, V. J. 1983. Making up characters for role play. *World Language English*, 2(4):249–250.

Cook, V. J. 1985. Bridging the gap between computers and language teaching. In Brumfit, C., Phillips, M. & Skehan, P. (Eds.) *Computers in English Language Teaching*. (ELT Documents, 122.) Oxford: Pergamon.

Cook, V. J. & Fass, D. 1986. Natural Language Processing in EFL. In Higgins, J. (1982). How real is a computer simulation? *ELT Documents*, 113. London: British Council.

Coote, A., Crookall, D. & Saunders, D. 1985. Some human and machine aspects of computerized simulations. In Van Ments, M. & Hearnden, K. (Eds.) *Effective Use of Games and Simulations*. Loughborough: SAGSET.

Covert, A. & Thomas, G. L. 1978. *Communication Games and Simulations*. Urbana, IL: ERIC Clearinghouse on Reading & Communication Skills.

Craig, S. & Martin, A. (Eds.) 1986. *Simulations and Games for Capability*. Loughborough: SAGSET.

Crookall, D. 1978. The design and exploitation of a role play/simulation. *Recherches et Echanges*, 3(1).

Crookall, D. 1979. Variations on the theme of ALIBI. *Modern English Teacher*, 7(1). Reprinted in Holden, S. (Ed.) 1983. *Second Selections from Modern English Teacher*. Harlow: Longman.

Crookall, D. 1983a. Learner training: A neglected strategy—Parts 1 & 2. *Modern English Teacher*, 11(1):31–33; 11(2):41–42.

Crookall, D. 1983b. Picture Stories. *Modern English Teacher*, 10(4).

Crookall, D. 1984a. The use of non-ELT simulation. *English Language Teaching Journal*, 38(4):262–273. Reprinted, 1985, in *Focus on English*, 1(1):11–22.

Crookall, D. 1984b. Review of Jones, K. (1982) *Simulations in Language Teaching*. *System*, 12(1).

Crookall, D. 1985a. Media gaming and NEWSIM: A computer-assisted, "real news" simulation. In Crookall, D. (Ed.) *Simulation Applications in L2 Education and Research*. Oxford: Pergamon. (Special issue of *System*, 13(3).)

Crookall, D. (Ed.) 1985b. *Simulation Applications in L2 Education and Research*. Oxford: Pergamon. (Special issue of *System*, 13(3).)

Crookall, D. 1986a. CALLS—Computer-assisted language learning simulations. In Cameron, K., Dodd, S. & Rahtz, S. (Eds.) *Computers and Modern Language Teaching*. London: Horwood.

Crookall, D. 1986b. Writing short stories for the BBC World Service. *System*, 14(3).

Crookall, D. 1988a. Combining the new technologies and simulations: An overview. In Crookall, D. (Ed.) *Simulation/Games and the New Technologies: Applications and Problems*. Loughborough: SAGSET. (Special issue of *Simulation/Games for Learning*, 18(1).)

Crookall, D. 1988b. Computerized simulation: An overview. In Crookall, D. (Ed.) *Computerized Simulation in the Social Sciences*. Durham, NC: Duke University Press. (Special issue of *Social Science Computer Review*, 6(1).)

Crookall, D. 1990. Task-based teacher training: CO-MADE (COoperative MAterials DEvelopment). *Papers in Applied Linguistics*, 1(2).

Crookall, D., Klabbers, J. H. G., Coote, A., Saunders, D., Cecchini, A. & Della Piane, A. (Eds.) 1988. *Simulation-Gaming in Education and Training*. Oxford: Pergamon.

Crookall, D., Martin, A., Saunders, D. & Coote, A. 1986. Human and computer involvement in simulation. *Simulation and Games*, 17(3).

Crookall, D. & Oxford, R. 1990. Dealing with anxiety: Some practical activities for language learners and teacher trainees. In Horwitz, E. K. & Young, D. J. (Eds.) *Language Anxiety: From Theory and Research to Classroom Implications.* Englewood Cliffs, NJ: Prentice-Hall.

Crookall, D., Oxford, R. & Saunders, D. 1987. Towards a reconceptualization of simulation: From representation to reality. *Simulation/Games for Learning*, 17(4).

Crookall, D., Oxford, R., Saunders, D. & Coote, A. 1988. Icebreaking via collective decision-making: ISLAND ESCAPE. In Saunders, D., Coote, A. & Crookall, D. (Eds.) *Learning from Experience through Simulations and Games.* Loughborough: SAGSET.

Crookall, D., Oxford, R., Saunders, D. & Lavine, R. 1989. Our multicultural global village: Foreign languages, simulations and network gaming. In Crookall, D. & Saunders, D. (Eds.) *Communication and Simulation: From Two Fields to One Theme.* Clevedon, Avon: Multilingual Matters.

Crookall, D. & Saunders, D. (Eds.) 1989. *Communication and Simulation: From Two Fields to One Theme.* Clevedon, Avon: Multilingual Matters.

Crookall, D., Saunders, D. & Coote, A. 1987. The SIMULATION DESIGN GAME: An activity for exploring the simulation design process. In Fitzsimons, A. & Thatcher, D. (Eds.) *Games and Simulations at Work.* Loughborough: SAGSET.

Crookall, D. & Watson, D. R. 1985. Some theoretical and applied perspectives on a jigsaw reading exercise. *ITL Review of Applied Linguistics*, 69:43–79.

Crookall, D. & Wilkenfeld, J. 1985. ICONS: Communications technologies and international relations. In Crookall, D. (Ed.) *Simulation Applications in L2 Education and Research.* Oxford: Pergamon. (Special issue of *System*, 13(3).)

Crookall, D. & Wilkenfeld, J. 1986. Information technology in the service of a worldwide multi-institutional simulation. In Damste, P. S. (Ed.) *Development of Educational Software and Courseware.* Oxford: Pergamon.

Cumming, A. 1984. Simulation or reality? A group project in writing. *TESL Canada Journal/Revue TESL du Canada*, 2(1):82–89.

Cunningsworth, A. & Horner, D. 1985. The role of simulation in the development of communication strategies. In Crookall, D. (Ed.) *Simulation Applications in L2 Education and Research.* Oxford: Pergamon. (Special issue of *System*, 13(3).)

Curtis, R. 1985. Cross-cultural communication: A simulation. Workshop at CATESOL Conference, April 1985.

Cziko, G. A., Lambert, W. E., Sidoti, N. & Tucker, G. R. 1980. Graduates of early immersion: Retrospective views of grade 11 students and their parents. In St. Clair, R. N. & Giles, H. (Eds.) *The Social and Psychological Contexts of Language.* Hillsdale, NJ: Lawrence Erlbaum.

DALEY THOMSON'S DECATHLON. Ocean Software. For Spectrum, Commodore and Amstrad computers.

d'Anglejan, A. 1978. Language learning in and out of classrooms. In Richards, J. (Ed.) *Understanding Second or Foreign Language Learning.* Rowley, MA: Newbury House.

Davies, N. F. 1980. Oral fluency training and small groups. *English Teaching Forum*, 18(3).

Davison, A. & Gordon, P. 1978. *Games and Simulations in Action*. London: Woburn Educational.

de Berkeley-Wykes, J. 1983. Jigsaw reading. In Oller, J. W. Jr. & Richard-Amato, P. A. (Eds.) *Methods That Work: A Smorgasbord of Ideas for Language Teachers*. Rowley, MA: Newbury House.

Debyser, F. 1974a. Simulation et réalité dans l'enseignement des langues vivantes. *Le Français dans le Monde*, 104 & 106.

Debyser, F. 1974b. Simulation et réalité. *Le Français dans le Monde*, 104:6–10.

Debyser, F. 1979. Recherches au BELC sur la simulation et la créativité. In Von Faber, H., Eichheim, H., Heid, M. & Maley, A. (Eds.) *Rollenspiel und Simulation im Fremdsprachenunterricht* (Pariser Werkstattgesprach, 1977). Paris: Goethe-Institut & British Council.

Delamont, S. 1976. *Interaction in the classroom*. London: Methuen.

de Margerie, C. 1979. CFTV et simulation. In Von Faber, H., Eichheim, H., Heid, M. & Maley, A. (Eds.) *Rollenspiel und Simulation in Fremdsprachenunterricht* (Pariser Werkstattgesprach, 1977). Paris: Goethe-Institut & British Council.

Dent-Young, J. 1977. Role-play in language teaching. *RELC Journal*, 8(1):61–68.

Diadori, P. 1987. Simulation strategy and communicative approach in CALL. In Crookall, D., Greenblat, C. S., Coote, A., Klabbers, J. H. G. & Watson, D. R. (Eds.) *Simulation/Gaming in the Late 1980s*. Oxford: Pergamon.

Dickinson, L. 1981. Have you got Mr. Bun the Baker?: Problems and solutions in the use of games, role-play and simulations. *English Language Teaching Journal*, 35(4).

Dickinson, L. & Carver, D. 1980. Learning how to learn: Steps towards self-direction in foreign language learning in schools. *English Language Teaching Journal*, 35(1).

Diffley, F. J. 1985. Course syllabus for business argumentation. Los Angeles: American Language Institute/USC (unpublished).

Di Pietro, R. J. 1981. Discourse and real-life roles in the ESL classroom. *TESOL Quarterly*, 15(1).

Di Pietro, R. J. 1982. The open-ended scenario: A new approach to conversation. *TESOL Quarterly*, 16(1).

Di Pietro, R. J. 1983. Scenarios, discourse, and real-life roles. In Oller, J. W. Jr. & Richard-Amato, P. A. (Eds.) *Methods That Work: A Smorgasbord of Ideas for Language Teachers*. Rowley, MA: Newbury House.

Di Pietro, R. J. 1984. Unpredictability in conversational discourse. The Tenth LACUS Forum 1983. Columbia, SC: Hornbeam.

Di Pietro, R. J. 1987. *Strategic Interaction: Learning Languages Through Scenarios*. Cambridge: Cambridge University Press.

Dixey, J. N. 1976. Sketches and role-play in your classroom. *Zielsprache Englisch*, 6(3).

Dixey, J. N. & Rinvolucri, M. 1978. *Get Up and Do It!* London: Longman.

DOCTOR. See ELIZA.

Donahue, M. & Parsons, A. H. 1982. The use of roleplay to overcome cultural fatigue. *TESOL Quarterly*, 16(3).

Dorry, G. N. 1966. *Games for Second Language Learning*. New York: McGraw-Hill.

Dresner, J., Beck, K., Morgano, C. & Custer, L. 1979. *It's Up to You*. New York: Longman.

Dubin, F. 1985. The use of simulation in courses for language teachers. In Crookall, D. (Ed.) *Simulation Applications in L2 Education and Research*. Oxford: Pergamon. (Special issue of *System*, 13(3).)

Dubin, F. & Margol, M. 1979. *It's Time to Talk: Communication Activities for Learning English as a New Language*. Englewood Cliffs, NJ: Prentice-Hall.

Dufeu, B. 1983a. Le jeu de rôle: Repères pour une pratique. *Français dans le Monde*, 176:43–44.

Dufeu, B. 1983b. Techniques de jeu de rôle. *Français dans le Monde*, 176:69–74.

Duke, R. D. 1974. *Gaming: The Future's Language*. New York: Halsted Press.

Duke, R. D. 1989. Gaming/simulation: A gestalt communications form. In Crookall, D. & Saunders, D. (Eds.) *Communication and Simulation: From Two Fields to One Theme*. Clevedon, Avon: Multilingual Matters.

Dulay, H. & Burt, M. 1978. Some remarks on the creative construction process in child language acquisition. In Ritchie, W. (Ed.) *Second Language Acquisition Research: Issues and Implications*. New York: Academic Press.

Dumas, D. 1985. La simulation dans l'enseignement de l'espagnol et des techniques d'expression. In Crookall, D. (Ed.) *Simulation Applications in L2 Education and Research*. Oxford: Pergamon. (Special issue of *System*, 13(3).)

Early, P. B. (Ed.) 1977a. *Games, Simulations and Role-Playing*. ELT Documents 77(1). London: British Council.

Early, P. B. 1977b. Postscript. In Early, P. B. (Ed.) *Games, Simulations and Role-Playing*. ELT Documents 77(1). London: British Council.

Edelhoff, C. 1979. Rollenspiel und Simulationsspiel als methodisches Mittel in der fremdsprachlichen Lehrerfortbildung. In Von Faber, H., Eichheim, H., Heid, M. & Maley, A. (Eds.) *Rollenspiel und Simulation im Fremdsprachenunterricht* (Pariser Werkstattgesprach, 1977). Paris: Goethe-Institut & British Council.

ELIZA. Weizenbaum, J. 1965. See Weizenbaum, J. 1965. ELIZA—A computer program for the study of language communication between man and machine. *Communications of the Association for Computing Machinery*, 9(1):36–45.

Ellis, G. & Sinclair, B. 1985. Learner training: Preparation for learner automony. *Les Cahiers de l'APLIUT*, 5(2).

Ellis, G. & Sinclair, B. 1989. *Learning to Learn English: A Course in Learner Training*. Cambridge: Cambridge University Press.

ELT Documents, 107. 1980. *University of Malaysia ESP Project*. London: British Council.

ELTA/OUP. 1981. London Workshop 1981. Beirut, Lebanon: Oxford University Press.

EMBEDDED STRATEGIES GAME, The. Oxford, R. 1990. In Oxford, R. 1990b. *Language Learning Strategies: What Every Teacher Should Know*. New York: Newbury House/Harper & Row.

Enright, D. S. & McCloskey, M. 1988. Integrating English: Developing English Language and Literacy in the Multilingual Classroom. Reading, MA: Addison-Wesley.

Entwistle, K. 1990. Prospects and constraints in using simulation/gaming for language instruction. In Oxford, R. (Ed.) *Using and Learning Language Through Simulations—II*. Newbury Park, CA: Sage. (Special issue of Reports and Communications, in *Simulation and Gaming*, 21(1).)

ESCAPE FROM UTOPIA. Cook, V. 1986. Unpublished. For Acorn BBC computer.

Evans, D. R. 1979. *Games and Simulations in Literacy Training.* Amersham: Hulton.

EXECUTIVE GAME, The. Henshaw, R. C. & Jackson, J. R. 1984. Homewood, IL: Richard D. Irwin.

EXPEDITIONS. 1986. St. Paul, MN: Minnesota Educational Computing Corporation. Diskette and Instruction booklet, containing three historical simulations: FURS, VOYAGEUR, and OREGON.

EXPORT ORDER, An. Littlejohn, A. & Hicks, D. 1986. See Littlejohn, A. & Hicks, D. 1986. Task-centred writing activities. In Candlin, C. N. & Murphy, D. (Eds.) *Lancaster Practical Papers in English Language Education.* Vol. 7. Oxford: Pergamon.

Farthing, J. 1982a. *Business Mazes.* St. Albans: Hart-Davis Educational.

Farthing, J. 1982b. *Out of the In-Tray.* St. Albans: Hart-Davis Educational.

Farthing, J. 1983. *More Mazes.* St. Albans: Hart-Davis Educational.

FAST FOOD. British Council. 1988. Cambridge: Cambridge University Press. For Acorn BBC computer.

Feldhendler, D. 1983. When the language prof becomes the inspiration for expression and communication. *Français dans le Monde,* 176:45–51.

Fernandes, J. 1983a. On the tip of my thumb: Developing awareness of oral traditions among deaf college students. In Crouch, I. & Owen, G. (Eds.) *Proceedings of the Seminar/Conference on Oral Traditions.* Las Cruces, NM: New Mexico State University.

Fernandes, J. 1983b. Sign language and "picture-talk": An experiential learning approach. *Communication Education,* 32(2).

Festinger, L. 1954. A theory of social comparison processes. *Human Relations,* 7:117–140.

Fillmore, C. J. 1981. Pragmatics and the description of discourse. In Cole, P. (Ed.) *Radical Pragmatics.* New York: Academic Press.

FINGAME (Financial Management Decision Game). Brooks, L. D. 1975 & 1982. Homewood, IL: Irwin.

Finocchiaro, M. 1977. Role-playing in the classroom. *Zielsprache Englisch,* No. 3:1–6.

Finocchiaro, M. 1978. Role playing in the language classroom. *Glottodidactica,* 11:25–31.

Fisher, D. 1982. *The Right to Communicate: A Status Report.* Paris: UNESCO.

Fiske, J. 1982. *Introduction to Communication Studies.* London: Methuen.

Fitzsimons, A. & Thatcher, D. (Eds.) 1987. *Games and Simulations at Work.* Loughborough: SAGSET.

Francis, D. 1987. The competent player: Some observations on game learning. In Crookall, D., Greenblat, C. S., Coote, A., Klabbers, J. H. G. & Watson, D. R. (Eds.) *Simulation-Gaming in the Late 1980s.* Oxford: Pergamon.

Francis, D. 1989. Game identities and activities: Some ethnomethodological observations. In Crookall, D. & Saunders, D. (Eds.) *Communication and Simulation: From Two Fields to One Theme.* Clevedon, Avon: Multilingual Matters.

Frank, C., Rinvolucri, M. & Berer, M. 1981. *Challenge to Think.* Oxford: Oxford University Press.

Frentzen, A. 1984. Using value orientations to introduce teachers to cultural communication content and training techniques. Paper at TESOL Convention, Houston, 1984 (unpublished).

Freudenstein, et al. 1981. *Language Incorporated.* Oxford: Pergamon.

Frisch, K. von. 1950. *Bees: Their Vision, Chemical Senses and Language.* Ithaca, NY: Cornell University Press.

Frohlich, M. & Paribakht, T. 1984. Can we teach our students how to learn? *ELT Documents*, 119, Language Issues and Education Policies. Oxford: Pergamon.

Gage, A. et al. 1981. Foreign language game plans for a successful season. ED 205030.

Gaies, S. J. 1985. *Peer Involvement in Language Learning.* New York: Harcourt Brace Jovanovich.

GALANTHIA (A Teacher Training Simulation). Geddes, M. 1979. Unpublished simulation/game.

Gardner, R. C. 1981. Second language learning. In Gardner, R. C. & Kalin, R. (Eds.) *A Canadian Social Psychology of Ethnic Relations.* Toronto: Methuen.

Gardner, R. C. 1985. *Social Psychology and Second Language Learning: The Role of Attitudes and Motivation.* London: Edward Arnold.

Gardner, R. C. & Kalin, R. (Eds.) 1981. *A Canadian Social Psychology of Ethnic Relations.* Toronto: Methuen.

Gardner, R. C. & Lambert, W. 1972. *Attitudes and Motivation in Second Language Acquisition.* Rowley, MA: Newbury House.

Gardner, R. C., Lalonde, R. N. & Moorcroft, R. 1985. The role of attitudes and motivation in second language learning: Correlational and experimental considerations. *Language Learning*, 35:207–227.

Gass, S. & Madden, C. (Eds.) 1985. *Input in Second Language Acquisition.* Rowley, MA: Newbury House.

Geddes, M. 1979. *GALANTHIA: A Teacher Training Simulation.* Unpublished manuscript.

Geddes, M. 1983. The word race game. In Holden, S. (Ed.) *Second Selections from Modern English Teacher.* Harlow: Longman.

Geddes, M. & Raz, H. 1979. Studying pupil-teacher interaction. In Holden, S. *Teacher Training.* London: Modern English Publications.

Geddes, M. & Sturtridge, G. 1979. *Listening Links.* London: Heinemann.

Genzel, R. & Cummings, M. G. 1986. *Culturally Speaking: A Conversation and Culture Text for Learners of English.* New York: Harper & Row.

Giles, H. & Smith, P. M. 1979. Accommodation theory: Optimal levels of convergence. In Giles, H. & St. Clair, R. N. (Eds.) *Language and Social Psychology.* Oxford: Basil Blackwell; Baltimore: University Park Press.

Giles, H. & St. Clair, R. N. (Eds.) 1979. *Language and Social Psychology.* Oxford: Basil Blackwell; Baltimore: University Park Press.

Giles, H., Robinson, W. P. & Smith, P. M. (Eds.) 1980. *Language: Social Psychological Perspectives.* Oxford: Pergamon.

Goethals, M. 1977. Creative and cognitive foreign-language learning. *ITL Review of Applied Linguistics*, 36:3–44.

Goethals, M. 1978. Role play in foreign language teaching: A description of the teaching strategy. *ITL Review of Applied Linguistics*, 41–42:87–119.

Goffman, E. 1962. *Encounters: Two Studies in Interaction.* Harmondsworth: Penguin.

GOING TO A NIGHTCLUB. Genzel, R. & Cummings, M. G. 1986. In Genzel, R. & Cummings, M. G. 1986. *Culturally Speaking: A Conversation and Culture Text for Learners of English.* New York: Harper & Row.

Goldberg, D. & Graber, M. (Eds.) 1980. *Simulation/Games in Education Research and Decision-Making.* Switzerland: ISAGA.

Goldhammer, R. 1969. *Clinical Supervision.* New York: Holt, Rinehart, & Winston.

Gonzalez, B. 1977. Small group activities for second language teaching. Meeting of American Council for Teaching of Foreign Languages & of American Association of Teachers of Italian, New York.

Gordon, T. 1974. *Teacher Effectiveness Training.* New York: Peter Wyden.

Graham, C. 1983. An excerpt from "Jazz Chants." In Oller, J. W. Jr. & Richard-Amato, P. A. (Eds.) *Methods That Work: A Smorgasbord of Ideas for Language Teachers.* Rowley, MA: Newbury House.

Gray, L. & Waitt, I. (Eds.) 1981. *Simulation in Management and Business Education.* London: Kogan Page/SAGSET/NELPCO.

Green, K. 1975. Values clarification theory in ESL and bilingual education. *TESOL Quarterly,* 9(2):155–164.

Green, K. 1983. Values clarification theory in ESL and bilingual education. In Oller, J. W. Jr. & Richard-Amato, P. A. (Eds.) *Methods That Work: A Smorgasbord of Ideas for Language Teachers.* Rowley, MA: Newbury House.

Greenblat, C. S. 1975. Teaching with simulation games: A review of claims and evidence. In Greenblat, C. S. & Duke, R. D. (Eds.) *Gaming-Simulation: Rationale, Design, and Applications.* New York: Halsted.

Greenblat, C. S. 1980. Group dynamics and game design: Some reflections. *Simulation and Games,* 11(1).

Greenblat, C. S. 1987. Communicating about simulation design: It's not only [sic] pedagogy. In Crookall, D., Greenblat, C. S., Coote, A. Klabbers, J. H. G. & Watson, D. R. (Eds.) *Simulation Gaming in the Late 1980s.* Oxford: Pergamon.

Greenblat, C. S. 1988. *Designing Games and Simulations: An Illustrated Handbook.* Newbury Park, CA: Sage.

Greenblat, C. S. 1989. Extending the range of experience. In Crookall, D. & Saunders, D. (Eds.) *Communication and Simulation: From Two Fields to One Theme.* Clevedon, Avon: Multilingual Matters.

Greenblat, C. S. & Duke, R. D. (Eds.) 1975. *Gaming-Simulation: Rationale, Design, and Applications.* New York: Halsted.

Greenblat, C. S. & Duke, R. D. 1981. (Eds.) *Principles and Practices of Gaming-Simulation.* Beverly Hills, CA: Sage.

Greenblat, C. S. & Gagnon, J. H. 1979. Further explorations on the multiple reality game. *Simulation and Games,* 10(1).

Grimshaw, A. D. & Holden, L. 1976. Postchild modifications of linguistic and social competence. *Items,* 30:33–42.

Guetzkow, H., Alger, C. F., Brody, R. A., Noel, R. C. & Snyder, R. C. 1963. *Simulation in International Relations: Developments for Research and Teaching.* Englewood Cliffs, NJ: Prentice-Hall.

Gumperz, J. 1978. *Language and Social Identity.* Cambridge: Cambridge University Press.

Gumperz, J. & Tannen, D. 1979. Individual and social differences in language use. In Fillmore, C. & Fillmore, L. W. (Eds.) *Individual Differences.* New York: Academic Press.

Gunderson, B. & Johnson, D. 1980. Building positive attitudes by using cooperative learning groups. *Foreign Language Annals,* 13(1):39–43.

Hall, E. T. 1959. *The Silent Language*. Garden City, NY: Free Press.

Halleck, G. 1990. Simulation in an ESL class. In Oxford, R. (Ed.) *Using and Learning Language Through Simulations—II*. Newbury Park, CA: Sage. (Special issue of Reports and Communications, in *Simulation and Gaming*, 21(1).)

Halliday, M. A. K., McIntosh, A. & Strevens, P. 1970. The users and use of language. In Fishman, J. (Ed.) *Readings in the Sociology of Language*. The Hague: Mouton.

Hare, G. & McAleese, R. 1976. Training the modern language assistant—A personalised approach. *Modern Languages in Scotland*, 9:104–109.

Hare, G. & McAleese, R. 1985. LAG: Development of a training simulation. In Crookall, D. (Ed.) *Simulation Applications in L2 Education and Research*. Oxford: Pergamon. (Special issue of *System*, 13(3).)

Harmer, J. 1984. Balancing activities: A unit-planning game. *English Language Teaching Journal*, 38(2):91–97.

Harper, S. N. 1977. Activities for motivation and real communication. ERIC: ED143208.

Harper, S. N. 1980. A teaching strategy for developing real communication in the foreign language classroom. *Hispania*, 63(3).

Harper, S. N. 1981. Game-like activities and the teaching of foreign languages. Great Lakes Colleges Association Foreign Language Conference at Albion; ERIC: ED206163.

Harper, S. N. 1985. Social psychological effects of simulation in foreign language learning. In Crookall, D. (Ed.) *Simulation Applications in L2 Education and Research*. Oxford: Pergamon. (Special issue of *System*, 13(3).)

Hart, B. 1987. The educational potential of interactive literature. In Crookall, D., Greenblat, C. S., Coote, A., Klabbers, J. H. G. and Watson, D. R. (Eds.) *Simulation/Gaming in the Late 1980s*. Oxford: Pergamon.

Hartig, G. 1978. For the classroom. Intermountain TESOL, Utah Foreign Language Association.

Hatch, E. 1982. *Psycholinguistics*. Rowley, MA: Newbury House.

Hawkins, E. 1984. *Awareness of Language: An Introduction*. Cambridge: Cambridge University Press.

Hayworth, F. 1978. *The Language of Discussion: Role-Play Exercises for Advanced Students*. London: Hodder & Stoughton.

Heap, J. L. 1971. The student as resource: Uses of the minimum-structure simulation game in teaching. *Simulation and Games*, 2(3).

Heard, L. E. 1972. Foreign language and the group context: Expanding student roles. *Foreign Language Annals*, 5.

Hendrickson, J. M. 1979. Getting students to communicate: Tips and techniques. Typescript presented at Ohio Modern Language Teachers' Association Conference, Columbus, OH.

Henzl, V. 1979. Foreigner talk in the classroom. *International Review of Applied Linguistics*, 17:159–167.

Herbert, D. & Sturtridge, G. 1979. *Simulations* (ELT Guide 2). London: British Council & NFER.

Herbolich, J. B. 1985. Box kites. In Swales, J. (Ed.) *Issues in ESP*. Oxford: Pergamon.

Hicks, D. & Murphy, D. 1979. Simulation procedures in remedial work. In Von Faber, H., Eichheim, H., Heid, M. & Maley, A. (Eds.) *Rollenspiel und Simulation im Fremdsprachenunterricht* (Pariser Werkstattgesprach, 1977). Paris: Goethe-Institut & British Council.

Higgins, J. J. 1982. How real is a computer simulation? *ELT Documents*, 113.

Higgins, J. J. (Ed.) 1986. *Computer-Assisted Language Learning: A European View*. Oxford: Pergamon. (Special issue of *System*, 14(2).)

Higgins, J. J. 1987. Artificial unintelligence: Computer uses in language learning. *TESOL Quarterly*, 21(1).

Higgins, J. J. & Johns, T. F. 1984. *Computers in Language Learning*. London: Collins.

Hill, L. A. & Fielden, R. O. S. 1974. *English Language Teaching Games for Adult Students*. London: Evans.

Hines, M. & Rutherfords, W. (Eds.) 1981. *On TESOL '81*. Washington, DC: TESOL.

Holden, G. W. 1988. Investigating social relations with computer-presented social situations. In Crookall, D. (Ed.) *Computerized Simulation in the Social Sciences*. Durham, NC: Duke University Press. (Special issue of *Social Science Computer Review*, 6(1).)

Holden, S. (Ed.) 1977. *English for Specific Purposes*. London: Modern English Publications.

Holden, S. 1979. *Teacher Training*. London: Modern English Publications.

Holden, S. 1981. *Drama in Language Teaching*. London: Longman.

Holden, S. (Ed.) 1983. *Second Selections from Modern English Teacher*. Harlow: Longman.

Holdzkom, D. 1979. *Ideabook: A Resource Manual for Teachers of English as a Second Language*. Silver Spring, MD: Institute of Modern Languages.

Holec, H. 1978. Jeux de rôle et simulations dans l'apprentissage de la compétence de communication: Degrés d'authenticité communicative—intégration pédagogique. *Recherches et Echanges*, 3:1–9. Reprinted in Von Faber, H., Eichheim, H., Heid, M. & Maley, A. (Eds.) 1979. *Rollenspiel und Simulation im Fremdsprachenunterricht* (Pariser Werkstattgesprach, 1977). Paris: Goethe-Institut & British Council.

Holec, H. 1981. *Autonomy and foreign language learning*. Oxford: Pergamon.

Holmes, J. 1978. Sociolinguistics in the classroom. In Richards, J. C. (Ed.) *Understanding Second or Foreign Language Learning*. Rowley, MA: Newbury House.

Holmes, J. & Brown, D. 1976. Developing sociolinguistic competence in a second language. *TESOL Quarterly*, 10(4).

Holmes, J. & Brown, D. F. 1977. Sociolinguistic competence and second language learning. *Topics in Culture Learning*.

Horn, R. E. & Cleaves, A. (Eds.) 1980. *The Guide to Simulation/Games for Education and Training* (4th ed). Beverly Hills, CA: Sage.

Horwitz, E. K. 1990. Affective factors in the communication-centered classroom: Current research on learner anxiety and beliefs about language learning. In Magnan, S. S. (Ed.) *Shifting the Instructional Focus to the Learner*. New York: Northeast Conference.

Horwitz, E. K. & Young, D. (Eds.) 1990. *Language Anxiety: Anxiety Reactions in Foreign and Second Language Learning and Performance*. Englewood Cliffs, NJ: Prentice-Hall.

Hughes, B. B. 1988. INTERNATIONAL FUTURES: History and status. In Crookall, D. (Ed.) *Computerized Simulation in the Social Sciences*. Durham, NC: Duke University Press. (Special issue of *Social Science Computer Review*, 6(1).)

Hutchinson, T. 1978. The practical demonstration. In *Practical Papers in English Language Education*, Volume 1. Lancaster: Institute for English Language Education.

Hymes, D. 1972. On communicative competence. In Pride, J. P. & Holmes, J. (Eds.) *Sociolinguistics*. Harmondsworth: Penguin.

HYPOTHETICA. See AGITANIA.

ICONS. Wilkenfeld, J. & Brecht, R. C. Undated. College Park, MD: University of Maryland.

ILLYRIA (A Teacher Training Exercise). White, M. 1979. Unpublished simulation/game.

INTER-NATION SIMULATION. Guetzkow, H. & Cherryholmes, C. H. 1966. Chicago: Science Research Associates.

Jaques, D. 1984. *Learning in Groups*. London: Kogan Page.

Jaques, D. & Tipper, E. (Eds.) 1984. *Learning for the Future with Games and Simulations*. Loughborough: SAGSET.

Joiner, E. G. & Westphal, P. B. (Eds.) 1978. *Developing Communication Skills: General Considerations and Specific Techniques*. Rowley, MA: Newbury House.

Jones, G. 1986. The KINGDOM experiment. In Higgins, J. J. (Ed.) *Computer-Assisted Language Learning: A European View*. Oxford: Pergamon. (Special issue of *System*, 14(2).)

Jones, K. 1974–1975. *Nine Graded Simulations*. London: ILEA (1974/75 ed.); Munich: Heuber Verlag.

Jones, K. 1980. Communication, language and realists. In Race, P. & Brook, D. (Eds.) *Simulation and Gaming for the 1980s*. London: Kogan Page/SAGSET.

Jones, K. 1981. Introducing simulations. *Practical English Teaching*, 4:15–16.

Jones, K. 1982. *Simulations in Language Teaching*. Cambridge: Cambridge University Press.

Jones, K. 1983. Who's for "We're not going to use simulations"? *Simulation/Games for Learning*, 13(4).

Jones, K. 1985. *Designing Your Own Simulations*. London: Methuen.

Jones, K. 1986. *Graded Simulations*. London: Longman. (Reprint of Jones, K. 1974–1975.)

Jones, K. 1987. *Simulations: A Handbook for Teachers and Trainers* (2nd ed.). London: Kogan Page.

Jones, K. 1988. *Interactive Learning Events: A Guide for Facilitators*. London: Kogan Page.

Jones, L. 1979. From presentation to role-playing: Methods used in a language course for upper intermediate and advanced students of English. In Von Faber, H., Eichheim, H., Heid, M. & Maley, A. (Eds.) (1979). *Rollenspiel und Simulation im Fremdsprachenunterricht* (Pariser Werkstattgesprach, 1977). Paris: Goethe-Institut & British Council.

Jones, L. 1981. *Functions of English* (2nd ed.). Cambridge: Cambridge University Press.

Jones, L. 1983. *Eight Simulations: For Upper-Intermediate and More Advanced Students*. Cambridge: Cambridge University Press.

Juleus, N. 1966. Akrestomije, ergahergahamah, and one. *Et Cetera*, 23(2).

Juleus, N. 1983. On inventing languages. *Communication Education*, 32(2).

Jupp, T. & Hodlin, S. 1975. *Industrial English*. London: Heinemann.

Kalidova, T. B. 1976. Communication in the foreign language classroom. *Hispania*, 59.

Katz, E. & Lazarsfeld, P. 1960. *Personal Influence*. New York: Free Press.

Kay, A. 1984. Computer software. *Scientific American*, (March) 53–59.

Kerr, J. Y. K. 1977. *Games and Simulations in English Language Teaching*. ELT Documents, 77/1. London: British Council.

Kerridge, D. 1985. The developments of an in-company language programme. *Language Training*, 6(1).

Kettering, J. C. 1975. *Interaction Activities in English as a Second Language*. Pittsburgh: Center for International Studies, University of Pittsburgh.

Khols, L. R. 1981. *Developing Intercultural Awareness*. Washington, DC: SIETAR.

Kimball, M. C. & Palmer, A. S. 1978. The dialogue game: A protypical activity for providing proper intake in formal instruction. *TESOL Quarterly*, 12(1).

Klippel, F. 1980. Games with aims: Classification and adaptation of foreign language teaching games. In Goldberg, D. & Graber, M. (Eds.) *Simulation/Games in Education Research and Decision-Making*. Switzerland: ISAGA.

Klippel, F. 1984. *Keep Talking: Communicative Fluency Activities for Language Teaching*. Cambridge: Cambridge University Press.

Knight, M. 1975. Video in oral proficiency training. *System*, 3(2).

Kollar, J. 1986. It's not a simulation, It's real! In Lightbrown, P. M. & Firth, S. P. (Eds.) *Both Sides of the Desk: Roles and Responsibilities in ESL/EFL Teaching and Learning*. Special Issue 1, November, of *TESL Canada Journal/Revue TESL du Canada*.

Krashen, S. 1980a. The theoretical and practical relevance of simple codes in language acquisition. In Scarcella, R. & Krashen, S. (Eds.) *Research in Second Language Acquisition*. Rowley, MA: Newbury House.

Krashen, S. D. 1980b. The input hypothesis. In Alatis, J. (Ed.) *Current Issues in Bilingual Education*. Washington, DC: Georgetown University Press.

Krashen, S. D. 1981. *Second Language Acquisition and Second Language Learning*. Oxford: Pergamon.

Krashen, S. D. 1982. *Principles and Practice in Second Language Acquisition*. Oxford: Pergamon.

Krashen, S. D. 1983. *Writing: Research, Theory, and Practice*. Oxford: Pergamon.

Krashen, S. D. 1985. *The Input Hypothesis: Issues and Implications*. London: Longman.

Krashen, S. D. & Terrell, T. 1983. *The Natural Approach*. Oxford: Pergamon.

Kreeft, J. 1984. Dialogue writing—Bridge from talk to essay writing. *Language Arts*, 61(2).

Lalonde, R. N. & Gardner, R. C. 1984. Investigating a causal model of second language acquisition: Where does personality fit? *Canadian Journal of Behavioural Science*, 16:224–237.

Lambert, W. E. & Tucker, G. R. 1972. *Bilingual Education of Children: The St. Lambert Experiment*. Rowley, MA: Newbury House.

Lasswell, H. 1948. The structure and function of communication in society. In Lyman (Ed.) (1948). *The Communication of Ideas*. Institute for Religion and Ideas; & in Schramm, W. (Ed.) *Mass Communications*. Urbana, IL: University of Illinois Press.

Lavery, M. 1985. The industrial language trainer. *Language Training*, 6(2).

Lawson, C. A. 1963. Language, communication, and biological organization. In

Von Bertalanffy, L. & Rapoport, A. (Eds.) *General Systems*, Vol VIII. Ann Arbor, MI: Society for General Systems Research.

Lederman, L. C. 1983. Intercultural communication, simulation and the cognitive assimilation of experience: An exploration of the post-experience analytic process. Paper presented at the 3rd Annual Conference of the Speech Communication Association of Puerto Rico, November 1983.

Lederman, L. C. & Ruben, B. D. 1984. Systematic assessment of communication simulations. *Communication Education*, 33(2).

Lee, W. R. 1979. *Language Teaching Games and Contests*. Oxford: Oxford University Press.

Legenhausen, L. 1988. The Dusseldorf CALL project. Paper presented at the Fourth International Conference on Second/Foreign Language Acquisition, May 5–7, 1988, Szczyrk, Poland.

Leong, H. 1979. The debate: A means of eliciting semi-spontaneous communication in the TEFL classroom. *English Language Teaching Journal*, 34(4).

Leong, H. 1983. The debate. In Oller, J. W. Jr. & Richard-Amato, P. A. (Eds.) *Methods That Work: A Smorgasbord of Ideas for Language Teachers*. Rowley, MA: Newbury House.

Lewis, M. 1982. *Partners 1, 2 & 3*. Hove: Language Teaching Publications.

Lian, A. & Mestre, C. 1983. Toward genuine individualisation in language course development. *Australian Review of Applied Linguistics*, 6(2).

Littlejohn, A. 1988. *Company to Company: A New Approach to Business Correspondence in English*. Cambridge: Cambridge University Press.

Littlejohn, A. & Hicks, D. 1986. Task-centred writing activities. In Candlin, C. N. & Murphy, D. (Eds.) *Lancaster Practical Papers in English Language Education*. Vol. 7. Oxford: Pergamon.

Littlewood, W. T. 1975. Role-performance and language teaching. *International Review of Applied Linguistics*, 13(3).

Littlewood, W. T. 1981. *Communicative Language Teaching*. Cambridge: Cambridge University Press.

Littlewood, W. T. 1984. *Foreign and Second Language Learning: Language Acquisition Research and Its Implications for the Classroom*. Cambridge: Cambridge University Press.

Livingstone, C. 1983. *Role Play in Language Learning*. Harlow: Longman.

LOBU ABU. See AGITANIA.

Locke, R. 1983. What's on TV tonight? In Holden, S. (Ed.) *Second Selections from Modern English Teacher*. Harlow: Longman.

LONDON ADVENTURE. British Council. 1988. Cambridge: Cambridge University Press. For Acorn BBC computer.

Lonergan, J. P. 1978a. *Clarity of Communication: Some Tasks for Teacher Training*. London: Centre for British Teachers.

Lonergan, J. P. 1978b. *Areas for Concern: A Role-Playing Exercise for Advisory Staff Working with Teachers*. London: Centre for British Teachers.

Lonergan, J. P. 1979. Management and tutorial skills for English language teachers. In Megarry, J. (Ed.) *Human Factors in Games and Simulation*. London: Kogan Page.

Lonergan, J. P. 1980. Using television to motivate adults to role-play in a foreign language. In Race, P. & Brook, D. (Eds.) *Simulation and Gaming for the 1980s*. London: Kogan Page/SAGSET.

Lonergan, J. P. 1984a. HOW CAN I PUT THIS . . .? In Jacques, D. & Tipper, E. (Eds.) *Learning for the Future with Games and Simulations*. Loughborough: SAGSET.

Lonergan, J. P. 1984b. Cooperation, competition, and the individual—Some games for beginners. In Jacques, D. & Tipper, E. *Learning for the Future with Games and Simulations*. Loughborough: SAGSET.

Lonergan, J. P. & Crookall, D. 1986. Jigsaw reading: Putting the puzzle into paragraphs. In Craig, S. & Martin, A. (Eds.) *Simulations and Games for Capability*. Loughborough: SAGSET.

Long, D. R. 1986. A case for case studies. *Foreign Language Annals*, 19(3):225–230.

Long, M. 1983. Native speaker/non-native speaker conversation in the second language classroom. In Clark, M. & Handscombe, J. (Eds.) *On TESOL '82: Pacific Perspectives of Language Learning and Teaching*. Washington, DC: TESOL.

Long, M. & Sato, C. 1983. Classroom foreigner talk discourse: Forms and functions of teachers' questions. In Seliger, H. & Long, M. (Eds.) *Classroom-Oriented Research in Language Acquisition*. Rowley, MA: Newbury House.

Lyman (Ed.) 1948. *The Communication of Ideas*. Institute for Religion and Ideas.

Lynch, M. 1977. *It's Your Choice*. London: Edward Arnold.

MacBride, S. et al. (Eds.) 1980. *Many Voices, One World: Towards a New More Just and More Efficient World Information and Communication Order*. Paris: UNESCO.

MacDonald, G. L. 1990. Creative chaos: The dynamics of competitive composition. In Oxford, R. (Ed.) *Using and Learning Language Through Simulations—II*. Newbury Park, CA: Sage. (Special issue of Reports and Communications, in *Simulation and Gaming*, 21(1).)

MacDonald, A. F. & MacDonald, G. L. 1989. ESL tutors: Simulated friends. In Oxford, R. (Ed.) *Using and Learning Language Through Simulations—I*. Newbury Park, CA: Sage. (Special issue of ISAGA News and Notes, in *Simulation and Games*, 20(4).)

Macmillan, D. & Brammer, M. 1982. EVA BRICK—A simulation for English language learning. *Simulation/Games for Learning*, 12(1).

Maley, A. 1984. "I Got Religion!" Evangelism in language teaching. In Savignon, S. J. & Berns, M. S. (Eds.) *Initiatives in Communicative Language Teaching: A Book of Readings*. Reading, MA: Addison-Wesley.

Maley, A. & Duff, A. 1982. *Drama Techniques in Language Learning: A Resource Book of Communication Activities for Language Learners* (new ed.). Cambridge: Cambridge University Press.

MANAGER, A Simulation. Smith, G. 1984. Boston: Houghton Mifflin.

Mandelson, L. R. 1977. Simulation works in the Spanish class. *Hispania*, 60(1).

MANEDES (Management Negotiated Decision Simulation). Crookall, D., Coote, A. & Saunders, D. 1984. See Coote, A., Crookall, D. & Saunders, D. 1985. Some human and machine aspects of computerized simulation. In van Ments, M. & Hearnden, K. (Eds.) *Effective Use of Games and Simulations*. Loughborough: SAGSET.

Manning, A., Martin, P. & McCalla, K. (Eds.) 1984. *The Tenth LACUS Forum 1983*. Columbia, SC: Hornbeam.

Mariani, L. 1983. Developing cuecards for group interaction. In Holden, S. (Ed.) *Second Selections from Modern English Teacher*. Harlow: Longman.

MARKETING STRATEGY. Boone, L. E. & Hackleman, E. C. 1971 & 1975. Columbus, OH: Charles E. Merrill.

Marshall, J. 1975. Ethics and values. In *Fourteenth Annual NASAGA Conference Proceedings*. Los Angeles: University of Southern California Press.

Martin, A. 1988. Out of the screen: Computers and simulation. In Crookall, D. (Ed.) *Simulation/Games and the New Technologies: Applications and Problems*. Loughborough: SAGSET. (Special issue of *Simulation/Games for Learning*, 18(1).)

Matheidesz, M. 1987. *SPEAKING FACES (96)*. Budapest: Babilon.

Matheidesz, M. 1988. Self-access language practice through CALL games. In Crookall, D. (Ed.) *Simulation/Games and the New Technologies: Applications and Problems*. Loughborough: SAGSET. (Special issue of *Simulation/Games for Learning*, 18(1).)

Matheidesz, M. 1989. Communication games: Some observations. In Oxford, R. (Ed.) *Using and Learning Language Through Simulations—I*. Newbury Park, CA: Sage. (Special issue of ISAGA News and Notes, in *Simulation and Games*, 20(4).)

McAleese, R. (Ed.) 1978. *Perspectives on Academic Gaming and Simulation: Training and Professional Education*. London: Kogan Page/SAGSET.

McAleese, R. & Hare, G. 1978. Language assistant game. In McAleese, R. (Ed.) *Perspectives on Academic Gaming and Simulation: Training and Professional Education*. London: Kogan Page/SAGSET.

McGinley, K. 1980. Use of simulation in ESP courses in a developing country. *Simulation/Games for Learning*, 10(1).

McGinley, K. 1985. ESP syllabus change and simulation. In Crookall, D. (Ed.) *Simulation Applications in L2 Education and Research*. Oxford: Pergamon. (Special issue of *System*, 13(3).)

McIver, N. 1974. Role playing in the commercial language class. *International Language Centres Research Bulletin*.

McMillan, N. & Madaras, S. W. 1974. *Games for the Foreign Language Classroom*. New York: ACTFL.

Mead, G. H. 1934. *Mind, Self and Society*. Chicago: University of Chicago Press.

MEDITANIA. See AGITANIA.

Megarry, J. (Ed.) 1977. *Aspects of Simulation and Gaming: An Anthology of SAGSET Journal, Vols. 1–4*. London: Kogan Page.

Megarry, J. (Ed.) 1979. *Human Factors in Games and Simulations*. London: Kogan Page/SAGSET.

Mehan, H. 1978. Structuring school structure. *Harvard Educational Review*, 45:311–338.

Mehan, H. 1979. *Learning Lessons*. Cambridge, MA: Harvard University Press.

Melville, M., Langenheim, L., Rinvolucri, M. & Speventa, L. 1980. *Towards the Creative Teaching of English*. London: George Allen & Unwin.

MEMORY TRICKS. Rinvolucri, M. 1984. In Rinvolucri, M. 1984. *Grammar Games: Cognitive, Affective and Drama Activities for EFL Students*. Cambridge: Cambridge University Press.

Menne, S. 1976. Conversation via role-playing. *Modern English Teacher*, 4:8–9.

Menne, S. 1977. Role-playing in an English conversation lesson. *Zielsprache Englisch*. 4:7–10.

MICROLANGUAGE LAB. Juleus, N. 1983. See Juleus, N. 1983. On inventing languages. *Communication Education.* 32(2).

Miles-Herman, M. 1978. The collection, creation and analysis of oral English games. ED 169750.

Miller, J. G. 1965. Living systems. *Behavioural Science,* (10):2–28.

Mohan, B. 1986. *Language and Content.* Reading, MA: Addison-Wesley.

Mohr, P. 1979. Zur Didaktik des Spielens im kommunikativen Englischunterricht. In Von Faber, H., Eichheim, H., Heid, M. & Maley, A. (Eds.) *Rollenspiel und Simulation im Fremdsprachenunterricht* (Pariser Werkstattgesprach, 1977). Paris: Goethe-Institut & British Council.

MONOPOLY. Darrow, C. W. 1935. Salem, MA: Parker Brothers.

Moore, B. 1978. *Australian Management Games.* Sydney: University of New South Wales Press.

Morgan, D. Y. 1967. Games and play-acting. *English Language Teaching Journal,* 21(2):182–185.

Morgenstern, D. 1976. Eight activities for the conversation class. *Modern Language Journal,* 60(1 & 2).

Morgenstern, D. 1987. Artifice versus real-world data: Six simulations. In Crookall, C., Greenblat, C. S., Coote, A., Klabbers, J. H. G. & Watson, D. R. (Eds.) *Simulation/Gaming in the Late 1980s.* Oxford: Pergamon.

Morrison, D. M. 1984. GAPPER: A microcomputer-based learning game. *System,* 12(2).

MORTAL REMAINS. Versluis, E. 1985. Ashland, OR: Southern Oregon State College.

Mugglestone, P. 1977. Role-play. *ELT Documents,* 77/1. London: British Council.

MULTI-NATIONAL MANAGEMENT GAME, The. Edge, A., Keys, B. & Remus, W. E. 1985. Plano, TX: Business Publications.

Murphy, J. 1972. *A Synoptic History of Classical Rhetoric.* New York: Random House.

Naiman, N., Frohlich, M. & Todesco, A. 1975. The good second language learner. *TESL Talk,* 6(1).

Nebraska State Department of Education. 1972. *Simulations in Foreign Languages.* Nebraska State Department of Education.

Neilsen, R. J. 1978. *Academic games, simulation games and computer games in foreign language education.* Master's Report, University of Texas, Austin.

Neuner, G. 1979. Soziologische und pedagogische Dimensionen des Rollenspiels im fremdsprachlichen Unterricht. In Von Faber, H., Eichheim, H., Heid, M. & Maley, A. (Eds.) *Rollenspiel und Simulation im Fremdsprachenunterricht* (Pariser Werkstattgesprach, 1977). Paris: Goethe-Institut & British Council.

Newcomb, T. 1953. An approach to the study of communication acts. *Psychology Review,* 60:376–386.

Nixon, U. 1989. NORZANZA: An evaluation simulation in teacher training. *English Language Teaching Journal,* 43(2).

Noel, R. C. 1987. The MUF CRISIS Scenario. See Noel et al., 1987.

Noel, R. C., Crookall, D., Wilkenfeld, J. & Schapira, L. 1987. Network gaming: A vehicle for intercultural communication. In Crookall, D., Greenblat, C. S., Coote, A., Klabbers, J. H. G. & Watson, D. R. (Eds.) *Simulation-Gaming in the Late 1980s.* Oxford: Pergamon.

NO RECUERDO. Undated. Cambridge, MA: M.I.T.

O'Callaghan, P. 1983. Foza's broken arm: An introduction to role-playing. In Holden, S. (Ed.) *Second Selections from Modern English Teacher.* Harlow: Longman.

Olsen, J. W-B. 1977. *Communication-Starters and Other Activities for the ESL Classroom.* Hayward, CA: Alemany Press.

Omaggio, A. C. 1979. *Games and Simulations in the Foreign Language Classroom.* Arlington, VA: Center for Applied Linguistics & ERIC Clearinghouse on Languages & Linguistics.

Omaggio, A. C. 1982. Using games and interaction activities for the development of functional proficiency in a second language. *Canadian Modern Language Review*, 38(3).

Omaggio, A. C. 1986. *Teaching Language in Context: Proficiency-Oriented Instruction.* Boston: Heinle & Heinle.

O'Malley, J. M., Chamot, A. U., Stewner-Manzanares, G., Kupper, L. & Russo, R. 1985. Learning strategies used by beginning and intermediate ESL students. *Language Learning*, 35(1).

Oppenheimer, J. & Winer, M. 1988. Using and creating a simulation authoring system: COOPERATION AND CONFLICT. In Crookall, D. (Ed.) *Computerized Simulation in the Social Sciences.* Durham, NC: Duke University Press. (Special issue of *Social Science Computer Review*, 6(1).)

Orbach, E. 1979. Simulation games and motivation for learning: A theoretical framework. *Simulation and Games*, 10(1).

O'Sullivan, T., Hartley, J., Saunders, D. & Fiske, J. 1983. *Key Concepts in Communication.* London: Methuen.

Oxford, R. (Ed.) 1989a. *Using and Learning Language Through Simulations—I.* Newbury Park, CA: Sage. (Special issue of ISAGA News and Notes, in *Simulation and Games*, 20(4).)

Oxford, R. 1989b. Use of language learning strategies: A synthesis of studies with implications for strategy training. *System*, 17(2).

Oxford, R. 1990a. Language learning strategies and beyond: Looking at strategies in the context of styles. In Magnan, S. S. (Ed.) *Shifting the Instructional Focus to the Learner.* Middlebury, VT: Northeast Conference.

Oxford, R. 1990b. *Language Learning Strategies: What Every Teacher Should Know.* New York: Newbury House/Harper & Row.

Oxford, R. (Ed.) 1990c. *Using and Learning Language Through Simulations—II.* Newbury Park, CA: Sage. (Special issue of Reports and Communications, in *Simulation and Gaming*, 21(1).)

Oxford, R. & Crookall, D. 1988a. Language learning strategies. In Berko Gleason, J. (Ed.) *You CAN Take It with You: Helping Students Maintain Second Language Skills.* Englewood Cliffs, NJ: Prentice-Hall.

Oxford, R. & Crookall, D. 1988b. Simulation/gaming and language learning strategies. *Simulation and Games*, 17(4).

Oxford, R. & Crookall, D. 1989a. Research on language learning strategies: Methods, findings, and instructional issues. *Modern Language Journal*, 73(4).

Oxford, R. & Crookall, D. 1989b. Review of SPEAKING FACES ("96"). *Simulation/ Games for Learning*, 19(1).

Oxford, R. & Ehrman, M. 1989. Psychological type and adult language learning strategies: A pilot study. *Journal of Psychological Type*, 16:22–32.

Oxford, R., Lavine, R. & Crookall, D. 1989. Language learning strategies, the communicative approach, and their classroom implications. *Foreign Language Annals*, 22(1).

Oxford, R. & Nyikos, M. 1989. Variables affecting choice of language learning strategies by university students. *Modern Language Journal*, 73(2).

Palmer, A. S. 1976. Communication games and the teaching of reading. 10th Annual TESOL Convention, New York.

Palmer, A. S. & Rodgers, T. S. 1982a. *DYADIC Communication Activities* (2 vols.). San Francisco: Alemany Press.

Palmer, A. S. & Rodgers, T. S. 1982b. Communicative and instructional considerations in language teaching. *Language Learning and Communication*, 1(3):235–257.

Palmer, A. S. & Rodgers, T. S. 1983. Games in language teaching. *Language Teaching*, 16(1):2–21.

Palmer, A. S., Rodgers, T. S. & Olsen, J. W-B. 1985. *Back and Forth: Pair Activities for Language Development*. Hayword, CA: Alemany Press.

Papalia, A. 1976. *Learner-Centered Language Teaching*. Rowley, MA: Newbury House.

Papert, S. 1980. *Mindstorms: Children, Computers and Powerful Ideas*. New York: Basic Books.

Paret, M-C., Therien, M. & Levesque, M. 1987. Simulation de dialogue pour l'apprentissage de la langue maternelle. In Crookall, D., Greenblat, C. S., Coote, A., Klabbers, J. H. G. & Watson, D. R. (Eds.) *Simulation-Gaming in the Late 1980s*. Oxford: Pergamon.

Paulston, C. B. 1971. The sequencing of structural pattern drills. *TESOL Quarterly*, 5:197–208.

Paulston, C. B., Britton, D., Brunetti, B. & Hoover, J. 1975. *Developing Communicative Competence: Roleplays in English as a Second Language*. Pittsburgh: Center for International Studies, University of Pittsburgh.

Paulston, C. B. & Selekman, H. R. 1976. Interaction activities in the foreign language classroom, or how to grow a tulip-rose. *Foreign Language Annals*, 9(3).

Petranek, C. 1985. The use of innocent deception in simulations. *Simulation and Games*, 16(3).

Pfeiffer, J. W. & Jones, J. E. (Eds.) 1975. *A Handbook of Structured Experiences for Human Relations Training* (vol. 5). La Jolla, CA: University Associates.

Phillips, S. 1972. Participant structure and communicative competence: Warm Springs Indian children in community and classroom. In Cazden, C., Vera, J. & Hymes, D. (Eds.) *Functions of Language in the Classroom*. New York: Teachers College Press.

Pike, G. 1983. Role-play simulation games. In Holden, S. (Ed.) *Second Selections from Modern English Teacher*. Harlow: Longman.

PINS AND STRAWS. Fromkin, H. L. 1975. In Pfeiffer, J. W. & Jones, J. E. (Eds.) *A Handbook of Structured Experiences for Human Relations Training* (vol. 5). La Jolla, CA: University Associates.

Piper, D. 1983. The notion of functional role-play. *TEAL Occasional Papers*, 7:23–31.

Piper, D. & Piper, T. 1983. Reality and second language role-play. *Canadian Modern Language Review*, 40(1):82–87.

Piper, T. 1984. Putting reality into role-play. *TESL Canada Journal/Revue TESL du Canada*, 1(2): 29–34.

Porter Ladousse, G. 1982. Role play and simulation in language learning. *Simulation/ Games for Learning*, 12(2).

Pote, M. 1979. A case for simulation games. In Von Faber, H., Eichheim, H., Heid, M. & Maley, A. (Eds.) *Rollenspiel und Simulation im Fremdsprachenunterricht* (Pariser Werkstattgesprach, 1977). Paris: Goethe-Institut & British Council.

Pratt, L. K., Uhl, N. P. & Little, E. R. 1980. Evaluation of games as a function of personality type. *Simulation and Games*, 11(3).

Pride, J. P. & Holmes, J. (Eds.) 1972. *Sociolinguistics*. Harmondsworth: Penguin.

PRISONER'S DILEMMA. Invented or discovered (?) by Merrill M. Flood; name given by Albert W. Tucker. Undatable. See Flood, M. M. 1958. Some experimental games. *Management Science*, 5:5–26. See also Oppenheimer, J. & Winer, M. 1988. Using and creating a simulation authoring system: COOPERATION AND CONFLICT. In Crookall, D. (Ed.) *Computerized Simulation in the Social Sciences*. Durham, NC: Duke University Press. (Special issue of *Social Science Computer Review*, 6(1).)

Propp, V. 1968. *Morphology of the Folk Tale*. London: Allen and Unwin.

Race, P. & Brook, D. (Eds.) 1980. *Simulation and Gaming for the 1980s*. London: Kogan Page/SAGSET.

Ramirez, A. 1986. Language learning strategies used by adolescents studying French in New York schools. *Foreign Language Annals*, 19(2).

Ramsey, G. 1978. *Play Your Part*. London: Longman.

Raz, H. 1967. *Dramatic Dialogues* (with posters). Otzar Ha Moreh.

Raz, H. 1972. Role playing in English. *English Teaching Guidance*, (23):14–17.

Raz, H. 1980. *Role-Playing in Foreign-Language Learning*. Doctoral dissertation, Hebrew University of Jerusalem.

Raz, H. 1982. Foreign-language teaching within the school framework: The educational challenge of a learner-centred approach. *World Language English*, 1(2): 108–111.

Raz, H. 1985. Role-play in foreign language learning. In Crookall, D. (Ed.) *Simulation Applications in L2 Education and Research*. Oxford: Pergamon. (Special issue of *System*, 13(3).)

Redfield, S. 1980. Role-play dialogues: An excellent way to practice "skill using." *English Teaching Forum*, 19(3).

RELATIONS. Coleman, D. W. 1988. See Coleman, D. W. 1988. Conversational simulation in computer-assisted language learning: Potential and reality. In Crookall, D. (Ed.) *Simulation/Games and the New Technologies: Applications and Problems*. Loughborough: SAGSET. (Special issue of *Simulation/Games for Learning*, 18(1):77–87).

Revell, J. 1979. *Teaching Techniques for Communicative English*. London: Macmillan.

Richards, J. (Ed.) 1976. *Understanding Second or Foreign Language Learning*. Rowley, MA: Newbury House.

Richards, J. & Rodgers, T. 1986. *Approaches and Methods in Language Teaching: A Description and Analysis*. Cambridge: Cambridge University Press.

Richards, J. & Schmidt, R. (Eds.) 1983. *Language and Communication*. New York: Longman.

Rigney, J. 1978. Learning strategies: A theoretical perspective. In O'Neil, H. F. Jr. (Ed.) *Learning Strategies*. New York: Academic Press.

Rinvolucri, M. 1980. Action mazes. *English Language Teaching Journal*, 35(1): 35–37.

Rinvolucri, M. 1983. Action mazes. In Oller, J. W. Jr. & Richard-Amato, P. A. (Eds.) *Methods That Work: A Smorgasbord of Ideas for Language Teachers.* Rowley, MA: Newbury House.

Rinvolucri, M. 1984. *Grammar Games: Cognitive, Affective and Drama Activities for EFL Students.* Cambridge: Cambridge University Press.

Ritchie, W. (Ed.) 1978. *Second Language Acquisition Research: Issues and Implications.* New York: Academic Press.

Rivas, M. 1975. Entrainement au débat public et à la négociation d'affaires en anglais. *Langues Modernes,* 69(2 & 3).

Rivers, W. 1976. Talking off the tops of their heads. In Rivers, W. *Speaking in Many Tongues: Essays in Foreign-Language Teaching.* Rowley, MA: Newbury House.

Rixon, S. 1979. Games and activities for unpromising circumstances. *ESPMENA Bulletin,* (January).

Rixon, S. 1981. *How to Use Games in Language Teaching.* London: Macmillan.

Roberts, G. W. 1985. A framework for a language simulation evaluation checklist. In Crookall, D. (Ed.) *Simulation Applications in L2 Education and Research.* Oxford: Pergamon. (Special issue of *System,* 13(3).)

Robinnett, B. & Schachter, J. (Eds.) 1983. *Second Language Learning.* Ann Arbor: University of Michigan Press.

Robinson, P. G. 1981. Role-playing and class participation. *English Language Teaching Journal,* 35(4).

Rodgers, T. S. 1978. *Games People Speak.* Honolulu: Hawaii English Program.

Rodriguez, R. J. & White, R. H. 1983. From role play to the real world. In Oller, J. W. Jr. & Richard-Amato, P. A. (Eds.) *Methods That Work: A Smorgasbord of Ideas for Language Teachers.* Rowley, MA: Newbury House.

Rogers, C. 1969. *Freedom to Learn.* Columbus, OH: Merrill.

Rogers, J. (Ed.) 1978. *Group Activities in Language Learning* (RELC Occasional Papers, 4). Singapore: SEAMEO Regional Language Centre.

Rogers, R. 1986. *Six Role Plays.* Esher: Lingual House.

Rosendale, D. 1989. Role-play as a data generation method. In Oxford, R. (Ed.) *Using and Learning Language Through Simulations—I.* Newbury Park, CA: Sage. (Special issue of ISAGA News and Notes, in *Simulation and Games,* 20(4).)

Ross, K. & Walmsley, J. B. 1976. Uberlegungen zur Erstellung und Durchführung einer Simulation. *Die Neueren Sprachen,* 75:39–51.

Ruben, B. 1972. General system theory: An approach to human communication. In Budd, R. & Ruben, B. (Eds.) *Approaches to Human Communication.* Rochelle Park, NJ: Hayden; New York: Spartan.

Ruben, B. 1975. Intrapersonal, interpersonal, and mass communication processes in individual and multi-person systems. In Ruben, B. & Kim, J. Y. (Eds.) *General Systems Theory and Human Communication.* Rochelle Park, NJ: Hayden.

Ruben, B. 1979. *Human Communication Handbook: Simulations and Games.* Vol. 2. Rochelle Park, NJ: Hayden.

Ruben, B. 1980. Communication games and simulations: An evaluation. In Horn, R. E. & Cleaves, A. (Eds.) *The Guide to Simulation/Games for Education and Training* (4th ed.). Beverly Hills, CA: Sage.

Ruben, B. 1984. *Communication and Human Behavior.* New York: Macmillan.

Ruben, B. & Budd, R. W. 1975. *Human Communication Handbook: Simulations and Games.* Vol. 2. Rochelle Park, NJ: Hayden.

Ruben, B. & Kim, J. Y. (Eds.) 1975. *General Systems Theory and Human Communication*. Rochelle Park, NJ: Hayden.

Rubin, J. 1975. What the "good language learner" can teach us. *TESOL Quarterly*, 9(1).

Rubin, J. 1981. Study of cognitive processes in second language learning. *Applied Linguistics*, 11(2): 110–131.

Rubin, J. 1987. Learner strategies: Theoretical assumptions, research history, and typology. In Wenden, A. & Rubin, J. (Eds.) *Learner Strategies in Language Learning*. Englewood Cliffs, NJ: Prentice-Hall.

Rudduck, J. 1978. *Learning through Small Group Discussion: A Study of Seminar Work in Higher Education*. Research into Higher Education Monographs, No. 33. Guildford, UK: Society for Research into Higher Education.

Rushby, N. & Schofield, A. 1988. Conversations with a simulacrum. In Crookall, D. (Ed.) *Simulation/Games and the New Technologies: Applications and Problems*. Loughborough: SAGSET. (Special issue of *Simulation/Games for Learning*, 18(1).)

Ryberg, C. R. & Versluis, E. B. 1987. Internal audiences in computer simulations. In Crookall, D., Greenblat, C. S., Coote, A., Klabbers, J. H. G. & Watson, D. R. (Eds.) *Simulation-Gaming in the Late 1980s*. Oxford: Pergamon.

Sacks, H. 1984. Notes on methodology. In Atkinson, J. M. & Heritage, J. C. (Eds.) *Structures of Social Action: Studies in Conversation Analysis*. New York: Irvington.

Sacks, H. 1987. On the preferences for agreement and contiguity in sequences in conversation. In Button, G. & Lee, J. R. E. (Eds.) *Talk and Social Organisation*. Clevedon, Avon: Multilingual Matters.

Sacks, H., Schegloff, E. & Jefferson, G. 1974. A simplest systematics for the organization of turn-taking. *Language*, 50:696–735.

Santoni, G. V. 1975. Using videotape in the advanced conversation class. *Foreign Language Annals*, 8(3).

Sato, C. 1981. Ethnic style in classroom discourse. In Hines, M. & Rutherford, W. (Eds.) *On TESOL '81*. Washington, DC: TESOL.

Saunders, H. V. 1974. *Fun and Games with Foreign Languages*. Charleston, WV: West Virginia State Department of Education.

Saunders, D. & Crookall, D. 1985. Playing with a second language. *Simulation/Games for Learning*, 15(4).

Savignon, S. J. 1972. *Communicative Competence: An Experiment in Foreign-Language Teaching*. Philadelphia: Center for Curriculum Development.

Savignon, S. J. 1983. *Communicative Competence: Theory and Practice: Texts and Contexts in Second Language Learning*. Reading, MA: Addison-Wesley.

Sawyer-Lauçanno, C. 1984. Case studies in the ESL classroom. *TESOL Newsletter*, Winter 1983–1984(4).

Sawyer-Lauçanno, C. 1986. *Case Studies in International Management*. Englewood Cliffs, NJ: Prentice-Hall.

Sawyer-Lauçanno, C. 1987. Intercultural simulation. In Crookall, D., Greenblat, C. S., Coote, A., Klabbers, J. H. G. & Watson, D. R. (Eds.) *Simulation-Gaming in the Late 1980s*. Oxford: Pergamon.

Scarcella, R. 1978. Socio-drama for social interaction. *TESOL Quarterly*, 12(1). Reprinted in Oller, J. W. Jr. & Richard-Amato, P. A. (Eds.) 1983. *Methods That Work: A Smorgasbord of Ideas for Language Teachers*. Rowley, MA: Newbury House.

Scarcella, R. 1990a. Communication difficulties in second language acquisition, performance and instruction. In Scarcella, R., Anderson, E. & Krashen, S. (Eds.) *On Developing Communicative Competence in a Second Language*. New York: Newbury House/Harper & Row.

Scarcella, R. 1990b. *Principles of Teaching Language Minority Students in a Multicultural Classroom*. Englewood Cliffs, NJ: Prentice-Hall.

Scarcella, R., Anderson, E. & Krashen, S. (Eds.) 1990. *Developing Communicative Competence in a Second Language*. New York: Newbury House/Harper & Row.

Scarcella, R. & Krashen, S. (Eds.) 1980. *Research in Second Language Acquisition*. Rowley, MA: Newbury House.

Schegloff, E. A. 1987. Recycled turn beginnings: A precise repair mechanism in conversation's turn-taking organisation. In Button, G. & Lee, J. R. E. (Eds.) *Talk and Social Organisation*. Clevedon, Avon: Multilingual Matters.

Schön, D. A. 1983. *The Reflective Practitioner*. New York: Basic Books.

Schramm, W. 1954. *The Process and Effects of Mass Communication*. Urbana, IL: University of Illinois Press.

Schramm, W. (Ed.) 1966. *Mass Communications*. Urbana, IL: University of Illinois Press.

Schrodt, P. A. 1988. PWORLD: A precedent-based global simulation. In Crookall, D. (Ed.) *Computerized Simulation in the Social Sciences*. Durham, NC: Duke University Press. (Special issue of *Social Science Computer Review*, 6(1).)

Schumann, J. 1975. Affective factors and the problems of age in second language acquisition. *Language Learning*, 2:201–235.

Schumann, J. 1978. *The Pidginization Process: A Model for Second Language Development*. Rowley, MA: Newbury House.

Schwerdtfeger, I. C. 1980. Perception-oriented FLL and teaching: Theory into practice—Notional syllabuses. *System*, 8(1).

Sciartilli, G. 1983. Canovaccio: Cuecards for role-playing. In Holden, S. (Ed.) *Second Selections from Modern English Teacher*. Harlow: Longman.

Scollon, R. & Scollon, S. 1983. Face in interethnic communication. In Richards, J. & Schmidt, R. (Eds.) *Language and Communication*. New York: Longmans.

Scott, A. M. 1988. Designing a societal simulation. *Academic Computing*, March/April.

Searle, J. R. 1969. *Speech Acts: An Essay in the Philosophy of Language*. Cambridge: Cambridge University Press.

Secretan, G. 1980. Role play and simulation techniques for advanced level ESP (science) students. *Al-Manakh*, 4(2).

SED (Scottish Education Department). 1987. *Learning and Teaching in Scottish Secondary Schools: The Use of Microcomputers*. Edinburgh: Scottish Education Department.

Seliger, H. & Long, M. (Eds.) 1983. *Classroom-Oriented Research in Language Acquisition*. Rowley, MA: Newbury House.

Semke, H. D. 1982. "Living" the language through simulation. *Central States Conference on Teaching Foreign Languages*.

Shannon, C. & Weaver, W. 1949. *The Mathematical Theory of Communication*. Urbana, IL: University of Illinois Press.

Sharrock, W. W. & Watson, D. R. 1985. "Reality construction" in L2 simulations. In Crookall, D. (Ed.) *Simulation Applications in L2 Education and Research*. Oxford: Pergamon. (Special issue of *System*, 13(3).)

Sharrock, W. W. & Watson, D. R. 1987. "Power" and "realism" in simulation and gaming: Some pedagogic and analytic observations. In Crookall, D., Greenblat, C. S., Coote, A., Klabbers, J. H. G. & Watson, D. R. (Eds.) *Simulation-Gaming in the Late 1980s*. Oxford: Pergamon.

Shaw, P. & Wilkinson, R. S. 1978. A roleplaying exercise for students of EFL. *ITL Review of Applied Linguistics*, 41–42:77–85.

Shirts, R. G. 1976. Ten "mistakes" made by persons designing educational simulations and games. *Simulation-Gaming News*, 3(May).

Simon, S., Howe, L. & Kirschenbaum, H. 1972. *Values Clarification*. New York: Hart.

Sinclair, B. & Ellis, G. 1985. Learner training: Preparation for learner autonomy. Paper presented at the TESOL New York Convention.

Sion, C. 1985. *Recipes for Tired Teachers: Well-Seasoned Activities for the ESOL Classroom*. Reading, MA: Addison-Wesley.

Sleeman, D. & Brown, J. (Eds.) 1982. *Intelligent Tutoring Systems*. London: Academic Press.

Smith, F. 1973. *Psycholinguistics and Reading*. New York: Holt, Rinehart & Winston.

Smith, F. 1982. *Writing and the Writer*. New York: Holt, Rinehart & Winston.

Smith, F. 1986. *Understanding Reading: A Psycholinguistic Analysis of Reading and Learning to Read*. Hillsdale, NJ: Lawrence Erlbaum.

Smith, L. E. & Via, R. A. 1982. English as an international language via drama techniques. *World Language English* 1(2): 102—107.

SOLIDANIA. See AGITANIA.

SOPHIE. Brown, J. et al. 1982. See Brown, J., Burton, R. & de Kleer, J. Pedagogical natural language and knowledge engineering techniques in SOPHIE I, II and III. In Sleeman, D. & Brown, J. (Eds.) *Intelligent Tutoring Systems*. London: Academic Press.

SPEAKING FACES ("96"). Matheidesz, M. 1987. Budapest: Babilon.

Spielberger, C. D. (Ed.) 1972. *Anxiety—Current Trends in Theory and Research*. New York and London: Academic Press.

Stadsklev, R. 1974. *Handbook of Simulation Gaming in Social Education—Part I*. Tuscaloosa: University of Alabama Press.

St. Clair, R. N. & Giles, H. (Eds.) 1980. *The Social and Psychological Contexts of Language*. Hillsdale, NJ: Lawrence Erlbaum.

Steinberg, J. 1983. *Games Language People Play*. Agincourt, Ont.: Dominie Press.

Stern, H. H. 1983. *Fundamental Concepts of Language Teaching*. Oxford: Oxford University Press.

Stern, S. L. 1980. Drama in second language learning from a psycholinguistic perspective. *Language Learning*, 30(1): 77–100.

Stern, S. L. 1983. Why drama works: A psycholinguistic perspective. In Oller, J. W. Jr. & Richard-Amato, P. A. (Eds.) *Methods That Work: A Smorgasbord of Ideas for Language Teachers*. Rowley, MA: Newbury House.

Stern, S. L. 1985. *Teaching Literature in ESL/EFL: An Integrative Approach*. Doctoral disseration, UCLA.

Stern, S. L. 1987. Expanded dimensions to literature in ESL/EFL: An integrated approach. *English Teaching Forum*, 25th Anniversary Edition, 25(4).

Stern, S. L. 1990. An integrated approach to literature in ESL/EFL. In Celce-Murcia, M. (Ed.) *Teaching English as a Second or Foreign Language* (2nd ed.). New York: Newbury House/Harper & Row.

Stevens, F. 1985. Simulation as research instruments. In Crookall, D. (Ed.) *Simulations Applications in L2 Education and Research*. Oxford: Pergamon. (Special issue of *System*, 13(3).)

Stevick, E. W. 1976. *Memory, Meaning and Method*. Rowley, MA: Newbury House.

Stevick, E. W. 1980. *Teaching Language: A Way and Ways*. Rowley, MA: Newbury House.

Stevick, E. W. 1981. The Levertov Machine. In Scarcella, R. & Krashen, S. (Eds.) (1980). *Research in Second Language Acquisition*. Rowley, MA: Newbury House.

Stirk, I. C. 1982. Role-plays: Bringing unreality into the classroom. *Chalk Face*, 2(2).

STRATEGY SEARCH GAME, The. Oxford, R. 1990. In Oxford, R. 1990b. *Language Learning Strategies: What Every Teacher Should Know*. New York: Newbury House/Harper & Row.

Stubbs, M. 1976. *Language, Schools, and Classrooms*. London: Methuen.

Sturm, D. 1979. Rollenübernahme und Identifikation. In Von Faber, H., Eichheim, H., Heid, M. & Maley, A. (Eds.) *Rollenspiel und Simulation im Fremdsprachenunterricht* (Pariser Werkstattgesprach, 1977). Paris: Goethe-Institut & British Council.

Sturtridge, G. 1977. Using simulation in teaching English for Specific Purposes. *Modern English Teacher*. Reprinted in Holden, S. (Ed.) (1983). *Second Selections from Modern English Teacher*. Harlow: Longman.

Swain, M. 1984. Large-scale communicative language testing: A case study. In Savignon, S. & Berns, M. (Eds.) *Initiatives in Communicative Language Teaching: A Book of Readings*. Reading, MA: Addison-Wesley.

Swain, M. 1985. Communicative competence: Some roles of comprehensible output and its development. In Gass, S. & Madden, C. (Eds.) *Input in Second Language Acquisition*. Rowley, MA: Newbury House.

Swain, M. & Lapkin, S. 1982. *Evaluating Bilingual Education: A Canadian Case Study*. Clevedon, Avon: Multilingual Matters.

Swain, M. & Lapkin, S. 1990. Aspects of the sociolinguistic performance of early and late French immersion students. In Scarcella, R., Anderson, E. & Krashen, S. (Eds.) *Developing Communicative Competence in a Second Language*. New York: Newbury House/Harper & Row.

Swales, J. (Ed.) 1985. *Issues in ESP*. Oxford: Pergamon.

Swift, S. & Fish, H. 1979. BAFA BAFA—A cross cultural simulation: Use of simulations designed for the native speaker in the foreign language classroom. In Von Faber, H., Eichheim, H., Heid, M. & Maley A. (Eds.) *Rollenspiel und Simulation im Fremdsprachenunterricht* (Pariser Werkstattgesprach, 1977). Paris: Goethe-Institut & British Council.

Talbott, V. & Oxford, R. Forthcoming. The ESL video variety show: Student-generated simulations. *Simulation/Games for Learning*.

TALKING ROCKS. Vernon, R. F. 1979. La Jolla, CA: Simile II.

Tarone, E. 1981. Communication strategies, foreigner talk, and repair in interlanguage. *Language Learning*, 30:415–431.

Taylor, B. P. & Wolfson, N. 1978. Breaking down the free conversation myth. *TESOL Quarterly*, 12(1).

TERRI. Coleman, D. W. 1985. See Coleman, D. W. 1985. TERRI: A CALL lesson simulating conversational interaction. In Crookall, D. (Ed.) *Simulation Applications in L2 Education and Research*. Oxford: Pergamon. (Special issue of System, 13(3).)

Thatcher, D. 1987. Comment made during a game session. See Crookall, D., Saunders, D. & Coote, A. (1987)

Thayer, L. 1968. *Communication and Communication Systems*. Homewood, IL: Irwin.

THREE BY THREE. Geddes, M. & Sturtridge, G. Undated (see Chapter 6).

TIGLET. Higgins, J. Unpublished. For Spectrum computer.

Tong-Fredericks, C. 1984. Types of oral communication activities and the language they generate: A comparison. *System*, 12(2).

TRIAD TEACHER TRAINING EXERCISE. In Davison, A. & Gordon, P. 1978. *Games and Simulations in Action*. London: Woburn Educational.

TUBES. Cook, V. 1985. See Cook, V. (1985). Bridging the gap between computers and language teaching. In Brumfit, C., Phillips, M. & Skehan, P. (Eds.) *Computers in English Language Teaching*. (ELT Documents, 122.) Oxford: Pergamon.

Tucker, G. R. 1974. Methods of second language teaching. *Canadian Modern Language Review*, 31:102–107.

Tucker, G. R., Hamayan, E. & Genesee, F. H. 1976. Affective, cognitive and social factors in second language acquisition. *Canadian Modern language Review*, 32:214–226.

Turnbull, R. M. 1981. An application of the interview role play. *English Language Teaching Journal*, 35(4).

Underhill, N. 1981. It's rude to interrupt. *Modern English Teacher*, 9(2).

Underwood, J. 1984. *Linguistics, Computers and the Language Teacher*. Rowley, MA: Newbury House.

Ur, P. 1981. *Discussions That Work: Task-Centred Fluency Practice*. Cambridge: Cambridge University Press.

van Ments, M. 1980. Games and simulations in education. In Cohen, L., Thomas, J. & Manion, L. (Eds.) *Educational Research and Development in Britain 1970–1980*. Windsor, Berks: NFER-Nelson.

van Ments, M. 1983. *The Effective Use of Role-Play*. London: Kogan Page.

van Ments, M. & Hearnden, K. (Eds.) 1985. *Effective Use of Games and Simulations*. Loughborough: SAGSET.

Via, R. 1976. *English in Three Acts*. Hawaii: East-West Center. University of Hawaii Press.

Villani, S. 1977. Communication in an experimental foreign-language class. *Canadian Modern Language Review*, 33(3).

Von Bertalanffy, L. & Rapoport, A. (Eds.) 1963. *General Systems*: Vol VIII. Ann Arbor, MI: Society for General Systems Research.

Von Faber, H., Eichheim, H., Heid, M. & Maley, A. (Eds.) 1979. *Rollenspiel und Simulation im Fremdsprachenunterricht* (Pariser Werkstattgesprach 1977). Paris: Goethe-Institut & British Council.

Wallace, M. 1979. *Microteaching and the Teaching of English as a Second or Foreign Language*. London: Overseas Development Administration.

Walmsley, J. B. 1976. Feedback and simulation. *International Review of Applied Linguistics*, 14(4).

Ward, M. D. (Ed.) 1985. *Theories, Models, and Simulations in International Relations: Essays in Honor of Harold Guetzkow*. Boulder, CO & London: Westview Press.

Watcyn-Jones, P. 1978. *Act English*. Harmondsworth: Penguin.

Watcyn-Jones, P. 1981. *Pair Work: Activities for Effective Communication*. Harmondsworth: Penguin.

Watson, D. R. & Crookall, D. 1987. Language, computers and simulation: An introduction. In Crookall, D., Greenblat, C. S., Coote, A., Klabbers, J. H. G. & Watson, D. R. (Eds.) *Simulation-Gaming in the Late 1980s*. Oxford: Pergamon.

Watson, D. R. & Sharrock, W. W. 1987. Some social-interactional aspects of a business game. In Crookall, D., Greenblat, C. S., Coote, A., Klabbers, J. H. G. & Watson, D. R. (Eds.) *Simulation-Gaming in the Late 1980s*. Oxford: Pergamon.

Weeks, T. 1983. Discourse, culture and interaction. In Robinnett, B. & Schachter, J. (Eds.) *Second Language Learning*. Ann Arbor: University of Michigan Press.

Weiner, B. 1972. *Theories of Motivation: From Mechanism to Cognition*. Chicago: Markham.

Weiss, F. 1984. Types de communication et activités communicatives en classe. *Français dans le Monde*, 183:47–51.

Wenden, A. 1985. Facilitating learning competence: Perspectives on an expanded role for second-language teachers. *Canadian Modern Language Review*, 41(6):981–990.

Wenden, A. & Rubin, J. 1987. *Learner Strategies for Language Learning*. Englewood Cliffs, NJ: Prentice-Hall.

WE'RE NOT GOING TO USE SIMULATION. Jones, K. 1982. In Jones, K. 1982. *Simulations in Language Teaching*. Cambridge: Cambridge University Press.

Westley, B. & MacLean, M., Jr. 1957. A conceptual model for communication research. *Journalism Quarterly*, 34:223–244.

Wheeler, M. 1977. The role of games, simulations and role-playing exercises in language training for specific purposes. In Holden, S. (Ed.) *Second Selections from Modern English Teacher*. Harlow: Longman.

White, M. 1979. *ILLYRIA: A Teacher Training Simulation*. Unpublished manuscript.

White, R. H. & Rodriguez, R. J. 1982. Appendix C: The open language experience; & Appendix D: Sample plan for an open language experience—Shopping at the supermarket. In *Mainstreaming the Non-English Student*. Chicago, IL: ERIC & NCTE.

Widdowson, H. 1979. *Explorations in Applied Linguistics*. Oxford: Oxford University Press.

Wiener, N. 1954. *The Human Use of Human Beings*. Garden City, NY: Doubleday.

Wilmot, W. 1979. *Dyadic Communication*. Reading, MA: Addison-Wesley.

Winn-Bell Olsen, J. E. 1977/1982. *Communication Starters: Techniques for the Language Classroom*. Oxford: Pergamon.

Wintjens, W. 1979. English role play in a Dutch classroom at intermediate level. In Von Faber, H., Eichheim, H., Heid, M. & Maley, A. (Eds.) *Rollenspiel und Simulation im Fremdsprachenunterricht* (Pariser Werstattgesprach, 1977). Paris: Goethe-Institut & British Council.

Wolfe, J. 1985. The teaching effectiveness of games in collegiate business courses: A 1973–1983 update. *Simulation and Games*, 13(3).

Wolfe, J. & Guth, G. R. 1975. The case approach vs. gaming in the teaching of business policy: An experimental evaluation. *Journal of Business*, 48:149–164.

Wolff, D. 1988. Structure and coherence devices in the speech of learners and near-native speakers of French. Paper presented at the Fourth International Conference on Second/Foreign Language Acquisition, May 5–7, Szczyrk, Poland.

Woodruff-Wieding, M. S. & Ayala, L. J. 1989. *Favorite Games for FL-ESL Classes*. Los Gatos, CA: Sky Oak Productions.

Wright, A., Betteridge, D., & Buckby, M. 1979. *Games for Language Learning*. Cambridge: Cambridge University Press.

Wright, D. W. 1979. The use of role play and simulations in the teaching of English as a foreign language. In Megarry, J. (Ed.) *Human Factors in Games and Simulation*. London: Kogan Page/SAGSET

Wright, D. W. 1980a. TEFL and ESP in French higher education—The case study and role-play approach. *System*, 8(2).

Wright, D. W. 1980b. Roleplay, simulations and video in the teaching of English as a foreign language (TEFL): Where are we now and where do we go from here? In Race, P. & Brook, D. (Eds.) *Simulation and Gaming for the 1980s*. London: Kogan Page/SAGSET.

Wright, D. W. 1981a. Simulation and gaming in TEFL: Resource list. *Simulation/Games for Learning*, 11(3).

Wright, D. W. 1981b. The business game and teaching English as a foreign language. In Gray, L. & Waitt, I. (Eds.) *Simulation in Management and Business Education*. London: Kogan Page/SAGSET/NELPCO.

Wright, D., Betteridge, D. & Buckby, M. 1979. *A Case for English*. Cambridge: Cambridge University Press.

YELLOW RIVER KINGDOM. For BBC range of computers, included in the WELCOME package, Acornsoft.

Yorkey, R. 1983. The appointment agenda: Practice in role-exercises in language training for specific purposes. In Holden, S. (Ed.) *Second Selections from Modern English Teacher*. Harlow: Longman.

Young, R. 1983. The negotiation of meaning in children's foreign language acquisition. *English Language Teaching Journal*, 37(3).

Zelson, S. N. J. 1974. Skill-using activities in the foreign language classroom. *American Foreign Language Teacher*, 4(3).

Index